Oyarekwa Emmanuel Ayebome

The Humanitarian Engagement
of the Church in Nigeria

Forum Religion & Sozialkultur

Abteilung A

Religions- und Kirchensoziologische Texte

herausgegeben von

Prof. Dr. Dr. Karl Gabriel (Münster)

Band 23

LIT

Oyarekwa Emmanuel Ayebome

The Humanitarian Engagement
of the Church in Nigeria

The Example of the Catholic Diocese of Idah

LIT

Cover image: Map of Nigeria showing the area of the Catholic Diocese of Idah.

This book is printed on acid-free paper.

Bibliographic information published by the Deutsche Nationalbibliothek
The Deutsche Nationalbibliothek lists this publication in the Deutsche Nationalbibliografie; detailed bibliographic data are available on the Internet at http://dnb.d-nb.de.

ISBN 978-3-643-91045-5 (pb)
ISBN 978-3-643-96045-0 (PDF)
Zugl.: Bochum, Univ., Diss., 2018

A catalogue record for this book is available from the British Library.

© LIT VERLAG GmbH & Co. KG Wien,
Zweigniederlassung Zürich 2018
Klosbachstr. 107
CH-8032 Zürich
Tel. +41 (0) 44-251 75 05
E-Mail: zuerich@lit-verlag.ch   http://www.lit-verlag.ch
Distribution:
In the UK: Global Book Marketing, e-mail: mo@centralbooks.com
In North America: Independent Publishers Group, e-mail: orders@ipgbook.com
In Germany: LIT Verlag Fresnostr. 2, D-48159 Münster
Tel. +49 (0) 2 51-620 32 22, Fax +49 (0) 2 51-922 60 99, e-mail: vertrieb@lit-verlag.de
e-books are available at www.litwebshop.de

Acknowledgement

Heaven is your throne and earth your footstool (Is 66,1)

To God, the author of life be praised for giving me this opportunity and blessing me with many generous men and women, who gave me all I needed to bring this work to an end.

My thanks to the late Bishop Ephraim Obot for laying the foundation that has made this path possible. I sincerely appreciate Bishop Anthony Adaji for his magnanimity in approving the undertaking of this study. I am deeply grateful to Rev. Msgr. Kenneth Enang, who ensured that I get a scholarship to embark on further studies. Thank you for believing in me. To my parents and siblings, I sincerely thank you for being there for me all these years.

I am indebted to Prof. Dr. Joachim Wiemeyer, my supervisor, for his fatherly direction, fraternal love and the financial support towards this publication. His critical analysis, contributions and the professional touch made me to see beyond the horizon of this work. I thank my second supervisor: Junior Professor Katharina Klöcker for her immense contribution too.

My gratitude goes to Bishop Heinzjosef Algermissen (the diocese of Fulda) and his auxiliary Bishop Prof. Dr. Karlheinz Diez, the Vicar General Prof. Dr. Gerhard Stanke and the Personnel administrator, Prelate Christoph Steinert for giving me the opportunity to work in the diocese of Fulda. I am forever grateful. My thanks to the late Parish Priest Edgar Hohmann of Volkmarsen, whose unflinching support saw me to the end of this work. I also appreciate the late Parish Priest of Zierenberg, Rudolf Bergmann for his support and for sharing his fountain of wisdom with me. May you both rest in peace, Amen.

I acknowledge the Parish Priest of *Pfarei zum Hl. Geist Kreuz* Zierenberg, Marek Prus, for all the wonderful care and support in the course of my stay in the parish. To all the priests living in *Wolfhager Land*: J. Kowal, M. Fischer and U. Trzeciok thank you for your support. Also thanks to the secretary of the parish in Zierenberg, Mrs Melanie Reisch, Mrs Zofia and the members of the Parish and Finance Council for the wonderful understanding and reception. To the other workers and parishioners of the *Heimerad-Verbund Wolfhager Land*: Naumburg, Volkmarsen, Wolfhagen and Zierenberg, I say thank you all for your brotherly/sisterly concern. Thank you Dr. Brigitte Turba-Jurczyk for taking your time to assist me in the corrections of the presentations I did in German language. I wish to appreciate Prof. Dr. Uchenna Okeja for the kind-hearted scholarly support towards the success of this project. This work would have been incomplete without the literatures, interviews and contributions of Frs. Anthony Agbali and John Oguche, Srs. Nora McNamara and Veronica Omata and finally Mr. Daniel S. Adah and Mr. Sylvester Idakwoji. Thank you for agreeing to share your experiences with me. My gratitude to you, Sr. O' Donnel, Nuala for taking out time to proofread this work.

Thanks to the members of the ecumenical prayer group: *Hauskreis-Dreamteam* in Zierenberg. I got to know this lively group through these two great men: Mr. Michael Turba and Mr. Joachim Backhofen. Your support and vitality to me have been amazing. May I appreciate the following Families for their support: Wiechens, Momodu, Sczygiol, Kroha, Stumpe, Backhofen, Chodjai, Linkenbach, Edmonds, Hejl, Gashi, Wagner, Lawal, Amaefule, J.P. Uba, Funke, Rumpf, Schöller, Marku, Mr. J. Hornfeck, Mrs M. Löber, Mrs. Amparo Alonso and children and the entire members of the *Seniorenkreis* Zierenberg and the *Kolpingsfamilie* Zierenberg. I am also grateful to Mucke and Monika; Rudi, Gertrude, Michaela, Martin for their prayers and support.

I appreciate Rev. Frs. Drs. F.E. Egbunu and Julius Abuh for their special support to me and my family. Thanks to Frs. Drs, John Abuh, , I. Oyibo, G. Atede, N. Okpe, T. Ejeh, Emmanuel Abuh, J.M. Aikoye, B. Okpanachi, S. Eseni, E. Antwi, I. Emejulu, and P. Omenukwa for all the support. Also my appreciation goes to Frs. S. Dim, E.T. Alih, T. Edogbanya, L. Illah, K. Edicha, A. Shaibu, L. Ohiemi, Elias Ojoma, M. Akubo, C. Abah, M. Odah, S. Etonu, L. Odidi, J. Eze, Abraham Adejoh, R. Adama, J. Ojo, Sebastian Musa, C. Akuh, M. Umameh, T. Akpa, S. Kure, J. Nduka, S. Udogbo CSSp., S. Adah, E. Njoku, B. Wazamda, D. Klarić, F. Offor and I. Achemu. Thank you to Srs. Mary Abuh, Mabel Abayol, Ojone Amedu, Mary Unwuchola and Ify Onyia. To my Friends in Freiburg Msgr. Waldraf, Frau Müller, Pfr. Stefan and the onetime Handmaid sisters: Gloria, Perpertua, Mary, Alextina and Rosemary, I am extremely grateful for your kindness. To my friends: Cyril Okeme, Jaime Armas, Femi Fowoyo, William Attah, Andreas Ekenberger, Simone and Bernd Geiersbach, I say thank you for everything.

Table of Contents

Abbreviations

AADP	Ayangba Agricultural Development Project
AIP	Agricultural Innovation Programme
ATR	African Traditional Religion
BNARDA	Benue Agricultural and Rural Development Authority
bpd.	Barrels per day
BRAC	Bangladesh Rural Advancement Committee
CARE	Cooperative for Assistance and Relief Everywhere
CBCN	Catholic Bishops' Conference of Nigeria
Cf.	Confer
CHAN	Christian Health Association of Nigeria
CI	Caritas Internationalis
CLCN	Catholic Laity Council of Nigeria
CMML	Christian Missions in Many Land
CMS	Christian Mission Society
CRS	Catholic Relief Service
CSM	Christian Social Movement
CSN	Catholic Secretariat of Nigeria
CST	Catholic Social Teachings
DCV	Deutscher Caritasverband
DDS	Diocesan Development Service
DESCO	Centro de Estudios y Promocion del Desarrollo
DFFRI	Directorate for Food, Road and Rural Infrastructure

DO	Divisional Office
DOI	Diocese of Idah
DSWD	Diocesan Social Welfare Department
DW	Diakonisches Werk
Ed.	Editor
Eds.	Editors
et al	and others
EU	European Union
FAO	Food Agricultural Organisation
FBO	Faith based Organisation
FC	Farmers Council
FLAIR	Farmers Level Agricultural Investigations and Response
FMH	Federal Ministry of Health
FNDP	Federal National Development Plan
FONWAN	Federation of Muslim Women in Nigeria
FS	Financial Service
FSRE	Farming Systems Research and Extension
FSRP	Farmer Self Reliance Programme
GATT	General Agreement on tariffs and Trade
GDP	Gross Domestic Product
GNP	Gross National Product
HDI	Human Development Index
Hrsg.	Herausgeber

IBASE	Institutio Brasileiro de Análises Socialis e Econêmicus
Ibid.	In the same place
ICRC	International Community of Red Cross
IDP	Internally Displaced People
IFRC	International Federation of Red Cross and Red Crescent Societies
IITA	International Institute of Tropical Agriculture
IMF	International Monetary Fund
NA	Native Authority
INGO	International Non-Governmental Organisation
IYY	International Youth Year
JCA	Joint Church Aid
JDPC	Justice Development and Peace Commission
KSN	Kolping Society of Nigeria
LBRBDA	Lower Benue River Basin Development Authority
LEA	Local Educational Authorities
LV	Local Variety
MDG	Millennium Development Goals
MOA	Ministry of Agriculture
MSF	Médecins Sans Frontières
NCV	New Crop Variety
NGO	Non-Governmental Organisation
OFN	Operation Feed the Nation
OFR	On-Farm Research

OPD	Out-Patients Department
OPEC	Organisation of Petroleum Producing Countries
ORT	Oral Rehydration Therapy
PHC	Primary Health Care
PMS	Prime Motor Spirit
QIM	Qua Iboe Mission
SAP	Structural Adjustment Programme
SEWA	Employed Women Association, India
SMA	Societas Missionum ad Afros
UAC	United African Company
UNICEF	United Nations Children's emergency fund
UNO	United Nations Organisation
UPE	Universal Primary Education
VDP	Village Development Programme
WAFF	West African Frontier Force
WCC	World Council of Churches
WCED	World Commission on Environment and Development
WDP	Water Development Programme
WHO	World Health Organisation
WMC	World Missionary Conference

Introduction:

The church from inception accompanies the proclamation of the gospel with the care of souls (cf. Matt. 14, 16, Acts 4, 32). It juxtaposes and highlights her evangelical foundation of both the spiritual and material care of souls. This spells out clearly the core message of healing that she continually offers to humanity as she mediates for the poor, underprivileged, oppressed, captives and the unheard in the society. Her mandate 'the great commission' to take this message to the ends of the earth has spread her influence and presence over the entire globe (cf. Mtt.28, 16-20). She exists side by side with modern societies and as such must deal with the changing norms and conditions of life in the modern state. The church's presence in global history and structure from the ancient world right to this post-modern age makes her aware of human society and her shortfall. Over time, human society has always experienced exasperating instability that has plunged humankind into colossal social disaster. Despite the church's active role, many societal ordeals are far from being resolved. This incapacity does not deter her but strengthens her role of standing in the gap and identifying with victims of social disorder through cushioning their pains.

The primordial world was perplexed with varying and asymmetrical pictures of humanity. In short, a typical mark of primitive human society was its self-centeredness, inequality and concerns for its members only and sometimes immediate neighbours. But humanitarian action today exceeds the immediate environment, the conventional definition of neighbours and as such cuts across racial, national, ethnic, religious lines and sexual difference. Through the designs of contemporary humanitarian viewpoint, the world today is dominated by an enormous and brilliantly encouraging picture of humanity. These ideas are consistently drummed into the human consciousness by the many institutional engagements of both secular and ecclesial humanitarian organisations. Thus they are enshrined today in many constitutions of the world. They unveil that inherent, prestigious nature of the human person endowed significantly with the right to life and indeed the non-hindrance to enjoy the goods of life. These rights are well articulated and profiled in Article 1 of the Universal Declaration of Human Rights by the United Nations Organisation (UNO) in 1948. It states that: "All human beings are born free and equal in dignity and rights. They are endowed with reason and conscience and should act towards one another in a spirit of brotherhood." That is why the social object of the humanitarian engagement today is to uplift the human person from the threshold of eternal servitude of human oppression, societal decadence, humanity-made or societal induced sufferings, modern slavery, failed economic prowess, ignorance and so on. Above all, it is propelled to reinstate the inalienable human rights and their accompanied dignity undermined centuries ago. Such teachings and consciousness in present-day human development carry the objective of change. It endeavours not only to unbind the human mind from frivolous lifestyles and practices but to provoke positive human insurrection. It is akin to vying for the desired freedom, to develop the self and to be emancipated from economic, cultural and psychological oppressions.

Humanitarian work will however remain vague in this work if the context reality of a people is not examined. It even becomes more pertinent in the case of the Nigerian people, where the positive freedom and choices of the human person is very much limited. The impact of humanitarian presence in Nigeria and particularly Idah diocese has prompted tremendous changes in the socio-political paradigm. This consequent impulse towards holistic emancipation of the human person has indisputably necessitated the creation of democratic capabilities. The success of such capabilities owes its humble beginning to the building of educational centres and the provision of other humanitarian assistance by the churches. It has consequently given a human face to the economic and political landscape of Nigeria and the diocese of Idah. Through her many humanitarian services, the church has delved into matters of development that were the supposed reserve of the state. However, the overt absence of governmental institutions definitely creates a perpetual humanitarian space to be covered. This inaction of the government, the supposed custodian of welfare and wellbeing of the people, makes the call for the presence of humanitarian agents louder. The missionary presence pioneered the human development process from the beginning of the mid 19th century in Nigeria and precisely the early 20th century in Idah diocese. Despite the missionary tutelage, its patronage still cuts across all faiths. This church's action is basically driven by her '*diakonein*' perspective and the belief that all humans are created in the image and likeness of God (Gen.1, 27). These humanitarian/*diakonein* roles were her social response towards pre-modern states devoid of social status and the failed development pace after independence. Nevertheless, to avoid the misery of eternal humanitarian gestures from neighbours and friends, true independence, self-reliance and sustainability are the lasting social answers, the permanent response to these humanitarian questions. This study therefore seeks to expose, reflect, compare and contrast with the aim towards making suggestions for potential breakthroughs in politics, education and production, beginning from the local environment in the Catholic diocese of Idah. It is with the hope to gather the requisite propensity to provoke proactive thinking and constructive developmental planning and above all its execution. Despite the focus of this work on Nigeria and particular reference to Idah diocese in Nigeria, its suggestions extend to humanity and not just the epicentre of Idah diocese alone.

Research question and methodology:

This dissertation is a contribution to the study of humanitarianism and the need to foster self-reliance, especially among Catholic dioceses in Africa, as the example of Idah diocese in Nigeria demonstrates. The goal is to provide a thorough, context-specific analysis of the different phases of humanitarianism in Nigeria and on that basis, to conceive a coherent path to self-reliance among emerging but resource-rich Catholic dioceses in Africa. The imperative for this study is grounded on the misleading implications of the current conventional idea about humanitarianism in available literatures. However humanitarian the abolishment of slave trade and the promotion of the rights of workers were, they were more or less humanitarian reactive actions. This convention of thinking of humanitarianism as a reactive endeavour makes it seem that it is all about containing past and prospective failures. This pattern of thinking about humanitarianism would seem to lend credence to David Rieff's idea that "humanitarianism is by definition an emblem of failure, not success. The disaster has already happened; the famine has started; the cholera is raging; or the refugees are already on the move."[1]

The foregoing gives rise to the question asked in this dissertation, namely: how can we conceive a form of humanitarianism that is not reactive but rather proactive? Although Rieff's assertion above is true about many current humanitarian efforts, it is only part of the entire story. The research, therefore, sets out to develop and defend the thesis that humanitarianism will continue to be less effective if it refuses to incorporate within its core the central idea of self-reliance which will ensure that it is proactive rather than reactive. To be successful in the sense of becoming a catalyst for the sort of change that leads to self-reliance, humanitarianism in this work avers needs to:

---

[1] David Rieff, A Bed for the Night, Humanitarianism in Crisis, Frankfurt Am Main, 2000, 21.

1) change some of its principles in order to integrate the ideal of self-reliance,

2) overcome the overbearing need for control by donor countries and

3) become proactive rather than reactive.

Through the analysis of the experience of humanitarian engagements in Idah diocese in Nigeria, this research will espouse the need for the integration of self-reliance into humanitarian core principles while also pointing the path to this ideal.

The proactive features of this conceived humanitarian venture projected in this work aims at self-reliance as its launch pad, which will serve the basis for its enquiry and exploration. Therefore this work is anticipated to look at the meaning of humanitarianism and how it connects to the lived experience of people in Nigeria, specifically, the people whose needs have been impacted by the humanitarian efforts of the safe and secured (mostly Westerners) in the diocese of Idah. Considering the humanitarian efforts put in place so far, one would give kudos to the Christian missions, who played and have continued to play major roles in the Nigerian society, alongside with the colonial and indigenous administrative setups. Today, church based humanitarian organizations continue to drive the humanitarian process in different directions. However, poverty still seems to be on the increase, despite the provision of educational/social services, health care deliveries, other amenities and the development of political, mainly, democratic capabilities. This raises the question:

1) How should we explain the paradox of more help but increasing need for help due to increasing poverty?

2) Can this dilemma be explained locally or are they also global dimensions to it due to the effects of the economic process of globalization?

The analysis of these challenges will be the connecting point between the context-specific study of the situation in Idah diocese and the global outlook of humanitarianism. Here, the research will focus on developing a model of understanding that is capable of coherently demonstrating how and why human dignity is the very basic driving force of humanitarianism. On this basis, it will be shown how globally it is in the interest of all human beings to ensure respect and protection of human dignity.

The social nature of this research work finds its place in the theological ambience of the Catholic Social Teachings (CST), as it deals with the social question of the people of Nigeria especially those within the geographical region of the Catholic diocese of Idah. The entire work is structured into five chapters: The focus of the first chapter (the preliminary observation) brings out the historical restructuring and the notion of humanitarianism. It analyses different definitions of the concept of humanitarianism in order to develop an integrative definition that captures its important dimensions. This part of the dissertation also reconstructs the account in the literature of the origins of humanitarianism and connects Nigeria, especially Idah diocese, to the global humanitarian understandings and practices as well.

The second chapter deals with the different phases of humanitarian works in Nigeria. Considering the geographical location of Idah diocese, humanitarian presence could not have begun like those in the coastal areas. However, the fact that Idah diocesan space belongs to Nigeria makes the Nigerian beginning very significant to this study. It brings out the historical phases of humanitarian practice in Nigeria so far. This will be done by mapping out a cogent means of categorizing and characterizing these different phases. It is divided into the epochs of colonial period through World War I and II period to the Nigerian independence; the civil war experience to the oil boom period and its aftermath. One question that runs throughout these humanitarian periods is: is it an act based on the appreciation of humanity or on convenience? The different phases of humanitarianism in Nigeria will set the stage for further considerations in Idah diocese.

The third chapter illustrates the socio-cultural, ethnic and religious dimension that pre-existed the dawn of Christianity in Igala/Bassaland. This background information launches the efficacy and importance of humanitarian engagements by outlining the historical trajectory of humanitarian works in the Catholic diocese of Idah in Nigeria. It is centred on the analysis of the projects carried out by Grimard Hospital, the Diocesan Development Service (DDS) and the Works Department of Idah Diocese. These are considered are examples of humanitarian projects conceived with the aim of fostering self-reliance. The discussions in this chapter will prepare the line of argument as regards the imperative of fostering self-reliance through humanitarian practice.

The fourth chapter deals with the imperative of self-reliance. Since Idah diocese exists within the Nigerian framework it is to be discussed and defended in the Nigerian context. The three elements of education, advocating structural changes and increasing capital development for wealth creation are to be linked together to foster self-reliance. A thorough survey of the current educational system will help to present a coherent system that could wean the people's mindset from dependency mentality and other acts of backwardness in the present society that deters progress. Also how does the church create a political impulse to bring about structural changes in a new social structure?

Finally the fifth chapter throws more light on the issue of humanitarian development in Igala/Bassaland and its relations to global phenomenon like globalisation. The utmost attention here is the implementation of the evolved humanitarian principles with greater emphasis on the Non Governmental Organisation (NGO), the DDS, its prospects and possibilities. The study of the past records of DDS and the Works Department, their successes and failures provide very essential insights and assessment towards setting benchmarks for self-reliance and sustainability.

CHAPTER ONE: BACKGROUND OF THE THESIS

1.   Historical restructuring

Over the last decades, the term 'humanitarian assistance' and 'humanitarianism' have made headlines in international politics. But to understand this concept of humanitarianism will demand exploring its etymology. From its components one could arrive at the following derivatives: 'humanit(y) -arian and –ism'. Even though humanitarianism is largely derived from humanity, the changing faces of human development and the picture of humanity has differed through the ages. All the same, humanity centres on the human person and the undeniable rights that come with being a human being. Humanitarianism therefore could be captioned as the act, service and the duty of humans towards other humans and above all towards the very ideal of our shared humanity. In spite of the presence of the suffix 'ism' in (humanitarian-ism), which bears a negative connotation, it is also "used to refer to a set of ideas or system of beliefs or behaviour".[2] Thus, in ethics, humanitarianism is considered as the ethical benevolence that describes humanitarian practices and principles. Its doctrine teaches that humanity is obliged and concerned with the welfare of the human race.[3] Humanitarianism is thus the action, state, result, teaching, feature and practice of welfare towards humans. The term *Humanitarismus* in the German language for example, is rarely used because of its negative connotation. In the English-speaking nations of the world and literature, humanitarianism is common vocabulary, which appears both as humanitarian teaching and as problem.

Humans are endowed with rights and as such belong to humanity. Humanity though a modern term,[4] connotes "a state of being a person rather than a god, an animal or a machine".[5] These natural rights of humans qualify the human person to enjoy the benefit of humanity, which is what

---

[2] Ism, in: Ed. Joanna Turnbull, Oxford Advanced Learner's Dictionary, Oxford, 2010, 826.
[3] Cf. Humanitarianism, in: Online Etymology Dictionary. © 2010 Douglas Harper. Retrieved November 24, 2014, from Dictionary.com website:
http://dictionary.reference.com/browse/humanitarianism. This ethical concept teaches also that the human person can achieve perfection through the use of his resources and without divine aid. Its theological meaning which is in defiance with Catholic theology believes only in the mortal nature of Jesus and as such denounces Jesus' divinity.
[4] Cf. Coustas Douzinas, Many Faces of Humanitarianism, in: Parrhesia number 2, 2007, Pp. 1-28, 1.
[5] Humanity, in: Oxford Advanced Learner's Dictionary, 760.

humanitarians are concerned with, through "reducing suffering and improving the conditions people live in".[6] Humanitarianism therefore is the respect, the recognition and the service to humanity. Michael Barnett, a renowned Humanitarian, describes humanitarianism as acts coming from compassion.[7] Though Johann Baptist Metz, the father of political theology is not an established humanitarian in the strict sense of it, this word compassion forms the central message of his political theological concept. His perception therefore could deliver the needed theological bearing for this discourse, since it is aimed at revealing God's memory about human suffering in the biblical traditions.[8] The picture of the God of both the patriarchs and Jesus was not just of monotheism but one through the historical trajectory of weak, violable and empathic monotheism. This was the outcome of God's word and His sensitivity towards human suffering. Therefore, Jesus' orientation through the parables was not to universalise sin, but towards universalising the suffering in the world.[9] In this discourse, J.B. Metz used a number of German expressions like *Mitleid*, empathy and so on; nevertheless none could match his intended political concept like the foreign word 'compassion'. This he described as the justice-searching-compassion, the keyword for the general programme of Christianity in this age of globalisation. For Europe, compassion is the biblical dowry of the European spirit, the Greek dowry of theoretical curiosity and the Roman dowry of legal thoughts. Compassion means to be aware, to feel and to understand the sufferings of others and also to address it. It is the absolute condition for future peace policy and the new form of solidarity in a growing world of inequalities between the rich and the poor. Besides, it is the promising understanding between the different cultures and the world religions.[10] The Christian humanitarian practice from this theological concept of compassion goes deeper than the secular humanitarian as it connects the human to the divine. The humanitarian is thus driven by this compassion to suffer in certain degrees with victims of oppression, to identify with the sufferings of victims of unjust systems and to assist people

---

[6] Humanitarian, in: Oxford Advanced Learner's Dictionary, 760.

[7] Cf. Michael Barnett, Empire of Humanity, A History of Humanitarianism, New Delhi, 2012, 19.

[8] Cf. Johann Baptist Metz, Compassion: Zu einem Weltprogramm des Christentums im Zeitalter des Pluralismus der Religionen und Kulturen, in: Eds., Johannes Baptist Metz, Lothar Kuld, Adolf Weisbrod, Compassion, Weltprogramm des Christentums, soziale Verantwortung lernen, Freiburg, 2000, Pp. 9-19, 9.

[9] Cf. Ibid., 10-11.

[10] Cf. Ibid., 13-14.

affected by disaster. David Rieff is of the view that "what we now call humanitarianism, our ancestors called charity."[11] An indication of this fact is the inscription on the tomb of Harkhuf, the governor of Upper Egypt in the twenty third century BC. The inscription read: 'I gave bread to the hungry, clothing to the naked, I ferried him who had no boat.' For that reason, humanitarianism could also be regarded as a modern term for charity.

One of the basic foundations for the charity practices after 1800 was the effect of the US political revolution in 1776, and the age of enlightenment heralded by the French revolution in 1789. These events sparked a wave of breakthroughs, the emancipation of the poor and the lower class from the aristocratic class. The previous society was comprised of nobles and the commons, the aristocrats and the lower class; it was the age of institutionalised societal inequality. The growing number of the middle class together with the poor fought for the total rejection of absolutism of the aristocratic class and the over bearing influence of the church. The fruit of the revolution was the recognition of the ordinary man in the society; a development which massively led to the eventual adoption of the equality of the human person. This development ushered in a people-oriented government in place of the aristocratic one, which consequently gave more attention and rights to the people. With the awareness of the ordinary citizens' rights and claims from the society and the state, charity was no longer from the perspective of the ruler's bounty to the lower class. The extension of this equality principle outside the shores of Europe necessitated and extended the consciousness of charity to other races of the world that were yet to experience such benefits of humanity.[12] This background gave momentum to further political liberation, for example the slave abolitionism in 1807.

The concept of humanitarianism is one that cannot be defined without complications. The reason for this is that it connotes different and often incompatible strands of thoughts. It may, for instance, mean assistance to the poor but also could be seen as the duty of the rich towards the poor. It may be understood not only as the alleviation of suffering, but also as an emblem of oppression and failure of the system of economic governance. Due to these difficulties associated with the definition of the concept, one

---

[11] Cf. David Rieff, A Bed for the Night, 57.
[12] Cf. Joachim Wiemeyer, Keine Freiheit ohne Gerechtigkeit, Christliche Sozialethik angesichts globaler Herausforderungen, Freiburg, 2015, 19.

will encounter different opinions in the literature. However, Ephraim Isaac offered a succinct definition that brings together the important aspects of the concept. He opines that humanitarianism is "a feeling of concern for and benevolence toward fellow human beings. It is a universal phenomenon manifested globally and throughout the ages."[13] The basic thought enshrined in this understanding above involves three main dimensions, namely:

1) the feeling towards people in a particular situation for example in pains or wants,

2) benevolence invoked by the feeling of sympathy and

3) teleological benevolence, a sort of benevolence that is meant to change the suffering situation of these fellow human beings.

Humanitarian thought has come a long way in the history of mankind; an indication is the high value of benevolence demonstrated towards fellow human beings caught in the web of suffering. Therefore the key role of a humanitarian "is to respond to the suffering of others regardless of their identity, to act selflessly, to do what can be done to save lives, and to place humanity above all considerations".[14] There are roles ascribed to people in every society and every role determines the level of duty and responsibility. Who is responsible towards the other? What are the responsibilities of parents/guardians towards their children/wards? What are the responsibilities of the state towards her citizens? When the responsible agents fail to curtail the crisis or care for the immediate needs of her subjects for many obvious reasons, therefore, 'any volunteering assistance' could then be referred to as humanitarian assistance, because it crosses the duty boundary.[15] Thus, every action designed to improve the conditions of those who are less well off could be described as humanitarianism. Humanitarianism must be embedded with altruism, as it seeks to assist only others not the self.[16] The action of the humanitarian in the strict sense is to

---

[13] Stephen A. Gareth, Doing Good and doing well, an Examination of Humanitarian Intervention. Westport CT., 1999, 6. (See also Andrew Natsios, Illusions of Influence.)

[14] Michael Barnett, Thomas G Weiss, A Brief History of the Present, in: Eds., Barnett Michael, Weis Thomas George, Humanitarianism in Question, Politics, Power, Ethics, Ithaca, 2008, Pp. 1-48, 6.

[15] Cf. M. Barnett, Empire of Humanity, 20.

[16] Cf. David C. Feason, The Rise of Emergency Relief Aid, in: Eds. Barnett Michael, Weis Thomas George, Humanitarianism in Question, Politics, Power, Ethics, Ithaca, 2008, Pp. 49-72, 51.

proffer solutions to the emergency needs of other human beings. From this concept of assistance, secular agencies believe that humanitarianism is a means towards building a global community; it "is a way of both expressing and bringing into existence an international community".[17]

The past actions of human beings based on compassion to rescue victims of different disasters were done primarily from simple charity and concern. They were mainly private affairs, where the privileged got assistance from the pious and philanthropic gestures of others. The yearning for organisational bodies to run the affairs of government and industries in the 19th century and beyond, informed the global quest for building governing institutions. Most governments were beginning to accept more responsibilities towards their citizens, through increased welfare, aids and other benefits. This encouraged organisational features in humanitarian practice to effectively assist victims of different disasters too. Though religious based organisations have been present on the charity venture, they now began to adopt organisational ideas to enhance their charity motives as well.[18] This fact encouraged the tailored organisational presence in humanitarian organisations and their operations today. Therefore another name for humanitarianism is 'organised help': thus "what distinguishes humanitarianism from previous acts of compassion is that it is organised and part of governance, connects the immanent to the transcendent, and is directed at those in other lands."[19] This transcendental role of humanitarian actions is drawn from the fact that it gives help to strangers in distant lands. It differs from the religious meaning of transcendence; it simply means there is something larger than us, which is humanity.[20] One could say affirmatively, it is rather the appreciation of humanity that is the driving force of such assistance.

From the foregoing, humanitarian activities could be subdivided in two main areas: Charity/help offered to people in times of need and the legal reforms, which pursue the eradication of poverty, the provision of justice to victims of violence and the pursuit of social- and structural reforms. The former which is reactive, gives assistance because fellow humans are caught in the web of lack/suffering, while the later which becomes proactive,

---

[17] M. Barnett, Empire of Humanity, 20
[18] Cf. Ibid., 21
[19] Ibid.
[20] Cf. Ibid.

pursues actions that will erase the original cause of the lack/suffering which eventually creates opportunity for justice. Humanitarian work is about pulling these two sides of the coin together. Reinhard Cardinal Marx addresses a prospective, feasible and effective example of these two sides of the coin in the parable of the good Samaritan (Lk 10,25-27). One side of the coin is to care for the victim of robbery while the other side is to ensure that through political commitments the road from Jerusalem to Jericho becomes safer.[21] The former is palliative and deals with the symptoms, while the latter is curative and heals from the root. Among the charity groups, there are personal charity/small groups, which is the face to face charity. Here the receiver has face to face contact with the donor and sometimes has personal knowledge of the donor; this could sometimes be another form of largesse. Another group is the organised charity, where organisations like Red Cross, Caritas and many other humanitarian NGOs give organised assistance. Beneficiaries receive institutionalized assistance/charity from these organised humanitarian organisations.

Many European nations today like the Nordic nations of Sweden, Norway, Denmark and Finland, and others like Germany, Netherland and Switzerland can be described as welfare states. The welfare state is a combination of democracy, welfare and capitalism. During the age of industrialisation from the mid-18th century, the nonchalant attitude of entrepreneurs towards the conditions of the working class and the growing abuse of workers provoked many fiery criticisms. Thus the advent of socialist idea was to address this inequality. As capitalism approved the possession of private property so was socialism opposed to it. The welfare economy, the combination of classless socialism and the laissez-faire but competitive capitalism was given birth to in Germany through the contributions of the church's social teachings and Ordoliberalism (a combination of social liberalism and neo-liberalism that did spread as economic policy to many European nations after World War II). The welfare state extracts the positive angles of the classless socialism and the competitive spirit of capitalism. The government plays a key role in the protection and promotion of the economic and social wellbeing of her citizens, by creating equal opportunities and equitable distribution of wealth.[22] In the developing nations, like Nigeria for example, where the idea

---

[21] Cf. R. Marx, Christ sein heißt politisch sein, Wilhelm Emmanuel von Ketteler für heute gelesen, Freiburg, 2011, 12.
[22] Cf. Ibid., 118-120.

of welfare state is still a mirage, the mention of child welfare and other similar programmes for example are mostly mummified with obsolete offices just bearing the name welfare. Moreover, when welfare services are really provided, they are interpreted as the bounty of the rulers towards the ruled. The nonexistence of such a welfare state or a similar government that caters for her citizens in the developing nations today, (like in the Middle Ages in Western Europe) creates the longing for assistance from international humanitarian agencies.

Michael Barnett establishes three different phases of global humanitarian development: the Imperial humanitarianism (1800-1945), the neo-humanitarianism (1945-1989) and liberal humanitarianism (1989-present). Each of these three periods was influenced and affected by the forces of destruction, production and compassion, consequently shaping the world's history in humanitarian works. The destruction responsible for the imperial humanitarianism was the great power wars displayed by western nations and the resultant effect of colonialism; thereby producing a new orientation toward commerce. Under the guise of the sympathy of civilization, services were rendered to the natives who were perceived as underdeveloped and savages. The second phase (the neo- humanitarianism) was as a result of the destruction occasioned by decolonisation and cold war. The institutional vacuum created by the end of colonialism brought many NGOs on board with lofty principles of helping the natives to achieve different humanitarian developments. It was to effect modernity and progress to the backward nations and the compassion was basically to create sovereignties. Finally the liberal humanitarianism came into effect through the force of destruction caused by the liberal peace and consequently producing globalisation. The force of compassion led to the collapse of boundaries that encouraged global liberal peace and the recognition of human rights.[23] These different developmental phases in the world have informed the different understandings and pursuit of humanitarian practices worldwide.

Whenever the term humanitarianism is mentioned today, what comes to the average mind is the relief materials given to victims of war, the military intervention for humanitarian purpose termed as 'responsibility to protect', to save victims of genocide, ethnic cleansing and innocent civilians who have fallen into the abyss of harsh economic and social conditions;

---

[23] Cf. M. Barnett, Empire of Humanity, 30.

most probably as a result of war or natural catastrophes.[24] This becomes all the more widespread today, as the homepages of the many humanitarian organisations publish their missions and achievements. Humanitarianism however goes deeper than that. Nonetheless, even within the humanitarian circle, there are pro and contra arguments as regards humanitarian military interventions. Conor Foley observes that military interventionism, the actions of the humanitarian NGOs during conflicts, disasters and the struggle for human rights, for example by Amnesty international have a common mission as they share the belief that human beings have indivisible, inalienable and universal rights. Thus, their collective action could be termed as political humanitarianism because the human rights organisations promote universal observance and respect of human rights. Through their political advocacy they are interventionist. The humanitarian NGOs from the understanding of universal standards, (primarily from the Geneva conventions) provide assistance during conflicts and natural disaster, which make them interventionists too; even though they rely on neutrality to gain humanitarian access.[25] For many humanitarians, humanitarianism is apolitical, since politics do not really fit into humanitarian action.

1.2   Philosophical idea of humanitarianism

The development of humanitarianism could be traced back to the European ideology of individualism. Though individualism is often seen as egoism and with negative connotation, it gave birth to the concept of respect for individuals, that all humans are equal; an idea derived from the philosophies of John Locke (1632-1704) and Immanuel Kant (1724-1804). This idea has been propagated through the works of many great philosophers of the enlightenment age, for example

> ...from Condorcet to the framers of American constitution to Kant, [they] were united in believing [that] every human being (or at least every male) had individual and inalienable rights. Because of this, they imagined what the Abbé de Saint-Pierre and later Kant called an international community that, if it could be realized would lead to a world of perpetual peace. But this idea of humanity, when it did not actually imply revolution, at least presupposed a commitment by the fortunate to improving the situation of the less fortunate and those in pain or in need. It was not exactly charity, in the traditional Christian and fatalistic sense, because Christian charity did not imply

---

[24] Cf. D. Rieff, A Bed for the Night, 314.

[25] Cf. Conor Foley, The thin Blue Line, How Humanitarianism went to War, London, 2008, 3-4.

equalizing the condition of different people, only of alleviating the pain of those worst off. But in the Enlightenment conception, the task for human beings is to realize the human happiness of all. This is a fundamentally democratic moral vision, one that rejects the notion of the accidents of birth and station as fate. And it would eventually provide the moral and intellectual underpinnings of the contemporary humanitarian project.[26]

The human person is an individual being and as such is responsible for the actions he takes. He is an indivisible being not a collective one, separate from the other human person in goals, needs and desires. The concept of Locke's individualism is interpreted to promote the goals and desires of the human person towards responsibility, independence and self-reliance. It upholds the rights of the individual to freedom and self-realization. The human person therefore has right to possessions and this right to property is referred to as Locke's theory of civil society and government. He maintains that, the greatest good is for men to unite themselves under a government for the preservation of their property. Also, man's freedom and actions with others are to be guided within the bounds of the law of nature. This bound (the law of nature) entails that all men are equal, independent and that no one ought to harm the other as they co-exist in a healthy state by creating room for liberty and possessions; what is implied is that, all men are equal and no one has natural jurisdiction over the other.[27] In this line of thought too, Kant describes the dignity of the individual as autonomous, because it is an end itself. Autonomy and freedom are necessary for an individual to be called a person; therefore he should not be seen as a means but an end. The human person has reason and is the only being whose existence has absolute worth and commands respect. For every law to be necessary, it must admit no exception.[28] These two philosophies served as pointers towards respect for the individual; that all humans are equal and as such attract same treatment and sympathy.

---

[26] D. Rieff, A Bed for the Night, 64-65.

[27] Cf. C.B. Macpherson, The political Theory of possessive Individualism, Hobbes to Locke, Oxford, 1962, 195-199. Some philosophers argue that Locke was a collectivist but not an individualist because he subordinated the wishes of the individual to the society. For this reason they crown him as the forerunner of Rousseau. Locke's individualism in an emerging capitalist state exacts the supremacy of the state over the individual. Though Locke was never a majority rule democrat, his view did rhyme with the wishes of the majority rule of the American political thinking in the late 18th and early 19th century.

[28] Cf. James R. Otteson, Kantian Individualism and political Libertarianism, Volume 13, Number 3, 2009, in: http://www.independent.org/pdf/tir/tir_13_03_4_otteson.pdf (15.10.14) 389- 409.

With the increasing global consciousness of human rights and human dignity from the UN and other continental unions, it has created a humanitarian consciousness to reach out to other regions of the world, where such issues were despicably hampered by tyranny, underdevelopment, wars and humanitarian disasters. This fact lends credence to one of the definitions of humanitarianism; -the act of building a global community through shared concern and assistance to other regions of the world.

1.3   Practical form of humanitarianism

In Michael Barnett's view, almost every student of humanitarianism will place the beginning of humanitarianism with the abolishment of the slave trade.[29] The abolishment of the slave trade and the acknowledgement of the rights of workers are paradigmatic examples of humanitarian acts. However there are diverse views toward the understanding that such actions are part and parcel of humanitarianism. On one hand they were conceived as ways of alleviating the condition of victims of unjust systems, which is part of what humanitarianism stands for. On the other hand, because of the complex nature of the social and economic events of slavery, the fight for abolition remains controversial for many scholars to be referred to as humanitarianism.[30] Nevertheless the sole objective of a humanitarian is to work to better the lives and living conditions of others. Humanitarianism aspires collectively through different actions to better the living conditions and to uphold the dignity of the human person.

The inherent and diverging views about humanitarianism make its history sometimes a very difficult one to comprehend. However, the conscious use of this term according to Michael Barnett, to connote humanitarian actions, may well date back to the 19th century experience. Hence, the experience of these two centuries (19th and 20th centuries) marked the 'conscious beginning' of the history of humanitarianism. Nevertheless, the fruits of the struggle for equality, liberty and fraternity through the America revolution (1765-1783) and the French revolution (1789- 1799) were restricted to only male Caucasians.[31] It was only from the 19th and 20th centuries that such rights were extended to women and other races of the world. These developments consequently made humanitarianism

---

[29] Cf. M. Barnett, Empire of Humanity, 57. (See also Brown Christopher, Moral Capital: Foundations of British Abolitionism. Chapel Hill: University of North Carolina 2016).
[30] Cf. Ibid.
[31] Cf. Walter Rodney, How Europe underdeveloped Africa, Enugu, 1982, 100.

a common vocabulary towards the ending of the 19th century. Most importantly too were the ravaging and demoralizing two world wars, especially World War II (1939-1945), which occasioned fresh and new humanitarian ideas.[32] It encouraged immense developments in the pursuit, structure and understandings of humanitarianism worldwide. This unique and unprecedented development transformed the concept and understanding of the human person vis-à-vis the concept of humanitarian actions. Many equate humanitarianism with cosmopolitanism, because of its ethical commitment about shared humanity that "extends our concrete realities to include some distant and generalized others, who, we are told, are our global neighbours".[33]

The historical development behind the term humanitarianism has made it experience two paralleled developments. Therefore the charity, compassion and philanthropy exercised by humans to ameliorate these deplorable conditions arrived on two fronts; assisting people in times of war and in times of peace, like natural catastrophes. The first global humanitarian agency is International Community of Red Cross (ICRC). What gave birth to this agency was 'The Memory of Solferino' written by Henry Dunant (1828-1910), a Swiss Banker and a Christian humanist. While on a business trip from Italy to Algeria to gain the favours of the French General, Emperor Napoleon III for his business intentions in Algeria, he witnessed the fierce battle of Solferino in 1859. There, the French and Piedmont battled the Austrian empire on Italian territory. Within the next 15 hours of battle, 6,000 of the 300,000 soldiers on the battle ground were killed, while 30,000 of them were wounded. The many deaths were as a result of lack of organised care, as many lay down with wounds for hours accompanied with injuries and flies; many died gradually and unattended to. His recommendation at the end of the memoir spurred the birth of ICRC. Through the charismatic assistance of Gustav Moynier (1826-1910), a Swiss lawyer, who became the chairman of a five man committee, with Henry Dunant as its secretary, many were inspired to think of the need for an organised humanitarian agency. On the 16th of October 1863, representatives from 16 European countries gathered in Geneva and thus founded the ICRC. This organisation is an inter-governmental agency, to be organised in every country. Her primary

---

[32] Cf. M. Barnett, Empire of Humanity, 19. Recognising compassion as humanitarianism makes humanitarianism both a modern concept and one that is as old as the human person.

[33] Kwame Anthony Appiah, Cosmopolitanism, Ethics in a World of Strangers, London, 2007, 157 (See also Robert Sibley).

responsibility is the provision of assistance to victims of war and those caught in war disasters. From its constitution, every government is to let ICRC have access to battlefields. ICRC is to possess neutral field hospitals and staff. In the course of her development, ICRC eventually found its endorsement in the Geneva conventions and human rights declaration. Since then, ICRC has enjoyed the permission for all-out humanitarian assistance in times of war and crisis.[34] This development made this institution to spread globally.

Therefore, these remarkable developments that came from Henry Dunant's trip made him the patriarch of ICRC. He was able to organise local forces to care for the needs of the wounded, the abandoned soldiers and victims of that war in Solferino. Even though such assistance may have been in existence in the past, the act of bringing in organisation into the system was his sole idea. The memoir eventually became a bestseller and is today for modern humanitarianism, what the treaty of Westphalia was to modern international politics.[35]

Another distinctive practical development in the history of humanitarian work was the ideas of Henry Davison (1867-1922), which was inaugurated in 1919, in Paris. It was the founding of the International Federation of Red Cross and Red Crescent Societies (IFRC). Henry Davison was the president of the American War Crescent Committee. This new agency was instituted to respond to the monumental humanitarian challenges after World War I. Its major objective was to improve the health of those who had suffered precariously during World War I (1914-1918), to strengthen health activities, to strengthen Red Crescent Societies and to create new ones. Unlike the ICRC's strict foundation of relief assistance during war, IFRC extended her frontiers of organised humanitarian activities to relief assistance in emergency situations and peaceful periods.[36] However, this was not without controversy, as the ICRC saw this new institution as a parallel organisation that had the tendency of undermining the leadership and presence of the ICRC. IFRC is today the largest humanitarian network and is part of the International Red Cross and Red Crescent Society, with 187 member national societies.[37] Another factor that led to the creation of

---

[34] Cf. C. Douzinas, The Many Faces of Humanitarianism, 5.

[35] Cf. M. Barnett, Empire of Humanity, 1.

[36] Cf. History, International Federation of Red Cross and Red Crescent Societies, http://www.ifrc.org/en/who-we-are/history/ (15.09.13)

[37] Cf. Ibid.

IFRC was the failure of ICRC to keep to the so much endorsed neutrality creed. The ICRC was accused of abandoning the neutrality code championed by Henry Dunant and Gustav Moynier. Hence from 1918, the IFRC was split on national lines to serve the medical corps of its respective army, while the ICRC was made to maintain its agreed neutrality code.[38] The IFRC works with the Red Crescent societies in the different nations. With these developments, many Red Cross Societies were established in many European states and the rest of the world.

These developments gradually defined the frontiers for organised humanitarian services: the former being strictly a neutral organisation for humanitarian assistance at war periods and the latter, a means of assistance during times of peace and human or natural catastrophes. Apart from these two groups, many humanitarian agencies exceed these strict boundaries. While some operate on both sides, others are strictly for the latter; besides, some take additional steps to eliminate the root causes and the likely causes of war and strife among communities, through programmes of reconciliation and so on.

The global increase in the need for humanitarian presence has led humanitarian organisations from one humanitarian emergency to the other today. It has landed humanitarian agencies in an unprecedented dependence on governments and the rich class. Because of this, many have opined that humanitarian organisations are on the brink of losing their identity, as politics continue to creep into humanitarian works by the day. This threatens and weakens the principle of neutrality, one of the defining principles of humanitarian organisation postulated by Jean Pictet of ICRC. Government's presences, rich individuals, being financiers of humanitarian projects, have been able to call the shots in recent times in the humanitarian circle.[39] Through this, humanitarians, both secular and faith motivated organisations have had to work to bridge the interest of the financiers and the needs of her beneficiaries. Owing to the church's dependence on public donations and the state to execute her humanitarian objectives, Pope Benedict XVI admonishes in the *Motu Proprio*, 2012 the danger of dancing to the needs of the financiers. Hence,

> ...the diocesan Bishop is to ensure that charitable agencies dependent upon him do not receive financial support from groups or institutions that pursue

---

[38] Cf. D. Rieff, A Bed for the Night, 330.
[39] Cf. M. Barnett, T. G. Weiss, A Brief History of the Present, 5.

ends contrary to Church's teaching. Similarly, lest scandal be given to the faithful, the diocesan Bishop is to ensure that these charitable agencies do not accept contributions for initiatives whose ends, or the means used to pursue them, are not in conformity with the Church's teaching.[40]

1.4   Church and Humanitarianism

Charity, compassion and philanthropy are Christian virtues and are humanitarian as well. They are indelible marks in the history of Christianity. They remain inseparable from the tenets of Christianity and are very deeply entrenched in the practice of Christianity. Moreover from the Church's perspective, "charity is not a kind of welfare activity which could equally well be left to others, but is a part of her nature, an indispensable expression of her very being."[41] As such it has made these virtues a commonplace in the Christian dominated western world. Whatever development humanitarianism has undergone today has its root and practice from the Christian background. This brings out the interesting wave of interrelationship in the history of Christianity and humanitarianism.

The right of slaves won through the efforts of the missionaries in 1807 in Britain has turned out to be one of the most remarkable beginnings of humanitarianism in history. The founding founders of this anti-slavery movement that led to slavery abolition were basically members of the Evangelicals and Quakers, including some other sects of Evangelicals and Protestants. They called for the equality of all humans and the slogan was: all humans are the Lord's children; therefore, they should be treated with equal respect and decency. The background of this development was as a result of the rising inspiration that all humans are capable of reasoning and are born inherently with rights. Slavery was viewed as an inhuman practice constituting a barrier to the moral, spiritual and physical development of the slaves.[42] For the Evangelicals, it was basically the human being, created in the image and likeness of God. This action of addressing "social justice is an expression of the eschatological tension between what is and what is yet to be about the salvation, in which we as church stand for, to the end of the

---

[40] Benedict XVI, Motu Proprio, on the service of charity, 2012, Art 10 §3.

[41] Benedict XVI, Deus Caritas est, 25.

[42] Cf. M. Barnett, The Empire of Humanity, 57-58. Inasmuch as many oppositionists of slave practice did a lot in favour of the freedom of slaves, it has been proven that the missionary/anti-slavery crusade leaders were not really against slavery but were opposed to the horrific treatment towards slaves. Their sympathy was directed towards the negative treatment as to its abolishment.

world."[43] The task of civilizing the slaves in the post slavery period too fell directly on the shoulders of these same liberators. It therefore became one of their major achievements, a humanitarian act of civilizing the slaves and to integrate them into the society.[44]

Towards the end of the 15th century, missionary activities began in different parts of Sub-Saharan Africa. The Portuguese missionaries had contacts with Congo since 1491, spreading the faith to Angola Mataba, Warri in Nigeria.[45] This Portuguese contact through their traders remained only at the coastal parts of the continent and never beyond. Their presence was very infinitesimal and as such, had no recorded humanitarian bearing on the people of the coast.

From 1830 onwards, after the abolition of slave trade, many slaves arrived Nigeria from Sierra Leone, Cuba and Brazil to spread Christianity. In Nigeria, it was only in the 1840s that Christianity began to spread to the hinterland through the Christian Mission Society (CMS), an organisation established by the same missionary abolitionists.[46] But the colonial invasion through trade and finally the post Berlin conference 1884-85 brought in more missionary presence. It was an age characterised by European exploitation, invasion, expansion and civilization. Man's perpetual quest to establish and expand his territory outside his original domain was once again made manifest in the human history, through establishing new territory outside her long-established territory.[47] Under the guise of mission of civilization, *mission civilisatrice*, the colonialists carried out an imperial and mercantile crusade. Civilization was just an aspect of the colonial exercise, nevertheless there was brutality, abuse, exploitation and the divisive politics practised during the colonial period and beyond.[48] As the scramble and partitioning of Africa went on by the European colonialists, so did the missionaries come with the zeal to Christianise this old, huge, but shattered and a 'European newly discovered' continent. Apart from this objective to Christianise the locals, missionaries helped to build and to train a working

---

[43] R. Marx, Christ sein heißt politisch sein, 98. (Translation is mine)

[44] Cf. M. Barnett, Empire of Humanity, 60.

[45] Cf. John Baur, 2000 Years of Christianity in Africa, an African Church History, Nairobi, 2005, 55. Even though they had the Papal bull to covert the 'heathens' the Portuguese because of economic and political reasons could not establish her raison d'être.

[46] Cf. Toyin Falola, The History of Nigeria, London, 1999, 41.

[47] Cf. Toyin Falola, Matthew M. Heaton, A History of Nigeria, Cambridge, 2008, 89.

[48] Cf. M. Barnett, Empire of Humanity, 62.

class for the colonial administration. The emerging new nations benefited from this exercise in the long run, as it encouraged the building of democratic capabilities among the newly grown African elites. It was the age of imperial humanitarianism. However, there was ambivalence in their mode of operation. It was that of cooperation, collaboration, support and opposition.[49] The missionaries and colonial administration's relationship was symbiotic. The missionaries trained the working force for missionary enterprise and for the colonial administration's interest; they taught the locals the need to be obedient towards God and constituted authorities, thereby toning down their volatile spirit and energy for revolt. Meanwhile the colonial administration provided the missionaries protection, (later funding of schools) to carry on with evangelism.[50]

For the missionaries, conversion to Christianity was their first humanitarian step in this new continent, Africa. In that process, many used derogatory words like converting savages and other terms. The use of militant languages rampart during the crusades in Europe between the 10th and the 13th centuries found its usage once again on the African soil, like: 'crusade against idolatry', 'war of salvation'. Their first humanitarian job was to win people for Christ. In addition, the evangelicals felt it was a means to atone for the sins of colonialism and slave trade.[51] The missionaries were sole decision makers. It was however a paternalistic humanitarianism, a situation where the fate of the people was decided only by the missionaries.[52] However, many have argued that the missionaries barely had the time to understand the indigenes; their major concern was Christianity and civilization.

From the 20th century onward, there was a paradigm shift from this Christian driven motive to humanism. This was precisely the resultant effect of the post-World War II development, the age of neo-humanitarianism.

---

[49] Cf. Chima J. Korieh, Conflict and Compromise, Christian Missions and New Formations in Colonial Nigeria, in: Eds., Chima J. Korieh, et al., Missions, States and European Expansion in Africa, African Studies, History, Politics, Economics, and Culture, New York, 2007, Pp. 147-166, 148.

[50] Cf. Waibinte Wariboko, West Indian Church in West Africa: The Pongas Mission among the Susus and Its Portrayal of Blackness, 1851–1935, in: Eds., Chima J. Korieh, et al., Missions, States and European Expansion in Africa, African Studies, History, Politics, Economics, and Culture, New York, 2007, Pp. 167-186, 173.

[51] Cf. M. Barnett, Empire of Humanity, 65.

[52] Cf. Ibid., 75.

Humanitarian goals for William Wilberforce (1759-1833) and the other missionaries were based on Christian ethics, that all humans are created in the image and likeness of God. But with the above development, the hitherto religious dominated agencies and motives in the humanitarian scenario were displaced, giving way gradually to humanism. Besides, secularisation and the massive development in the universal version of humanity and community of people gradually edged out the stratified humanity. It was a shift from the spiritual needs to the material needs. Hence humanitarians began to concentrate on assisting humanity and not teaching the bible or Christianity any more. By implication, humanitarian work became *ipso facto* a service to humanity, the recognition and the appreciation of humanity.[53] Even though Christian Ethics, drawn from charity, compassion and philanthropy were manifested in the humanitarian practice, they however became humanistic gestures across boundaries of human presence.

The period of neo-humanitarianism (1945-1989) gave birth to the idea of self-reliance. The growing quest to end colonial occupation in the world was gradually in the offing. Many agencies in the decolonising world saw the need to move from a paternalistic humanitarianism to 'help to self-help' humanitarianism.[54] This is the principle of subsidiarity in the CST, a practice that has become a very strong axiom in the humanitarian drive of the German Caritas today.[55] The different churches, impressed by this wind of change, adopted this practice in their many charity and humanitarian agencies. It sowed an inspiration of self-reliance into the newly evangelized churches in Africa, with the driving maxim that: 'give a man a fish and he eats for a day; teach a man to fish and he eats for a lifetime.'[56] This corroborates the human history that is ever "replete with efforts and attempts at... survival".[57] With this, the old humanitarian goal of providing the immediate needs of the people was gradually jettisoned; giving way to a new humanitarian practice, that is the imperative of self-reliance.

---

[53] Cf. Ibid., 119.
[54] Cf. Ibid., 122.
[55] Cf. Thomas Bohrmann, Subsidiarität, in: Ed., Marianne Heimbach-Steins, Christliche Sozialethik, Bd. I, Regensburg, 2004, Pp. 293-301, 297
[56] Cf. M Barnett Empire of Humanity, 122.
[57] Uchechukwu Obodoechina, The Imperative of Self-Reliance for the Churches in Africa, Frankfurt Am Main, 2006, 7.

1.4.1 The World Missionary Conference (WMC) and its humanitarian effects

Another development that had a profound effect on Christianity in Africa was this World Missionary Conference (WMC) of 1910 held in Edinburgh Scotland. It crowned the period of classical missionary activity as many renowned publications encouraged the use of every possible means to bring about conversion of 'heathens'. This was the only sustained humanitarian activity during the age of European expansion and colonialism.[58] Despite the fact that Africa was one of the key issues of this conference, she was only represented by expatriates working on mission in Africa. The conference and its outcome shaped especially the Protestant Churches in Africa. However, the global nature of the conference cannot be undermined, as it focused attention on Japan, China, India and Africa. Latin America was taken as a reserve of the Catholics and as such was not part of the focus.[59] This was the Vatican I era when the Catholic Church still had frosty contacts with the Protestants; as such Catholic bishops, priests and religious workers had no authorisation to be part of the WMC. The WMC recognised the successes of the Roman Catholic mission school enterprise over the Protestant missions in many parts of Africa, for example the eastern part of Nigeria. Therefore, the Catholic Church's absence and by implication her missed inputs during this conference was regretted.[60] The reduced circle made the outcome and its effect more or less Protestant. However, one of the outstanding resolves during the conference was the indigenization of the church. Its objective was to create self-governing churches that would be rooted in their respective local communities and would no longer need foreign support.[61] Even though the Protestant undertone of self-governing churches goes contrary to the Catholic Church's understanding of

---

[58] Cf. M. Barnett, Empire of Humanity, 64.

[59] Cf. Ogbu U Kalu, To Hang a ladder in the air: Talking about African Education in Edinburgh in 1910, in: Eds., Chima J. Korieh, et al., Missions, States and European Expansion in Africa, African Studies, History, Politics, Economics, and Culture, New York, 2007, Pp. 101-106, 102.

[60] Cf. Ibid. 110.

[61] Cf. M. Barnett, Empire of Humanity, 72; Toyin Falola, The History of Nigeria, 41. The idea and strategy behind the self-governing, self-propagating and self-supporting church, known also as 'native agency' was also meant to reduce the cost of mission and to save European lives from tropical illness. West Africa for example was regarded as the white man's grave because many Europeans fell because of malaria. Finally it was to use the locals too to accelerate the establishment of Christianity among the natives.

ecclesiology, hierarchy and tradition, the deduced goal of self-reliance as a fruit of this conference is tenable within the 'one, holy and apostolic church'.

1.4.2 Advocating change in the social structure

Human society is continuously in a state of flux, experiencing evolution and change. One of the shortcomings of primitive societies was not only the technological backwardness but the total absence of the present day social status accorded to the human person. The conditions of the ruled in most of these societies, who were peasants and living on the bounties of the rulers were totally devoid of any social preference. Change, according to Heraclitus (535BC - 475BC), is the only constant thing in nature. Therefore the humanitarian breakthroughs since the 1800 changed this fate with ground-breaking developments in the recognition of the human person and the equality of all humans. Thus human societies evolved from institutionalised inequality to equality of humans and from oligarchic, monarchical to democratic governments. Though many of these changes came through peaceful agitation, others were violently achieved.

There were times when the Church was part of the unjust systems, (as evident in the Church before the French Revolution of 1789-1799) and other times when she fronted the liberation of the masses (as will be seen in the political reforms to be discussed in this context.) In colonial times in Nigeria, like in many developing nations, the missions were sometimes accused of double-dealing. Regardless of some negative attachments of missionaries/colonial administration's relationship, some landmarks were created by the church as regards the increased social awareness of the people through the efforts of the missions.

Reinhard Cardinal Marx maintains that: *Christ sein heißt politisch sein*, meaning: to be a Christian also means to be politically conscious. He exclaims that, body and soul, earthly wellbeing or welfare and eternal salvation are inseparable and as such interrelated. In essence, Christianity cannot exist without taking cognisance of political activities, because it is within the circle of politics that the welfare policies of the Christians are determined.[62] Therefore staying away from politics mars the representation of his welfare interest in the body politics of his nation. Bishop Wilhelm

---

[62] Cf. R. Marx, Christ sein heißt politisch sein, 13. To be a Christian is to be politically conscious or minded.

Emmanuel von Ketteler, (1811-1877) is one of the most prominent church leaders, whose contribution has shaped the German social society. Thus, he became the founder of the *Katholische Arbeitnehmer Bewegung* (KAB) (Catholic Employers Movement) and the pioneer of Catholic Social Teachings in Germany. In his first Advent sermon, Ketteler underscored that the most important challenges of today were the social questions.[63] He confronted the growing hostility and enmity between the haves and have-nots with the teachings of St. Thomas Aquinas on the ownership of property. This was also because of the increasing hold on the rights of private property and a blatant denial of property rights in the midst of growing poverty. Thomas emphasizes that God the creator of the universe is the primal owner of all possession, therefore private property is only legitimate when it serves God's will and public welfare.[64] Therefore Ketteler affirms that "we are called to solidarity with the poor and the weak in the society, however it should not only be solidarity through personal contact but also in our actions for social justice".[65] Social issues for Ketteler form the centre of the faith, therefore the human person according to the church's social teachings and *Gaudium et spes* is "the focal point and the central socio-ethical standard for all political and economic actions";[66] that is why his political activity towards his welfare is paramount to his faith. The presence of these humanitarian services and benefits enshrined and embedded today in the constitution of welfare states like Germany came from the arduous efforts of the churches, under the umbrella of *Christliche Sozialbewegung* (the Christian Social Movement) (CSM).

Ketteler was famous for his social issues in the parliament from 1871. Even though the parliament came to an abrupt end two years later, his contributions are rated with excellence in the German society for the obvious

---

[63] Cf. Joachim Wiemeyer, Alte und neue soziale Frage, Wilhelm Emmanuel von Ketteler als Arbeiterbischof, in: Eds., P. Klasvogt et al., Amosinternational Gesellschaft gerecht gestalten, 6 Jg., Heft 2, 2012, 47-53, 48. The emphasis of Ketteler's sermon on the challenges of social problem and not the constitution or state system may not be tenable in the Nigerian context. Inasmuch as social problems are preeminent, the state system and the constitution must have the permeable status to accommodate these social questions. This was probably right in the previous German society with state consciousness and experiencing the overwhelming humanitarian changes since 1800. What Nigeria today needs is a sound state system with a people's constitution. It is the only platform that can articulate and accommodate the welfare of the Nigerian people.

[64] Cf. Ibid.

[65] Cf. R. Max, Christ sein, 97. (Translation is mine)

[66] Ibid., 42. (Translation is mine)

fact that the social issues he stood for were later accepted in the constitution.[67] As a Catholic representative in the struggle for the nation's constitution, he did not only represent the social issues but also fought vehemently for the constitutional inclusion of the freedom of religion and the right of self-determination of churches. This credit endeared him to the hearts of the people and it eventually made him the forerunner of CST in Germany.[68] His criticism too was directed against the selfish attitude of factory proprietors towards their workers. Unlike the socialist Karl Marx (1818-1883) and Fredrick Engels (1820-1895), he was never against the possession of private property. For Ketteler, communism would never make the poor to be rich and worst of all it would make all humans to be poor.[69] His contribution as regards the right to private property was accepted over a hundred years later into the German constitution, (*Grundgesetz*) with the clause that, its use shall serve the general welfare.[70] It consequently made his contribution to the emerged social market economy in Germany an impressive one.

The industrialisation according to Ketteler turned the working class into mere objects, what he described as the slave market of liberal Europe. Beginning from 1860 and beyond, the liberalist lawyer Hermann Schulze-Delitzsch (1808-1883) proposed the cooperative idea (*Genossenschaft*) and the socialist philosopher Ferdinand Lassale (1825-1864) projected the 'Workers Movement' (*Arbeiterbewegung*) as instruments to curb the prevailing social issues. Lassale is known worldwide for the principle of the 'iron law of wages'. It is a panacea for the misery of the workers, to also share in the profit of the firm by receiving the minimum wage necessary to sustain their lives. Ketteler welcomed and used this principle to reiterate the church's commitment towards the care of the poor.[71] He also adopted Schulze-Delitzsch and Lassale ideas partly but termed it productive cooperatives (*Producktivgenossenschaft*). Unlike Schulze-Delitzsch, he accepted with Lassale that this proposed productive cooperative could be the driving instrument to alleviate the plight of the workforce. However, in contrast to Lassale, he proposed that the cooperative should not be financed with tax payer's money. Instead he was hoping for funds from Christian

---

[67] Cf. J. Wiemeyer, Alte und neue soziale Frage, 50.
[68] Cf. R. Max Christ sein, 14.
[69] Cf. J. Wiemeyer, Alte und neue soziale Frage, 48.
[70] Cf. R. Max, Christ sein, 30.
[71] Cf. J. Wiemeyer, Alte und neue soziale Frage, 48.

charity and the generous contributions of the rich towards such projects. Ketteler found out he overrated the cooperatives, but he finally found great advantages with the new market economy, which could generate enormous wealth and economic growth; for this reason he concentrated more on the pursuit of social reforms. Social reform therefore is about giving the market development the opportunity to grow through regulatory and social policy, which will provide and guarantee every one the required human dignity, a fair and level playing ground for healthy competition. It was this development that made Germany, after the World War II, embrace the social welfare known today as social market economy *'Soziale Marktwirtschaft'*.[72] This contribution of the CST towards the welfare of the masses could serve as a template to churches in the developing world. Like the church in Germany, the local church could champion such a course for constitutional reform of the social institutions, by asserting the importance of welfare as it points to the principle of self-reliance. The call for social reforms is imperative because, despite the goodwill behind Christian charity, it remains as a cheap substitute that has only temporary effects on the masses. But the only visible, sustainable and long-term effect is social reforms. Such reforms form the basis of these humanitarian studies, since they are directed towards the provision of fundamental answers to the many contemporary social problems. It is a *diakonein* call for churches in the developing world like Nigeria and through this political *diakonia* the church lends her voice to fight for structural reforms in the politics as undertaken by the CSM.

1.4.3   Schools, Hospitals and *Caritas* work

The missionary task of civilization began with the establishment of institutions of learning, hospitals and charity works. Because of the need to educate the locals, missionaries became first-hand educationists especially in the hinterland. As part of their Christian services, that is the *diakonein* work, they were involved in the building and administering of clinics, mobile clinics, medical facilities, maternities, dispensaries and so on to the locals. For the missionaries, humanitarianism was inseparable from evangelism. "For them, missionary work was humanitarian, and humanitarianism was best served by Christians."[73] Religious groups have assiduously been very strong in the provision of educational and health facilities both in their

---

[72] Cf. R. Max, Christ sein heißt polittisch sein, 39-40.
[73] M. Barnett, Empire of Humanity, 66.

homes and foreign nations, most times long before the nation-states began.[74] This factor gives Faith-based Organisations (FBO) an unrivalled presence in rural areas so that the UN generally sees the FBOs today as a very vital instrument for the mobilisation of local people towards the achievement of the Millennium Development Goals (MDG).[75]

In the discharge of this *diakonein* role, the funds and the experts who ran these organisations were products of the missionary expatriates. This trend has continued partly even till today, despite the increased demand for local support. Many agencies, like Caritas International, *Propaganda Fidei,* German Caritas, *Misereor, Missio,* Church in need, diocesan partnership, parish partnership, international congregations, orders, Catholic Relief Service (CRS),[76] other Caritas units in Europe and America, individuals, who have established relationship with dioceses and parishes have continued to provide assistance, sponsorship and support in different ramifications towards church projects, training of would be ministers in many African countries. These are geared towards the encouragement of the faith, to counter economic difficulties, natural and man-made disasters, to improve the life standards of the poor, the neglected, the socially disadvantaged; besides, they provide succour to the masses because of the overwhelming failed government's presence and institutional collapse and vacuums in the developing nations of the world.

1.4.4 Theological meaning of humanitarianism

The descriptive analyses of the philosophical thoughts of humanitarianism are as well embedded in theological thoughts. However the theological goes deeper as it captures the totality of the life of the human person and God the author of life. According to J.B. Metz, for every theology to have a meaning, it must address the evils of its time, the current issues related to the faithful and must also have a bearing on the reality of

---

[74] Cf. Matthew Clark, Understanding Faith-based Organizations: How FBOs are contrasted with NGOs in international development literature, in: Progress in Development Studies 15, I, 2015, Pp. 37-48, 39.

[75] Cf. Ibid., 44.

[76] Cf. Catholic Relief Service, http://www.crs.org/ The Catholic Relief Services CRS is the official international humanitarian agency of the Catholic community in the United States. She is also the official overseas relief and development agency of the U.S. Conference of Catholic Bishops and a member of Caritas International and the National Catholic Development Conference. (14.03.15)

the faithful in question. Theology is very accommodating and elastic as it incorporates not only private corrective trends but also the eschatological message into the current issues of the society.[77] Such eschatological promises of the biblical tradition include freedom, peace, justice and reconciliation of the human person.[78] Theology takes into consideration the totality of the human person and how it deals with his being in question. It is the incarnation theology and it implies "that the timeless God relates in history with a particular people, and assumes or takes into serious consideration, their culture, their language, and their general socio-political and economic context."[79] Incarnation theology is a mystery that brings the messiah to humanity, where the poor have Jesus present in the flesh with them.[80] As the word becomes flesh, so does the word take root among the faithful to address the sufferings, the plight, pains and sorrows, with the hope to finding deliverance. Therefore, the joys and pains of the people are deep-seated in incarnation theology. This brings out the relevance and meaning of the word and the sacrament, the sacrifice of Jesus, the mediator and redeemer that is celebrated on the altar, for and with God's people. The gospel according to the apostolic exhortation of Pope Francis responds to the deepest needs of the human person. Her answers descend deep in the heart to support and to raise the human person. For that reason, Jesus' way of life and his dealings with the poor, his actions, generosity, integrity and the giving of himself reveals the preciousness and the mysteries of his divine life. The colossal sadness associated with the human person can only be resolved by the infinite love of Christ.[81] All this corroborates the Jesus mission policy in Lk 4:18 to assist, provide for and to heal human brokenness.

Theology therefore can never be extricated from the living conditions of the people of God. The church as represented by the missionaries and to date stands for the poor and the afflicted. Like Vatican II, the church serves and aspires to give joy and hope to the poor and the marginalised. She shares in the grief and pains of the people. Since the

[77] Cf. Johann Baptist Metz, Zum Begriff der politischen Theologie, 1967-1997, Mainz, 1997, 9.
[78] Cf. Ibid., 15.
[79] George O. Ehusani, A Prophetic Church, Ibadan, 2003, 56.
[80] Cf. Alberto Melloni, Poverty of the Church,- Poverty of Culture,: A contribution of Giuseppe Dossetti to Vatican II, in: Ed., David G. Schultenover, Theological Studies, Vol. 75, Number 3, New Jersey, 2014, 485-501, 498.
[81] Cf. Francis, Evangeli Gaudium, 265.

human being is at the centre of salvation, his wellbeing, and his entirety becomes as well the mission of the church.[82] Such aspiration qualifies the Church as an "expert in humanity [who] offers by her social doctrine a set of principles for reflection and criteria for judgement as well as directives for action so that the profound changes demanded by situations of poverty and injustice may be brought about in a way that serves the true good of humanity."[83]

The church remains God's dwelling place among humans. Her solidarity role includes the recognition of every human person, sharing in their conditions and bringing them the gospel of God's kingdom as initiated by Jesus Christ. This church represents in the world the sacrament of love, which is the greatest hope that can inspire humans and support every true project that pursues the deliverance, development, betterment and the good of the human person. This church, being the dwelling place of God, offers humans the zest to improve this world not by man's power alone but by Gods intervention and support. The church believes that when humans lose this divine viewpoint, their actions are reduced to vanity. Therefore, the human person needs continuously the saving love of Christ, which the church midwifes as the healing servant that has been present in human history, as she answers God's call to initiate His plan in human life.[84]

The role of the church transcends conversion and the preaching of the gospel. The feeding of the five thousand by Jesus (Mt.14:13-21) gives a lucid picture of a humanitarian Jesus. The care of the souls is as important as the conversion. The gospel of Christ captures the entire human person, body and soul, his wellbeing and the life after. It deals with the presence and the eschatological dimension of the human person. Therefore, "the purpose of evangelisation is to bring the good news into all strata of humanity."[85] Since humanitarianism is about alleviating the conditions of the human person, the action of Jesus is even deeper as it deals totally and completely with the human person. That makes theology central to humanity, where Jesus' action is for the human deliverance, alleviation, betterment and

---

[82] Cf. Paul VI., Gaudium et Spes, 1.

[83] Congregation fort the Doctrine of Faith, Instruction on Christian Freedom and Liberation, 1986, 72.

[84] Cf. Kompendium der Soziallehre, Päpstlicher Rat für Gerechtigkeit und Frieden, Freiburg, 2004, 64.

[85] G. O. Ehusani, A Prophetic Church, 88. (See also Paul VI Evangelii nuntiadi, 18).

...teaches the way of the kingdom of God. He cures the sick, he opens the eyes of the blind, he gives freedom to captives, liberates the demonised, he feeds the hungry, he forgives sinners, he teaches the ignorant, he challenges the sinful structures in society that push people into sub-human existence, and he promises eternal life to those who follow him faithfully. So Jesus is the way to integral development. The salvation he offers is all-embracing.[86]

Theology then is all-embracing and all-encompassing. The church over the years has continued to develop on these humanitarian traces of Jesus, as her *diakonein* role. These, she has carried out and continues to do over centuries through the different agencies, private organisations, churches, dioceses, parishes, religious orders (monks and nuns) and individuals in different dimensions, by attempting to provide answers to social questions. The church's *diakonein* perspectives have created landmarks in the emerging nations of the world, as they alleviate the misery of the masses, providing alternative lifestyles, building democratic capabilities and improving the socio-political life of the people in question.

1.4.5 Humanitarianism and justice

Human history from antiquity has been beleaguered and plagued by series of inhuman and violent acts perpetrated on one side, by humanity acting wilfully against humanity and on the other side, by factors beyond the immediate control of the human person. Since life in the primitive society according to Thomas Hobbes (1518-1679), 'was short, lawless, brutal and full of atrocities', it gave rise to the need and existence of a government, whose principal objective was and is to control and manage the affairs of her subjects.[87] It is against this precarious background of the society too, that humanitarians most times work to improve the scenes affected by failing, weak or lack of government presence. They also complement the roles of government, through helping to recuperate humanity and to restore the supposed dignity of the human person, by establishing their presence through some humanitarian concerns. Their exerted actions to curb inhuman acts against humanity have raised the confines of humanitarianism by many to include curbing injustices and savagery as well.

The global defeat of the evil of slavery, which for many centuries had been practised in different parts of the world by natives and foreigners,

---

[86] Ibid.,71.
[87] Cf. Robert L. Heilbroner, The Worldly Philosophers, the Lives, Times and Ideas of the great Economic Thinkers, New York, 1992, 39.

began with the abolition in 1807 in Britain and in 1833 in other parts of the world; it was an uphill task to prevent other nations from engaging in such illicit trade. However, it was only in the 1860s that slave trade was eventually brought to a halt worldwide.[88] This criminal and callous practice was possible because of the absence of the organ called sovereign state today. A sovereign state is a human creation, with embodiment of law and order for safe living in a society. She is meant to create efficient and functioning institutions that uphold human rights and human dignity. She is not meant to create situations that bring about humanitarian disaster, as it was in the primitive times and still a practice in emerging nations today.

Every sovereign state therefore is endowed with the responsibility to care for, and protect her citizens. The citizens "do not exist for the state but rather the state exists for the wellbeing of [its citizens] and families entrusted to its care".[89] It is the responsibility of the state to make and implement policies that will shape the entire welfare of her citizens. When a part of the state is affected with disaster, it is expected that the state and the citizens respond to the humanitarian needs of the affected. At such moments, the state's actions may not be referred to as humanitarian, simply because it is her duty. However in recent times government response has been termed humanitarian too. The Hurricane Katrina in 2005 is a perfect example, where the Bush administration was said to be acting humanitarian. Humanitarians ask the question, whether the government was acting or failing to act.[90] However, seasoned Humanitarians like Michael Barnett understand humanitarianism as actions that cross such boundaries.

Because of this dividing line between humanitarianism and the state, the state may be referred to as doing her duty of caring for her citizens.

---

[88] Cf. D. Rieff, A Bed for the Night, 58. Britain too has been accused of pushing for slave abolitionism only after two centuries of immense benefits from this crime; M. Barnett, Empire of Humanity, 57, Like every other development in Africa, the freedom of the slaves came because at that time, slave trading was becoming no longer economically viable, due to alternative use of labour and the inventions of modern machines for farming; Cf. Emmanuel Ayandele, The Missionary Impact on Modern Nigeria, 1842-1914, A Political and Social Analysis, London, 1971, 3. British pursuit of abolitionism was for economic and philanthropic reasons. Through her superior naval forces, she was able to end this nefarious traffic 60 years thereafter.

[89] Cf. Michael E. Allsopp, Subsidiarity, The New Dictionary of Catholic Social Thought, in: Ed., Judith A. Dwyer, The New Dictionary of Catholic Social Thought, Minnesota, 1994, 927.

[90] Cf. M. Barnett, Empire of Humanity, 20.

However, states do vehemently support humanitarian organisations. In the western states, humanitarian organisations have benefitted massively from state support. Due to the special church/state relationship in Germany, the church enjoys a great deal of state support, which has earned charity organisations like the German Caritas (*Deutscher Caritasverband)* and the Lutheran agency (*Diakonisches Werk)* the advantage to receive heavy financial support from the federal government of Germany yearly; to execute special projects, during serious emergency situations or humanitarian projects within and outside Germany.[91] Likewise the CRS too receives enormous assistance from the US government.[92] When governments act on this premise, a humanitarian government may suit the conclusion of such an argument.[93] However, states have been known today to cross boundaries through assisting other states in cases of emergencies. Military presence and victories of western nations have been accompanied by heavy humanitarian actions today.[94] Here soldiers execute the double task of protection and attending to the immediate humanitarian needs of the besieged people.

One of the strongest criticisms against humanitarian services is that of Karl Marx. He holds the view that humanitarianism spurs the reproduction and expansion of capitalism. Capitalism is the structure, whereas humanitarianism is the superstructure that supports and helps capitalism to thrive. In *Communist Manifesto*, he classifies humanitarians, economists, philanthropists, activists, charity organisers and reformers as agents who work on one side to eliminate social injustices in the society, and on the other hand, promote the growth and existence of the rich class. Probably, that is why some critics label humanitarianism as the mendicant orders of the west, as they solicit for assistance from the rich to pacify the

---

[91] Cf. Emmanuel Ayebome, The Nigeria-Biafra War and the negotiating Role of Carlo Bayer, (unpublished Master thesis) Freiburg, 2013, 26. These two organizations received a lot of financial support from the German government during the 'Operation Biafra' in 1968-1970.

[92] Cf. M. Barnett, Empire of Humanity 109, there are criticisms on such state's support to NGOs. It could serve as a means to control and therefore NGOs are used as conduit of state ideologies.

[93] Cf. E. Ayebome, The Nigeria-Biafra War and the negotiating Role, 46. The USA government during the Operation Biafra declared she was acting humanitarian; to this effect she sent relief material through CRS and UNICEF. (See also L.N. Aneke The Untold Stories of the Nigeria-Biafra War, New York 2007, 112.)

[94] Cf. Laura Hammond, The Power of Holding Humanitarianism hostage and the Myth of protective Principle, in: Eds., Barnet Michael, Weis Thomas George, Humanitarianism in Question, Politics, Power, Ethics, Ithaca, 2008, Pp. 172-179, 172.

49

oppressed and supposedly revolting people.[95] A good example was during a community crisis in August 1993 in the Ogoni community of South-South Nigeria, a crisis believed to have been incited by the military. The Irish Sisters of Charity who were helping on the invitation of Dr. Owen Wiwa, got relief materials from the Shell Oil company; the same multinational accused of complicity in the attack and the environmental degradation that was responsible in the first place for the uprising. The natives on hearing the source of the relief materials rejected the offer. Even their spokesperson, Ken Saro Wiwa could not even convince them to swallow their pride and accept the relief materials.[96] Such actions propel the likes of Karl Marx, a proponent of socialism to assert that humanitarianism encourages the growth in the margins between the rich and the poor class. Their presence and work pacify the victims of an unhealthy system from revolting. In other words, humanitarianism sustains the uneven and unhealthy capitalist system. If humanitarianism is truly the responsibility of the rich towards the poor, it hereby sustains the argument of Karl Marx. However, humanitarianism truly exists beyond this border, as it shares in the pains of the afflicted community and people.

While the State is political, humanitarianism is supposedly apolitical. During wars and in disaster areas, humanitarians always search for a humanitarian room or space from the state to enable her reach out to the affected. After the fall of Kabul in December 2001, Colin Powell the US secretary of State visited Tashkent the capital of Uzbek to secure a commitment for the opening of the bridge for humanitarian passage to the north of Afghanistan. This was a typical example of interventionism termed as state humanitarianism.[97] In doing this, it brings humanitarians sometimes into politics. This has raised a lot of ethical questions about the supposed neutrality of aid agencies. The ethical question remains; when does politics begin and end? At what point is humanitarianism really (a) political? However, the fact remains that

> Humanitarians depend on others to do good, especially on states and others who have political and military power. Humanitarians often need the cooperation of the very groups that are responsible for the suffering or who will help only so long as it furthers their interests. The ICRC needs the

---

[95] Cf. M. Barnett, T. Weiss, Humanitarianism, Brief History, 16.
[96] Cf. Cf. J. Timothy Hunt, The Politics of Bones, Dr. Owens Wiwa, The Struggle for Nigeria's Oil, Toronto, 2005, 131-134.
[97] Cf. David Rieff, Bed for the Night, 262.

cooperation of those states who are suspected of abusing prisoners of war, political prisoners, and detainees. Aid organisations often seek funding from the same governments that they believe have caused the suffering they want to alleviate. Relief convoys often must negotiate with the same rogues that are causing, and frequently benefitting from, mass starvation. Aid agencies try to minimize the compromises the make, but compromise they must.[98]

This brings out the ambivalence of the humanitarian work and how it sometimes goes in circles. Nevertheless, it is still the "tireless lobbying, pleading, cajoling, and shaming on the part of humanitarian organizations [so] that, on occasion, states have responded to the tragedies around the world, adopted more progressive foreign policies, and harnessed their considerable power for good."[99]

The scope of humanitarian practice varies. In the western nations, it may be assistance to the very poor and disadvantaged, or people in crisis, whereas in the developing world humanitarianism also helps to cover up loopholes created by failed governmental policies, non-governmental presence and state failures. The state presence of the many developing nations for example in Nigeria has been very negligible. This worsens as you move into the interiors because remote settlements from cities and villages hardly have government presence. Owing to this shortcoming, humanitarian challenges are being attended to by immediate families, friends, well-wishers and external hands, like aid agencies, NGOs, FBOs, Foundations and so on. One of the strongest and greatest contenders among the humanitarian agencies especially in the hinterlands is the church based organisations.

1.5   Contextual situation of humanitarian work in this study

Over the last five hundred years Africa and the African people have been captioned with ambivalent strands of conception: a people of excitement but facing underdevelopment, where primitivism reigns despite modernity, with prevailing destitution and hunger in the midst of global abundance, a disease infested colony in spite of modern technology, the list could go on. The media and literature profiling makes it expedient to underscore the present level of humanity consciousness, the psychological as well as economic growth and development. Do the present findings correlate with the former conceptions? Has the church the capability today to rewrite a

---

[98] M. Barnett, Empire of Humanity, 33.
[99] Ibid., 41.

new history? Can the church answer this question, being that she lives closest to the common people? Or like the church in Europe did for example, as she played enormous and significant roles towards European liberation from humanitarian distortions? Her participation, though not immune to criticism, has been a milestone in providing for the needy, influencing national development policies and the social life of her people. On the contrary, church ministers in the developing world sometimes befriend government authorities/officers for pecuniary assistance, which most times affect their stance to influence governmental policies for the good of the masses. Nonetheless, African churches in this flourishing age of evangelism and 'church boom' have the God-given mandate and the capacity to genuinely pursue programmes, that will lead her people away from the shackles of poverty, through self-awareness and self-consciousness of their worth. Thus "given the infinite human resources available to the churches in Africa, there is no gainsaying that the churches in Africa can move the whole of Africa forward. It requires the foresight and the preparedness to set the pace."[100] The church today, like the missions in the colonial times, stands therefore as the true beacon of change towards true independence, autonomy through self-reliance and sustainability. She can assist to contain this deadly economic and social virus in Nigeria and Africa at large, by looking inwards to be able to pull her disenchanted millions out of the wriggles of poverty and misery.

The humiliation arising from poverty has reduced the church in Africa vis-à-vis the western churches from being partners to dependent churches. The accident of history has guaranteed the western world with Christianity and has thus created a western dominated Christianity. Nevertheless, the poverty in the developing world distracts the contributions, the attention and the level of participation of the churches and their leaders on critical issues about the faith; thereby inheriting and living in a church like "a big Euro-American multinational corporation, ...[that sells] the same product everywhere".[101] This is because local inputs are rarely heard or presented. In essence the status quo left by foreign missionaries has not changed much under the management of the indigenous pastors, as the attention and energies are geared toward sustaining the system rather than the content of the faith itself. The question remains, should Africa continue

---

[100] U. Obodoechina, The Imperative of Self-Reliance, 48.
[101] George Omaku Ehusani, An Afro-Christian Vision "Ozovehe" Toward A More Humanized World, Lanham, 1991, 205.

to beg and dance through the pains of relegation and shame? It affects the quality of the faith. It is time for the church in Nigeria to contain this trend. It is time for an African solution to be adopted, and not the solution through western lenses. It is true, 'Rome was not built in a day', but the journey of a mile begins with a step. The affluence of the western churches came through the wealth of the people. Nigeria, however is not poor, she has all it takes to be well off, because "all societies used to be poor. Most are now lifting out of it, why are others stuck?"[102] Paul Collier observes further that though most developing nations today are immersed in development traps because of many international factors and development today, it is becoming more difficult for developing nations to come out of such predicaments.[103] Notwithstanding the presence of these traps and their inherent enigmas, breakthrough is still feasible, but it demands serious political will, increasing local production quotient to be accompanied with a sound and authentic education.

True independence and autonomy will enhance mutual respect and the dignity of the human person towards the other. A self-reliant being is able to reflect und ensure his/her objectives. Elochukwu E. Uzukwu a Nigerian Theologian advocates for true autonomy of the local church; a kind that still possesses the universal mission of the resurrected Christ, to be able to face the challenges of the time, by bearing witness to Christ.[104] This local church is one "that is committed to social transformation of Africa and leads by example–a church which is, for example, self-reliant at all levels".[105] Such autonomy is only possible through self-reliance driven programmes. Another Nigerian theologian George Omakwu Ehusani, stresses the need for a prophetic church; a church of visionaries and seers, to change the corporate amnesia and collective myopia plaguing the nation.[106] This is evidently possible through self-reliance, as he canvasses for empowerment of the poor. That is why the clarion call for the church is "to lead Africa in an interior journey of self-discovery and social restoration".[107] The entire exercise is to

---

[102] Paul Collier, The Bottom Billion, Why the Poorest Countries Are Falling and What Can Be Done About it, Oxford, 2008, 5.
[103] Cf. Ibid. (An adoption of the works of Jeffrey Sacks)
[104] Cf. Elochukwu E. Uzukwu, A Listening Church, Autonomy and Communion in African churches, Eugene Oregon, 1996, 48.
[105] Ibid., 3.
[106] Cf. G. O. Ehusani, A Prophetic Church, 71.
[107] U. Obodoechina, The Imperative of Self-Reliance, 48. (See also F. Nwatu, The Church's Prophetic Role, 172-187).

curtail the culture of begging and undue dependence which has been the practice of the African churches towards the 'mother church' in Rome and the 'sister churches' in Europe and America; besides "the beggar has no self-respect. Self-respect for the churches of Africa, and indeed for the African nations, will continue to be elusive until there is a certain level of self-reliance on the material level."[108] It is with the hope of exterminating such practices in the future. It is time to move away from the naive accusation of the twin forces of colonialism and slave trade, coupled with failed and weak governments in Africa, which actually are and have been taken as the bane of economic woes of many African countries. The church since its origin in Africa relies on foreign funds to execute church projects, feeding and training of her ministers and would be-ministers, assisting the poor, the destitute, people at the margins of the society and the socially deprived in the society. This has maintained the status quo ante by the founding missionaries, as virtually every project must see the light of western contribution. Even though the call for self-support has been on the increase, the craving for foreign support is still very strong. To stem the tide of begging and looking up to the west consistently for help, local churches have to be proactive and productive, by mobilizing and harnessing their rich but scattered resources. The objective of this work is a call to self-consciousness and the need for true independence and autonomy. If a people put their acts together; they shall find ways to rescue the church from the present and the threatening pains and disaster staring in the future.

As the different and diverging views about humanitarianism are important to the background of this study, it is however imperative too, that the focus of this study be restricted to the humanitarian services; precisely the *Diakonia* exercised by the church agencies in this part of the globe. It is a study on the collective efforts of the founding missionaries and how it has influenced, affected and impacted changes in the life of her beneficiaries in Nigeria, but more importantly in the vicinity of the Catholic diocese of Idah Nigeria. The Catholic diocese of Idah is the centre and locus of this humanitarian study. The conspicuous poverty, despite the past gigantic humanitarian actions, provokes the study of the prevailing causes of poverty towards a new impulse of humanitarian work that is imperative of self-reliance.

---

[108] E. E. Uzukwu, A Listening Church, 88.

The humanitarian achievements of the mission in Nigeria cannot be disregarded. Its presence has brought in unique and distinctive changes in the economic, psychological, educational, physical, structural and religious life of the average Nigerian. Despite the roles played by the colonial and the different national administrations, the mission's role was very special. With the meagre income compared to the secular administrative bodies, she reached even the fabric of the society, where she unlike the secular state enjoys the confidence of the masses. Till today, this factor (like Caritas) makes the church the first to note the social problems of the indigenes even before the state.[109] The church today has continued in this humanitarian drive, but poverty seems on the increase by the day. The inferring innovations from this case study 'Idah diocese' are meant as a catalyst to stimulate modern and pragmatic approach towards an independent and self-reliant church especially in this part of the nation. The church as *Diakonia* must fashion self-reliance as the backbone and the principal target of her humanitarian actions. Through this 'mission of self-reliance and eventual sustainability', the local church would not only be alleviating the plight of her people but also improving their living standards; thereby enhancing her prophetic credibility of bearing witness *Marturia*, the proclamation of the word and the celebration of the sacrament *Liturgia*. This expresses the true nature of the church integrated "in her three-fold responsibility: of proclaiming the word of God (*kerygma-martyria*), celebrating the sacraments (*leitourgia*), and exercising the ministry of charity (*diakonia*). These duties presuppose each other and are inseparable".[110] It will invariably enhance the *Koinonia*, where all churches could truly relate in the spirit of true oneness.

---

[109] Cf. Wollasch H.J., Lorenz Werthmann, Charismatiker und Visionär, in: Eds., Neher Peter, et al., Freiburg, 2008, Pp. 30-32, 30.

[110] Cf. Benedict XVI, Deus Caritas est, 25.

CHAPTER TWO: HUMANITARIANISM IN NIGERIA

2.   The different phases of humanitarian works in Nigeria

The concept of humanitarian work from the last chapter was basically on the varying understandings and the traces of such gestures in different parts of the world and over the last centuries. This was done in view of creating a better world and offering a better lifestyle to the people. These conscious activities carried out in different parts of the world have carved a niche for the place of humanitarian works in world history. It was part of the driving philosophy and ideology of the human person and the changes in the society. The increasing welfare consciousness reflected in many constitutions of states towards their citizens today and the organisational presence of many humanitarian organisations have instigated a longing for humanitarians to save the world, especially states with failed welfare activities. Saving the world through humanitarians also triggered countless historic developments among different organisations and nations. These human activities and global changes echo the growing need to explore the historical and developmental pace of the concerned nation, as it pertains to the humanitarian action of saving and improving lives. Nigeria like any other sub-Saharan African nation has had her unique humanitarian history since her contact with the rest of the globe. Her humanitarian record, which is a communication of the past and present, was shaped by different activities over the years. This chapter outlines these different phases of humanitarian works in Nigeria and the role they have played in the nation. Among the many humanitarian agents were the colonial administration, the regional/central governments, the self-help groups, the secular and the missionary organisations. However, the humanitarian focus here centres on the perspective of the Christian missionary contribution in Nigeria.

Global calamities like the World Wars affected Nigeria like every other nation of the world, coupled with national events like colonial and self rule. Thus, the history of humanitarian development in Nigeria could be subdivided into three different epochs: The colonial period (1840-1945), the post World War II development (1945-1973) and the post oil boom period (1973 to present). The colonial period lasted from the mid 19th century to the end of the World War II; this was characterized by the dominant activities of colonialists and missionaries as humanitarian agents. The second period, the post World War II development in 1945, commenced with the political awareness for self rule and nationalistic movements that galvanised echoes for independence in 1960; this continued down to the early years of nation building, the civil war period of 1967-70 until the oil boom period of 1973. This was the age of agro-dominated economy; where the regional together with the later central government and self helps groups became part of the humanitarian agents. Finally the post oil boom period, the oil oriented economy comprises the oil boom period of 1973, the oil bust after 1975 and the subsequent upsurges in oil price for example in the 80s and recent times; its economic effect and the general aftermath made oil the mainstay of Nigerian economy. The many internal factors and the global forces of demand and supply of oil have affected the gullible Nigerian mono-economy, with its resultant humanitarian challenges. These different periods are strictly from the humanitarian perspective of the missions in Nigeria and in Idah diocese. There were other humanitarian undertakings, for example the fundraising of 1917 in Lagos for Red Cross to assist the returnee soldiers of the World War I.[111] However, this work deals extensively with the *diakonein* undertakings of the Christian missions especially the Catholic missions, the changing demands on these mission and the corresponding services at every epoch. Therefore the standpoint here is to explore the humanitarian level of these missionary engagements.

2.1   Humanitarianism in colonial Nigeria. (Ca.1840-1945)

The arrival and presence of the missionaries in Nigeria marked the epochal beginning of missionaries' contribution to humanitarian work. Benin and Warri had some feeble Portuguese missionary activities in the mid 15th century that soon faded with their departure. The dominant Afro-Euro relationship then was strictly trade and commerce.[112] The ending of slave trade encouraged the arrival of many slaves from 1830s onwards. Missionary activities began between 1842 and 1892 in Lagos and in the south[113] with the arrival of Rev Thomas Freeman and Mr. and Mrs. de Graft of the Wesleyan Methodist mission on 24th September 1842.[114] The activist evangelical Christians under the aegis of Church Missionary Society, CMS, (founded in 1799, which fought hard for the slave trade abolition) committed also towards social reforms and world evangelisation began the Christian evangelisation in southern Nigeria. The CMS Bishop Samuel Ajayi

---

[111] Cf. Nigerian Red Cross Society, http://www.redcrossnigeria.org/history.html (06.02.15)
[112] Cf. E. Ayandele, The Missionary Impact, 3.
[113] Cf. T. Falola, The History of Nigeria, 41.
[114] Cf. Leonard James Lewis, Society, Schools and Progress in Nigeria, Oxford 1965, 24.

Crowther, (1809-1891) an ex Yoruba slave was charged with the responsibility to establish CMS missions.[115] The Catholic presence began on the 18th April 1861 in Whydah with the pioneer missionary *Societas Missionum ad Afros* (SMA), commonly referred to as Society of African Missions.[116] Since colonialists and missionaries came by sea, settlements at the coast had the geographical advantage to first experience such humanitarian works before the interiors.

Another epoch-making development that brutally institutionalised colonial control was the Berlin conference, 1884-1885, 'the scramble and partitioning of Africa'. Through conquest and military subjugation with mercantile capitalism at the background, the present Nigeria came under colonial rule from 1900.[117] Hence the colonial administration began to build roads, railways, telegraphs and telephones. These facilities were limited and originally planned to ease the transportation of African resources to the coastal cities for export to their home countries. The colonial rule oversaw the day to day running of the state, provided security for their firms, established a few schools, piped water and sanitation. These social amenities were built primarily for settlers' needs; they were unevenly established and mostly concentrated in the resource areas and newly grown urban areas, where the colonialists were mainly resident.[118] These actions were hardly humanitarian and if ever they were, it was humanitarianism from convenience; in essence the people ate from the crumbs. The missionary task was the teaching of the bible and the spread of Christianity by winning new converts. This task was accompanied by humanitarian objectives of establishing schools, building health institutions, provision of social amenities and doing charity works.

However, what became Nigeria today was the amalgamation of the southern and northern protectorates in 1914 by the British colonial system for administrative convenience. From this very moment, both the north and the south came under one administration until independence in 1960.

---

[115] Cf. Waibinte Wariboko, The CMS Niger Mission, Extra-Territorial Forces of Change, and the Expansion of British Influence in the Niger Delta during the Nineteenth Century, in: Eds., Chima J Korieh, et al., Missions, States and European Expansion in Africa, African Studies, History, Politics, Economics, and Culture, New York, 2007, Pp. 35-53, 36.

[116] Cf. Blaise Okpanachi, Nigerian-Vatican Diplomatic Relations, Würzburg, 2011, 51. The Latin name serves as the acronym SMA and not SAM as in English language.

[117] Cf. T. Falola, The History of Nigeria, 67.

[118] Cf. Adekeye Adebanjo, The Curse of Berlin, Africa after the cold War, London, 2010, 20.

2.1.1 Humanitarianism and the missions

The humanitarian projects of the missions were to alleviate the people's poverty. Preaching was to expound the Christian faith and doctrines, the schools were the medium to impart western cultural values, while the hospital provided new ways to tackle health challenges. However, their fundamental goal was the establishment of Christianity.[119] For many obvious reasons, missionaries were warmly received in many parts of Nigeria. From the spiritual angle, natives felt that the supernatural power of the missionary's God could avail them spiritual advantage over their enemies. For commercial reason, the mission schools taught reading, writing and spoken English which was the emerging official language, thereby enhancing trade between the foreign and local merchants.[120] However, some of native's expectations were not met and mission intentions were rather misconstrued. Thus,

> many indigenous leaders welcomed Christian missionaries in the belief that these missionaries would help them gain influence with their god and with British political agents against their rivals in times of political instability and economic transformation. The missionaries however were more concerned with spreading their religion and ending slavery and the slave trade than with helping indigenous rulers meet their political goals.[121]

The strong humanitarian perspective projected by the CMS in West Africa was influenced by the experience of her founders the 'activist evangelical Christians' for abolitionism.[122] They viewed the mission as the machinery for spreading the gospel and civilization; a move termed as humanitarian by many authors. It was humanitarian, because it came to liberate Africans from the pains, ravages and effects of the just ended inhuman action of slave trade. Its blighting effects were still conspicuous and precarious to the people. As such, their response through preaching the gospel and spreading civilization was to cushion the suffering of the people and to improve their living conditions. It was a very challenging

---

[119] Cf. Jude C. Aguwa, Mission Colonialism and the Supplanting of African Religious and Medical Practices, in: Eds., Chima J Korieh, et al., States and European Expansion in Africa, African Studies, History, Politics, Economics, and Culture, New York, 2007, Pp. 127-146, 132.

[120] Cf. T. Falola, Matthew M. Heaton, A History of Nigeria, 87-88.

[121] Ibid., 89.

[122] Cf. F. Deaville Walker, Project Canterbury, The Romance of the Black River, The Story of CMS Nigerian Mission, London: Church Missionary Society, 1930, in: http://www.anglicanhistory.org/africa/ng/walker1930/index.html (09.02.15).

humanitarian mission. Because of her history, Africa at this time was in dire need of the gospel of liberation, which according to some authors required massive and compassionate effort.[123] This humanitarian role was inseparable from evangelism, since the mission believed she was humanitarian and that humanitarian services were best carried out by Christians.

The missions were very emphatic about creating economic opportunities for the converts. This huge mission's commitment towards enabling economic development to take effect was questioned by many missionaries. These critics separated evangelical work from the humanitarian perspective. For them humanitarian work was a sort of distraction from evangelism. These missionaries argued from the viewpoint that it was the duty of the government to provide economic opportunities for the natives. But the substantive regime, by implication the colonial rule and the respective native authorities were preoccupied with personal interests, such that the common people were hardly ever considered. Irrespective of these opinions, many denominations over time still endorsed an active church in humanitarian practice. The Catholic Church had been a very vehement voice, but was still trailing behind in her practice. Many of the Protestant bodies too were convinced of the need to raise both the spiritual and physical nature of the converts.[124] One of the missionaries made a humanitarian statement that: "I do not see how you can raise a man's spiritual life unless you raise the bodily life to correspond."[125] Apart from the humanitarian desire to care for the natives, another antecedent led to the missionary's strong involvement and encouragement of the economic life of the natives. It was to help find an alternative means of trade and a legitimate commerce to replace the slave trade. [126]

The Missions, being the home of charity,[127] were acting as last resort for many in the colonial period; this trace is still common today in some communities or to communities during environmental disasters. In these missions, the practice of Christian charity became the fundamental answer to the looming underdevelopment and poverty. The missions became the place

---

[123] Cf. J. C. Aguwa, Mission Colonialism and the Supplanting of African Religious and Medical Practices, 133. (See also R. Rweyemamu) The Christian Mission in Africa, before and after the Berlin conference (1884-1885).
[124] Cf. Ibid., 418.
[125] Ibid. (See also Olivier)
[126] Cf. T. Falola, M. M. Heaton, A History of Nigeria, 89.
[127] Cf. Kompendium der sozialen Lehre, 61.

of fraternal love, caring for the least of the brothers cf. John. 13:34, Mt. 25:40. However, charity posed its own problem as well. It was like the growth of the faith was dependent on the influx of material and charitable goods. How was this going to affect the new faith? It raised questions, besides it threatened the resilience of the faith. It created a dependency syndrome among the natives 'that the missions had it all'. The missions were confronted with difficult and challenging questions like who was really in need and how were they to be helped? On one hand should the missionaries give them work, an appreciation of human dignity to evade the begging syndrome? On the other hand, there were hardly any works to be given; besides not all could work for their needs. All the same, many missionaries have been remembered today for the enormous charities channelled through them to the natives.[128]

Since humanitarian works were virtually inseparable from the missions, wherever the missions existed, humanitarian works were present. Therefore the presence of the missionaries was itself a humanitarian presence. Many communities despite their reluctance towards accepting the faith saw the missionaries' presence as opportunities that created new perspectives and alternative lifestyles that were very attractive.

2.1.2 The humanitarian impact of the missions

One obvious effects of the humanitarian aid by mission in contemporary Nigeria for example is the glaring socio-economic difference between the south and the north. This goes back to the insulation of the northern region from missionary activities in colonial Nigeria called 'Christian non-interference pact'. This prohibition included humanitarian/charity works and as a matter of fact everything missionary. Given that the missionaries were pioneers of schools and a very strong force in medical institutions, the north was left with only the services provided by the colonial administration. Missionaries were forewarned by the colonial administration and the Royal Niger Company (RNC), the custodians of security not to violate this pact; hence they ceased to be under the protection of the colonial administration.[129] This pact invariably slowed down the pace of modern development and impoverished the entire region such that even up till the close of colonialism in 1960, the north despite her overwhelming

---

[128] Cf. J. Baur, 2000 Years, 419.

[129] Cf. B. Okpanachi, Nigerian-Vatican Diplomatic Relations, 154.

landmass had just 14 secondary schools, as against 842 in the south.[130] Consequently, of the entire number of western educated Nigerians, only a tenth were from the north.[131] During this period too, 185, 000 children from the north were attending primary schools, while the south had 2,300,000 children.[132]

These educational and health institutions were sources of revenue, employment opportunities and alternative source of living to the people, thereby increasing the masses' economic activities and potentials. Negatively too they encouraged the consumption of European goods; a fact that promoted importation of foreign goods. Missionaries were able to generate other economic activities as they supported and encouraged many of their converts and members in new economic and cash crops production like cocoa, sugar cane and so on, which eventually emerged as major exporting commodities of the time.[133]

2.1.3   Schools

The Christian missions were the centres of western education during the colonial era. Schools were almost identical with the missions and the most visible and important institutions by the missionaries. In southern Nigeria for example, the missions were so associated with schools that the acquisition of western education was tantamount to conversion to the new faith.[134] Therefore mission presence meant establishment of schools and the nursery ground for Christianity. For some historians the schools in sub-Saharan Africa were "the barometer of Africa's development".[135]

---

[130] Cf. J.A. Daly, A.G. Saville, The History of Jointchurchaid, Vol 1-III, Copenhagen, 1971, 2; T. Falola, M. M. Heaton, A History of Nigeria, 146. Another statistic states that the entire North had over 40 secondary schools while only south west had over 700.

[131] Cf. Nigeria's Dawn, Last Chance for a patchwork state? Understanding Global Issues 99/2 in: Ed., Richard Buckerly, England, 1999, 2.

[132] Cf. Johannes Harnischfeger, Zur Entstehung religiöser Konflikte in Nigeria, in: Ed., Josef Thesing, Konrad Adenauer Stiftung (KAS) 11/1996. 41 (See also Okeke Okechukwu, Hausa-Fulani Hegemony, 23)

[133] Cf. T. Falola, The History of Nigeria, 44.

[134] Cf. William Neher, Nigeria: Change and Tradition in an African State, Massachusetts, 1999, 75.

[135] J. Baur, 2000 Years, 412. He breaks down the school developmental period in sub-Saharan Africa into four epoch: From 1900- 1920 (World War I period), was the age of the CRI school; from 1920- 1940 (between World War I and II) could be called the age of primary school; from 1945-1960, (after the World War II) could be termed as the age of secondary

The early missionary schools were at the beginning tuition free with cheap running cost and were mostly below standard. It took the model of schools in the dark ages in Britain. Missionaries taught the faith, catechism, reading and writing. Missionaries sometimes went from house to house to persuade parents to send their children to schools. Some of the parents in return requested payment so as to let their children off to mission schools. But despite its poor standard, parents and pupils came to appreciate the school as a mode of social emancipation and a road towards economic development.[136] The missions in no time were able to 'harvest' readers, teachers, interpreters and catechists through the schools.[137] Virtually every mission had a central school for academically excellent pupils, who eventually became catechists, learnt a craft and probably could be employed by the missions or the colonial administration. But its objectives were basically to raise people for settlers' needs and the colonialist shared this same view too. Therefore the educational programme that would launch the converts into other walks of life was not incorporated into the school curriculum. Apart from these schools serving the evangelical viewpoints, to win converts and to enable them develop their own church, the different denominations had additional motives. The Lutherans desired the converts to be capable of reading the bible; the Anglicans proposed a self reliant church, while the Presbyterians and especially the Catholics pursued the spread of Christian civilization.[138] This humanitarian effort to impart new art of knowledge to the people was geared towards achieving that anticipated notion of self-reliance that was proposed by the founders of the CMS mission.

Unlike the missionaries, the colonial administration was not interested in the establishment of primary schools. But after the institution of

---

schools; and finally from 1960 was the university age, the year of independence, the advent of universities. This development was not equally the same in sub-Saharan Africa. The famous public university, the 'Fouray Bay College' in Freetown Sierra-Leone for example was founded in February 1827. She is the oldest university and the first western styled university built in West Africa. In Nigeria for example the first tertiary institution was the Yaba Higher College, built in 1934.

[136] Cf. Andrew G. Onokerhoraye, Social Services in Nigeria, An Introduction, London, 1984, 15. Letting children to school constituted wastage to agricultural practice, which needed many hands for the manual labour.

[137] Cf. John Mibiti, African Religions and Philosophy, London, 1971, 226.

[138] Cf. J. Baur, 2000 Years, 413; Cf. E. Ayandele, The Missionary Impact, 286. Apart from the society of the Holy Ghost Fathers and the Presbyterians, other missionaries restricted educational achievement to only evangelistic objectives.

colonial rule in 1900, the colonial rulers made a change of policy. It promulgated an education code in 1903 that gave the rules for the provision of primary and secondary schools. By 1912, the colonial administration had 59 primary schools while the missions had 91 in the south. This changed the thinking that schools were the strict preserve of the missions. The expansion of the post primary schools was very slow because the pioneer missionaries did little to improve the status quo; many felt that providing the common people with post primary education was superfluous and could make them intellectually arrogant and materialistic. This argument was not tenable because even between 1859 and 1914 some post primary schools were already established by the missions.[139] Another factor that gave rise to more secondary schools was the anti-colonial move of the emerged superpowers after World War II, as Moscow and Washington placed colonial authorities under pressure for decolonisation.[140] The increased number of secondary schools was meant to step up Africa's preparedness for self rule and independence.[141] Thus these factors coupled with nationalists' movements created democratic capabilities and groundbreaking thrust for independence of many nations under colonial rule.

The World Missionary Conference in Edinburgh in 1910 adopted the education-strategy as the best means to Christianise the African population. Apart from the Christian and the humanitarian goals inherent in education, it thus became "the instrument for colonizing the Africans' mind".[142] Bishop Shanahan is known for the popular statement that if he captures the hearts of the children, he was sure their hearts were in Catholic hands.[143] A system some authors refer to as the 'school magic' because of the increased number of Christian population it has garnered in Eastern Nigeria.[144] This 'school magic' presented a mutual game of deception and exploitation between the missionaries on one hand and the people on the other hand. The villages wanted the schools for socio-economic reasons, while the village school was the principal means of evangelisation by the missions then.[145] However there was some local participation in the payment of fees, financing school

---

[139] Cf. A. G. Onokerhoraye, Social Services in Nigeria, 15-16.
[140] Cf. Chniweizu, The West and the Rest of us, New York, 1975, 103.
[141] Cf. J. Baur, 2000 Years, 413.
[142] O. U Kalu, To hang a Ladder, 101
[143] Cf. Ibid., 110.
[144] Cf. E. Ayandele, The Missionary Impact, 265; J. Baur, 2000 Years, 143.
[145] Cf. Innocent O. Dim, Reception of Vatican II in Nigeria/Igbo Church with Reference to Awka Diocese, Frankfurt am Main, 2004, 75.

buildings and scholarships from kinships and ethnic unions especially in the rural areas.[146] Bishop Shanahan's dynamic pursuit of this educational drive made the inspectors from Lyon in 1929 wonder whether the Holy Ghost Fathers had not derailed from evangelism. This educational dynamism made the World Missionary Conference in Edinburgh to adopt education as the best strategy for winning African converts. According to the report from J.R. Mott, one of the attendees of this conference, in a German adage, he attested to this point: that 'what you would put into the life of a nation, put into its schools.' Education however served the instrument that mediated this Christian message.[147]

The missions involved in the task of civilization pursued education, modelled to the west to transform the indigenous African milieu into modern states. The missions, through this Christianising role in the nation would provide the masses with the opportunity to respond to present and future social and economic structures. This was another humanitarian sign from the reports of the conference in Edinburgh that would positively influence Christianity. The ensuing suggestion was to have a native agency trained, to shoulder the envisaging challenges and burden of the proposed self governing, self-funding, self-propagating Churches. Therefore education was the instrument to serve this purpose of raising native Christian Churches, to be national and yet capable as an independent church that is devoid of foreign influence and support.[148] As mentioned earlier, however realistic this view may be to other denominations, it is not tenable in the Catholic Church for her central nature of governance; nevertheless, the inferred self-reliance and self supporting idea is important from the Catholic perspective. It is a foresighted humanitarian practice that is embedded with self-reliance. From the Protestant perspectives, it did not only end with autonomy in the church's leadership, or Nigerians becoming church ministers; it extended to all branches of the faith in question. To this effect, the WMC "recommended changes in the content and method of education, with emphasis on agricultural and industrial training."[149] This was to prepare the indigenes culturally and economically, to lead both the church and the state in responding to the challenges of their time and that of the future.[150] All these

---

[146] Cf. T. Falola, M. M. Heaton, A History of Nigeria 139.
[147] Cf. O. U. Kalu, To hang a Ladder in the Air, 110.
[148] Cf. Ibid., 115. (See also World Missionary)
[149] Ibid., 115.
[150] Cf. Ibid., 115.

stress the objective of the practised humanitarianism of this period that was imperative of self-reliance.

The school strategy consequently produced the democratic capabilities, the foundation and the springboard that propelled the agitation for self rule and independence in many African nations. These newly grown African elites became the nationalists and some eventually became presidents of the newly independent nations in sub-Saharan Africa. Out of the 16 who eventually emerged as first citizens of these independent nations, 11 were Christians and 5 were Moslems and all had mission school background.[151] The benefits of this humanitarian work of setting up schools were the stepping stone to many developments in Africa. The great majority of Nigerian elite especially in the areas of politics, medicine, law, in civil service and education owe their beginnings to the success of the mission schools. It offered the African elites the opportunity to define and document their native languages into written form; coupled with the spread of the bible in the African languages, which created the possibility of learning these languages from the book.[152] Some observe that the educational work of the missions and the development of indigenous languages into written form were the greatest legacy of the missions.[153] All these perspectives created through the dawn of mission schools were humanitarian as they created new opportunities for the new nations and the means to live together.

Another landmark created by the advent of the schools was the possibility of women's emancipation. Even though the percentage of the pupils was conspicuously male, it however created gender awareness, social breakthrough and self consciousness for the women. It prepared women for many modern occupations like nursing and teaching, gave them the opportunity to earn their living and be able to determine their future, for example the choice of husband, the family structure and the kind of care they were comfortable with.[154] This development gradually reduced the stereotyped picture of the woman reduced to domestic work. Even though such liberation is an ongoing process, the schools did set this humanitarian task in motion.

---

[151] Cf. J. Baur, 2000 Years, 281.

[152] Cf. E. Ayandele, The Missionary Impact, 304.

[153] Cf. Hauwa Imam, Educational Policy in Nigeria from the Colonial Era to the Post-Independence Period, 182, in: Italian Journal of Sociology of Education I, 2012, Pdf, Pp 181-204.

[154] Cf. J. Baur, 2000 Years, 415.

In spite of the fortunes of education, the art of breaking ties with traditional norms which was one aim of western education[155] created a rift between the traditional life style of the average African and the educated African. This development took the pattern of the Greek philosopher Stoic, who differentiated the human man and ordinary man, the educated man and the brute respectively.[156] Even though it was a give and take relationship, it affected the culture and consequently the African Traditional Religion (ATR), which was intertwined and seemingly inseparable from the African culture and lifestyle. It lessened the patronage and practice of ATR; today many Africans regard the ATR as backward and lacking the sophistication of the present age. The school, despite its economic and political advantages watered down some societal values and traditional means of treatment/healing. From the foregoing, some of the traditionally established ethnic groups were sceptical of the adverse effect of this new lifestyle, as it threatened their traditions, structures, traditional lifestyles and local institutions.[157] The people were blinded by the humanitarian advantages of the schools and they got wrapped up in the attractive options and opportunities the system presented even to the detriment of the societal development. These distorted developments, like broken native institutions and local medications for example became the fallout of western education.

Regardless of the ambivalences, hindsight, religious motives, the force created by the advent of schools can never be underestimated. It was about the greatest humanitarian good to the natives, even though there were traces of a humanitarianism practised from convenience. The aspect of the appreciation of humanity was however very glaring too. Therefore,

> ...whatever the motives on both sides, in the sociological perspective the mission schools were the greatest service done to our developing African nations. It is in this respect that Dr. Kwame Nkrumah, himself a former student of a Catholic mission school, said at a students' seminar shortly after the achievement of independence: "the rise of our country is properly due to the missionaries. To their work and their assistance I and others owe what we are now." Yes, without their educational work independence would have been delayed for several decades or, if imposed by political events, it would have

---

[155] Cf. O. U. Kalu, To hang a Ladder in the Air, 119.
[156] Cf. C. Douzinas, The Many Faces of Humanitarianism, 1. A concept that was later adopted by the Romans too. The Homo Humanus was the educated Roman and the Homo Barbarus, the ordinary Roman.
[157] Cf. E. Ayandele, Missionary Impact, 290.

left the new nations without the necessary leadership and manpower to run the country.[158]

In short, the missionaries were mostly trailblazers in many rural areas before the coming of the private and government owned schools. The first generation of Christians were the products of these schools, while others received only the education, they probably learnt the rudiments of the Christian faith and the many Christian virtues embedded in the mission schools. However, the modern day humanitarian may question why should the gospel precede the humanitarian task? The provision of answers to social problems is part of evangelisation and the church's *diakonein* role. This service to humanity makes the church humanitarian, since humanitarianism is about improving the social life of others. She is also humanitarian because she is concerned with both the spiritual and material care of all humans and not her adherents alone, because all are created in the image and likeness of God. This trait brings out her altruism and an impartial gesture which in itself is humanitarian. Besides while the secular humanitarian acts on one hand only from the angle of humanity, the church on the other hand acts from the foundation that humanity comes from God and not by itself.

2.1.4 Medical institutions

Colonialism and the spread of Christian missionary enterprise remain the two most important factors that have shaped contemporary Africa. As the colonial administration concentrated on the political and economical restructuring, the missionaries focussed on the social and cultural life of the people.[159] The colonial administration, through her support to the missions to establish schools and medical institutions, felt the natives would in the long run appreciate the colonial rule. But it was the missionaries' ability to explore these social needs of the Africans that made this humanitarian enterprise unique, interesting and attractive.[160] The medical institutions were so important that they "clearly occupied a second place in missionary activity. Education was considered a direct response to Christ's commission 'go and teach all nations'; healing diseases seemed to have been an activity used mostly to support Christ's own teaching mission."[161] Therefore, medical institutions became another arm of the

---

[158] J. Baur, 2000 Years, 414-415. (See also Pax Romana Seminar Accra, 1957)
[159] Cf. C. J. Korieh, Conflicts and Compromise, 154.
[160] Cf. Ibid., 157.
[161] J. Baur, 2000 Years, 416.

missions through the establishment of hospitals, dispensaries, mobile clinics and other medical installations.[162] This medical perspective was humanitarian, because the missions saw the care of the souls as inseparable from the wellbeing of the people.

The presence of the missionaries, being all things to the natives, posed a social healing to the natives for example through administering first aid and other medical services like injections. This system gave birth to the first Catholic medical initiative, a sixty bed hospital in 1908 in Kwararafa.[163] This factor, a pure humanitarian service was more in the interior, where medical services were like luxury because of non-government's presence and thus became a daily routine of the missionaries. Many indigenous Nigerian communities since 1914 were beginning to feel the impact of missionary presence through the establishment of missionary hospitals. From 1914, missions began to establish hospitals; the CMS founded Iyi Enu Hospital near Onitsha, (Eastern Nigeria) the Baptist established a hospital in Ogbomosho. The Wesleyan Guild Hospital was founded in Ilesha and the Sacred Heart Hospital, the first real Catholic Hospital by the SMA in Abeokuta (the last three are all in western Nigeria). Because of local scepticism and suspicions about these medical institutions, they did not flourish immediately until after 1914. However the increasing number of converts automatically gave credence to the missions and increased the patronage of mission medical establishments.[164] The Sacred Heart Hospital in Abeokuta gave meaningful recognition to the little Yoruba Catholic Community presence in a town that was then dominated by Islam, Protestantism and ATR.[165] The colonial administration too established a few outreach clinics in Lagos and Asaba in 1898. Moreover, in 1898 the colonial administration constructed a sturdy hospital in Calabar. As from 1900, many military makeshift hospitals were built in Jebba and Lokoja. The

---

[162] Cf. J. Mbiti, African Religions and Philosophy, London 1971, 233.
[163] Cf. Anthony Attah Agbali, The Catholic Church, Social Justice Teachings and Healthcare Delivery in Nigeria, in Eds., Toyin Falola, Matthew M. Heaton, Traditional and Modern Health System in Nigeria, Trenton, 2006, Pp. 37-90, 44. Kwararafa is the name of the kingdom of the Jukuns in today's Taraba State, Nigeria.
[164] Cf. E. Ayandele, Missionary Impact, 343.
[165] Cf. J. Baur, 2000 Years, 147.

commencement of World War I encouraged the building of such hospitals from 1915 for military reasons.[166]

Due to the importance of medical practice to the missions and the people's dependence on the mission hospitals, European missionaries for example the White Fathers, from 1920 began adding special courses like tropical medicines to their formation. Among the missionary sisters on African mission, at least one was earmarked as a trained nurse, to help in the establishment of medical services like dispensaries. This dispensary, a mini hospital became one of the most attractive institutions even in the Moslem dominated areas, where conversion to Christianity was least expected. It granted missionaries the opportunities for contacts with women, by winning their confidence through maternity services. This also helped to reduce the high mortality rate that was common before the advent of western medicine. From the statistics of *Propaganda Fidei* in 1930, some 1100 dispensaries were at the services of over 11 million consultations. About 20 years later, dispensaries had risen to 1500 with corresponding 30 million consultations.[167] Over the years, as the hospitals and other medical installations increased in number, size, operations and patronage, missionaries were faced with the challenge of the low number of qualified personnel. To this effect, some female congregations like the Medical Missionaries of Mary (MMM) and Medical Missionary Sisters (MMS) began the training of sister doctors for their respective missions. CMS as well had to employ the services of minsters that had medical knowledge at the beginning, to cover for the required expertise.[168]

In 1930, Nigeria had 71 hospitals, 47 of them were established by the colonial administration, while 23 by missionaries and one privately owned hospital.[169] From this number, the colonial administration provided 12 modern hospitals for the services of 4000 Europeans, whereas the remaining 59 were established for well over 40 million Nigerians,[170] bringing a contrast that necessitated the very demanding presence of the

---

[166] Cf. A. G. Onokehrhoraye, Social Services in Nigeria, 102. These hospitals were built as sub-stations for wounded soldiers in transit. Nigeria became a temporary military base for British soldiers en route to the East and other parts of the world.
[167] Cf. J. Baur, 2000 Years, 416.
[168] Cf. Ibid.
[169] Cf. A. Onokerhoraye, Social Services in Nigeria, 102.
[170] Cf. A. Adebanjo, The Curse of Berlin, 20, (See also A. Adu Boahen, African Perspectives on Colonialism, 109)

missionaries to fill in such complex gaps. By 1945 the number of hospitals rose to about 116; 46 of them belonged to the missions and 69 were colonial administrative owned and a private one. The mission in her uniqueness concentrated her health facilities more in the interior, unlike the colonial owned, who were more in the urban areas.[171] From 1860 till 1960, Nigeria had over 200 hospitals; slightly over 50% of them were missionary facilities. But by 1970, the number had tripled.[172] Despite government's plans after the 1960, health facilities still remained negligible for the teeming Nigerian population. Thus the mission's resourcefulness to cover these humanitarian breaches is worthy of praise.

2.1.5 Professional training and centres for skill acquisition

Centres for skill acquisition or vocational schools were also one of the remarkable developments of the missions. In these centres, new types of craft works other than the well known indigenous ones were taught. But the issue of skill acquisition and professional training has faced a long and twisted history of questionable success and failures in Nigeria. Over the years, voluntary agencies have shown less interest in such schools than in primary or secondary schools, making it a reserve of the government. Unfortunately, technical and vocational schools are wrongly viewed by many as avenues for dropouts from secondary schools. Their establishment and running cost is thrice more than the academically oriented secondary schools and that alone makes such vocational institutions scarce and inadequate.[173]

The indigenous technical and professional knowledge from craftsmen and farmers was entirely missing. This was because of the oral tradition in the African background, which hampered the documentation and transfer of skills, coupled with the subsistence and crude agricultural practice that was facing a sudden confrontation of a much more technically advanced

---

[171] Cf. A. Onokerhoraye, Social Services in Nigeria, 102- 103.

[172] Cf. Daniel E. Harmon, Nigeria, 1880 to the Present: The Struggle, the Tragedy, the Promise, London, 2000, 121. Cf. A. Onorkerhoraye, Social Services in Nigeria, 103. On the part of the Nigerian government, she was still lagging behind to catch up with the required health institutions and personnel after the nations independence. However, there were a few efforts by government to increase medical facilities for example, the ten year development plan 1946-56, the Federal national development Plan, (FNDP) 1962-68 and the Second National Development Plan, 1970-74.

[173] Cf. Ibid. 22-23.

and developed agricultural practice from Europe. It created a missing link between the traditional agricultural practice and the modern one. The missionaries, for reasons of self-reliance, established model farms and plantations in the course of their settlement; (a system which unfortunately from the records, were not successful), with the intention to assist the natives in developing new skills. This task was curtailed by the lack of local skills. As a result, the natives resorted to learning only the foreign agricultural skills from the book, which eventually encouraged the book-learning that is mostly devoid of practice.[174] Besides, since the early mission schools were observed to be bereft of industrial education, the social and economic needs of the people, their curriculum never had the thrust to improve agriculture and handicraft. However in 1897 the first industrial institution was established by CMS in Brass and Onitsha.[175] But the fact still remains that such schools were scarce and the few that were built were out of reach for the majority of the populace, especially the rural dwellers.

From the foregoing, missionaries who were all things to all men were handicapped in proffering solutions to the agricultural practices then, for the obvious reasons that, some of the food items were strange to them. However their presence facilitated the documentation of skills. It gradually made the practice of obscurantism (as practised by the local medicine men/women too) a thing of the past. It helped to evolve new strategies, for the simple fact that it made people aware that there were alternative ways, even though such later inventions too were still seemingly crude. These missionaries' efforts, however minute were humanitarian; it was the appreciation of humanity and above all a gesture towards self-reliance.

Critics believe that the advent of the superior and cheaper imported goods like chairs, tables, umbrellas, drawers, plates and so on, from the West damaged the little indigenous handicraft. Of course, humans by nature would prefer superior goods to the home-made, thereby belittling domestic production. The option on the table for the missionaries was to teach their converts these new superior skills, which had to do with massive importation of new tools.[176] The missionary presence created new technical skills like carpentry, masonry, brick-making, cabinet-making, tailoring and different artisanship. It encouraged the setting up of small modern businesses, which

---

[174] Cf. J. Baur, 2000 Years, 415.
[175] Cf. E. Ayandele, The Missionary Impact, 296-297.
[176] Cf. Ibid., 296.

subsequently created new opportunities and alternative lifestyles.[177] Although the superior goods edged out inferior ones of the natives, it was the product of change, the only constant thing in nature. These new opportunities for economic growth were however a gradual move from the agriculturally dominated economy to a multifaceted one.

2.1.6 Curbing societal vices

Despite the evils of colonialism, it helped to check some societal ills which were prevalent among the people then. For example, in some of the old kingdoms, human sacrifice was highly practised to avert calamities as prescribed by a deity or a god.[178] Also at the death of a local chief for example, it was customary to bury along with the deceased some innocent persons. But the coming of colonialism and Christianity opposed many of these practices.[179] Since the colonial administration was at the helm of affairs, communities that practised such acts in the past were put under spotlight. Christian churches performed progressive tasks as they abhorred the trial by ordeal and the killing of twins which was rampant in some parts of the country.[180] Due to the poor state of local medicine and the high mortality rate, mothers of twins often faced greater danger of non-survival and complications at delivery. Besides, the surplus births of twins in some parts of Africa were misconstrued with some superstitious beliefs, therefore subsequent drought or one mishap or the other in the society could be ascribed as the repercussion from the birth of twins.[181] Thanks to science accompanied by western education, which denounced such beliefs and with the presence of the missionaries a natural end was created. Efforts to abolish the killing of twins in some parts of Nigeria have been credited to

---

[177] Cf. T. Falola, The History of Nigeria, 44.

[178] Cf. Fidelis Eleojo Egbunu, Igala traditional Values versus Modernity, Nsukka 2009, 20. The sacrifice of Inikpi and the other virgins were evidence of human sacrifice too. However, its uniqueness has turned out to be a thing of pride in the Igala kingdom for its military victory and the consequent liberation.

[179] Cf. R.S. Seton, Installation of An Attah of Idah (Nigeria), in: The Journal of the Royal Anthropological Institute of great Britain and Ireland, Vol. LXVI, London, (no year) Pp 255-679, 257. One of the commonest features after the death of the Attah of Igala was the silent period. Some have interpreted this period as the grace interval to gather enough slaves for the funeral ceremonies; Fidelis Eleojo Egbunu, Chieftaincy Titles among Igala, Problems and Prospects for Christians, Idah, 2001, 140. He enjoins Christian Chiefs to aspire for necessary reforms and modifications.

[180] Cf. W. Rodney, How Europe underdeveloped Africa, 278.

[181] Cf. Ali Mazrui, The African Condition, The Reith Lectures, London, 1981, 46.

missionaries, for example Mary Slessor (1848-1915), a Scottish missionary in Calabar the present South-South Nigeria.[182] With the growth and presence of Christianity, numerous societal vices perpetrated against humanity gradually faded away from different communities.

2.1.7 Human rights and human dignity

The Nigerian people like every other society had her questionable history of human rights and dignity, coupled with the petty wars, fear of raid and attack from the other ethnic groups that fuelled the atmosphere of fear of disaster. These created insecurity around many kingdoms. Some historians are aligned to the success and the positive side of colonialism for the relative peace it offered during the colonial period, which was never so in the preceding period. Alan Burns (1887-1980) and some other historians believe it was the best thing that happened to Nigeria. Though it was forceful, it did create some level of peace, some governance in place of tyranny and abolished human sacrifice and slavery. Besides, it gave the indigenes stability and some room for business interactions, thereby permitting trade and subsequently creating internal wealth. It doused the fear of sudden raid and attack on farm, roads, at home or in the market by other ethnic groups and tribes, which without the advent of the British rule was very often.[183]

The motivating humanitarian phrase of the Quakers and other missionaries that 'all are children of God' empowered the missions to advocate for equal treatment and to stand against cultural practices that were inconsistent with the practice of human rights and dignity.[184] The mission presence gave the relegated in the society some recognition, for example many of the slave children given away by local chiefs for western education turned out to be at the helm of affairs in the new dispensation, wielding strong influences in independent Nigeria.[185] The missions played this role, like other *diakonein* duties, to uplift the social status of the people

---

[182] Cf. Wholesome words, Missionary Biography,
http://www.wholesomewords.org/missions/bioslessor2.htm l . (07.07.14)
[183] Cf. B. Okpanachi, Nigerian-Vatican Diplomatic Relations, 43 (See also Alan Burns, History, 307-308). There is every tendency for Alan Burns to go into this line of argument, since one of the British imperial intentions was mercantilism. Without economic activities among the natives, it was going to affect the volume of trade between the indigenes and the settlers. However this does not undermine the above mentioned advantages to the natives.
[184] Cf. I. O. Dim The Reception of Vat. II, 77.
[185] Cf. E. Ayandele The Impact 290.

irrespective of ethnicity or religion. This neutrality that the church has maintained in her humanitarian actions, has earned the church a good name and record in contemporary Nigeria.

2.1.8 The ethical relationship between missions and colonial authority

The colonial administration and the missions became the most dominant humanitarian actors in colonial Nigeria; these two most important bastions of British colonial rule[186] were humanitarian in varied ways. The missionaries with meagre means and dependent on the government were subordinate to the colonial administration. Since they were dependent on the colonial administration for security, support and some funding, "the government frequently took advantage of this dependency to control the missionaries and their mission station residents."[187] It created a crisis identity for the missions: how were they to relate with the imperial interest of the colonial administration that they were heavily dependent upon, even for transport of goods and materials from their home countries to their mission territories?

> As they ministered to, and interacted with Christians and non-Christians alike, missionaries struggled with the conflict between their „universalist Christian religious values and the imperial context of those values. One audience might describe this relationship as a conflict between faith and power, another as the relationship between universal egalitarian ideals and an exploitative imperial presence.[188]

The imperial spirit of the colonial heads offered no space for the brotherhood that was embedded in the Christian message. Hence missionaries were torn between the lordship role imparted on them from the imperialist *zeitgeist* and the Christian message of brotherliness.[189] Even though the collaborative and cooperative spirit was very high, there was however some level of

---

[186] Cf. W. Wariboko, The CMS Mission, 36. The author uses this phrase to describe the south eastern Nigeria. However it was a common fact in the colonial Africa that the colonial rule and the missions were about the strongest foreign body among the indigenous Africans. In the Nigerian case, this was more common in the southern part of the country, because of the obvious Christian domination unlike the north with a dominant Muslim population.

[187] Roger B. Beck, All Things to all people: Christian Missionaries in Early Nineteenth Century South Africa, in: Eds., Chima J. Korieh, et al., Missions, States and European Expansion in Africa, African Studies, History, Politics, Economics, and Culture, New York 2007, Pp. 11-34, 15.

[188] Ibid., 11.

[189] Cf. Ibid.

opposition from the missionaries as regards some colonial policies; this helped the missionaries occasionally to maintain some level of independence.[190]

Since the mission was a place of charity, she was easily accepted by the commoners, who were primary beneficiaries. As such, she made very swift inroads into the interior where colonial control and presence was negligible. But sad enough, this mission soon became a requisite factor to extend colonial rule to the hinterlands. As the colonial administration sought for mission support so as to gain access to the grassroots, the mission consequently and sometimes became a conduit of the colonial rule.

> Missionaries, because of the moral values they preached and the close relationships they maintained with their converts in the mission-stations, were often considered as custodians and guardians of the people's moral conscience, including their political conscience. For this reason the secular authorities used them as one other means of keeping a close surveillance on the political pulse of society throughout the period of the informal empire, including the initial decades after the imposition of colonial rule.[191]

To this effect, missions were at times turned into colonial quasi-administrative centres. Missionaries in some places were meant to do some unpleasant and odious jobs for the colonial administration. In some parts of Africa, they even issued travel documents, acted as spies and were subjected into making regular reports of activities and the conduct of the indigenes in the interior. Missionaries acted often as informants and advisers to the colonial administration as well as to the indigenes they lived with. As they represented both sides of the imperial frontline, it was breeding some level of mistrust and suspicion in the missions. Inasmuch as the missionaries' first role was that of evangelization, they became representatives/agents of colonial administration. They were answerable to the colonial administration for the numerous roles the colonial administration was playing in the success of the missions, for example their security and funding. In return, they were obliged to pay back by implementing and enforcing colonial administrative policies.[192]

The European attempt to penetrate Africa for political and economic reasons acted as a fertile ground for expansion of evangelism. Even though

---

[190] Cf. Ibid., 18; W. Wariboko, The CMS Mission, 37.

[191] W. Wariboko, The CMS mission, 43.

[192] Cf. R. B. Beck, All Things to all people, 34; W. Wariboko, The CMS Mission, 43.

there were signs of conflicts and differences between the two bastions, "they [however] worked concertedly to impose the British colonial state on the indigenous populations."[193] There are schools of thoughts that the memos of the colonialists together with the missionaries served as the sources of intelligence gathered for the scramble and partitioning of Africa.[194] It counters the probity of the Christian missions and their humanitarian objectives. However, one can submit to the fact that the

> colonial agents and missionaries mutually exchanged *avant-garde* roles, and they collaborated in other ways in the pursuit of their respective aims. There are reasons for this collaboration. First, their respective goals sometimes traversed each other. Second, they shared a common religious and cultural background. Third, they shared the same ideologies about racial differences, as well as stereotyping. Both considered their subjects and potential converts barbaric, and so it was justified to use any means available, to subdue them into accepting Western notions of civilization along with the Christian faith. Fourth, in the mission and colonial lands, missionaries and colonial agents faced common traits of resistance and physical dangers.[195]

The entire mission of civilization brought down in different facets "was firmly predicated on the notion that Europeans were racially superior to non Europeans—in this case Africans".[196] Since Africa was more or less a passive receiver and never an active interventionist,[197] she received paternalistic humanitarian services. Decisions were solely taken by the initiators of the projects in question, this was however a common thing in the age of imperialism. Therefore paternalism was an offshoot of imperial humanitarianism. In this task of civilization with colonialism serving as the background, the officials of both bastions believed it was the best way to effect civilization. The indigenous societies must be exposed to the influences and values of British civilization, commerce and Christianity. These three Cs served as the ground for the mission of civilization. In this division of labour, the different arms were more or less doing different but coherent things towards the goal of imperialism, in the name of civilization. This included the military subjugation of the people, in order to create a political atmosphere and environment for merchants and missionary patronage under a mercantile system, so as to ease the implantation of the

---

[193] W. Wariboko, The CMS Mission, 36.

[194] Cf. Chinweizu, The West and the rest of us, 52.

[195] J. C. Aguwa, Mission, Colonialism and the supplanting of African Practices, 131.

[196] W. Wariboko, The CMS Mission, 36.

[197] Cf. A. Mazrui, The African Condition, 16,

values of Christianity and capitalism. Many interpreted this action as the proverbial breaking of the eggs to make the omelette.[198] This governance, trade, commerce and Christianity altered the life of the colonised forever.

Why should missionaries in their relationship with the colonial administration be subjected to play roles that were unchristian, thereby subjecting their missions to mistrust? Some missionaries however held the view that whenever western civilization arrived without such accompanied religious atmosphere and sanctions, it was likely to generate dangerous and unacceptable influences. From this foregoing, it was necessary for the missions to be co-partners in the civilization cause, to effect the required socio-cultural and religious structure.[199] In essence, the missions were responsible for imparting British culture to the indigenes, she was responsible for training, even manipulating and 'forming' the minds of the indigenes and probably to serve as some kind of 'impotent observer' of the colonial excesses. In all this, it is clear the mission played an immense role in the institutionalisation of the British political power and presence in Nigeria. Arnold Toynbee is of the opinion that missionary exercise ceases to be a legitimate one, when it strives in the name of evangelism to bring another nation under the political extension and advantage of her own mother nation.[200] Was this ambivalent position the only and possible way the missions and the missionaries were able to practice their evangelical task and humanitarian works? Was it a question of the missionaries scratching the backs of the colonial administration so as to have theirs scratched in return? In whichever way the analysis may go, the missions had good intentions, but they were perpetually the 'unavoidable' link between the colonial officers and the indigenes. Occasionally some missionaries were carried away by the enshrined and the already induced European supremacy in the psyche of the indigenes. However, many schools of thoughts have maintained that the colonial administration and the missionaries had a united and collective ideology, to promote British imperial interest.

To summarise the mission enterprise and her humanitarian contributions towards modern Nigeria, the certainty remains that "of all the

---

[198] Cf. W. Wariboko, The CMS Mission, 37.
[199] Cf. Ibid., 38.
[200] Cf. Ibid., 45. (See also Arnold Toynbee, Change and Habit: The Challenge of our Time, Oxford: One World, 1992, 191)

agencies which have contributed to the regeneration and development of ... [Nigeria], missionary effort has been the most potent‒is an axiom."[201]

2.2   Humanitarianism in post World War II period (1945-1973)

The pressure of the superpowers for decolonisation and the nationalist's agitation for self-rule after World War II brought about some constitutional transfer of power to the early Nigerian elite.[202] Through this concession, regions were granted some constitutional autonomy in the new political dispensation that increased their role towards their people, for example the free education policy of western Nigeria in 1957, which became exemplary to other regions.[203] The increased role made regional blocks humanitarian partners as well. Their economic activities and sustenance were centred on agricultural products, like cocoa, palm oil and groundnuts. Through the political independence on 1st October 1960, the Nigerian government inherited fully the past roles performed by the British colonial rule.

Some factors made the Nigerian economy to be tied to the British, for example the imposition of British currencies as legal tender and her export quest that made the cash crop production for economic purpose in colonial period a commonplace. It thereby displaced the cultivation of food crops for the domestic needs of the nation.[204] This consequently created enormous challenges for the post colonial government to effect a quick transformation from this inherited status quo 'the agro-economy' to an 'industrially producing one'. The first step was "to accelerate the pace of economic development and improve the welfare of the... citizens through expanded health and educational system, in part to satisfy the massive expectations aroused during the transfer of power".[205] The central government, caught in this transformation web proposed the Federal National Development Plan, FNDP, focussing on agriculture, industry and education. With an anticipated growth rate of 4 percent, savings and investments rate of 15 percent annually, the FNDP was to complement the

---

[201] E. Ayandele, The Missionary Impact, 304. (See also Lagos Weekly Record, 6 Jan. 1894)

[202] Cf. T. Falola, The History of Nigeria, 89.

[203] Cf. T. Falola, M. M. Heaton, A History of Nigeria, 146.

[204] Cf. Alaisdair Tenquist, Nigeria, A Study on an economically Developing Country, East Sussex England, 1966, 31; T. Falola, M. M. Heaton, A History of Nigeria, 111.

[205] John Healey, Mark Robinson, Democracy, Governance and Economic Policy, Sub-Saharan Africa in Comparative Perspective, Nottingham, 1992, 23.

political independence project of post World War II with economic independence; thus political independence without economic independence would amount to nothing. The mining sector was the most thriving industrial development, rising from 0.9 percent in 1960 to 4.8 percent in 1966. Petroleum sector was gaining momentum from 1961 to 1967, growing from 46,000 barrels per day (bpd) to 600, 000 bpd. Nonetheless other manufacturing units like tobacco, food processing and beverages were on steady growth from 3.6 percent in 1960 to 6.2 percent in 1966. Agriculture which was the major means of resource generation stagnated between 1960 and 1966 and fell from 63.4 percent to 55.6 percent of GNP. The economy was growing at an annual rate of 5 percent. The per capita income rose from N48.1 in 1960 to N53.8 in 1966. The GNP rose from N2, 244.6 in 1960 to 3,140.8 million in 1966. With this steady growth despite the myriad socio-political problems in the background, many optimists were still enthusiastic about a promising Nigeria.[206] Also the economy was affected by internal and external factors and the fact that over 70 percent of the firms were owned and managed by foreign hands alone [207] excluded job opportunities for Nigerians.

The humanitarian question is how much of these developmental plans did translate to the ordinary people? Only the urban areas saw trickles of these developments, many Nigerians like the peasant farmers, the poor, rural dwellers were barely Nigerians by name.

2.2.1 Nigerian Civil War experience

The amalgamation of the southern and northern protectorates into one colony in 1914, a political decision solely by the British colonial rule, remains one of the underlying controversies in modern Nigeria. Since the bonding of the regions was devoid of self determinism and consent, the eventual independence in 1960 only marked a journey of myriad social problems like discord, scepticism and mutual distrust among the many nations in Nigeria. Most particularly was the entrenched animosity among the three big ethnic groups: the *Hausa/Fulani* in the North, the *Yorubas* in the South/West and the *Igbos* in the South/East, as they struggled among themselves to dominate the nation. The central government was represented by a *troika* government, practised by these three majority ethnic groups. As

---

[206] Cf. T. Falola, M. M. Heaton, A History of Nigeria, 163.

[207] Cf. T. Falola, The History of Nigeria, 113.

the three fought for political supremacy, the other ethnic groups, over 250, were mostly used as pawns to achieve the political advantage of the three major ethnic groups. These stark differences, the lopsided regionalism and the flawed federal structure were posing very conspicuous challenges to the nation. Thus, modern Nigeria is "a conservative, army-disciplined north and an ebullient, individualistic and trade minded south".[208] The background of the war bore the signs of misgivings and misunderstanding within the context of one Nigeria that was impalpable among the many ethnic groups.

The Nigerian civil war lasted for thirty months, spanning from July 1967 till January 1970. There have been irreconcilable statistics of estimated casualties between one and three million. Humanitarian work before the civil war was still on peaceful ground, until the 1967 experience, when humanitarianism was carried out on a wide scale to alleviate the plight of the Eastern Nigerians. It shifted attention from the suffering of the masses to relief materials. As these plights took centre stage, humanitarian actors and the military administration were mostly preoccupied with the palliative task and the struggle to end the war respectively. Thus industrial development and agriculture were retarded during this period.[209]

2.2.2 The action of the humanitarian organisations and the diplomatic fallout

The economic blockade in the secessionist state created a humanitarian lack that made her suffer economic strangulation. Hunger and starvation became one of the weapons of the war and a synonym of the civil war. There was little media coverage at the beginning of the war, which has been interpreted as media conspiracy to keep Biafra out of the press. Without publicity, humanitarian organisations would lack funding opportunities for relief action. But the greatest media publicity that lunched Biafra into western limelight was by Markpress, owned by an American William Bernhardt, based in Geneva. The photographs of kwashiorkor afflicted children, the bombings and strafing evoked deep sympathy. This publicity provoked humanitarian response all over the world especially in the western world.[210] Their donations helped to boost humanitarian support in the Biafran state.

---

[208] Nigeria's New Dawn, Understanding Global Issues, 1.
[209] Cf. T. Falola, The History of Nigeria, 132.
[210] Cf. http://www.spiegel.de/spiegel/print/d-44914623.html.

Prominent among the humanitarian agencies that came on board were, the ICRC, the *Caritas Internationalis* (CI), which was the umbrella of all other Catholic humanitarian agencies. The German presence was very conspicuous, coupled with the support of their federal government through the *Diakonisches Werk* (DW) and the *Deutscher Caritasverband* (DCV). Also were the Swiss Caritas, *Misereor*, War on Want, Oxfam, *Nordchurchaid*, World Council of Churches (WCC), USA, Britain, the Scandinavian countries. Later, the Church organisations operated under the umbrella of Joint Church Aid (JCA). But because of the centralistic nature of the Catholic Church and the Catholic presence in the Biafran community, the name Caritas (implying, CI) became more dominant in this operation. Caritas was also able to coordinate large shipments from CRS and UNICEF. This project 'Operation Biafra' lasted for 22 months,[211] with a total number of 27 agencies.[212]

Since it became difficult to secure a safe humanitarian corridor to deliver relief materials, agencies resorted to airlifts. Goods were ferried by planes from Sao Tome (a nearby island belonging then to Portugal) to Uli in Biafra. Virtually all the foodstuffs that came to this closed society were through airlifts. However "the most heart-breaking tasks and the dirtiest work were undertaken by the Roman Catholics."[213] At the end of the operation, JCA had recorded 5310 flights into the enclave through supplying foodstuffs, accommodation medication and clinical assistance worth DM. 166 Million. It was termed then as the largest humanitarian aid since after World War II.[214]

As the economic blockade cut off Biafra from the rest of the world, only the ICRC had diplomatic rights to supply relief materials. However this was truncated too when a Red Cross plane was bombed in June 1969, leaving behind only the church agencies on the humanitarian scene. The CI and other church agencies, being propelled by Christian charity, went through all odds to deliver food and relief materials. They were accused of

---

[211] Cf. E. Ayebome, The Nigeria-Biafra War and the negotiating Role, 24. (See also Archive, Generalversammlung)
[212] Cf. Ibid. 32. (See also Archive, Generalversammlung)
[213] Fredrick Forsyth, The Making of an African Legend: The Biafra Story, New York, 1978, 210.
[214] Cf. Christian Heidrich, Carlo Bayer, Ein Römer aus Schlesien und Pionier Caritas Internationalis, Arbeiten zur schlesischen Kirchengeschichte, Bd. VI, Sigmaringen, 1992, 237.

prolonging the war and being accomplices in the smuggling of ammunitions to the secessionist administration. After the war, the foreign resident missionaries in Biafra during the war suffered the diplomatic brunt, like deportation and other diplomatic issues. The remaining relief materials from JCA were rejected and labelled as blood money by the Nigerian military administration.[215]

2.2.3   The post civil war relief programme

After the capitulation, the military regime initiated the programme of Rehabilitation, Reconstruction and Reconciliation, (RRR). This programme was extended to the conscripted soldiers to help integrate them into civil life. All relief materials were to be channelled through the Nigerian Red Cross.[216] Many humanitarian programmes were prepared to work for the re-integration of Eastern Nigeria and to create sustainability in the long run. The Ministries of Works, Education, Agriculture, Health, Rural Development Division were to work in tandem with the State Rehabilitation Commission to achieve the desired humanitarian objectives in another programme named 'Food for work Programme'.[217] The church organisations participated in the post war humanitarian work as well. Prominent among them is the Christian Council of Churches (CCC) in Nigeria. They lauded the federal government for the many humanitarian programmes to resettle Eastern Nigeria. However, the problems were still monumental and therefore called on donations and supports from firms and individuals for this humanitarian task.[218]

2.2.4   Global/internal changes and modifications arising from the civil war experience

Owing to the large scale relief in the Operation Biafra, it affected global humanitarian practice. There are variant opinions about the position of Biafra in the history of humanitarian practice. The Nigeria-Biafra War in this work belongs to one of the long journeys of self rule and nation building that constitutes the humanitarianism in post World War II era (1945-73). However some humanitarians observed that Biafra opened a new phase of

---

[215] Cf. Ibid.
[216] Cf. Luke Nnaemeka Aneke, The Untold Story of the Nigeria-Biafra War, New York, 2007, 627.
[217] Cf. Daily Post, Monday April 20, 1970, 5.
[218] Cf. E. Ayebome, The Nigeria-Biafra War and the negotiating Role, 61.

humanitarianism.[219] The logjam, administrative stalemate and the misunderstanding between the Nigerian and Biafran authorities created the difficulty of an agreed humanitarian spigot for agencies to access the war region. Many of the humanitarian organisations especially the church agencies felt that to circumvent the Nigerian administration was the only way out. But this resulted in heavy diplomatic outbursts. The effect of the diplomatic crack between the Nigerian state and the Vatican authorities for example did not just end with the ousting of Carlo Bayer the General Secretary; his exit was to pave way for many reforms.[220] Among the many reforms thereafter was the creation of the office of *Cor Unum* in 1971. Today, she is charged with the "special responsibility for supervising and guiding the activity of *Caritas Internationalis* ... a Confederation of over 160 charitable agencies, usually the national entities responsible for charitable activity recognized by the Bishops' Conferences".[221]

All the aid agencies were shaken by the effects of the civil war, but the fate of ICRC was swinging more in the crisis of legitimacy. Many questioned its ability to fight contemporary and future challenges or 'new wars'. The civil war was interpreted by the UNO as an internal crisis and that posed hindrance to the interventions of the ICRC. It was only in 1977 that the review of the Geneva conventions was made to include two protocols, one dealing specifically with matters of internal crisis. Due to this diplomatic hindrance encountered by ICRC during this civil war, a few officials of the ICRC who were not comfortable with the 'political silence' of the ICRC, decided to found a new humanitarian agency that could address issues like the Biafran case. Consequently, the agency *Médecins Sans Frontières*, (MSF) meaning, Doctors without Borders, was born. Therefore the concept of Doctors without Borders became an emblem of humanitarian practice that is devoid of such political silence, as in the case of Biafra.[222]

---

[219] Cf. M. Barnett, The Empire of Humanity, 133. Desgrandchamps Marie-Luce, 'Organising the unpredictable': the Nigeria–Biafra War and its impact on the ICRC, in: International Review of the Red Cross, Vol. 94, Number 888, Winter 2012, 1409-1432, 1409. The author's view is that, the 2nd century humanitarian action began with the Biafra experience. Also, that Biafra marked the before and after in the history of humanitarian aid. (See also Philippe Ryfman, Une histoire de l'humanitaire, La Découverte, 48–49).

[220] Cf. C. Heidrich, Carlo Bayer, 324.

[221] The Roman Curia, Pontifical Council, Cor Unum, http://www.vatican.va/roman_curia/pontifical_councils/corunum/corunum_en/profilo_en/istit uzione_en.html (01.07.14)

[222] Cf. M. Barnett, Empire of Humanity, 142.

This agency, however had its French background too, therefore "MSF also represented the latest version of a longstanding French ideology that justified foreign intervention for improving human welfare, symbolized by the colonial doctrine of *la mission civilatrice* (sic) and personified by Charles Lavigerie Archbishop of Algiers, and the missionary society known as the Pères Blancs (White Fathers)."[223]

The propaganda story of the Biafran authorities generated a lot of misgivings among humanitarians after the civil war. The religious argument was irrelevant, as against what many humanitarians and average westerners were made to believe in. No one would deny the famine in the enclave, but the excesses of the hired press firm 'Markpress' and the Biafran authorities has been frowned upon by many humanitarians today;

> The Biafris (sic) hired a public relations firm Markpress, to publicise their plight and then exaggerated and manipulated the effects of the famine in order to generate more international assistance. And, because they now had an incentive to keep the famine alive, the Ibo (sic) leadership showed little urgency in trying to get an agreement with Lagos to open the relief spigot. Only years later did the aid agencies realise how the savvy Biafran rebels had manipulated them.[224]

Humanitarians under Oxfam like Tony Vaux agrees passively, unlike Aengus Finucane, who totally admits after 30 years that, "the Biafrans fought a good propaganda war."[225] The Nigerian Civil War "was the first large scale civil war to be covered by the television based media".[226] This happened during the period of the global spread of the TV media, beginning from the 1960s. Since Oxfam was very much involved in gathering humanitarian relief for this cause, the generated humanitarian action from this media hype gave Oxfam a national prominence.[227] It created media awareness in the humanitarian circle today, that "people do care; obtaining support is a question of getting the message to them."[228] The propaganda became the only tool of the Biafrans to garner international support, since

---

[223] Ibid., 145. (*La Mission Civilisatrice*)
[224] Ibid., 135.
[225] D. Rieff, A Bed for the Night, 84.
[226] D. E. Harmon, Nigeria 1880 to the Present, 125.
[227] Cf. D. Rieff, A Bed for the Night, 84.
[228] Ibid., 85.

the religious slant had failed and the issue of genocide was no longer tenable.[229]

2.2.5 New Problems and the resultant national policies

Within Nigeria, few changes had taken place. The mission's dominance in the building and management of schools in the colonial period of Nigeria until after the civil war was curtailed by a military decree: the indigenisation of schools, popularly known as 'Government takeover of schools'. This policy of government's control of education began from 1968 and was tenaciously pursued till October 1972.[230] States were mandated to take complete ownership and control of educational institutions belonging to voluntary agencies within their area of jurisdiction. The previous school policies and practices by the missions were criticised as western oriented, irrelevant to Nigeria and divisive, thereby breeding unhealthy rivalry, ethnic and religious bigotry.[231] On the part of the military administration this was part of the indigenisation policy of the state but for the missions, this argument was a camouflage. The enforced discipline and the Christian virtues crafted into the curriculum by the missions were relegated. The schools only retained their Christian name. It was the dark age of mission presence in school administration. This setback later crumbled the general standard of education especially with the growing loss of confidence in government institutions and the slogan that 'everything government is for nobody'.

2.3   Humanitarianism in post oil boom period (1973 to the present)

The discovery of oil in Oloibiri dates back to 1956 in the 'oil region' referred to politically as 'Niger Delta'. Its population stands at 33 million today, with a predominant population of 14 million *Ijaws* and at least 40 minority ethnic groups. It is one of the largest wetlands in the world, the largest mangrove eco-zone in Africa. It is Nigeria's largest ecological region and the last intact lowland rainforest, with over 850 tree species and over

---

[229] Cf. Alex de Waal, Famine Crimes, Politics &the Disaster Relief Industry in Africa, Bloomington, Indianapolis, 2011, 74. (See also speaking on: Bifara Fighting a War without Guns, Timewatch, BBC 2,1995)

[230] Cf. Nora McNamara, Stephen Morse, Developing Financial Services, A case against sustainability, County Cork, 1998, 59.

[231] Cf. Nicholas A. Nwagwu, The State Take-over of Schools in Nigeria: a controversy", Journal of Educational Administration, Vol. 17, iss: 1, 1979, 75.

250 fish species.[232] Since the last three centuries, the Niger Delta has experienced a changing baton of international trade; from the slave trade to palm oil trade (where she first got the name oil region) and the present baton of international trade, the black gold, Petroleum. The different trades represent repeated and massive exploitation of the people by foreign aggressors and mercantilists; just very few concessions have been given to the masses. Through the complicity of successive Nigerian government in the oil business, 'big oil' trade has brought untold hardship, extreme poverty, violence, environmental degradation, extortion in the Niger-Delta. These have led to vast humanitarian challenges that have consequently altered the socio-economic life of the people.

Unlike the oil from many Arab nations of the world, the Nigerian crude oil popularly known as 'Bonny light' has less sulphur, making it easier to refine and well priced.[233] Some have opined that one could run a diesel car with the Nigerian oil even without refining it.[234] Commercial drilling began in 1958 but gained precedence from 1960 and beyond, however the civil war slowed the developmental pace of the oil industry. The production rate from the 70s went so high that it singlehandedly made Nigeria the 6th petroleum producing nation and the wealthiest nation in Africa with an increasing international role and in the sub-region. However, this was unevenly translated to the public. Proceeds were mismanaged by successive military regimes and civilian governments. This only drove the country into a culture of kleptocracy, to the benefit of opportunistic elites, politicians, entrepreneurs, top civil servants, military officers and their cronies, while the masses languish in abject poverty.[235]

2.3.1 The Nigerian oil boom (1973)

After the civil war there was an exponential growth in the oil sector. Crude oil from 1970 grew from 396 million bpd, to 643 million bpd in 1972 and 823 million bpd in 1974. Increase in the dividends of oil brought about enlarged budget, planning and expenditure. But what occasioned the oil boom was the controversy from the war in Yom Kippur. The embargo of the Organisation of Petroleum Producing Countries (OPEC) on western nations

---

[232] Cf. John Campbell, Nigeria, Dancing on the Brink, Wisconsin, 2013, 65.

[233] Cf. Michael Peel, A Swamp of Dollars, Pipelines and paramilitaries at Nigeria's Oil frontier, New York, 2009, 7.

[234] Cf. F. Forsyth, The making, 109.

[235] Cf. T. Falola, M. M. Heaton, A History of Nigeria, 181.

for supporting Israel in the war jacked up the petroleum price from $3.80 per barrel in October 1973 to $14.70 by January 1974. Nigeria being a member nation of OPEC, benefitted massively from this (global energy crisis) controversy. This unprecedented rise in the cost of petroleum products brought in enormous wealth in the coffers of the state. This global scarcity increased Nigerian productivity and profit in the petroleum sector.[236] However like Paul Collier observes, in every boom there is a bust too,[237] therefore the bust and other factors brought in unparalleled development in the country that changed the humanitarian scene of this young nation.

2.3.2 Oil resources and the humanitarian challenges of the post civil war

With the accrued oil revenue, the Military Regime was able to overcome some economic and humanitarian challenges after the civil war, by initiating series of programmes to contain the pains, the destructions and the trauma of the war. The central objectives were to promote social and economic development, with the expansion of social and educational institutions. Among their achievements were the restoration of farms, airports, industries and roads damaged during the civil war, the expansion of schools from primary to university level and the building of low cost houses.[238] The humanitarian challenges were still grave despite the oil resources. On one side, the flamboyant lifestyle of government officials and the stark difference among the masses became a monster, like a loaded gun powder waiting for a trigger. On the other side, the military administration gave the impression she could handle all the needs of the masses, coupled with her boasting that she had more money than she could spend, but she was far from achieving that.

2.3.3 The benefits of oil on the social services and infrastructures

The quick wealth fortunately changed the perception and lifestyle of the average Nigerian. New states were created with the hope to spread development to the interior and to address marginalisation. With the whopping surplus of US$5 billion from oil proceeds in 1975, the military administration embarked on a five year developmental plan to build seven new universities, a new federal capital, thirteen new television stations, thirty

---

[236] Cf. Ibid. 182.
[237] Cf. P. Collier, The Bottom Billion, 38.
[238] Cf. T. Falola, The History of Nigeria, 139.

four new prisons and 20,000 kilometres of paved road.[239] The quest to achieve industrialization within a short space of time extended the spending spree to capital, technological, developmental programmes and projects like steel mills, new refineries and petrochemical plants and so on, but many eventually became white elephant projects.[240]

Through increased funding, educational facilities were to be expanded to prop up the envisaged free educational policy termed 'Universal Primary Education' (UPE). Polytechnics and universities were established in nearly every state. On the other side, the government did not foresee the problems of management, finance, job opportunities for graduating students.[241] This growing economic phase was short-lived because of the endemic corruption, the oil glut, the world recession and the fall of oil price.[242] The good aspect of the school development was that it reduced the financial burden on missions. More so through the indigenisation policy of schools, government took over the financial burden that missions for years were saddled with. But this decision became a huge challenge to the missions later.

New health institutions were added to already existing ones, coupled with the expansion of five teaching hospitals and the building of five new ones, the upgrading of three hospitals to the status of teaching hospitals, the building of an eye specialist hospital and 362 health care clinics were established all over the country.[243] Economic and structural developments are evidence of increased government's presence and the sustenance of such projects reduces the vacuums for humanitarian interventions. It lessens the burdens of humanitarians who could channel their resources and energy into other sensible areas; besides a buoyant economy stands better to assist others in cases of humanitarian lack. That was the hope and joy of this age of oil boom.

2.3.4 The Udoji Award and the growing middle class

The military administration in a haste to trickle down the benefits of oil to the masses and to buy public support came up in 1975 with the 'Udoji

[239] Cf. A. Tenquist, Nigeria, 32
[240] Cf. T. Falola, The History of Nigeria, 139
[241] Cf. Ibid., 168.
[242] Cf. A. Tenquist, Nigeria, 32.
[243] Cf. T. Falola, The History of Nigeria, 168

Award'. It included comprehensive administrative reforms and changes in scale and remunerations. The fear of impending inflation made the government of the day reluctant to implement these recommendations, but it was met with serious protests. The salaries and wages of workers were increased outrageously, some were doubled, others backdated to 1. April 1974. Provisions were made for arrears to be paid in lump sums, half the arrears were to be tax free and car loans were given at much reduced rates. Very generous benefits were poured into the hands of the masses. This over 100% increment created amazing opportunities for workers on one hand; on the other hand it provoked protest from many quarters. Public servants with professional qualification, disconcerted with the increment protested their exclusion from such benefits. It sparked nationwide protests and wage agitation among workers in public corporations, the private sector, the technical, scientific and medical sectors. On the contrary, there was an exorbitant increase in the prices of goods in anticipation of this increment, causing widespread labour unrest and leading to an eventual chain of wage increase in all sectors of the economy.[244] This clamour for wage increase since the oil boom has plunged the Nigerian economy into serious strikes; "In 1980 alone, the Nigerian workforce lost over 2, 5 million worker days, involving over 220,000 workers, in 416 registered strikes. In May 1981 general strike shut down nearly all essential services and businesses in Nigeria."[245]

The fortunes of oil gave Nigerians the feeling of a better life; she became an emerging power, an industrializing nation with an increasing middle class and millionaires. However great the opportunities that came with these increments, they later caused great havocs to the economy as inflation for example went up to double digits. The consumer price index rose from 150 in 1970 to 423 in 1977 with an arbitrary rise in food price to 500%.[246] The vacuum created by this development caused one of the greatest humanitarian challenges Nigerians have ever had. There was so much money, improved lifestyle, good living, but that the state machinery could not control the resources was itself posing a threat that would require more humanitarian presence later.

---

[244] Cf. Ian. Campbell, Army Reorganisation and Military Withdrawal, in: Ed., Keith Panter-Brick, Soldiers and Oil, the Political Transformation of Nigeria, Studies in Commonwealth Politics and History, No 5, London, 1978, Pp. 58-100, 74-75.
[245] T. Falola, M. M. Heaton, A History of Nigeria, 205.
[246] Cf. T. Falola, The History of Nigeria 144.

2.3.5 Oil and resource trap

The sudden wealth became simultaneously a blessing and a curse and oil became the glue that held the nation together. The military class obsessed by the military victory of the civil war, held on to power and purported herself as the most secure government. Theirs was the most lucrative occupation and the driving force of Nigerian government and politics by gaining access into other sectors of the economy, especially the oil sector. When politicians were eventually given democratic opportunities in 1979, it was only a minimal difference from the military. Very few changes were seen through the structures on the ground and poverty still went on the increase. Some have observed that Nigerians became even poorer than they were at independence. The picture of the Nigerian society is a perfect juxtaposition of stupendous wealth and mammoth poverty.

Societies with large mineral deposits and raw materials have been described as the hotbed of unprecedented greed and corruption. They are able to cause and entrench the misuse of power, dictatorship and insecurity, because they are dealing with natural deposits, unlike the manufacturing sector that is grown out of diligence and thus creates a culture of hard work and discipline.[247] Corruption became endemic, contracts were inflated outrageously with kickbacks, the patron/client relationship waxed stronger,[248] 'Prebendalism'[249] loomed higher. Adekeye Adebajo describes Nigeria as the 'Gulliver's Travel' that has been perplexed by the sorry site of corruption and mismanagement. Hence, "while Nigeria, as the most populous country and one of the most powerful states in Africa can be likened to Gulliver, the metaphor of Lilliputian can equally be applied to many of its leaders whose petty ambitions and often inhumane greed−like the creatures in Swift's tale−have prevented a country of enormous potential from fulfilling its leadership aspirations and development plans."[250] An

---

[247] Cf. Raimund Bleischwitz /Florian Pfeil, Global Resource Governance, Perspektiven nachhaltiger globaler Rohstoffpolitik, in: Eds., Raimund Bleischwitz , Florian Pfeil, Globale Rohstoffpolitik, Herausforderung für Sicherheit, Entwicklung und Umwelt, Nomos, Baden Baden, 2009, 25.

[248] Cf. T. Falola, M. M. Heaton, A History of Nigeria, 183.

[249] The usage of the term Prebendalism began with Richard A. Joseph, the Director of African Studies in North-western University USA. It describes patron/client relationship or Neopatrimonialism commonly found among the Nigerian ruling class. It is an informal social hierarchy, where patrons use state resources to secure the loyalty of clients.

[250] A. Adebajo, The Curse of Berlin, 124.

estimated sum of US$380 billion from oil proceeds has been lost to corrupt practices, measuring about two-third of entire African aid during this period.[251] Unlike in modern economics where the economic strength is measured from the growth of the manufacturing sector, the Nigerian government lives on royalties from crude oil. A rent-seeking government is independent of the electorates and as such it negates accountability and disconnects the ruler from the ruled.[252] Consequently the politicians use mischievous ways to gain access to power, besides the "boom and bust phenomenon... [even] makes it very hard for electorates to sort out when a government is making mistakes."[253] The Nigeria's case study is such that the discovery of oil almost paralleled the period of independence; a period that lacked visible and credible home-grown institutions to handle such volume of unanticipated wealth. While nations like Norway, U.S.A had such institutions that helped to streamline the development and management of such proceeds, Nigeria became rich even before she had the wisdom and vision of reasonable spending.

The myriad economic and social illnesses were the offshoot of what Paul Collier describes as the resource trap. Through resource exports, the Nigerian currency rose very high in value against other currencies of the world. This eventually made the nation's other export activities very uncompetitive; they were in fact the hitherto leading economic activities and the best vehicles for technological progress.[254] The agricultural sector was the most hit by the 'Dutch disease',[255] falling by 1% annually, while the oil sector was growing at 10%. Oil was a blessing, but the unjust distribution of the resources and the unpreparedness for rainy days posed hazardous humanitarian challenges. The displacement of workers in the other sectors increased unemployment, thus leading to additional economic sclerosis. The sudden exodus of the thriving sectors before the oil boom was another humanitarian disaster. The environmental degradation, pollution and the loans to offset expenditures became not only a curse but multiplied the humanitarian problems. From the economic indices, every indication points to a government that was too naive, ill-prepared and immature to handle such volume of money. The oil boom created a revenue allocation crisis and

---

[251] Cf. Ibid.
[252] Cf. T. Falola, The History of Nigeria, 143.
[253] P. Collier, The Bottom Billion, 40.
[254] Cf. P. Collier, The Bottom Billion, 39.
[255] Dutch disease is an economic term that describes the sudden decline of one sector of the economy for example agriculture, by the exploration of a newly discovered natural resource.

a culture of economic laziness as there was suddenly so much money; how was it to be invested, shared or spent or economically distributed? It brings out the view that "volatile revenues are obviously difficult to manage."[256] The Nigerian economy is tied to the petrodollars and it accounts for three-quarters of her revenue and over 95% of export; in fact the Nigerian economy is not diversified and her principal 'industry' today is administration,[257] where corrupt civil servants and politicians are served with jumbo pays that even outweigh the wages of their western counterparts.

The oil corporation Nigeria National Petroleum Corporation (NNPC) has inflicted pains on Nigerians through increase cost of Prime Motor Spirit (PMS). Refineries were purposely snuffed out of maintenance by the junta government, until they wore out the refining capacity for domestic consumption. Despite Nigeria's record of oil production, she imports refined fuel for domestic use. This portrayed another corruption window. It has made the price of PMS to soar exponentially over the last two decades; causing uprisings, riots, strikes and civil unrest. The subsidy, the only direct economic gain to the masses has been under threat of removal by the central government but, has always met stiff opposition[258] The January 2012 fuel crisis recorded a few deaths and some humanitarian challenges, where the Red Cross and some church organisations participated in the humanitarian relief. But in 2015, the new administration bowed to the pressure to remove the subsidy.

2.3.6   NGOs and the aftermath of the oil bust

The suspension of capital projects and the failing sectors of the economy increased the unemployment rate and reduced the sudden exorbitant lifestyle. The middle class melted back into the poor class and that widened the poverty margin. It opened another conspicuous humanitarian angle, to fill the vacuum created by the government's inaction, failed policies and also to complement government's lapses. These failures have increased the longing for NGOs to arrest the humanitarian disasters associated with the bust; it thus chronicled the making of the NGOs and humanitarian agencies as 'humanitarian saviour'.

---

[256] P. Collier, The Bottom Billion, 40.

[257] Cf. W. Rodney, How Europe underdeveloped Africa, 27.

[258] Cf. J. Campbell, Nigeria, Dancing on the Brink, 22. (See also National Catholic Reporter)

Many disaffected with the system embraced religion. Many peaceful organisations were founded to assuage the falling human standard. These were self-help organisations, who through community solidarity wanted to change the social situation, by offering the masses other alternatives. Some other religious organisations were founded aiming to influence and bring changes in the system. The churches and their Muslim counterparts became a voice of the masses through heavy criticisms against the government.[259]

2.3.7 The emergence of church's NGOs

Many Christian NGOs have come up in recent times to join the humanitarian communities. One of the dominant names is the Catholic arm of 'Caritas' in Nigeria, known today as the Justice Development and Peace Commission (JDPC). Its birth coincided with the post oil boom era in Nigeria. The establishment of JDPC was a response to the papal teachings of Pope Paul VI: *Motu proprio, Catholicam Christi Ecclesiam*, in 1967, which led to the establishment of the Pontifical Council for Justice and Peace. The church, through this medium was to attend to issues relating to justice, peace, development and human rights. What is JDPC today was called the Catholic welfare committee in 1960, but since 1976 it came under the Catholic Bishops Conference of Nigeria CBCN as JDPC.[260] She is today present in the 53 dioceses in Nigeria, beginning from the diocesan level down to the parish level. She is a registered NGO with the corporate affairs commission in Nigeria. Her objective is to bring the kingdom of God to men and women, to liberate them from the oppressive forces that keep them under such bondage. JDPC is definitely neutral and her services cut across age, race, creed, gender and social status because she believes also that all men and women are made in the image and likeness of God. Her campaigns are to push back the frontiers of hunger, ignorance, poverty, endemic diseases and so on.[261]

One of the JDPC's objectives is to respond to the signs of the time. Since her creation, she promotes many humanitarian projects like gender/women and youth empowerment. With the growing conflicts in Nigeria, she is involved in conflict and dispute resolution among

---

[259] Cf. T. Falola, M. M. Heaton, A History of Nigeria, 205.
[260] Cf. Justice Development and Peace Commission, Ikeja Office, http://jdpcstleoikeja.org/origin.html (07.10.14)
[261] Cf. Justice Development and Peace Commission Ijebu-Ode Diocese, http://www.jdpcijebuode.org/. (06.10.14)

communities. In the area of human rights, she has been very prominent, through assisting prisoners with legal aid to fight against unjust arrest and the decayed judicial system. She has been actively involved in election monitoring since 1999; her campaigns among youths is to forestall the recruitment of youths as political thugs and to contribute towards good governance and democracy. She is very much in the area of micro finance to indigents. Her humanitarian relief and presence during disaster and emergency aid has been very visible. She is also involved in the training and education of the poor, assisting people to learn new skills, and assisting Internally Displaced People, (IDPs).[262] Despite these activities humanitarian challenges are still conspicuous. JDPC is sponsored through local and foreign support, but her major setback remains in the area of inadequate finances.

Another Faith Based Organisation FBO that has made great strides in the area of health care is the Christian Health Association of Nigeria CHAN, founded in 1973 by the CBCN, the Christian Council of Nigeria CCN and the Northern Christian Medical Advisory Council NCMAC. Originally she was founded to represent the views of the Nigerian Voluntary Medical Organizations to the government. Her duty was to advise ways of integrating this organisation into the overall governmental planning and to act as a central point for exchange of views and ideas. CHAN is a non-profit organisation with the motto: 'reaching the unreached'. She provides medical services and coordinates church sponsored health programmes through her member institutions (MIs) nationwide, except in Zamfara state (North-West). Her services are good, qualitative, affordable and patient friendly. She believes in the continuation of the healing task of Jesus Christ. Her ecumenical strength is visible through her 23 member churches and is represented at federal, state and local levels. CHAN reaches all in need irrespective of religious affiliation, gender and origin. She is regarded as the oldest and largest health care institution in Nigeria and second to government. Over 40% of health care institutions today, especially in the rural areas are ascribed to the efforts of CHAN. Through the grants from some members in 1979, a CHAN Drug Supply Services (CHANmedi-Pharm) was established to produce safe, quality and affordable medication to its members. Her established Primary Health Care services PHCs collects

---

[262] Cf. Catholic Institute of Development Justice and Peace (CIDJAP), http://www.cidjap.org/justice-development-and-peace-commission-jdpc-its-implication-in-the-nigerian-church.html (07.10.14)

and disseminates information about holistic knowledge of health care issues like, HIV/AIDS and so on. Today she has almost 400 MIs, comprising 140 hospitals and 187 clinics, carrying out maternal and primary health care; also she has 23 rural health programmes, 4 Leprosy treatment clinics and operates a total of 4000 outreach health facilities mostly in the rural areas. [263]

2.3.8 Islamic NGOs and humanitarian concept

One of the commonest Muslim NGOs is the Federation of Muslim Women in Nigeria (FONWAN), established in 1985 to ensure the protection of the rights of Muslim women. Her view is that Muslims stand better chance of solving fellow Muslim's problems. Her objective is the education of the Muslim women and promoting the understanding of the Islamic religion through the Quran and *Sunnah*. She pursues the education of Muslim women at all levels, caring for school dropouts, children not enrolled in schools, girl-child education and adult education. She supports the provision of health services mostly maternal and women's empowerment through capacity building. Her mission is basically the propagation of Islam through the establishment of schools and improvement of the socio-economic status of women, youths and children. FONWAN is a registered NGO by the National Corporation; represented in all the states of the federation and has a consultative status with the UN. Her many projects have received funding from USAID, British High Commissions, National Action Committee of Aids (NACA), UNICEF, Save our Children, federal and state government in Nigeria and so on.[264]

Among the listed FBOs, the JDPC and CHAN have a very secular approach in their humanitarian gestures while the FONWAN is faith saturated and has strong religious language in her name, mission statements and humanitarian target audience.[265] From the foregoing the former possess the neutral trait of humanitarian work, while the latter is restricted to her religions members.

---

[263] Cf. Christian Health Association of Nigeria, http://www.channigeria.org/index.html (08.10.14)
[264] Cf. Federation of Muslim Women Association of Nigeria, (FOMWAN) http://www.fomwan.org/about_fomwan.php (05.10.14)
[265] Cf. Omobolaji Ololade Olarinmoye, Faith-Based Organizations and Development: Prospects and constraints in; Transformation: An International Journal of Holistic Mission Studies 2012 29: 1:in http://trn.sagepub.com/content/29/1/1 online: DOI: 10.1177/0265378811427985, Pp. 1-15, 7 (15.10.14).

2.3.9 Secular NGOs, Foundations and charity organisations

The exceptional rise in the need for NGOs in the post oil boom era has encouraged the founding of many pressure groups with multitask objectives like civil societies, pro-democracy groups, Labour unions and like the case of the Niger Delta groups. Even though they were not founded with humanitarian objectives, they were accompanied with humanitarian drives, as they provided for their members. The special traits of such civil organisations in Nigeria is that they

> ...have often been constituted to meet the needs of their members in a way that is completely separate from the state. Sometimes civil society organizations serve both functions: making their needs known to the state while simultaneously meeting the needs of their constituencies in ways that are completely separate from state involvement. The fundamentalist Christian charismatic movement for example, serves both these purposes for its congregation.[266]

The survival syndrome created different religious activities for economic gains. Religious activism became a response to economic deterioration. Consequently, it intensified the politicisation of religion between Christians and Muslims and furthered the clash of these civil societies against governmental policies.[267] Apart from the faith driven humanitarian agencies, litanies of private and foreign NGOs, foundations from well meaning Nigerians and those who have benefitted from the kleptocratic practices have been established for humanitarian objectives. Basically they provide funds for training the poor in schools in face to face charity and also meeting the immediate needs of some poor. Its prominence today hinges on the fact that the masses see the largesse of state rulers as humanitarian assistance.

---

[266] T. Falola, M. M. Heaton, A History of Nigeria, 210.
[267] Cf. Ibid. 222.

CHAPTER THREE: THE LOCAL CHURCH: IDAH DIOCESE AND HUMANITARIAN WORKS

3. The traditional politics and economy of the Igala/Bassa kingdom

The preceding chapter was largely about the humanitarian work concentrated on the entire Nigerian landscape, which Idah diocese is part of. The present chapter will outline the prehistoric activities, antics, leadership structure, economic activities and religious settings of beneficiaries in Idah diocese. These facts are very important to humanitarian studies, because they form their very nature and weltanschauung. Over the last century, Igala/Bassaland in a state of flux recorded a lot of modifications and innovations in the lifestyle, mode of governance and trade among her people. Her political and economic success through coercive means made her a formidable state. Nevertheless later alterations in her history created enormous upheaval to politics and trade. To understand this underlying political setting would demand painstaking studies about her numerous neighbours that have influenced her socio-cultural, economic and political life.[268] Apart from the immediate neighbours, the Benin (Edo), Igbos and Idomas, her history has been influenced by many other ethnic groups like the Yoruba, Hausa/Fulani, Nupe, Jukuns and Igbira. From a historical trajectory, Igala evolved out of a continuous intermingling of different people and ethnic groups of the lower Niger Basin who collectively belong to the kwa branch of Niger-Congo family of languages.[269] The intense migration of people caused by internecine feuds, political, economic and security reasons brought about the settlement of different families and clans in Idah from about the first millennium A.D.[270] The strategic location of Idah, the seat of Igalaland on the Niger with its resources and physical attributes has exposed this town to a great variety of cultures and peoples. Though the bulk of Igala runs inland,[271] historical facts maintain that these families migrated to the

---

[268] Cf. S.F. Afolayan, The Evolution of the Igala Kingdom to 1800, A Reconsideration, in; The Africa Historian, Journal of the History Students' Society, University of Ife, Ile-Ife, Vol. XII, 1986, 24-31, 24.
[269] Cf. Joseph N. Ukwedeh, History of the Igala Kingdom, c.1534-1854, A Study of Political and Cultural Integration in the Niger-Benue Confluence Area of Nigeria, Kaduna, 2003, 1-2, 45.
[270] Cf. Ibid., 26.
[271] Cf. Ibid., 29.

inlands at different points in the Igala history, consequently commingling with other migrating families from other parts of the Niger basin too.[272]

The settler families in their different *Olopu* clans metamorphosed into *Ewo* towns and eventually galvanised into an ethnic group for mutual support and for security reasons in moments of foreign aggression. The emergence of governing roles was the result of increased population and such leadership was hierarchical and patrilineal.[273] The initial settlers, the *Igalamela* (Nine Igalas), and later settler *Igalogba* (first Igala) formed a federation in the pre-*Attah* Igala kingdom. But from the 17th century, Ayegba Om'idoko emerged as the new and powerful King the *Attah* (father) of the land. The credit of winning the war against the Jukuns made him the most renowned *Attah* of all time. His reign witnessed a firm structural organisation of the royal dynasty, the consolidation of the Igala leadership structure and the politics of expansionism.[274] The Igala kingdom became a powerful kingdom at the close of the 17th and early 18th century extending over a vast territory including some parts of the Koton Karfi, Asaba, Aboh, Aguleri, Nkpologwu, Asaba, Onitsha, Nsukka, Opi, Ogurgu, Lokoja and Nupeland;[275] nevertheless its suzerainty was a loose one.[276] The *Attah* was both a political and religious leader and in the consolidation of power, the *Igalamela* emerged as the kingmakers or counsellors while the *Igalogba* became the *Achadu,* the prime Minister or head of Kingmakers. This structure served as checks and balances when the king was unpopular or a tyrant.[277] There were a litany of chiefs and royal functionaries who were

---

[272] Cf. P.E. Okwoli, A Short History of Igala, Illorin, 1973, 16.

[273] Cf. J.N. Ukwedeh, History of Igala Kingdom, 25-27.

[274] Cf. P.E. Okwoli, A Short History of Igala, 26, 42. The Igala share historical trajectories with Benin and Jukun and has thus integrated some aspects of these cultures. The strong semblances from costumes, regalia, royal rites and kingship system in Igala support these claims. This is substantiated by historical claims that the *Attah* was initially chosen first from among the first settlers but they were overpowered by the Benin dynasty and reduced the kingmakers. The Benins were later toppled by the Jukuns the present dynasty. Besides, the *Attah* at a time was under servitude of both Benin and later the Jukuns, but Igala was liberated from both kingdoms in two bitter wars.

[275] Cf. Anthony Agbali, The Igala Response to Colonial Destabilization and Fragmentation, in: Ed., Toyin Falola, Perspectives on Colonialism in Africa, Durham, 2003, Pp.97-135, 98; R.S Seton, Installation of An Attah of Idah, 255.

[276] Cf. J.S. Boston, The Igala Kingdom, 1968, Ibadan, 3.

[277] Cf. J.N. Ukwedeh, History of Igala Kingdom, 120-121; Mohamed Sanni Abdulkadir, A Political and Economic History of Igalaland, Central Nigeria: 1896-1939, Saarbrucken, 2011, 7. Nonetheless this office was scrapped in 1835 for the alleged conspiracy in the murder of an

appointed from the different clans and other minor power blocs within the kingdom. Political offices were associated with titles and the great majority are hereditary. Also both hereditary and non-hereditary are vested in patriarchs. The non hereditary include eunuchs, slaves and palace officials, whereas the hereditary are a privileged elite who represent a descent group or a group of villages in the central administration. They were responsible for the collection of tribute from the groups they represent. They also bear title names, special greeting names and wear beads or other regalia.[278] The ruling house at Idah was privileged with "eighteen hereditary titles, including the kingship and all the posts of chief councillors. All these offices rotate through the four major lineages that make up the ruling sub clan at Idah. The kingship is inherited by the eldest surviving son of the last king to hold office in each lineage."[279]

The ancestral lineage of Ayegba Om'Idoko was very prominent in trade. This factor gave him the political clout and the needed loyal crew to ascend and consolidate power.[280] Therefore Igala trade under his control was vital to his political hegemony. With the aid of the appointed offices alongside a coterie of hereditary chiefs and clan heads, the different districts (former mini Igala states) were administered from Idah.[281] Idah belongs to one of the major towns along the Niger River and they are collectively referred to as the Lower Niger; it was the busiest waterway in the West African sub region in the colonial era.[282] During this era, there were trade

---

Attah in 1833. Even when the office was restored in 1919, it lacked the previous powers and functions

[278] Cf. J.S. Boston, Igala Political Organisation, in: African Notes, Institute of African Studies, University of Ibadan Nigeria, Vol. 4, Num. 2, 1967, Pp 18-31, 19.

[279] Ibid., 20. At the coronation of a new *Attah* the former 18 hereditary titles must give way for their offices to the new officials.

[280] Cf. J.N. Ukwedeh, History of Igala Kingdom, 99, The family of Abutu Eje to Ayegba Om'Idoko were famous for iron smelting and trade. The latter was into horse trading and travelled far outside the vicinity of Idah plains.

[281] Cf. Ibid., 131.

[282] Cf. Anthony Danladi Ali, The Colonial Economy in the Lower Niger Region, in: Arabian Journal of Business and Management Review (Oman Chapter) Vol. II., No.7, February 2013, Pp. 47-54, 47. The Lower Niger stretches from Lokoja, the confluence of River Niger and Benue flowing southward to the other towns like Onitsha, Warri, Asaba, Sapele, Burutu and Forcados and finally emptying itself into the sea. This route was very important for conveying goods for both export and internal use during the colonial period. The absence of other means of transportation made this route the busiest waterways in the West African Sub-region. Water transportation has contributed immensely to the growth of these towns right from the

activities with the neighbours through the "exchange of slaves and ivory for luxury goods such as horses, beads and bronze."[283] Nevertheless palm oil wholesale was one of the most important trades around Idah and "for nearly two hundred years until the late 1960s, ships and barges were loaded with palm produce from Igalaland and beyond at Idah. From here they were taken across the world. This trade was very lucrative and its demise, accelerated by the civil war and later concentration on petroleum products, was a very real blow to Igalaland."[284] The trade opportunities associated with the water transportation encouraged other economic activities, like the presence of a British multinational the United African Company UAC from the 1870.[285] However, from every index the Afro-Euro relationship was strictly trade; there was hardly any humanitarian service either from their firms or from the colonial regime much later. It was a purely mercantilist affair. The control of the Niger-Benue confluence which is the meeting point of trade from both rivers made Igala a major political and commercial power in the lower Niger.[286] The strategic importance of the River Niger for trade and security of the kingdom gave revenue advantage to the *Attah*, as tax and custom duties from these water ways went into the coffers of the royal house.[287] The ruling family and the retinue of chiefs profited massively from tax and tributes. Like in Aboh, trade in Idah was under royal monopoly; therefore every trade in commodity goods was with the authorisation or under the control of the king's trusted lieutenants on the ground.[288]

---

pre-colonial days and consequently making them also as ferry terminals, inland river ports and trading stations.

[283] Kate Meagher, Identity Economics, Social Networks & the informal Economy in Nigeria, New York, 2010, 30. The Igala people were a link between the Igbos and the Hausas and consequently the trans-Saharan trade.

[284] N. McNamara, S. Morse, Developing Financial Services, 69.

[285] Cf. A. D. Ali, The Colonial Economy in the Lower Niger Region, 47-49. The UAC was a later creation, the fusion of all the British firms within the lower Niger Region. Before this development, the respective companies conducted their trades through the local chiefs, but as soon as the conglomerate was achieved, it changed the rule of the game to direct contacts with the local suppliers.

[286] Cf. Ebere Nwabuani, The political Economy of Aboh, 1830-1857 in; African Economic History, Vol. 27 1999, Pp. 93-116, 108.

[287] Cf. J.N. Ukwedeh, History of Igala Kingdom, 126-128. One-ninth of the contents in every canoe passing by was collected as revenue on behalf the *Attah*; M. S. Abdulkadir, A Political and Economic History, 63, Tributes were paid according to local economic good of the people. For example a hunter usually gives the hind leg as tribute whereas the palm oil producer gives a measure of palm oil and so on.

[288] Cf. E. Nwabuani, The Political Economy of Aboh, 105.

There are both internal and external factors that led to the gradual fall of the Igala nation from the late 18th century and beyond. The internal rancour in the political institution that led to the scrapping of the office of the kingmakers created administrative imbalance. With the absence of checks and balance, it heightened the autocratic tendency of the Attah, which increasingly weakened the kingdom coupled with a dwindling economy.[289] The advancement of the Caliphate, the Jihad of Usman Dan Fodio in 1804 to the lower Basin also destabilized the Igala state. Though Igala was not conquered, a few of the districts in the far north were affected with far-reaching economic importance, for example the confluence was lost to Nupeland.[290] Within the kingdom too, it raised questions of new loyalty and marked the beginning of self- liberation and determination of some weaker nations like the Bassa- Nge and Kwomo from the suzerainty of Igala kingdom.[291]

The 'final straw that broke the camel's back' was the colonial subjugation. By 1896 and 1903 Idah and Dekina districts were absolutely under British rule respectively.[292] With the aid of the West African Frontier Force (WAFF)[293] the last siege was laid on Ankpa in 1904-05, such that by 1906 the whole of Igala/Bassaland was entirely under colonial administration.[294] Therefore political and economic control became the strict preserve of British West Africa. Monetary and economic policies were determined by the British colonial officers and therefore salt and cowries ceased gradually as legal tender. As colonialism gathered momentum in the Igala interior coupled with the plummeting and changing economy, loyalty to the *Attah* diminished and the kingdom became a shadow of itself.[295] The highhandedness and shrewdness of the colonial firms thwarted every trade towards the colonial advantage. Since the *Attah's* economic power waned in the mid 19th century and beyond, the usual collection of annual tribute could

---

[289] Cf. P.E Okwoli, A Short History of Igala, 49.

[290] Cf. E. Nwabuani, The Political Economy of Aboh, 109.

[291] Cf. M.S. Abdulkadir, A Political and Economic History, 71.

[292] Cf. A. Agbali, The Igala Response, 125. As part of the punishment for the stiff resistance of the Attah against colonial conquest, the divide and rule (divide and conquer) was adopted in Igalaland, thus the kingdom was broken into two: Idah and Dekina provinces.

[293] WAFF was a military expedition in British West Africa to advance the colonial subjugation. Here it was composed of the Hausa/Fulani and northern ethnic groups who were mostly Muslim on the mission to quell a political uprising in Ankpa.

[294] Cf. A. Agbali, The Igala Response, 89.

[295] Cf. E. Nwabuani, The Political Economy of Aboh, 109.

no longer be enforced, thus "river piracy, organised highway robberies, extortion and the sale of titles"[296] became new revenue alternatives for the ruling house. The *Attah* subtly sanctioned this piracy on the Niger to fend for financial resources because the royal ships for example plied the Niger without paying taxes. This guerrilla attack provoked a British bombardment of Idah; subsequent arson against British monopoly of trade in Idah led to two other military attacks on the local people.[297] Other European and Asian Nations were excluded from the trade in the Niger. Idah like other towns on the Niger lost her importance from the late 19th century, the river was only a highway to the hinterlands and once the access to the interior was achieved the river became a backwater. With the opening of railways, new roads and other viable routes the Niger became obsolete.[298]

Apart from agriculture, hunting, fishing and palm oil trade, there were a few other local industries that thrived in the Igala state like, "spinning, weaving cloth, baskets and mats, salt making and brewing. Outside crafts by groups included smiting, dyeing, pottery fishing, canoe making and flooring. Individual crafts comprised charcoal burning... tanning leather making and wood carving."[299] Till the mid 19th century the ruling elite exercised absolute control over these forms of trades and production of Igala.[300] However, Igala export trade from 1900 and 1913 which was already the period of UAC/colonial control was made up of palm oil, palm kernel, rubber and cotton. About 70% of the rubber in the north came from Igalaland.[301] There were innumerable internal and external factors responsible for the production fall; but there is a general colonial contention that the poverty of many old states in Nigeria was the result of laziness, whereas other explorers attested to the hardworking nature of these people.[302] Nevertheless, I believe the pre-independent Nigeria and particularly the Igala nation lacked the unity and the capacity in their

---

[296] Cf. The Rise and Fall of the Igala State, in: Ed., Onuora Nzekwu, Nigeria, Magazine no. 80, March, 1964, Lagos, Pp. 17-29, 29.
[297] Cf. M.S. Abdulkadir, A Political and Economic History, 85. Idah was bombed thrice under British military order; P.E. Okwoli, A Short History of Igala, 78.
[298] Cf. E. Nwabuani, Political Economy of Aboh, 111.
[299] Cf. M.S. Abdulkadir, A Political and Economic History, 23.
[300] Cf. Ibid., 59.
[301] Cf. P.E. Okwoli A Short History, 99; M.S. Abdulkadir, A Political and Economic History, 108. The reason for the decline in rubber production was the new supplies from Malaya, Indonesia and later Liberia.
[302] Cf. M.S. Abduklkadir, A Political and Economic History, 155.

different states to understand the changing nature of trade, the need for cohesion to collate their interests, how to confront their collective challenges and settle their differences. The people and the local economy were confronted and overrun by unforeseen shock beyond their grasp.

The peak of the political assault perpetrated on the Igala leadership structure by colonialism was the preference of the Hausa/Fulani Muslim officials in Igala administration. The British raised the Hausa/Fulani to key positions and reduced the Igala traditional leadership institution and structure to rubble. The once deified *Attah* was demystified by many organic and foreign factors beyond his control. *Attahs* were deposed and elected at the colonial will and ultimately Igala was psychologically shattered by the breaking of the kingdom into two in 1906.[303] Such division defied hitherto relationships, loyalty of the people and the established patterns of commerce, administration, culture and communication. With its artificial boundaries like the many straight lines in Africa, it altered the political contours of the kingdom. Even though the kingdom was reunited in 1918, this menace sowed bitter rivalry among the earlier mini Igala states; as it eroded the Igala leadership structure and weakened her unity.[304] The real reason for the re-unification was not far from the British intent for centralisation of power on the *Attah* for effective administration of the indirect rule.[305] Though the powers of the *Attah* increased, it was dependent on his cooperation and the goodwill of the colonial administration.[306] The colonial administration's preference of an authoritarian and a coercive force for revenue generation, recruitment of labour, production and market for the actualisation of colonial interest gave birth to the Native authority (NA). The Native Treasury was founded alongside for the formulation of budget, payment of staff, provision of funds for capital and recurrent projects.[307]

Today the *Attah's* office does not really hold much political clout. Such political seats in contemporary Nigeria are under the jurisdiction of a state government where they are domiciled. Their political powers, loyalty and sustainability are largely determined by the state structure, such that they

---

[303] Cf. Ibid., 93-95.
[304] Cf. Yusuf Etu, Tom Miachi, The Mahionu War (1916-1917) and the History of Igala, in; Ed., Brian Dawtrey, Journal of Igalaland, Vol. 2, No 2, Ayangba, 1980, Pp. 34-37, 35; M.S. Abdulkadir, A Political and Economic History, 89.
[305] Cf. P.E. Okwoli, A Short History, 95.
[306] Cf. M.S. Abdulkadir, A political and Economic History, 119.
[307] Cf. Ibid., 126-127.

could be deposed or appointed at any point in time by the sitting governor of the state.[308] Also, the *Attah* like other traditional rulers in Nigeria today represents a political rallying point especially during electioneering periods. It is an informal but a quasi-reconciliation house or centre for settling differing political factions, fracas and internal political disputes.[309] Nevertheless their go-between role in the society must not be underestimated especially in the hinterlands. It is imperative that NGOs recognize their presence for smooth and successful implementation of projects because of the stratified and hierarchical structure of the society.[310] At the opening of the DDS in the 70s the founder had to pay a visit to the Royal Father *Attah*. Also, in all the villages that DDS projects were executed, the local chiefs, (*Madakis* and *Gagos*) were contacted and given due recognition as royal elites. Thus, inasmuch as modern state structure has almost eclipsed their importance, they still play enormous roles in the background especially in the hinterland.

3.1   Ethnic and religious interrelationship

Traditional religion was the only religion in the pre- and the early Igala state. Between the 14th and 15th century, contacts with the old Bornu Empire brought about Muslim traders in the Niger-Benue Basin. The 17th century marked the official recognition of Islamic religion in Igala state by the *Attah*. Islam was well received by Igala because of its many similarities with the Igala traditional religious practices. Even though Islam came from the Arab world it had experienced some forms of 'cultural expression' among these Hausa/Fulani states and as such could easily find religious space in the Igala tradition too.[311] Also, the 30 years WAFF settlement

---

[308] There were such cases in the mid 90s when the Ejeh of Ankpa was deposed by the state governor. This office is almost sterile as the Nigerian constitution does not give a straightforward path towards their duties.

[309] During election periods, electoral candidates pay enormous attention to the demands of the traditional rulers.

[310] Cf. Thomas Bierschenk, George Elwert, Dirk Hohnert, Long –Term Effects of Development Aid: Empirical Studies in Rural West Africa, Pdf, Pp. 83-112, 92.

[311] Cf. P.E. Okwoli, Introduction to Igala Traditional Religion, Idah, 1966, 73-74; M.S. Abdulkadir, Islam in the non-Muslim Northern Area of Nigeria, c. 1600-1960, in; Illorin Journal of Religious Studies, Vol. 1, No. 1, 2011, Pp. 1-20, 4. These were Hausa/Fulani Muslims from Bebeji in Kano from whom the Attah solicited assistance to defeat the war against the Jukuns. Through the help of a prepared charm, the Attah won the war and thus pleaded with them to stay back in the kingdom. Where they settled in both Idah and Ankpa were named *Angwa*.

(1903-1933) in Ankpa encouraged a spatial Islamic settlement.[312] Christianity unlike Islam was more or less regarded as a western religion and was totally alien to many practices of the traditional faith.[313] Despite the reluctance associated with the reception of Christianity, it opened the door of modernity to the people in Igala/Bassaland. Though the missionaries understood less the significance of the unwritten culture of the Aborigines, they spent themselves by taking evangelism to the doorstep of the natives. In the process, they gave the first step of western education, the first medical assistance, the first contact with the rest of the world and by implication the rest of humanity, the first defence of human rights and the general knowledge that is perceived today as common culture.[314] It thus made them humanitarian pioneers in Igala/Bassaland. Besides, all the practices and institutions built by the missionaries operated on the basis and ideal of humanitarian charity.[315]

In spite of the heavy Muslim settlement in Igala/Bassaland there is hardly any religious hostility for many reasons. The Jihad which violently islamised other parts of Nigeria never surfaced in Igala/Bassaland, so much so that family members and relatives live side by side with both faiths. However some historians believe that the Jihad shook the foundation of the Igala traditional religion and demeaned the priest/king role of the *Attah*, which is intrinsically tied to the Igala traditional religion.[316] The religious scenario is generally a relaxed one despite the diversity of religion in Igala/Bassaland. The people have very high religious tolerance, but the engraved religious sentiment in the political mainstream of the nation today is beginning to raise some religious concerns.[317] Such a religio-political worldview at the federal seat for example is beginning to affect the

---

[312] Cf. P.E. Okwoli A Short History, 114.

[313] Cf. P.E. Okwoli, Introduction to Igala Traditional Religion, 75.

[314] Cf. A. A. Agbali, The Catholic Church, Social Justice Teachings, 45. (See also Pope Paul VI, "Africae Terrarum" A Message from Pope Paul VI to Countries of Africa, African Ecclesiastical Review AFER 10, no. 1, January 1968, no. 24, 78.)

[315] Cf. Anthony Attah Agbali, Ritualizing Communal Wellbeing: The Igala Anthropology of Healthcare and Contemporary Nigerian Healthcare Delivery, in: Eds., Toyin Falola, Matthew M. Heaton, Traditional and Modern Health Systems in Nigeria, Trenton, 2006, Pp. 305-363, 325.

[316] Cf. M.S. Abdulkadir, A Political and Economic History, 76.

[317] The religious undertone today generates an atmosphere of bigotry and it thus dictates informally the balancing of every contestable position and political appointments between Christian/Muslim; without such consideration, the appointment is bound to face protest and misunderstanding from the masses and the political class.

sociological viewpoint of the masses, thus raising political questions and confrontations between the adherents of these two religions.

At the state level, there are ethnic tensions among the Igala, Igbira and the Okun. But within the old Igala state, there exists solidity in the midst of some pockets of disagreement among the ex- mini Igala states. Ankpa district is the only exception, where a long history of opposition and rivalry has existed with Idah the ancestral home. Despite the age-long interrelationship with the neighbouring ethnic groups, there exist sentiments, prejudices and misconceptions too. Some emanated from the long rivalry of wars, coercion, factions, fracas and misunderstanding that still affect the spirit of cooperation and trust.

3.2   The primitive picture of humanity in the Igala/Bassa kingdom

The human person in the pre- and during the Igala state era was not with the kind of dignity accorded to humans today. Though the society is hierarchical and teaches respect of elders, its practice was devoid of the recognition of rights and dignity of the human person. Unfortunately, this teaching of respect towards elders has sometime built fear among younger ones to challenge wrong decisions, actions and to confront injustice from existing autocratic leadership structures. In a development study, the Igala hierarchical tendency was proved as antithetical to development growth, because of the consistent acceptance of every development package in its entirety without any critical exercise or contribution.[318] At the early engagements of the DDS, her foreign personnel had to come to terms with this issue. But it did improve over the time, because inordinate claims in the name of seniority could hinder developmental ideas and contributions.[319]

Within and outside the Igala kingdom there were issues of slave trade; war indemnity for example was paid with slaves.[320] This was a source of revenue to the *Attah* and like most of the traditional rulers they made false

---

[318] Cf. T. Bierschenk, et al., Long –Term Effects of Development Aid, 93. Whereas this study described the Tiv in Benue state as acephalous neighbours, who unlike Igala accept specific aspects of development package and adapt other aspects to local conditions.

[319] Cf. Irene Christina Lynch, Beyond Faith and Adventure, Irish Missionaries in Nigeria tell their extraordinary Story, Wicklow, 2006, 127.

[320] Odigwe A. Nwaokocha, A.D. Nzemeke, Aspects of Igala Influence on the Oshimili People of Western Igboland in Pre-Colonial Times, in; Nsukka Journal of the Humanities, No. 12, 2002, 169-179, 174.

claims that the slaves were from distant raids, as if distance negates humanness.[321] The Ikiri market under the control of the Igala state for example was recorded with over 11,000 slaves of Nupe origin annually.[322] Even when the treaty for abolishment of the trade was signed on the 6th September 1841 by the *Attah*,[323] pockets of internal slave trade still existed during the economic depression of 1932 after World War I.[324] Some development experts have observed the lack of cooperation and the existing spirit of distrust among the local people today as the consequent indications of the past slave trade's shock.[325]

The slavery raid, the mutual suspicion leading to internecine feuds, other military expeditions, the struggle for state formation and nation building must have discouraged early settlement in the present Igalaland. But between 17th -18th centuries when Igala feudal state emerged a strong kingdom, her population including the nations under her servitude must have grown exponentially because of the relative stability.[326] However, lack of records gives a very feeble estimation of the population. For example "Oldfield describing a festival in Idah town in 1833 reports that 'there were nearly 15,000 people assembled in the town'. [While] Trotter in 1841 estimated that there were 2000 huts in Idah with a probable population of 8000 to 9000 people."[327] Whereas during Crowther's visit in 1841, he concluded that the population was less than the above figures and that was probably because of the decentralisation of Igala due to the politics of expansionism.[328] Even though the explorers' and missionary estimation could serve as historical guides they were still by mere guess. Many factors were responsible for the unfeasibility of a practical population census, for

---

[321] Cf. E. Nwabuani, The Political Economy of Aboh, 100. These were the claims of Obi Ossai the king of Aboh to the colonialists that the raids were directed against other ethnic groups who waged war against his kingdom. However he failed to mention in the first place the insinuating role his kingdom must have played in the attack.

[322] Cf. P.E. Okwoli, A Short History of Igala, 62

[323] Cf. Ibid., 74.

[324] Cf. M.S. Abdulkadir, A Political and Economic History, 101. The famine of 1904 still prompted another slave trade. Indigent parents sold their children to buyers from Abeokuta; Ibid., 145, such prospective buyers sometimes were rich women who had no children.

[325] Cf. I. C. Lynch, Beyond Faith and Adventure, 130.

[326] Cf. A. Agbali, The Igala Response, 107. This stability comes from the fact that Igala was a powerful and established state and thus gave rise to the expansionist drive and strong political consciousness.

[327] The Rise and Fall of the Igala State, 21.

[328] Cf. Ibid.

example the internal political/economic feuds and the migration of people into the forest and inhabitable places to evade tax payments and tributes. Also the successive military attacks by the Royal Niger Company at Idah, the WAFF settlement at Ankpa and the insecurity created by the fall of the Igala state decimated the population too. Nevertheless population census in contemporary Nigeria has remained a perennial problem. Igala believes she is over 2.5 Million and succinctly rejects the estimated population of 2 million by the national census commission.

If by pre-colonial human standards the picture of humanity were adduced with less human dignity than obtains today, what is a 'person' today in the Igala and Bassa concept? In the course of enlightenment and education many notions and perspectives on humanity have changed over time. Nevertheless there are some undesirable points on the human person still very prevalent among the people today and need humanitarian attention. Issues like equality, indigenes' and settlers' question, family background and preferential treatment to the haves and in some parts of the diocese marital status of ex-slaves are still current social issues today. The basic question of every humanitarian is to assist humanity; therefore every humanitarian's attention is to ensure the recognition of all human beings as part of humanity and to jettison every other opposing human standard.

3.3 The Igala/Bassa kingdom and its social reality

By the 1850s and the 1860s ordinary people, immigrants and even clans were getting discontented with the overbearing state control and the *petite* political and economic space granted them in the midst of a gradual and global changing economy. Inasmuch as the divided loyalties, mutual suspicion and new alliances in the state weakened the economic and political foundations of the state they also created new social perspectives.[329] The displacement of old patterns of commerce by the treaty contributed to the weakness of Igala but increased the human consciousness by expunging the slave trade mechanism. The inland penetration of the British conglomerate too gave rise to new ways of life, new opportunities, increased rights, and demeaned the fear of instant raid for slavery or for any reason at all. But with the merchants having the privilege of unflinching access to local producers, the purchase of commodity goods came at its lowest price, so much so that the market control right from the bottom of the society came

---

[329] Cf. M.S. Abdulkadir, A Political and Economic History, 71.

under colonial dominance. The Igala economy could not resist the shocks arising from the changes in the European market and the consequent effect was the global depression of 1932. Thus Igala economy became integrated into the global economy.[330] As a matter of fact, there were social welfare provisions in Britain like "soup lines, bread queues, charity soup kitchens, relief and public works to alleviate the suffering of her citizens"[331] but these were never the case in the Igala and in the colonies in general.

The aristocratic Igala state was heavily abused by tribute collection, extortion through tax, bribery and corruption. As the kingdom grew larger, these proliferated appointed chiefs were into exorbitant and arbitrary charges because every politically exalted position was entitled to both official and unofficial tributes and privileges. The distance of other plains from Idah and the overemphasis of the *Attah's* spiritual role to the detriment of the political, contributed to the misery of the administration. These political factors hampered possible social resonance in the state.[332] Therefore the outcome was a state under the control of the royal counsellors, the coterie of chiefs and other officials who perpetually undercut the *Attah's* might for selfish interests. In an autocratic state the maxim of 'might is right' thrives and the Hobbesian conjecture of 'survival of the fittest' becomes the norm. These officials were the custodian and the bridge between the King and the people and as such had the power to lock out the political pulse and wishes of the masses from the hearing of the *Attah*. The consequence of such politics of exclusion was an example of an excessively authoritative system saturated with innate greed amidst a suffering people. Such tendencies have persisted into the contemporary age so that the greater part of Igalaland today carries the attributes and features of a command state. It is the consequent effects of nonexistent judiciary, an authoritative power setting and the lingering prototype system of the pre-colonial feudal state that has wangled its way into modern states.[333] Igala as an authoritarian peasant state lacked the medium to formulate her interests and the formidable channel to articulate her demands. That there was no social structure for compromise like in the

---

[330] Cf. Ibid., 83. The fluctuations in the demand and supply of palm oil affected local production and income, whereas imported goods became more expensive. Also the commercial exploitation of oil in USA affected the demand of palm oil.
[331] Cf. Ibid., 172.
[332] Cf. The Rise and Fall of the Igala State, 26.
[333] Cf. T. Bierschenk, et al., Long –Term Effects of Development Aid, 97-98. Because of the absence of the judiciary or non separation of power, people are subjected to obey arbitrary regulations and directives from officials and pseudo-officials.

modern age complicated the poverty and travail of the people,[334] at worst the people grumbled in silence and found other ways to evade the rapacious system.

Even the presence of the colonial administration worsened the taxation later. The failure to "maintain a single [tax] assessment policy after the conquest was the result of an unhealthy combination of indecision, incompetence, diplomacy and fear".[335] There was no clear policy and means of taxation, yet it was heavily demanded to cover up for insolvency in the colony. It was also an expansionist strategy of the British market that real wealth be transferred to Britain and the burden of such taxes created feelings of resentment.[336] There was a new social order, consisting of new elite schooled by the missionaries and working for the colonial administration. The traditional structure and the new elite became parallel institutions and the latter was meant to take sides with the colonial administration. The ensuing tension from such division was a calculated attempt by the colonial administration to further her imperialist mission through the 'divide and rule' tactic.[337] Such local tax officials for example were under pressure to deliver so as to maintain their appointed position. Also coupled with their selfish interests, it inadvertently led to unimaginable taxation on the poor people.[338] Fifty percent of the taxes collected by the N.A. were handed over to the colonial administration while the rest were retained by the Native Treasury. This fifty percent went basically for the salaries, from which the *Attah's* was ten percent. The chiefs and the workers in this new structure continued to use the native administrative structure to extort from the people even after colonialism.[339] Therefore the colonial and post colonial structure was basically resumed in a new structure, which is precisely an archetype and a continuum of the pre-colonial system.

The Igala nation arrived unprepared into the global economy and the consequent global depression of the 1932-33, thus there were no social linkage and plans for any cushioning policy. Besides, the absence of a central administration later, which even from the beginning was very self-centred and lacked social package, dragged the ensuing poverty in

---

[334] Cf. Ibid., 103.

[335] M.S. Abdulkadir, A Political and Economic History, 99.

[336] Cf. Ibid., 100.

[337] Cf. A. Agbali, The Igala Response, 118.

[338] Cf. M.S. Abdulkadir, A Political and Economic History, 103.

[339] Cf. Ibid., 163, 167.

Igala/Bassaland into the period of World War II; whereas Britain could come out of the recession after a year or two.[340] Also the stringent and mercantile British policies increased the poverty and extortion through multiple taxes and duties thereby affecting the flow of Igala trade and production to the advantage of the colonial nation. Since the European firms paid better prices at the beginning of their contacts with local producers, it encouraged the people to desert the traditional structure that they were already tired of. However, it was just a competitive strategy to arm-twist the *Attah's* monopoly. As soon as the European firms had the monopoly it was a déjà vu, the sale of the commodity goods were forced down to unbearable prices.[341] Therefore from the *Attah*-Igala state structure till the colonial age, there was no iota of social security. There were no relief packages or assistance to ameliorate the suffering of the people during moments of pest attack, drought or moments of bad harvest; yet the people were subjected to regular and arbitrary tribute and tax. It suffices to say the state of affairs was habitual extortion by the ruling elite and the subsequent colonial structure.[342] The missionaries were about the very first western institution with some feeble picture of social welfare packages and humanitarian endeavours to cushion the harsh economic and social questions of the time. Even though they were aligned to their home states, they "were agents of social change as well as planters of the seed of hope...and also significant agents of people centred progressive social change."[343]

3.4   Idah diocese

The Catholic diocese of Idah lies in the present-day Kogi State (the middle belt Nigeria) that is referred to today as North-central geo-political zone. Idah diocese is composed of the Igala speaking people as its dominant ethnic group; the others include Bassa-komo, Bassa-Nge and the Igbirra Mozum speaking people as the minorities. Also, there are Igbos at the boundary with Nsukka and the Ika Igbo (along the Niger River line boundary). This vicinity of the Catholic diocese of Idah is also referred to politically today as 'Kogi-East senatorial zone' and it covers about 15,113

---

[340] Cf. Ibid., 146.
[341] Cf. Ibid., 84. It was such monopoly that led to the several insurrections, which were quelled with the British naval ship in several bombardments in Idah and like in many pre-colonial African states.
[342] Cf. Ibid., 107, 151.
[343] A. Agbali, The Igala Response, 122.

square kilometres.[344] From the projected census of 2006, she has an estimated population of over 1.5 million people with a Catholic presence of 246,852, which is about 12.1%.[345] Idah the seat of the diocese is the ancestral home of the Igalas, where the local chief known politically as the *Attah* of Igala too is resident.

The penetration of the CMS Mission into the southern Nigeria already extended the Christian frontiers to Idah as far back as 1865.[346] The principal agents of Catholic Evangelization were the Holy Ghost missionaries from Ireland, France, Germany and later Canada. Catholic Missionary activities began first in Dekina, the political and military headquarters of Bassa province from 1902 by Rev. Fr. Joseph Lichtenberger C.S.Sp. Among the members of this mission was the legendary and great missionary priest, who is famously remembered as Bishop Joseph Shanahan (known for the 'school magic' in Eastern Nigeria). The mission was closed down in 1905 because of the stiff resistance and lack of co-operation mostly from the Muslim indigenes.[347] The proximity of the area to the northern part of Nigeria, that is highly Muslim populated, raised a strong Muslim presence even before the advent of the Christian missions. It thus made missionaries to be influenced by fear and caution, despite their humanitarian intentions that were opened to all.[348] However, the period of Catholic absence as observed by some schools of thought retarded the socio-economic and educational growth of this region.[349] While the Catholic mission was closed

---

[344] Cf. Idah Diocese Catholic –Hierarchy, http://www.Catholic-hierarchy.org/diocese/didah.html (04.02.15). There are disparities regarding this geographical exactness. For example, Oguagha P.A's version in 1981 is 13,665 square km.

[345] Cf. Ibid. Population census remains one of the most controversial political issues in Nigeria because it determines the revenue sharing formula. It is however difficult to come out with very distinct figures. What is represented here is the Catholic view of 2014.

[346] Cf. W. Wariboko, The CMS Niger Mission, 36.

[347] Cf. Welcome to Catholic Diocese of Idah, http://netministries.org/frames.asp?ch=ch09029&st=KOGI&name=CATHOLIC%20DIOCESE%20OF%20IDAH&city=IDAH (02.03.15).

[348] Cf. Ali Mazrui, The African Condition, The Reith Lectures, 51. Even though other parts of Igalaland had reasonable number of Muslims; one could accept the assertions that the possibility of backlash from religious zealots was evidently prevalent with such communities that had religions with highly established culture and structure, for example Christianity, Islam, Hinduism and Buddhism. Thus, the absence of such structure in ATR could not have warranted such a unified force to attack other religions trying to settle down in new places.

[349] Cf. John Oguche, The Contributions to the infrastructural and social development of Idah Diocese in: Ed., Pub./Hist. Sub-Committee of the Idah Diocesan Silver Jubilee celebration, Catholic Diocese of Idah at twenty five, Enugu 2003, Pp. 38-45, 39.

down, other Protestant groups had in between broken into this area. The quest to reopen the missions rose up from 1930 and was finally fulfilled in 1934 through this second missionary attempt by Fr. Anthony Konrath, a German Holy Ghost priest resident then in the Utonkon mission (in Otukpo, a neighbouring diocese today). Due to this successful launch of the Catholic faith, many new missions were founded in different parts of the diocese including the old abandoned Dekina mission.[350] The present Idah diocese had her beginning from the Lower Niger Prefecture with headquarters in Onitsha in 1930 and was later joined to the Benue region in 1934 with headquarters in Makurdi. From 1947 to 1968 she came under the Kabba prefecture and from 1968 to 1977 she attained the stature of a prefecture. Finally, on the 17th December 1977 she was raised to the status of a diocese by Pope Paul VI.

Between 1934 and 1978, the religious working force comprised many expatriate priests of the Holy Ghost Congregation. However, a few Nigerian priests, Frs. J.C. Anyogu and Anthony Nwedo from the Archdiocese of Onitsha joined this crew between 1946 and 1948.[351] Their primary mission was the establishment and the building of churches, schools and doing charity works. It was only in 1968 the diocese witnessed the ordination of her first priest, Fr. Dominic Arome; the diocese from then witnessed sporadic vocations, but the establishment of the St. Kizito Minor Seminary since 1982 massively encouraged vocation to the priesthood and male religious.[352] The contributions of the expatriate priests were very conspicuous and a landmark in the affairs of Idah diocese up to the 80s. There was a considerable reduction in their presence beginning from the 90s, due to age and illness; the last among them, Fr. Dennis Guertin, who for over fifty years lived and worked in Odomomoh-Ibaji (the swampy region of the diocese), returned to Canada in 2014.

Among the early working force also were the German Holy Ghost Brothers, the Franciscan Brothers, the Canadian Holy Ghost Brothers and the Marist Brothers. The religious Brothers, mostly expatriate, were

---

[350] Cf. P.E. Okwoli, An Outline History of the Catholic Church in Idah Diocese, Nsukka, 1984, 8.
[351] Cf. Ibid. 24.
[352] Cf. John Abuh, The Contribution of St. Kizito's Seminary to the growth of Vocation in Idah Diocese in: Ed., Pub./Hist. Sub-Committee of the Idah Diocesan Silver Jubilee celebration, Catholic Diocese of Idah at twenty five, Enugu 2003, Pp.54-56.

basically involved in educational and charity activities.[353] The presence of female congregations in the diocese began with the Holy Rosary Sisters from Ireland on the 15th September 1951 with Srs M. Regina and Philips. Apart from the management of the diocesan medical institutions like the Grimard Hospital, the establishment of DDS through Sr. Nora McNamara became one of the greatest contributions of the Holy Rosary to the diocese. Other congregations like Holy Ghost Sisters and the Handmaid of the Holy Child Jesus came into the diocese thereafter. Since then many female congregations have come into the diocese and are contributing to the growth of the diocese based on their respective charism and apostolate such as education, medical, pastoral and social work. Monastic presence in Idah diocese was only realised on the 21st December 2001 when the female contemplative order of the Benedictines joined the pastoral team of the diocese.[354] Idah before 1930 had a considerable number of Catholic Igbo traders and soldiers of WAFF;[355] these lay people formed the crop of the early working force of the diocese. It was the gathering of this group of people for Sunday prayers that encouraged the coming of Fr. Konrath to open the new mission at Idah. At the inception of this mission, prominent members of the aforementioned group and other indigenes became instructors, interpreters to the expatriate team and many eventually became catechist too.[356]

3.5   Idah diocese in the context of the Nigerian state structure

For the purpose of peaceful coexistence, every nation has a set of rules that determines the rights, duties and limits in the relationship of the different components and organs within her territory. The Nigerian case has been a long, vague and twisted relationship of state and religion, coupled with the consistent tendencies for domination and mutual distrust between the two biggest religions, Muslims and Christians. It has beclouded the state/religion relationship and thus created an obscure scenario of ambiguous laws. However, since 1999 there has been a constitution even though it has

---

[353] Cf. P.E. Okwoli An Outline History, 75.

[354] Cf. Dorothy Okpanachi, A brief History of Religious Congregation for Women in the Diocese in: Ed., Pub./Hist. Sub-Committee of the Idah Diocesan Silver Jubilee celebration, Catholic Diocese of Idah at twenty five, Enugu, 2003, Pp 57-59.

[355] In this case WAFF was composed of soldiers from the southern part of Nigerian, who were already Christian converts.

[356] Cf. P.E. Okwoli, an Outline History, 84.

been pilloried as a non- 'people oriented constitution', it remains today the only legal framework to describe the current church/state relationship.

Chapter one, article 10 of the 1999 constitution of the Federal Republic of Nigeria states that, "the government of the federation or of a state shall not adopt any religion as state religion." This makes Nigeria constitutionally a secular state. Chapter 4, Article 32, Paragraph 1, also states that "Every person shall be entitled to freedom of thought, conscience and religion, including freedom to change his religion or belief, and freedom (either alone or in community with others, and in public or in private) to manifest and propagate his religion or belief in worship, teaching, practice and observance." The churches are registered under public corporation and as such operate within the specified rights and privileges granted in the constitution. Therefore churches like other organisations have the right to ownership of properties, but depend mainly on gifts, donations and contributions from within and outside the nation. Sometimes fund raising and launching appeals are made to execute projects. Financially, the state does not have a constitutional duty and commitment toward the churches. Whatever comes from the state is usually through contacts and connections with state's personnel(s).

With the aforementioned church/state relationship and the case of Idah diocese with a predominantly peasant agricultural occupation, it suffices to say that Idah diocese is a rural diocese. It is obvious that, apart from the iron-cast coal mining and the timber companies, there are no industries and commercial cities in this part of the nation. This makes her case of poverty a glaring and peculiar one.[357] The state capital does not reside in this territory and so there is very little government presence except at the local government level. The traditional population is no longer only into agrarian and semi-fishing today, but into civil service in educational institutions as teachers, petty traders and people who practice menial jobs. A few small scale businesses exist like merchandise, provision stores, petty trading, crafts work like carpentry, tailoring and departmental stores. These 'petty' businesses do not have the financial weight to create wealth and improve living conditions as modern economy entails. Hence this part of the nation is very much socio-economically disadvantaged.[358] The absence of

---

[357] Cf. N. McNamara, S. Morse, Developing On-Farm Research, The Broad Picture, County Cork, 1996, 26.
[358] Cf. John Oguche, The Contributions of the Diocesan Works Department, 40.

economic activities that brings about improved standard of living in this part of the nation and the paradox of the Nigerian state with abounding opportunities is itself a dangerous monster for the teeming and growing young population today.

3.6 Humanitarian works in Idah diocese

The wave of humanitarian works and its progression from the coast to the interior was a journey of time and space. It was sometimes conflict-ridden, strenuous and was delayed by a number of factors like the absence of roads and other means of transportation. This further access was easier for riverine communities, since water transportation was the commonest means of transportation. Thus communities in the interior (without access to rivers) experienced late humanitarian influx because of the rigours of land transportation as it took days crossing through the different terrains and different ethnic groups; besides this presented its own challenges like distrust, insecurity and so on. On one side, these factors, to mention but a few were unfortunate hindrances to the arrival of the missions and their humanitarian activities into the present Kogi-East senatorial zone, on the other, it fortunately slowed down the colonial invasion till about 1903.

Before the colonial era, there were also forced movement of people as slaves, traders and religious evangelists through the length and breadth of the nation. Communal relationships, social exchanges and marriages existed among these different ethnic groups. However the colonial administration's presence and the dawn of foreign religious activities encouraged and "increased the magnitude, the frequency and the intensity of these movements"[359] and other relationships among the different ethnic groups. The colonial assault and religious intrusion into the affairs of the people in this part of the globe came along with exceptional development. It awakened a wave of development of an estranged people and the triviality of the idea of the 'dark continent'. The changes were informed by factors beyond the immediate control of the traditional society. While these societies were still at their communal stage en-route from feudalism, Europe with her capitalistic quest on a mercantile journey had already transformed from

---

[359] Akin L. Mabogunje, Changes in socio-economic and cultural patterns caused by the industrialization of Nigeria - a regional differentiation in: Afrika Spectrum, Wirtschaftsplannung und Wirtschaftspolitik in Nigeria, Deutsches Institut für Afrika-Forschung Hamburg, 1972, Pp. 34-45, 39.

feudalism to other forms of government.[360] This European advancement from feudalism to capitalism, the first ever in human history gave Europe "a headstart over humanity in the scientific understanding of the universe, the making of tools and the efficient organisation of labour";[361] it consequently gave Europe an easy access into Africa. The colonial access ignited a wave of alteration in the affairs of these 'new' environments, which were forcefully positive and negative. Nevertheless, they were accompanied by humanitarian developments that opened new perspectives for new economic development, democratic capabilities, leadership restructuring and a Eurocentric view of humanism. Also they were tremendous and ambivalent changes from the spread of the gospel. However, there is no gainsaying that these developments transformed the traditional environment in different dimensions beginning from the settlements around the coast, which later confirmed the importance of humanitarian activities in the hinterland. Besides, the many social challenges among the people ordinarily welcomed the call for humanitarian presence. This segment of this chapter is intended therefore to spell out the humanitarian perspective of the churches especially the Catholic Church; its role in the territory of the Catholic diocese of Idah, its answers to social questions from *diakonein* standpoint. Also it intends to trace the social principles of human dignity, common good, solidarity, subsidiarity and sustainability expressed in the light of the undertaken projects. It would further point out the commendable role and the immeasurable achievements of the church in this part of the globe despite the fact that she was far away from the coast and had little mineral resources that never really attracted colonial presence and even indigenous administration. Nonetheless, through the advent of the mission, humanitarian opportunities arose and the church in her *diakonein* response pursued these humanitarian works like other regions too.

3.6.1 The Dekina Mission and its humanitarian viewpoint

A flashback on the thesis of Michael Barnett that every new student of humanitarianism is likely to identify humanitarianism with abolitionism, will help to elucidate the importance of the Dekina mission and the significant humanitarian gesture of this eventful but failed mission from 1903 to 1905. The Dekina Mission was also to serve as the centre for the

---

[360] Cf. W. Rodney, How Europe underdeveloped Africa, 88.
[361] Ibid.

redemption of slaves.[362] In view of this agreement between the missionaries and the colonial administration, the acting High Commissioner of the colonial rule recommended Dekina[363] in Bassa province as the most suitable place to establish a mission with schools and a village for liberated slaves. One humanitarian adventure of the missions was to establish a day school for the local children, primarily for the pagan children, a boarding school for children from the remote environs of Dekina. Also an industrial school was to be established that would provide vocational training for carpenters, gardeners, farmers and in general for training artisans and finally it was to become a village of freed slaves.[364] This model of school and vocational school by the missions was known both in the government and commercial circles as the Basle method. It was geared towards making missions self-supporting and the provision of a trade section to dispose of their surpluses.[365] The colonial administrator was to liberate the slaves and turn them to the mission in Dekina, while the mission as promised was to abide by the regulations of the colonial administration and to care for the slaves. The missionaries were very optimistic that "the Dekina mission will support itself after a few years by its own industry."[366] For many selfish political reasons the colonial administration tactically avoided the slave redemption project and only very few slaves were given to this mission. According to Shanahan, "Until now, we have only received fourteen slaves from the Government, seven of whom are children between two and seven years old."[367] The Dekina Mission was a very challenging experience and unlike past missions, she did not grow because of its proximity to the Muslim north that made Dekina very Muslim dominated. Consequently, the people's

---

[362] Cf. D. Rieff, A Bed for the Night, 58. Despite the frantic efforts employed to contain the trade slave, it persisted in the hinterlands. After the abolition in 1807, slavery only came to a global halt after almost seventy years. This phenomenon was more in the interiors than in the coast; Cf. F. Deaville Walker, The Romance of the Black River, The Story of CMS Nigerian Mission. in: http://www.anglicanhistory.org/africa/ng/walker1930/index.html (09.02.15). Also the Hausas from the north were still into raids, for example the raid that took Ajayi Crowther and his family into slavery in 1822.

[363] Cf. N. McNamara, S. Morse, Developing Financial Services, 70. The choice of Dekina from all indications goes back to this historical background after the establishment of colonial rule in 1902. The kingdom was traumatized and divided into two: Idah came under the southern protectorate and Dekina became the Igala capital of the northern protectorate, until 1918 when they were again re-united.

[364] Cf. B. Okpanachi, Nigerian-Vatican Diplomatic Relationship, 109.

[365] Cf. L. J. Lewis, Society, schools and Progress in Nigeria, 27.

[366] B. Okpanachi, Nigeria-Vatican Diplomatic Relationship, 109.

[367] Ibid., 114.

unwillingness to send their children to the mission school held back the growth of the Mission. The eventual shutting down of the mission was after the mission premise was razed to the ground by fire; there are dissenting views as regards the cause of this inferno.[368] Although resilient efforts were put in place to rebuild the house, so many factors still worked against the mission.[369] Nevertheless, the missionaries at the close of the mission in 1905 went away with the freed slaves, who eventually became the workforce of the missionaries in subsequent missions through their artisan works.[370]

3.6.2   The post civil war relief action

The proximity of the Eastern region to Idah diocese created a pre-civil war Igbo influence and presence. The Igbo presence was very pronounced in this area and in the Idomaland of present Benue state. The exodus of the Igbo traders, tailors, wine tappers, mechanics, and little merchandise, brought about humanitarian distortions to the present Idah diocesan terrain. The popular Onitsha market was the main source of manufactured goods for the Igala/Bassaland; also other Igbo towns, where the agricultural products of the Igalas and the Idomas found market, came to a close. This created depression even till after the civil war.[371] Parishes like Odomomoh and Akpanaya at the borders were the most affected during and after the civil war. Thus, Msgr. Leopold Grimard, the Prefect of Idah Prefecture in 1969 set up the Diocesan Social Welfare Department (DSWD), led by Fr. Y. Frechette. Arrangements were made for some rehabilitation assistance to the parishes and many of the war victims, prominently the IDPs in the diocese. These affected parishes at the borders were therefore closed down till after the war. Their parish priests were made to supervise these

---

[368] Cf. Eugene Groetz, The First Contacts of the Spiritans with the Middle Belt, 10-18. Since Dekina was Muslim dominated, naturally every suspicion pointed at the Muslims. But from the report of the missionaries a bush fire fanned by strong Harmattan wind swept through Dekina village and destroyed everything including the mission premises, leaving the missionaries with only the clothes they had on them. It took them four days journey to trek back to Onitsha.

[369] Cf. Ibid. Despite the attempts made to rebuild the mission later, the animosity between the different ethnic groups created strife and violence, the mission was too poor and never achieved self-sustenance as envisaged. It was too tough for the missionaries and they were eventually called back from Onitsha and the Dekina mission was closed. The Dekina journal ended with the word 'DEKINA VIXIT' Dekina is dead.

[370] Cf. P. E Okwoli, An Outline History, 5.

[371] Cf. N. McNamara, S. Morse, Developing Financial Services, 70.

humanitarian tasks of rehabilitating the IDPs.[372] The advent of this social welfare department marked the beginning of such humanitarian consciousness and aid to war victims. The later growth of such consciousness could be likened to the establishment of DDS. However, the magnitude of the DDS far outweighs the DSWD.

3.6.3   Increasing educational institutions and opportunities

Like the other parts of the nation, the mission school was the most remarkable tool of evangelization. The school became not just the vehicle for the spread of the faith but also the humanitarian standpoint as it cared for the spiritual, material and social welfare of the new converts. The CMS attempt by Bishop Ajayi Crowther was the very first effort to introduce western education into Idah in 1857, which led to the establishment of a mission station. But he left with his church members in 1866 after they were maltreated by the natives. The return of CMS in 1925 came through another side of Kogi-East, the Bassaland and spreading further to Dekina, Idah and other places.[373] The presence of the different missions in the present Kogi-East provoked a chain of establishments of many mission institutions beginning with the mission schools to churches and some humanitarian projects/concerns. After the establishment of the colonial rule in 1900, missionaries came directly under the colonial rule and thus had to work with the NA and the Divisional Office (DO, the representative arm of the colonial rule); the NA was directly under the DO. Through the process of indirect-rule orders were passed by the colonial rulers and executed by the NA.[374] The 'early schools' (chapter 2.1.3) was also commonplace in this territory in the early years of the missions, before the establishment of real primary schools began. The curriculum of these early schools was centred on religious instructions and the preparation of converts for the reception of the Christian faith. Apart from the three Rs (Reading, Writing and Arithmetic) they offered, they had no modern pragmatic relevance since they only served

---

[372] Cf. P.E Okwoli, An Outline History, 41, 103.

[373] Cf. Lawrence Achimugu, History of Education, in Igalaland, Lagos, 2005, 39; Ibid. 45. The CMS school was closed down in 1889. This report provokes an open-ended question like, who was managing the school in the absence of the CMS mission, owing to the fact that this was the first attempt ever in the history of Igala/Bassaland? However, the author cites *Fafunwa,* whose works suggested that educational historians probably did not document anything about the school since it was closed down; W. Wariboko, The CMS Niger Mission, 36. This author opines that CMS presence began in 1965.

[374] Cf. T. Falola, The History of Nigeria, 71.

religious purposes. However, they created a literate society that consequently added new dimensions of knowledge to the community and to the beneficiaries at large.

Among the many humanitarian works done by the missions in this interior, the institution of primary school education was the most striking and foundational development. The second Catholic missionary attempt of 1934 opened this new chapter of evangelisation through the school strategy, whereas the CMS began their second expedition later in 1925. The Christian Missionary in Many Lands (CMML) was already in operation since the 1919 and the Qua Iboe Mission (QIM) began from 1931. The outings of these churches were also felt in these environs through the establishment of schools. The Catholic Church was however a latecomer and from 1932 she began to apply to the DO to open new schools. This development was stalled by a few factors; among them was the presence of other pre-existing denominations who lobbied to keep the Catholic Church out of the scene. The DO was displeased with this development as it created some divisive traits and scepticism that became a pointer to future rivalry. From the NA viewpoint, the Catholic missionaries did not pass through the due process. Despite these challenges the Catholic Church eventually got her breakthrough in June 1934. The approval was given for the founding of ten primary schools in different strategic locations of the diocese and on the 16th August 1934 all these schools began full operation with a considerable number of pupils. Between 1934 and 1939 the Catholic mission had 250 pupils from all the primary institutions in the diocese. This major breakthrough heralded the Catholic presence in this vicinity and thus became a catalyst to other developments. The Catholic mission's dominance in educational institutions in other parts of the nation also became conspicuous in Idah diocesan terrain. The number of pupils increased tremendously over the years so that communities without schools often made the school-request as first priority whenever they came in contact with the missions; so much so that the building of churches and the spread of the faith that was the primary target of the missions became secondary to the schools. Consequently, the Catholic church/faith though a latecomer overcame this shortfall through the school strategy.[375]

The working force of these Catholic primary schools comprised of both male and female expatriate missionaries. Because of the benefits of the

---

[375] Cf. P. E Okwoli, An Outline History, 59-64.

'School Magic', the Igbos of Eastern Nigeria descent featured among the early staff too; a recruitment that was facilitated by the universal nature of the Catholic Church. The early schools like other parts of Nigeria were basically tuition free, but the founding of real primary schools attracted school fees, this was more or less a token from the pupils to finance the schools. Nevertheless, the schools were heavily subsidized by the mission to redress the educational backwardness of the entire area. In effect, the staff remuneration, the cost of building, maintenance and the general running cost was a result of effective management and donations through the missions. Thus, like the Western and Eastern Nigeria, the majority of educational provision and finances for school management in Kogi-East took the typical template of mission schools. Accordingly, "it was dependent upon the efforts of the Christian missions supported by their home churches and gifts from friends."[376] Although "the colonial education policy of financing of education [was] based on cost sharing between the proprietary bodies, local community, parents/guardians and the government,"[377] this system never worked fully in Idah Diocese as the missions bore most of the costs. Nevertheless, it was a perfect strategy in Eastern Nigeria, where the idea of the village school was a give and take relationship. The case of Idah diocese was not as precarious as the far north, as the people still welcomed education, nonetheless, it created a slogan like: 'Father's church' and 'Father's school'. Thus whatever was inclined 'Father's' was more or less captioned a free venture.

The movement for self-government after World War II that ignited change in the educational approach led to the promulgation of the 1948 educational ordinance. Thus, educational administration was decentralised, the colonial administration reviewed its ten years' educational plan, a director of education was appointed and procedures to access grants-in-aid were carefully laid out.[378] Before the 1948 educational ordinance, the

---

[376] L. J. Lewis, Society, Schools and Progress in Nigeria, 27.

[377] H. Imam, Educational Policy in Nigeria, 190.

[378] Cf. Ibid., 184; L. J. Lewis, Society, Schools and Progress in Nigeria, 27. The colonial administrator's concern about education began in 1822 as the ordinance to govern education in West Africa was passed with a follow-up visit from 1864-5 by the Commissioner Ordinance to check the status of schools. The case of 'grant' was first reported in 1877 till 1882 by the Lagos administration. The sum of £200 was given annually to each of the three missionary societies carrying out educational work in this colony. However, the administration did nothing else other than this financial support. But from 1882, the West African Education Ordinance became operational in Lagos and a board of education was

different regions, (north, west and east) operated different systems, but were united under one system with the effect of the 1948 ordinance. Nevertheless, the creation of the three regions led to the promulgation of the 1952 education ordinance that empowered each region to develop its educational policies and system; thus, the colonial education board was abolished. From 1951 to 1954, two constitutional conferences emerged between the colonial administration and Nigerian politicians in the course of the march towards self government. These gave birth to new constitution in 1954 and Nigeria subsequently became a federation of three regions. Each region had constitutional rights to make laws for its territories, citizens and educational policies. Hence the regions began to promulgate their educational policies, beginning from the west in 1955 while the East and the North were in 1956. But one established fact remains that these regional educational laws and acts were basically served from the same source: the educational act 1944 of Wales and England. Though they had little variations in their definitions and components, they basically comprised primary, post-primary and further education.[379] From 1956 to 68, the northern administration encouraged the missions to work towards upgrading the primary schools to full-fledged primary schools. By 1968 during the government take-over of schools from all voluntary agencies, the Catholic Church had a total number of 51 primary schools, while the QIM owned 28, CMML with 6 and CMS (Anglican Church today) numbered 6, bringing a total of 51/40; the NA had less than 40 schools at this period. Within the space of 34 years (1934-1968) the Catholic Church had overtaken all the Protestant churches. The Catholic schools had reputable and well disciplined teachers that so much attracted even the Muslim's patronage.[380]

From the background of the different missionary groups one could infer the possible reasons for the Catholic dominance in the school set-up in Kogi-East during the colonial episode till the period of 1968. There must have been a repetition of CMS's refusal to key into grants from the colonial administration like it happened in the Eastern Nigeria.[381] Such a factor must

---

consequently set up to advice the general board on the conditions for grants. Lagos from this moment became open to grant-in-aid from the colonial administration for schools.

[379] Cf. H. Imam, Educational Policy in Nigeria, 184-185.

[380] Cf. P. E. Okwoli, An Outline History, 64-66.

[381] Cf. E. Ayandele, Missionary Impact, 302. The overriding catholic presence in schools in southern Nigeria was through the charismatic Bishop Shanahan's ability to key into colonial administrative grants, while the other churches like the CMS rejected these government's grants.

have retarded the spread of her educational activities in Igala/Bassaland. Besides, the fact that the CMS was into agitation and plan for self-governing and self-supporting African churches lends credence to this factor.[382] The missionary group the CMML was a corporation of independent churches from England, Canada and the USA that grew from the Plymouth Brethren in England and supports their missionaries in distant lands. From its foundation, funding sources must have been restricted to the aforementioned nations.[383] CMML was into versatile ministry and above all ventured into schools for the disabled, which is usually more expensive than the regular schools. Though the departure of its founders has watered down its managerial strength today, the CMML remains the only institution that has such a humanitarian undertaking in the entire Kogi-East until date.[384] Thirdly, the QIM (known today as United Evangelical Church UEC) is one of the indigenous founded churches in Nigeria that originated from the present South-South Nigeria and later spread to Igala/Bassaland.[385] The translation of the bible as far back as the 1930s into native languages, Igala and Bassa, and their mass production are one of her greatest achievements.[386] Being locally founded unlike the other churches, she was more or less preoccupied with the establishment of her raison d'être and hold in Kogi-East, whereas the others had passed such a foundational level. Just like in southern Nigeria, the Catholics were more 'forceful' towards the opening of schools than the other missions. Moreover, the growth and increased patronage of the Catholic schools is likened probably to the number of overseas missions who were funding the Catholic schools. While the CMS was into self-sustenance the QIM was partly dependent on funding from her foreign missionaries from England and likewise the CMML; the Catholics were opened to donations from the entire Catholic world. Thus, the universal nature of the Catholic Church must have encouraged multiple sponsorship and funding opportunities. The humanitarian importance of the missions through the opening of schools remains a fact that cannot be underestimated.

---

[382] Cf. F. D. Walker, Project Canterbury, The Romance of the Black River, 50, 91.

[383] Cf. A. A. Agbali, Ritualizing Communal wellbeing:, 328; Christian Missions in Many Lands, http://www.cmml.us/about (01.09.15)

[384] Cf. L. Achimugu, History of Education in Igalaland, 37.

[385] Cf. Dictionary of African Christian Biography, http://www.dacb.org/stories/nigeria/bill_samuelalexander.html (01.09.15). The idea of the Qua Iboe Church in 1927 came from a British Missionary to Nigeria, who offered to work with the Efiks at the mouth of the Qua Iboe river. He worked with the Efiks and the Anang people of south-south Nigeria.

[386] Cf. L. Achimugu, History of Education in Igalaland, 38.

Therefore, the school game as observed earlier between the missions and the local communities presented profound and immense opportunities to the growth of the new emerging literate society. Without the schools the whole Igala/Bassaland would have been lagging behind the other communities at the coast in the modern dispensation. For this reason, it subsequently made the schools so welcomed, revered and appreciated by many.

Like those at the coast of Nigeria the opening of post primary schools in Kogi-East took a longer time as well. The Catholic presence in the project of post primary education from 1958 to 1968 became very sturdy. Four post primary schools were established: Our Lady's Teachers College Ayangba in 1958, Holy Rosary College Idah in 1962, St. Peter's College Idah in 1963 and the St. Charles College Ankpa in 1967. There was Protestant presence too between the years 1960 to 1969: the Ochaja Secondary Schools 1960, Ochaja Teacher's College 1962 and Bassa Nge Anglican College Gboloko 1969, and just one government owned secondary school, the Dekina Government Secondary School. A good number of the staff of these Catholic secondary schools were expatriates; their sense of dedication and commitments were very high. Some members of staffs were trained through church scholarships at home and overseas so as to beef up the educational standard of the schools. The indigenisation policy, known also as the 'government takeover' of schools that began from 1968 in the northern region shook the foundations of the missions. Consequently the missions halted further school plans and only the last founded secondary school (St. Charles in 1967) built a year before this programme still received a facelift from the mission.[387] The first group of elite in the Kogi-East senatorial zone owe their appreciation to the zealous and benevolent sacrifices of the missions. Through the schools, the church was able to establish her presence, changing the perspectives of life, offering free education, sometimes cheaper or subsidised tuition fees and through that she was able to fulfil her initial objective which is the conversion of souls.

The provision of social services is the utmost responsibility of the state, but spanning from the period of the self rule to independence, only one secondary school was built in this locality in spite of its population of over a million inhabitants, which has doubled today. This educational loophole tells the inefficiency and the lack of government's presence that the missions had to cover for. Unlike communities close to the coast, there were no schools in

---

[387] Cf. P. E. Okwoli, An Outline History, 67.

the present Kogi-East, from 1859 to 1887, when missions solely built and managed their schools without any support from the colonial administration. However the period of school establishment in Kogi-East, came during the dual mandate era, as the colonial administration began to issue grant-in-aid to voluntary agencies from 1887 to 1963;[388] this prompted the building of schools too by the colonial administration from 1908.[389] Despite the colonial and later the national government's performance in setting up schools, the mission's prime step was a scrupulous humanitarian task that set the ball rolling for other developments.

After the takeover of schools by the government in 1968, the missions were forced out of the educational scene and the management of such schools were left in the hands of the Local Educational Authorities (LEA). There were no agreement, compensation and provision for the voluntary agencies that had built these schools. The outcome of this development set in terrible precedents, changes and setbacks in the nation's educational system. The nonchalant attitude, the poor working ethics and the loss of loyalty and patriotism on the part of the teachers towards their jobs resulted in low output. However, the reasons for the indigenisation have been contested in present day Nigeria.[390] Nevertheless, this period marked the worst period of education coupled with consistent numbers of strikes and the consequent *laissez-faire* attitude of the teachers. The much cherished sense of dedication during the mission days could not survive the flames of government decay at all levels, it consequently led to the production of illiterate and semi-illiterate pupils. This encouraged examination

---

[388] Cf. L. Achimugu, Education in Igalaland, 13.

[389] Cf. Ibid., 29

[390] There are different claims to the government takeover of schools, some opined the religious undertone in the policy, that it was meant to stall the growth of Christianity, which was waxing stronger through the schools.; Lawrence O. Obibuaku, Qualitative Education: The Role of Government Take-Over of Schools, Nigeriaworld, http://nigeriaworld.com/articles/2005/sep/061.html (03.07.15). However, there are pros and contra views too, that the indigenisation policy was relevant as it gave teachers a national recognition; their conditions of service were harmonised with their fellow civil servants in the civil service and their career ladder was established and clarified accordingly. It gradually countered the slogan that a 'teacher's reward is in heaven'. Thus, the indigenisation was never a bad thing as it also helped in the rebuilding of the schools in the war affected area. It is the monster of corruption and government inefficiency that has crumbled education, beginning with poor funding and the general lukewarm attitude towards government jobs. It is evident from the fact that virtually every sector today is in shambles; because individuals and officials basically 'develop' themselves and not the state institutions.

malpractices at all levels coupled with the crumbling and most times total absence of training and vocational schools (especially with the drop-out syndrome attached to it). Thus achieving a post secondary result became a 'do or die' factor for the future, it was like the biblical saying that everyone must 'pass through the eye of this needle'.

Owing to the falling standard of education all over the nation, a new strategy of education commenced from 1978 in the diocese. It was the beginning of another era of education, therefore this governmental policy was historical as it marked 'the schools before' and 'the schools after' the indigenisation policy. The coming of Kogi-East, 1976-1990, under Benue state coincided with the UPE period that recorded massive expansion of both primary and secondary schools in the state. A new policy of the Benue state 'the liberal policy towards private ownership' led to unprecedented opening of schools by private proprietors and communities. Consequently from 1978 a number of primary/secondary schools rose understandably. This educational policy stressed the 6-3-3-4 system and the need for the 3Ts 'toil, tolerance and team work' as against the earlier 3Rs.[391] In line with this policy, a new diocesan educational policy under Bishop Ephraim Silas Obot (1936-2009) was conceived to produce well educated people with the divine mission of the church to 'teach all nations'. This policy was to set up nursery/primary schools in all parishes of the diocese. Thus different congregations of missionary sisters and brothers were invited to manage these schools. This exercise began in 1979 with the establishment of the Holy Family Nursery/Primary School Idah.[392] This action set the motion for parish's venture in nursery/primary school, such that the diocese today has 32 nursery and primary schools. The participation of the private sector in education has earned credible resonance since the enactment of the liberal policy. Albeit the proliferation in the schools, they stand out better than the public schools as their pupils perform excellently in external examinations and competitive common entrances. These achievements are the effects of the quality of education, teaching staff's discipline and adequate teaching materials. At this level the private sector has absolute control of these schools, for example the remuneration of staff, school contents and uniforms

---

[391] Cf. L. Achimugu, History of Education in Igalaland, 51.
[392] Cf. Joseph F. Aduku, Development of Education in the Diocese 1978-2003, 33-37, in: Ed., Pub./Hist. Sub-Committee of the Idah Diocesan Silver Jubilee celebration, Catholic Diocese of Idah at twenty five, Enugu 2003, Pp. 33-37; L. Achimugu, History of Education in Igalaland, 57

and so on. In spite of the exorbitant fees charged, many parents prefer to have their children in such schools. Nevertheless some of the schools do not meet the required standard and many proprietors today are more or less into business than the mission to educate.[393] Because of the cost effect of building and maintaining these schools the Catholic Diocese of Idah has in recent years made moves to maintain good quality and a minimum price that the poor could afford. Through the Catholic flair, the presence of the services of nuns and brothers has helped to address the cost effectiveness and the quality of learning. Although the nursery/primary schools are noted for good learning, the staffing is a problem. Often their members of staff are not under the state package and are consequently not entitled to the salaries, allowances, emoluments, pension, gratuity and other bonuses like their counterparts in the open schools. Even though the teachers employed by the government deliver poor quality services, they have a better pay package than their colleagues in the private schools. It explains why teachers in the private schools are perpetually on the lookout for government paid jobs. This factor sometimes raises tension between the religious in such schools and the lay teachers. The same problem of teachers' remuneration addressed at the government takeover is still a dominant issue today.

This educational plan was extended to the secondary school establishment too. All these efforts were to restore that decency, academic performance that soon went with the whirlwind of government takeover of schools and government failed educational policy. The falling standard of education later created a feeling of sympathy during the democratic dispensation among some politicians to return the schools to the missions. Accordingly, the respective churches who formerly owned these schools were granted some concessions by the government: the appointment of the principals and the vice principals of these schools.[394] This educational lacuna also encouraged the founding of private secondary schools all over the diocese and the relegation of the public schools, thus, public schools today are consigned as quarters of the 'not haves' in the society.

Education remains the best humanitarian good the missions have served the people with. Today the diocese controls 20 secondary schools:

---

[393] Cf. L. Achimugu, History of Education in Igalaland, 55.
[394] Cf. J. F. Aduku, Development of Education in the Diocese, 37.

S/N	List of Schools	Year of establishment	Status	Type	Ownership
1	Our Lady of Schools Anyigba	1957	Boys and Girls	Day and Boarding	Government and Diocese
2	Holy Rosary College, Idah	1962	Girls only	Day and Boarding	Government and Diocese.
3	St Peter's College	1963	Boys only	Day	Government and Diocese
4	St. Charles College Ankpa	1967	Boys and Girls	Day	Government and Diocese
5	St. Kizito Seminary Idah	1982	Catholic Boys only	Boarding	Diocese
6	Daughters of Mary Mother of Mercy Secondary School Sheria	1997	Boys and Girls	Day and Boarding	Daughters of Mary Mother of Mercy
7	Redeemer Secondary School Ankpa	2001	Boys and Girls	Day and Boarding	Diocese
8	Christ the good Shepherd Academy of Sciences, Anyigba	2002	Boys and Girls	Day and Boarding	Marist Daughters
9	Sacred Heart Marist College Ejule	2003	Boys and Girls	Boarding	Marist Brothers
10	Christ the Good Shepherd Academy of Sciences Dekina	2004	Boys and Girls	Day	Marist Daughters
11	SS Peter and Paul Academy Egume	2006	Boys and Girls	Day and Boarding	Diocese
12	St Mary's Secondary School Abejiukolo	2007	Boys and Girls	Day	Diocese
13	Christ the Good Shpeherd Academy of Sciences, Ogbadu	2007	Boys and Girls	Day	Marist Daughter
14	Dr. Williams Kupiec Girls Academy Agbaduma Okpo	2009	Girls only	Boarding	Diocese
15	St John of the Cross Secondary School, Ogugu	2010	Boys and Girls	Day	Diocese
16	Holy Spirit School	2010	Boys and	Day	Diocese

	Imane		Girls		
17	St Matthew's Secondary School Odeke	2010	Boys and Girls	Day	Diocese
18	Pope John Paul II Academy Okenyi	2011	Boys and Girls	Day	Diocese
19	Holy Ghost Secondary School Okura	2013	Boys and Girls	Boarding	Holy Ghost Fathers north/west province
20	Mary Immaculate Secondary School Iyegu-Idah	2014	Boys and Girls	Day	Diocese and Catholic Women Organisation CWO

Even though the first-four schools on the above table are at present still joint-owned by government and church, they were initially built by the church. Together they have stepped up the literacy level of the diocese and the entire Kogi-East senatorial zone. The church has remained today the greatest humanitarian saviour of this illiteracy tendency. Another strong humanitarian feature is that the tuition fee of these new schools was made affordable to the peasants at reduced or subsidized rate. Most of the monies are donations from agencies and friends from Europe, America and within. Through these donations school halls, classrooms, learning materials were secured even without having the poor people taxed; a fact that still makes the tuition fees of these Catholic institutions cheaper than other private schools today. This *diakonein* aspect of the church wins laudable resonance and is worth the humanitarian spirit, the selfless spirit through organised help to assist societies that have less government presence like the case of Idah diocese.

3.6.4   The Grimard Hospital and outreaches

The project of medical services in Idah diocesan terrain like the development among the people at the coast took the second place in humanitarian attention of the missions. The mission was not the pacesetter of medical institution in Idah diocesan terrain. The WAFF stationed at Ankpa from 1905 came with the establishment of the first medical facility and was operated primarily for their soldiers.[395] Nevertheless the first joint work between the state and the church was initiated in 1934 at the very beginning of the mission's history. This came on the heels of the resignation of the European medical officer in Idah General Hospital in June 1934. The mission was invited by the NA to take over the management, while the NA provided the funds for running the hospital. Unfortunately the mission declined this offer for lack of personnel. This joint work was realised in 1951 when the mission took over the running of the General Hospital through the help of the Holy Rosary Sisters. The General Hospital was situated in Idah, the NA's headquarters for the services of all people within the confines of the present Kogi State East Senatorial Zone. The history of the General Hospital presents a case of one hospital for over a million people, in such a vast area. Besides she was inefficient, which portends a humanitarian vacuum, thus this mission participation and her later activities speak volumes. The medical services came with a lot of advantages as it availed the missionary sisters the contact with the people by creating a culture of confidence in the Catholic missions. Through this contact with the Holy Rosary sisters, many consented to sending their female children to the Holy Rosary Primary School, which was to be run by the Holy Rosary Sisters; then, it was not common to send girls to school.[396] This advantage paved the way for both evangelical development and the girl child education that was scarce to find. It was a humanitarian breakthrough for the female folks through the mission institutions, as it opened the door for a new kind of development. Since the General Hospital was the major health provider in the whole region, by implication, the force of mission's presence and humanitarian task helped to spread the mission's potency and faith all around the region.

The above stated medical services were the mission's participation in the open corporation. The second phase of the mission's tireless medical services was the building of her own medical centres like hospitals, dispensaries and health centres. The plans of building a mission health institution was conceived by the German Holy Ghost Fathers in 1938. It drafted a health plan for the provision of health centres beginning from Idah town. This project was however abandoned for lack of workforce. In addition, the idea was truncated by the unfortunate outbreak of the World

---

[395] Cf. A. A. Agbali, Ritualizing Communal wellbeing, 323.
[396] Cf. P.E. Okwoli, An Outline History, 72.

War II in 1939, as German fathers had to leave.[397] But with the arrival of the Holy Rosary Sisters in 1951 this plan was reactivated. This development spurred on the building of other medical institutions and outreaches in strategic areas of the diocese: Ayangba Catholic Hospital in 1960, Ankpa Mobile Clinic in 1971, Egume Catholic Maternity in 1970, Odomomoh Dispensary in 1960, Immaculate Heart Maternity in Awo-Akpali in 1982 and Sheria Health Centre in 1982. All were managed by different religious congregations within the diocese. Also the missionary sisters opened up large antenatal child welfare clinics in different parts of the diocese. To reach out to more persons in the rural areas, they adopted the mobile clinics services. Through this medium they moved from one parish to the other, reaching out to people who came as well from neighbouring dioceses (in the present Enugu and Edo states) to receive medical services.[398] The services were usually at a subsidized rate and in some cases indigent communities were given free treatments. They reached even the farthest village and were at the services of all, irrespective of religion. The spectacular humanitarian presence of the missions in the hinterland is to be appreciated because "outside the mission settlements..., the ...[colonial administration] provided doctors and medicine for their own officials and families, but not for all the people in the colony."[399] This case was worse in the interior like Idah diocesan territory, where "missionaries were willing to go... and endure hardships that the profiteers [the colonialists] had avoided."[400]

The diocesan health institution drew new impulse from the World Health Organisation (WHO) campaign in the early 1980s against diseases like malaria, cholera, diarrhoea and respiratory infection. WHO consequently laid more emphases on the Primary Health Care (PHC) than curative medicine and gave guidelines on the preventive nature of this illness. That was the advent of the Oral Rehydration Therapy (ORT). All diocesan health institutions began the implementation of this policy and in collaboration with the DDS, the health institutions were able to set up their goals. The emphases were on "health of the earth, utilisation of locally produced foods, weaning foods, inputs and skills for their production, clean water, child care, income generation activities with special reference to

[397] Cf. Ibid., 16.
[398] Cf. Ibid., 72.
[399] D. E. Harmon, Exploration of Africa, Nigeria, 51.
[400] Ibid., 35.

widows and disadvantaged."[401] There were also efforts to create capacity building opportunities for women. Through this, many were able to gain self confidence that helped them have the desired control of their lives. The religious sisters managing the ORT programmes took the message out, helping people on compost making, soya milk production, child welfare and several skills that helped to augment the meagre income of the masses. This ORT programme led to the stationing of the PHC centre at Ankpa and that later made this centre a full-fledged clinic.[402] The services of the diocesan hospitals and clinics lent some credence to the success of the ORT programme, therefore this complementing role and the charismatic spirit of the missionary sisters was very humanitarian as it taught the ordinary people alternative ways of dealing with health issues. Even though some were sceptical of the ORT programmes others were assisted with these new skills. This act of assisting poor people with new skills to better their living conditions qualifies it to be called a humanitarian achievement.

The greatest Catholic health provider in Idah diocese today is the Grimard Hospital Ayangba founded in 1960. She is named after the last apostolic prefect of Idah Prefecture, Msgr. Leopold Grimard, who began the extension of the centre to a fulltime hospital from 1968 to 1978. She began as Ayangba Maternity/Dispensary under Bishop Delisle in 1960 and was managed by the Canadian secular nursing sisters from the missionary group known as Mundo. It was an integrated approach as they assisted orphans, taught local girls sewing and provided treatments for the common diseases. Later the Holy Rosary sisters took over its operation in 1964 and extended its services and operations through the mobile clinics with outreaches in different neighbouring communities within the diocese.[403]

Grimard hospital enjoys the patronage of patients from all over the diocese for her missionary flair. She also serves as a referral to numerous health institutions in the length and breadth of Kogi-East. As a full time hospital she offers laboratory services, ultra sound scanning, x-rays, child welfare, Out Patients Department OPD and maternity services and so on.[404]

---

[401] Albert Shaibu, Health Policy/History of Health Care Idah Diocese, in: Ed., Pub./Hist. Sub-Committee of the Idah Diocesan Silver Jubilee celebration, Catholic Diocese of Idah at twenty five, Enugu, 2003, Pp 22-29, 26.
[402] Cf. Ibid., 27. The ORT solution is a mixture of salt and sugar.
[403] Cf. Ibid., 22.
[404] Cf. Health/Justice Development & Peace Commission Abuja Province, 2008 Annual Report, 2008, Abuja, 25.

These services have also been extended into many ramifications as she partners with many agencies like CRS, Catholic Agency for Overseas Development (CAFOD), AIDSrelief, and Irish AID. The CRS has been very dominant in the care and support for HIV/AIDs Patients, through the provision of test kits and anti retroviral, assisting orphans and vulnerable children OVC, Prevention of Mother to Child Transmission (PMTCT), HIV testing and counselling. After the celebration of the Holy Mass on the World Aids day of 1st December 2011, an awareness campaign was launched by the HIV/AIDS unit of the hospital to sensitize the masses on the effects of this dreaded disease. The HIV/AIDS sector has been very strong in the diocese through the Diocesan Action Committee on Aids, (DACA). She operates through all parishes of the diocese as Parish Action Committee on Aids (PACA). All these activities are sponsored by CRS and managed by Grimard Hospital.[405] The support of CRS in the campaigns against HIV/AIDS, the treatment and unequalled care Grimard Hospital establishment provides within the diocese, furthermore that her assistances too are offered to all irrespective of religious backgrounds makes her bear the humanitarian hallmark of neutrality.

Another monumental development was the opening of the Grimard school of Midwifery Ayangba in 1996 by the diocese to complement the efforts of the government in the provision of manpower for the health sector.[406] Though the institution has lived abreast with challenges since its foundation, its complementary role to government's inadequacy makes the move humanitarian.

3.6.5   The Diocesan Works Department

The Diocesan Works Department is a building unit of the diocese that constructs, supervises and undertakes building projects in the diocese for diocesan needs, her agencies, private individuals and governments' structures. It is like a little 'firm' within the diocesan structure. Its establishment had her antecedents from the building works of the early

---

[405] Cf. Ibid., 28.

[406] Cf. Health/Justice Development & Peace Commission Abuja Province, 2011 Annual Report, 2011, Abuja, 15. In 2005 she was granted provisional accreditation but was closed down in 2008 by the Nursing and Midwifery Council of Nigeria for deficiencies in the accreditation requirements. Since then frantic efforts have been made towards the restoration of the accreditation however in 2012, she was granted another provisional accreditation but with limitations in the admission of students.

Catholic institutions in the diocese, which were done mostly by the joint effort of the expatriates and the local people. While the missions provided the lion share of the funds, the expertise and the transport, the laity's self-finance was augmented with direct labour. Through these actions many houses, bridges, culverts, reservoirs and other infrastructures were erected. The expatriate missionaries were everything to the people; the parish priest for example, was sometimes the foreman, the 'quantity surveyor' and the 'Engineer' on site. From 1943 to 1969, virtually all the churches, parish houses, schools, hospitals, convents, many roads and bridges constructed by these expatriates came through this direct labour investment. The enormous savings that this system brought about for a diocese whose finances were very low made this medium of construction a commonplace. This ingenuity that created massive savings prompted Msgr. Leopold Grimard, the then prefect of Idah prefecture in 1969 to organise a 'central building team' that would supervise and coordinate building projects all over the prefecture. It was this building team that eventually matured into the Works Department. The birth of this building team like a 'little building firm' was more or less a child of necessity and thus, became one of the greatest ventures ever in the history of the diocese.[407]

This building team was pioneered by Msgr. Leopold Grimard, Fr. Peter Bergeron, Mr. Gabriel Akeje and Mr. Daniel S. Adah beginning from 1974. The last two were involved in different construction works in the diocese from the 1950s like the Grimard hospitals, all the four secondary schools owned by the diocese and some other projects. But they were not under any 'organised' body. Therefore the founding of the building team led to new policies under the umbrella of the works department. Their objective was basically the construction of building, but new goals were added later: to coordinate all building projects within the prefecture, to assist in the training of new staff and interested people in mason works and building, to ensure income generation for the diocese and to maintain all buildings in the diocese.[408] This was about the first income generating medium of the diocese, it was the first time to look inwardly not relying solely on the donations of well meaning people, because "excessive dependence on external help does harm to individual and collective efforts at the

---

[407] Cf. J. Oguche, The Contributions of the Diocesan Works Department, 41.
[408] Cf. Ibid. 41-43.

grassroots."[409] Thus, the Works Department inevitably created the first self-reliance machinery of the diocese.

Ever since then, the Diocesan Work became heavily involved in construction works in the diocese, beginning from the many buildings of St. Kizito Minor Seminary in 1982, the building of the diocesan nursery/primary schools, new parish buildings and convents. Almost every building in the diocese was basically constructed by the team; even though some were contracted to other agents, it however passed through the team. She became popular for the quality of work done, the precision and the affordable cost; all that soon attracted the patronage of the masses. The first of such jobs was the building of the guest house for Idah local government, (it belongs to Igalamela/Odoru local government today). Subsequently she was contracted for the building of some classrooms for some public schools, for example, the Government Secondary School Okenya and the Commercial Secondary School Idah. The Works department because of her effectiveness and trust even attracted contracts from private persons, thereby giving the people great confidence in this church establishment. The groundbreaking contract was the building of the new secretariat for the new local government in Ajaka in 1998.[410]

Through foreign assistance, the Works Department was able to purchase heavy duty vehicles. These vehicles under the transport division of the Works Department offer different services and deliveries (like sand, chippings, stones, gravels for building and water supply) to people and mission establishments. She offers cheaper services than the average vehicles of other individuals around Idah town. Despite the income generating objectives, the Works Department still placed consideration on the prices and the quality of service.[411] The Works Department was not strictly a profit oriented venture in the strict sense of capitalism but had a friendly business atmosphere under Fr. B. Beaulieu CSSp. Her *diakonein* perspective was for the services of both the diocese and the local people.

---

[409] U. Obododechina, The Imperative of Self-Reliance for the Churches in Africa, 14.

[410] Cf. J. Oguche, The Contributions of the Diocesan works Department, 44.

[411] I remember in the 80s and 90s when my parents were building at Idah, they paid for the services of the DOI to supply sharp sands and stones. Their prices were relatively better, at least N1 cheaper than other contractors. Also unlike other firms they delivered on time and had lesser complications. Even when we were relocating in the late 80s, we took patronage of the DOI vehicles and they were at relatively fair cost. The faith aspect and her reasonable formal treatment made her contract friendly and less strenuous.

Despite its price reduction, it had no statutory exemption, the cost of registration and tax payment to the government and other co-operative/obligatory charges were like other firms of its kind.

As at 2003 she had at least 50 members of staff and a number of contract staff, comprising people of different faith and religious background; what for many was 'strange' with the Catholic church, since many denominations and religious groups would prefer to offer such employments strictly to their members. The works department became "this guiding criterion for fraternal cooperation between believers and non-believers [which] is undoubtedly the principle of subsidiarity".[412] That she became an employer of a sizeable number of workers for a mini firm and into many infrastructural works so much raised the reputation of the diocese. The Works Department through effective management was able to experience economic gains for the diocese. It helped the diocese in the savings of incredible finances that would have been lost to normal contracting. The gains of the Works Department is better than having to keep waiting for funds from agencies to run the diocese. Even though some of the projects were awarded by agencies, the diocese reaped the benefits that soon increased her self-reliance. The employment opportunities the works department provided gave a means of livelihood to the workers and she was also *diakonein* through her spiritual services to the workers. At a time in the history of the Diocesan Works, the holy Mass was offered regularly for all the workers to corroborate the importance and the centrality of the sacrament of the Holy Eucharist. Though the field workers sometimes could not make it, the church through this spiritual contact was sharing in the joys and sorrows of her people. The Works Department was both a mini building firm and the diocesan building department within the Idah diocesan Secretariat. The job opportunities, the effectiveness of her services, the reliability and moderate charges were *diakonein* and humanitarian. Moreover raising revenue for the diocese made the establishment a model of self-sustenance and self-reliance operation. It overwhelmingly gave a new platform of organisation, which is also the principle of subsidiarity.

3.7 National agricultural policies and the rural area

Before discussing the humanitarian work on agriculture, it is pertinent to review the national agricultural policies and how they connect

---

[412] Cf. Benedict XVI, Caritas in Veritate, 58.

with the everyday life of the common people. Aquiculture lies at the heart of the of every nation's economy because it is tied to other sectors of the economy. It is a consequent factor that generates a broad base growth for national development and as such it is geared towards sustaining the nation and its people. This is the fundamental of agriculture and it thus explains why agriculture forms the bedrock of economic development, through the provision of the required nutrients for the growth of the people and the needed raw materials for the industry.[413] Moreover, adequate nutrition spurs the health, physical and mental development of the human person.[414] Also a thriving agricultural industry becomes the banner of national peace and unity and this could be buttressed by the words of the onetime German Chancellor Willy Brant for example: that where there is hunger, peace cannot exist or last.[415] The UN body 'Food Agricultural Organisation' (FAO) in 2003 asserts that societies define themselves by way and degree of their success at increasing agricultural production.[416] By implication issues of increased poverty, hunger and malnutrition reflects a nation's agricultural status quo. Unfortunately agricultural policies over the years have been beleaguered as the bane of agricultural practices in Nigeria. This informs the need for a careful survey of the different agricultural policies in the Nigerian agricultural voyage and their impact on Kogi-East. They are motivating factors of a broad based agricultural policy to enhance the projected growth and development of the nation. Therefore, the success of every modern nation is hinged on her agricultural policies. The abounding poverty and destitution in Kogi-East provokes questions like, are there no agricultural policies in Nigeria? Are the policies also the very factors that stifle agricultural production or are there other factors? F. Deaville Walker of the CMS, the pioneer missionary of Nigeria as far back as 1930 observes that,

> ...there is comparatively little poverty in West Africa and hardly anything that can be called destitution. In this it differs from India or China, where literally millions of people live from year to year perpetually below the hunger line. Nature is bountiful to West Africa; the rains never fail completely, and famine is practically unknown. The very poorest villagers have food enough and to

---

[413] Cf. Agricultural Research Council of Nigeria, http://www.arcnigeria.org/index.php/explore/the-council/our-vision/152-arcn/about/71-agricultural policies (29.06.15).

[414] Cf. Franz Nuscheler, Entwicklungspolitik, Lern- und Arbeitsbuch Entwicklungspolitik, Bonn, 2005, 230.

[415] Wo Hunger herrscht, kann Frieden nicht Bestand haben.

[416] Cf. J.C. Iwuchukwu, E,M. Igbokwe, Lessons from Agricultural Policies and Programs in Nigeria, 1.

spare. Under normal conditions there is work for all, and all are able to provide for the simple needs of their families.[417]

The same China and India that West African situation differed from and was better off in terms of nutrition and otherwise have become globalisation giants, agricultural giants and emerging nations today. In the words of Chinua Achebe, "when did the rain start beating us?"[418] Until a people find an answer or answers to fundamental questions of when, how and where their travails began, feasible headway may ever remain elusive. However, many authors have it that "hunger is the direct repercussion of the negative development in the political, legal and economic segment of a nation."[419]

Agro-policies from the colonial times in 1900 till present day Nigeria are notoriously known to be hasty, swift and opaque; their different drafts basically reflect the ruling administration at a point in time. The colonial agricultural policy promoted output growth and the extraction of surpluses. This surplus extraction philosophy was meant to generate immense products from the rural areas to satisfy the growing demand for raw materials in metropolitan Britain.[420] Apart from this colonial policy that encouraged the production of economic/cash crops like cocoa, rubber, groundnuts and so on for export, all other agricultural policies have practically been the same, like a chameleon maintaining same substance but undergoing accidental changes of different regimes, acronyms, governments or administrations. Sometimes to discredit previous administration, subsequent ones employ different strategies and coinages, but they basically "emphasize almost [the] same objectives like: to provide food for the inhabitants of the nation (food security and sufficiency) ..., export excess to other countries and to provide rural dwellers and farmers with extension services, agricultural support and rural development services."[421] Even though the average farmers in the Kogi-East for example were basically subsistent, because farming was a means of livelihood, their surpluses found

---

[417] F. D. Walker, The Romance of the Black River, The Story of CMS Nigerian Mission, 90.

[418] Chinua Achebe, Nigeria's promise, Africa's Hope, the New York Times, Jan., 15, 2011, http://www.nytimes.com/2011/01/16/opinion/16achebe.html (12.09.16)

[419] Deutsche Bischofkonferenz, Den Hungern bekämpfen 8. Unsere gemeinsame Verantwortung für das Menschenrecht auf Nahrung, Bonn Mai 2012. (translation is mine)

[420] Cf. J.C. Iwuchukwu, E,M. Igbokwe, Lessons from Agricultural Policies and Programs in Nigeria, in: Journal of Law, Policy and Globalization www.iiste.org ISSN 2224-3240 (Paper) ISSN 2224-3259 (Online) Vol. 5, 2012, Pp. 11-21, 12.

[421] Ibid., 11.

market among the neighbouring peoples. However, the commercial aspect in the colonial economy and the present dispensation has widened the business horizon. Therefore good governance in the agricultural sector was to enhance bountiful production and to prop up small scale farmers. The idea of economic crops from the colonial era and the new breeds in subsequent times opened farmers to different crops and varieties. Besides, the average farmers were being introduced into a global world; a world with options and choices, where their needs and wants were bound to increase. Even though "pre-colonial Africa may have been poor by contemporary western standard ...they did not necessarily know that they were poor, in fact, by their own criteria, some of them might have been extremely rich;"[422] Nevertheless, through contacts life is improved upon as people learn from the other and also discover other needs and are able to compare and contrast. But the sharp and conspicuous differences in the choices and opportunities between contemporary affluent nations and African nations for example are the effects of huge increase in global production by these affluent nations since the 1970s; whereas African nations experience stagnating and depreciating production.[423]

Between 1966 and 1999 Nigerians witnessed only one democratically elected government for a period of five years and several military administrators.[424] Their different agricultural policies have compounded the agricultural scenario and practices over the time. All the evolved policies have consequently been eaten up by the locust of corruption, mismanagement, gross misconduct and the oil curse. The first agricultural policy began in western Nigeria in 1959 and became a nationwide programme by 1960 after the independence. It was called 'Farm Settlement Scheme'; its aim was to settle youths and young school leavers in the rural areas with land and improved agricultural practices so as to avoid the exodus of young people into the cities. This post independence policy 1960-1966 was to create agricultural growth in connection with the pre-colonial principle of surplus extraction policy. Hence the three regions were partitioned and recognised according to their agricultural preeminent production: western-cocoa, eastern-Palm oil and northern-groundnuts; this

---

[422] Aylward Shorter, Religious Poverty in Africa, Nairobi 2001, 11.

[423] Cf. Giles Bolton, Poor Story, An insider uncovers how globalisation and good intentions have failed the World's poor, London, 2007, 169.

[424] The second tenure of the Shagari administration was ousted in a coup d'état, bringing his reign to a tenure and a year, 1.10.1979- 31.12.1983.

was to enhance export trade for revenue generation. Since 1966-1999 it has been jumping from one policy to another and shrouded with different names but a shadow of itself. Such programmes include: National Accelerated Food Production Programme, (NAFPP) in 1972, the Agricultural Development Project (ADP) known as Integrated Agricultural Development Project (IRDP) in 1974, a joint project of Nigeria government and World Bank, which were unproductive in the long run (The DDS had contacts before the programme collapsed). In 1976 there was the Operation Feed the Nation (OFN), which paralleled the River Basin Development Authority in 1976 (RBDAs).[425] OFN was the height of the administrative disaster of the military regime that petrodollars could buy technology.[426] In 1980, the 2nd republic greeted the nation with the Green Revolution (GR) programme and like the past ones, it amounted to colossal waste. Again the military resumed its presence with the Directorate for Food, Road and Rural Infrastructure in 1986 (DFFRI); it lacked focus and accountability and was a futile journey. Besides it operated like a construction firm. So were other subsequent programmes under the military administration like: Better Life Programmes for Rural Women (BLP), National Agricultural Land Development Authority (NALDA), Family Support Programmes (FSP) and Family Economic Advancement Programmes (FEAP) and their likes.[427] In summary, the failure of governmental policies to establish a technological strategy that is consequent and particular to national development is the main reason for the 'merry go round' in the agricultural landscape today.[428]

However, since the democratic era in 1999, several reasonable agricultural policies have been propounded but still bear relatively weak economic importance. The Growth Enhancement Scheme (GES) under the Agricultural Transformation Agenda (ATA) of the Jonathan administration 2010-2015 "recorded a laudable performance in improved production of

---

[425] Cf. J.C. Iwuchukwu, E,M. Igbokwe, Lessons from Agricultural Policies and Programs in Nigeria, 20

[426] Cf. Rolf Goldstein, Landwirtschaftliche Beratung, im Gebiet der Diözese Idah/Benue State, Nigeria, in: Ed., Theodor Dams, Integrierte ländliche Entwicklung. Theoretische Grundlagen und praktische Erfahrungen. (Entwicklung und Frieden : Materialen 8), München, 1980, Pp. 237-250, 237.

[427] Cf. J.C. Iwuchukwu, E,M. Igbokwe, Lessons from Agricultural Policies and Programs in Nigeria, 20.

[428] Cf. Benjamin Ofori-Amoah, Technological Change Strategy for Economic Development in Africa, in: Eds., Fidelis Ezeala-Harrison, Senyo B-S-K. Adjibolosoo, Westport, 1994, 85-102, 90.

arable crops and livestock through the provision of subsidised inputs to farmers."[429] However "as laudable and well-intended as these economic blueprints are, the associated challenges have been poor implementation as evidenced by the weak plan-budget link since 1999."[430]

The past programmes in the 70s and 80s were optimistic and presented more resonance, but the hurricane of corruption and repeated unproductiveness have marred people's attention and hope of a thriving agricultural policy. Some of the programmes like DFFRI in 1986 were meant to create feeder and commercial roads so that investors and marketers could access the villages.[431] Even the second National Development Plan 1970-74 came up with such lofty ideas to improve transportation, which ordinarily would have increased rural productivity and consequently expanded the market for industrial goods, but there was failed determination to implement these plans.[432] The failures of these plans have rendered the status quo of the villages unchanged, as they bear both the cost of production and transport. Sometimes, middlemen facilitate the movement of these goods to the cities, with economical advantage on their side but to the detriment of the local producers. The lack of paved roads, poor food preservative methods, non-cohesive planning and weak transport organisation for movement of foodstuffs create wastage, artificial scarcity and high cost of food. The prices of foodstuffs are very cheap at harvest periods, which explain the state of affairs of increased supply and low demand in the months of August to January for example; this results in massive waste because of the lack of preservation. Whereas the same product in the dry season between February and July could attract over 300% price hike due to increased demand and less supply. It encouraged the importation of foodstuffs during the oil boom, which stifled agricultural production because the cheap imports were better preserved and packaged. Sometimes their transportation was easier, coming through the sea and finding their ways into supermarkets and groceries. Most times the local and national transport cost of many African nations "are around twice as high as those of the average Asian country, [therefore] hitting hard at [their] citizens' ability to buy cheap

---

[429] National Human Development Reports, December 2015, 19.
[430] Ibid., 21.
[431] Cf. J.C. Iwuchukwu, E,M. Igbokwe, Lessons from Agricultural Policies and Programs in Nigeria, 20.
[432] Cf. A. L. Mabogunje, Changes in socio-economic and cultural patterns caused by the industrialization, 43.

produce and [their] country's ability to export competitively".[433] Dealers sometimes prefer to avoid such internal rigours of transportation, like the rickety and lack of paved roads from the villages to the cities.[434] This accounts for the inherent difficulties with the movement of agricultural products from the place of production to consumption. Despite the significant improvements in the availability of paved roads today, transportation still remains a major handicap due to lack of maintenance of the already paved roads, substandard asphalted roads and lack of modern transportation network like rails system and so on. Moreover, there are basically no roads on these farms; hence transportation of goods from the farms to the so-called roads is still crude and physically tasking.

The provision of fertilizers for example to increase production during the 'Operation Feed the Nation' OFN in the late 70s was carried out haphazardly. The ineffectiveness of subsequent fertilizer distribution today has been furthered by political issues, where party stalwarts use fertilizers as handouts. The problems associated with failed agricultural policies are numerous as they affects any rural area; however they are basically "(1) the land tenure problems, (2) problems of fragmented holdings, (3) lack of capital, (4) poor farming techniques, (5) lack of storage facilities and (6) inefficient distribution and marketing".[435] In spite of the emphasis and repetition of credit facilities and micro finance for example in the many evolved programmes, the take-off grant at the planting season has eluded the peasant/local farmers.

One very common feature with Agricultural policies of many African nations which was very much a practice in Nigeria is the preeminent consideration and advantages given to the cities. Even from the colonial times, it was a policy to always keep the cities fed; such that in the event of food subsidies urban dwellers were also prominent beneficiaries of such policies. This factor as a matter of a fact is facilitated by the presence of trade unionism and nationalist sentiments among civil servants in the urban settlements. This is unlike the rural settlements with a predominant illiterate

[433] G. Bolton, Poor Story, 59.
[434] Cf. N. McNamara, S. Morse, Developing Financial Services, 86. The absence of rail system and bad roads affect the movement of agricultural goods. For example, travelling from one end of the diocese for example Idah to Anyigba on the road before the 70s, which is a journey of less than 75km, took 3-4 hours; today it takes about an hour. Also travelling from Lagos to Kaduna, about 800km took about a week; today it takes about 9 hours.
[435] L. J. Lewis, society, Schools and Progress in Nigeria, 65.

population. Basically this policy creates a political imperative of keeping the cities fed. It also explains sometimes the seeming stronger guarantee of food security in the urban areas than rural areas, even though the bulk of home grown agricultural products come from the rural areas. [436]

The oil boom of 1973 flawed the agricultural production, as it transformed but subsidised almost every aspect of life in Nigeria. Increased quest for imports due to the high currency value made commodity prices to fall, for example "imported rice could even be found on sale in markets of rice producing areas. Nigerian farmers found it difficult, if not impossible, to get good prices for their produce."[437] The consumption of foreign rice became gradually and conspicuously a thing of 'class', thereby leading to a large neglect and relegation of the locally produced rice as a substitute. The farmers in Kogi-East had to compete with these cheap agricultural imports; the Ibaji area of Kogi-East for example, whose predominant agro-products are rice and yam had to suffer the fate of cheap imports of rice from the Asian markets. These imported goods were not only found in the local markets but also in government owned stores. As a result, many farmers abandoned their faming business in search of menial jobs in some of the newly built firms that were products of the sudden effect of the oil boom, like the dilapidated Iron and Steel industry in Ajaokuta today.[438]

3.8   The Land Use act and the fate of agriculture

The popular decree 6 'land use act' was enacted primarily to ameliorate the problem of land tenure in Southern Nigeria and to contain other myriad problems associated with land tenure in Nigeria. This was promulgated on the 29th March 1978 on the recommendation of a panel set up by the military administration on the future of land policy. Thus it marked the beginning of the impasse on land acquisition and rights.[439] Its implementation led to the vesting of all land (except land owned by the federal government) in each state in the governor (military governors) of the state. Therefore state governors became the custodians of land, to issue right of occupancy to land owners, but this action became a clog in the wheels of modern development. Also, that the decree was tenaciously pursued by

---

[436] Cf. Alex de Waal, Famine Crimes, 32.

[437] N. McNamara, S. Morse, Developing Financial Services, 48.

[438] Cf. N. McNamara, S. Morse, Developing Financial services, 74,

[439] Cf. J.C. Iwuchukwu, E,M. Igbokwe, Lessons from Agricultural Policies and Programs in Nigeria, 13,

subsequent military administrators and has found its way into the 1999 constitution as the 'land use act', makes it a constitutional case binding on all Nigerians.[440] Even though it was aimed at introducing a uniform right of occupancy to counteract the numerous customary laws that pre-existed the decree in 1978, the echoes and call for reforms today have won sympathy but met very little success. However the fact still remains today that,

> ...the true implication of a uniform right of occupancy system for the indigenous land tenure system has not been fully articulated by lawyers, grasped by the courts, or appreciated by laymen. This is evident from the conflicting decisions of courts, controversial commentaries of learned writers, and the continuous alienation of land by laymen in complete disregard of the rights of occupancy system. [441]

The multiplicity of land tenures operated in Nigeria since the pre-colonial era till 1978 could be narrowed into four land tenure systems. Two of them pre-existed the British conquest and the last two were intra-colonial structure. The oldest tenure system was the 'indigenous tenure' under customary law and was very widespread in Southern Nigeria. It was the traditional concept of land because land for them has social, political, economic and religious background/significance. Land is considered a sacred institution from God to sustain all members of the family, the dead, the living and the yet unborn. The living were only conferred an ancestral trust, thus it was absolutely out of question to sell the land because it was community owned and not individual property as the English were conversant with. This was the general belief system among many West African communities before the colonial occupation. Secondly, the 'tenure under land tenure law' came with the Islamic subjugation of Hausa land in ca. 1820; the northern tenure system was displaced by the Fulani Jihadist and was replaced with a feudal system. The colonial conquest of 1903 inherited this Fulani established feudal system of over-lordship; thus land rights were consequently ceded to the colonial administrator. Further land rights were introduced, enacted and subsequently re-enacted by the colonialists. Such enactments between 1916 and 1962 made regulations that secured some designated land as native land. Power was subsequently vested in the Minister or commissioner of land and survey under the governor to

---

[440] Cf. Akin L. Mabogunje, Land Reform in Nigeria Problems, Progress, Prospects, Chairman Presidential Technical Committee for Land Reform, (online) (01.07.15), Pp. 1-25, 1.

[441] P. Ehi Oshio, The Indigenous Land tenure and Nationalization of Land in Nigeria, 43, in: Online- Boston College Third World Law Journal, Vol.10, Iss. 1, Art. 3, 1990, Pp. 42-62, 42.

administer such land to the benefit of natives and also to issue certificate of occupancy.[442] Therefore, natives and native communities using land lawfully under this native law and custom enjoyed a right of occupancy, they were protected by the ordinance and such rights attracted no rent. Also, the ordinance specified and limited the use of not more than 1,200 acres and 12,500 acres for agricultural and grazing purposes respectively.[443] Thirdly, the 'tenure under the received English law' played out for example after the annexation of Lagos in 1861, which led to the establishment of a freehold system in 1863. Finally, the 'tenure under state laws'; these were pieces of land acquired by the British crown through agreement, cession or conversion during the colonial period and have become state properties today.[444] These laws were rather makeshift rules and the problem of land was never really given a conclusive solution. Besides, the north south dichotomy was a factor against a uniform right of occupancy of land. In a resume, these factors put together have made land allocation, alienation and ownership matters of litigation; the feeling of might is right, rivalry and violence.

The changes that came with colonial economy brought adverse effects on the land policies and just like other goods, land also became monetised. The southern Nigeria viewpoint of land as community good has gradually been replaced by the new economy resulting in the multiple sale of the same piece of land to several buyers by a land owning family; all because of the absence of an acceptable registration mechanism. Also, it encouraged increased cost of land after independence for developers and for government structures. Moreover, both the northern and southern Nigeria never factored land as a capital good like today's capitalist worldview, thus one had to depend on kinship and allegiance to local sovereignty to gain ownership of land. Accordingly, the sale of land to a visitor posed a security threat to the natives. This issue made land acquisition very difficult even for the colonialists at the beginning of the colonial administration's reign. To this effect the colonial powers in 1912 had to set up a special land committee to investigate land tenure system in the British West Africa. However, the ideas of land as community property began to give way to the extensive labour movement and modernisation coming from the colonial economy, consequently making land to be alienated to strangers, migrants and women.

---

[442] Cf. Ibid, 44-46.
[443] Cf. A. L. Mabogunje, Land Reform in Nigeria Problems, Progress, Prospects, 2.
[444] Cf. P. E. Oshio, The Indigenous Land tenure and Nationalization of Land in Nigeria, 45-46.

It made transaction of land both in the south and north very widespread. Unlike in the pre-capitalist society, land became an individual good and at the demise of the owner, it was sometimes subjected to multiple owners because of ownership through inheritance. The use of land for long term farming of perennial crops like cocoa, rubber, palm tree and so on, also raised the question of the transient ownership to a permanent ownership of land.[445] These were issues that the land act set to deal with but have remained inconclusive.

Since the rural areas were the abode of agriculture in the Nigerian economy, access to such lands was only by conveyance, inheritance or through a nexus of relationship with the local sovereignty. Such setbacks opened up negative sentiments between who is a 'stranger' and a 'native' and also who really should have access to land. The location of Idah diocese makes it inherit the southern land tenure system; and following national development too, land issues have become matters within the family, relatives and village set up. However, there is enough land and to acquire an expanse of land for agribusiness is very easily possible but through the traditional rulers. The major agricultural setback today is that the small farmers are still very dependent on the use of local tools like cutlass and hoe and worst of all they are still very superstitious in their practices. In addition, governmental bottlenecks have warped access to credit and modern machines, and the sales of insecticides, herbicides and fertilizers for example are very much under the control of the informal market.[446]

The monetisation of land, the exodus of workers from one part of the nation to the other and the sudden return to agriculture since the days of SAP in the 80s have made land distribution in Kogi-East more sensitive today than in the past. However the opportunity for leasing the land is very much in practice for small-scale and casual farmers. But they face the danger of food security, because "closeness of plots and farmland to the compound has also become critical to ensuring the crop is not stolen. Food security and human security are thus more inextricably entwined."[447] In a study in the early 2000 by DDS titled: 'Sustainable Livelihood Approach: A critical analysis of theory and practice', the authors observed that the four

---

[445] Cf. A. L. Mabogunje, Land Reform in Nigeria Problems, Progress, Prospects, 2-4.
[446] Cf. R. Goldstein, Landwirtschaftliche Beratung, 239.
[447] Cf. Stephen Morse, et al., Sustainable Livelihood Approach: A Critical Analysis of Theory and Practice, Geographical Paper No.189, November 2009, 1-67, 36.

households involved in the programme rented their land for the aforementioned programme.[448] Since the land is not the farmer's own property, how much would that farmer be ready to invest in such land for a real agribusiness? Despite the improved land scenario in Kogi-East, the acquisition of land for extensive agricultural purpose could be problematic like other parts of the nation. Therefore land reforms could still be faced with difficulties, especially where rights of land are still within the extended families and not individuals. However, the more precarious and demanding cases are lands that belong to the community.[449] All these raise a consortium of problems to the average farmer who intends to begin a farming business. The land use act did not appropriately state the kind of relationship between a landowner and tenants, especially long term tillers of the lands; because, the pre-existing relation was the payment of tribute either in cash or kind to cement the relationship.[450] Another increasing spate of land controversy was a case of "traditional chiefs, as well as individuals [today that] soon saw land as a means of enriching themselves at all costs. Chiefs would appropriate income from corporate holdings for their personal benefit rather than hold it in trust for the benefit of the members of the group. Greed and unprecedented racketeering thus characterized administration of group-owned lands."[451]

In spite of the land use act, the various community heads and chiefs who acted as trustees of land within their locality have not given up such duty, which equals an utter disgust of the right of occupancy of land as enacted by the land use act. Thus, their "...various Communal Lands Allocation Wards are still functioning effectively although they were meant to be supplanted by the Land Use Allocation Committee and the Land Allocation Advisory Committee established under the Act."[452] The land issue has extraordinarily encouraged corruption, where land ownership is backdated to 1978 to avoid the land use act implementation.[453] It creates legal cases from land issues which are inevitable because of the litanies of problems, intrigues, interests and greed.

---

[448] Cf. Ibid., 39.

[449] Cf. A. L. Mabogunje, Land Reform in Nigeria Problems, Progress, Prospects, 19. The rights of these lands were conferred on male members of the family, but with the growing free market on land issues today, women too are able to purchase land for personal use.

[450] Cf. Ibid, 20.

[451] P.E. Oshio, The Indigenous Land tenure and Nationalization of Land in Nigeria, 49.

[452] Ibid., 56.

[453] Cf. Ibid.

The aforementioned factor shows clearly that the people of Kogi-East are largely settlers and farmers are entirely arable and not a nomadic people.[454] Nomadic cattle rearing is mainly associated with the Fulanis from northern Nigeria, whose annual grazing activity today creates tension between the nomads and the indigenes.

3.9   Diocesan Development Service (DDS)

The DDS is a Catholic NGO and as such a humanitarian arm of the Catholic diocese of Idah. The establishment of the DDS derives its background from many diverse but seemingly bonded factors: beginning from the special effects of the social teachings of the church in the 60s, the global economic scenario, the peculiar nature of Idah diocese along with the depression after the civil war, the historical development of the aid industry and the many horrible economic incidents in Nigeria. The Catholic diocese of Idah up till the 1960s was more into other *diakonein* services like schools and hospitals alongside the teaching and the preaching of the gospel. But from the 60s, a new wave and a social consciousness were awakened from the papal encyclicals of John XXIII, *Mater et Magistra* 1961 and *Pacem in Terris* 1963.[455] The Pope's address was against a world of increasing gap between the poor and rich nations/class; the sub-human conditions and the depreciating socio-economic realities of many developing nations including hunger and starvation. While a few nations lived in the ocean of affluence and with remarkable technological growth, others wallowed in poverty because of global economic imbalance from the unfair terms of trade. These consequently undermine the socio-political freedom and the fundamental human right of the poor nations of the world, hence constituting a major threat to global peace. In addition, despite the fact that many nations were decolonised, the agony of economic dependence was still very glaring, as wealthy nations offered a pittance for the raw materials from these poor nations in return for expensive finished goods.[456] The emphases of these social teachings through *Mater et Magistra* to all nations gingered the social awareness of the local church towards finding answers to the social needs of

---

[454] Cf. S. Morse, et al., Sustainable Livelihood Approach, 30.

[455] Cf. Diocesan Development Services, Functional Guidelines, 4.

[456] Cf. George O. Ehusani, The Social Gospel: An Outline of the Church's Current Teaching on Human Development Ibadan, 1992, 22.

her faithful. Such Church's concern for the poor is one of the many attributes that inspired the establishment of the DDS.[457]

Also, one of the outcomes of the Vatican II council was the relevance of the church to the local situation. This relevance was unequivocally instrumental to the ideas of the DDS as it thus became a break-away from the traditional school/medical services and works of charity provided by the missions to more humanitarian and self-reliance driven programmes. What was sacrosanct here was the underlined dignity of the human person, created in the image and likeness of God. That force propelled the church into a change of strategy from doing things for people to doing things with people.[458]

According to John Paul II in the encyclical *Sollicitudo rei socialis*, solidarity is much deeper than mere compassion and a show of concern towards distressed people or people in pains and misery. Therefore, "it is a firm and persevering determination to commit oneself to the common good; that is to say to the good of all and of each individual, because we are all really responsible for all."[459] This commitment towards the common good of the human person was one factor that influenced the founders of the DDS towards the people. Hence the founders resolved on the use of the evolved reflection-action-reflection process, a product of the Latin American church, where the hierarchy encouraged the poor at the grass roots to work together with the church so as to help diagnose the problems of the society. The evidence of this evolved method proved that understanding the people was only through critical study of their political, economic, social and cultural background; these combined to form the background of their problems.[460] This system became a very significant humanitarian factor used by the DDS to diagnose the background of her beneficiaries, towards working a self reliant programme; it thus made the DDS the hallmark on a humanitarian approach towards the maxim of self-reliance.

To keep this papal message alive, the Catholic Secretariat of Nigerian (CSN) from 1969 moved to establish a development structure that would assist Catholic dioceses. Thus, the appointment of a development coordinator in every diocese was approved. By a stroke of luck, some of the

---

[457] Cf. Diocesan Development Services, Functional Guidelines, 4.

[458] Cf. N. McNamara, S. Morse, Developing On-Farm Research, 16.

[459] John Paul II, Sollicitudo rei socialis, 38.

[460] Cf. N. McNamara, S. Morse, Developing On-Farm Research, 16.

scientists on the ground, who were members of the International Institute of Tropical Agriculture IITA in Ibadan South-West Nigeria, were also members of the Catholic team. This lucky beginning encouraged the church/state collaboration in the field of agriculture. The CSN's call for the appointment of a development coordinator came through in Idah prefecture in 1971 and thus the idea of a 'DDS' was born. DDS is an NGO that "...represents the 'development arm of the Catholic diocese of Idah (DOI). Its remits and functions are guided by Christian principles: loving your neighbour as yourself, justice and equality.' The DDS reaches out to all peoples; Muslims, Animists and the various Christian denominations. Its staff includes people from faiths other than Catholic."[461]

The birth of the DDS paralleled the era of global shift from humanitarian relief to third world development in the aid history of African development. Dambisa Moyo substantiates this development as the age of third world development in the 1970s. It succeeded the industrialisation age of the 60s (the age of independence of many African nations).[462] The loss in the age of industrialisation was grave; it only exposed the naivety of the government in the new nations, the unpreparedness of her leaders and the anxiety of swift industrialisation which led to many rash decisions coupled with the harsh tropical climate and diseases. The limited infrastructure, large number of uneducated, subsistence agriculture and virtually no industries in the African nations at this early stage of development after independence, prepared the ground for another phase of aids development programme.[463] The 1970s then saw a gradual move of foreign aid into poverty alleviation. The major aim was a redirection of aid from large infrastructural development to direct humanitarian projects like, agricultural- rural development, social services, adult education campaigns, the fight against malnutrition and provision of health services like inoculations. The 1960 strategy (the age of industrialisation) failed to deliver the humanitarian objectives, as the rising level of poverty, unemployment and other social ills plagued these new nations. More so was the eventual ugly scenario perpetuated by the inability of borrowing nations to pay back loans, hereby accruing interest.[464] Thus, this period of humanitarian shift encouraged many

---

[461] Ibid., 22.
[462] Cf. Dambisa Moyo, Dead Aid, Why Aid is not working and how there is another way for Africa, London, 2009, 14.
[463] Cf. Carol Lancaster, Aid to Africa, So much so little done, Chicago, 1999, 21.
[464] Cf. D. Moyo, Dead Aid, 14-17. The Industrialization age began in the 1960s when many African nations got independence. Funds for development aids were transferred to these

NGOs into the humanitarian scene in the developing countries, especially faith based humanitarian organisations or church aid organisations for example DDS; they were actively involved in raising awareness about the need for humanitarian work in developing nations, through gathering donations for help in emergencies and in difficult situations. The social, ethical and theological movement in the developing countries, especially liberation theology, was another factor that provoked this development.[465] Besides the extra-parliamentary oppositions of the late 1960s in central Europe irked the feelings of resentment that galvanised these provocations. This increased the frontiers of humanitarian operations into justice and human rights development. The papal encyclicals *Pacem in Terris* in 1963 and *Populorum Progressio* in 1967 contributed vehemently to this development, as they propagated justice, peace, preservation of creation, they provoked change of strategy in the NGO's operations in the developing world. However, many have observed that, these NGOs were sometimes an 'overrated beacon of hope' among the people.[466] Some humanitarian authors have tagged this period and the aftermath as 'third worldism'; it was the "failure of the so-called development decades in the poor world, and the discrediting of the 'third worldist' ideology that went with it".[467] Nonetheless, the most important trait during this period was the global awareness towards humanitarian development in the developing world.

The principal foundation of DDS was basically to lead a way forward from the poverty trap and the financial dependency of the diocese. It was to assist individuals to achieve their personal potentials and that of their

---

nations for large industrial projects and thus marked the genesis of the sudden rain of billion-dollar-aids to African states. These were projects that rarely attracted the patronage of private investors. The age of poverty alleviation in aid history 1970, was the period of the energy crisis created by the war of Yom Kippur in 1973. Many oil exporting nations like Nigerian benefitted massively from the sanctions through increased oil price (chapter 2.3.1), it jacked up the prices of foodstuffs and other commodities in many African nations. The oil exporting nations deposited their reserves with some international banks, from which these banks made enormous capital and later dispensed some loans to developing nations at outrageous rates. Loans were given arbitrarily without due respect, who was credit worthy or not. Some African Despots/dictators for example Nigeria (after the oil bust), despite they lacked credibility in leadership were heavily financed at this period too.

[465] Cf. A. A. Agbali, The Catholic Church, Social Justice Teachings, 46. Though the liberation Theology having its origin from Latin America has been judged of Marxist slant, it caught the attention of the Nigerian church in her care of the poor.

[466] Cf. F. Nuscheler, Entwicklungspolitik, 564.

[467] Cf. D. Rieff, A Bed for the Night, 101.

respective communities.[468] The major thrust of DDS is agriculture and agro-related projects. These projects inform its broad base of self reliance in the present Eastern Kogi vicinity that is more or less devoid of industrial and government's presence. Out of necessity, DDS has evolved into an Integrated Rural Development Project (IRDP) to ensure equality between gender and different socio-economic groups.[469] The DDS does not impose its principles on people, its credo is unity and thus DDS believes that,

> ...we [the DDS and the beneficiaries] depend on each other and when we fail to do this there is IMBALANCE. When we build each other up as individuals, the group grows and from this strength develops a condition of greater self-reliance. Self-reliance makes sense only in a group or community, so when self reliance is mentioned we see it as more of sharing, trusting and acknowledging individual talents, skills and abilities. No one is self-reliant, hence the urgency of UNITY. Without this there is no solid foundation on which to build any project. This is a most difficult task.[470]

Since the DDS was imbued from onset with the principles of self-reliance and human development, it consequently believes in the human potentials and strives with the people towards achieving this concept. This bespeaks the principle of subsidiarity, because "subsidiarity is first and foremost a form of assistance to the human person via the autonomy of intermediate bodies. Such assistance is offered when individuals or groups are unable to accomplish something on their own, and it is always designed to achieve their emancipation, because it fosters freedom and participation through assumption of responsibility."[471] This gesture made her exceed the hitherto church humanitarian concept of merely relieving the people of their pains to doing things with them. The DDS recognises the individual and the endowed capabilities and consequently helps each one to develop these qualities. Thus the DDS does not "take [away] from [the] individuals what they can accomplish by their own initiative and industry",[472] instead she assists the people to accomplish joint initiatives, where the people themselves become involved and responsible actors.

---

[468] Cf. N. McNamara, S. Morse, Developing Financial Services, 81.
[469] Cf. N. McNamara, S. Morse, Developing On-Farm Research, 35. There are pros and contra argument as regards IRDP.
[470] Diocesan Development Services, Functional Guidelines, 7.
[471] Caritas in Veritate, 57.
[472] Quadragesimo Anno, 79.

The recognition of human dignity and the appreciation of humanity could be interpreted as the driving humanitarian motive of the DDS. Thus, it began by initiating programmes that could empower the people and their communities. But it was first of all through studying the local environment and helping to find ways of adapting already existing local structures into modern pragmatic structures that could lead to financial empowerment. By so doing, the people would be better off to identify their inherent developmental obstacles and would consequently find ways to tackle the general poverty scenario around them.[473] This is predicated on the fact that sustainable development could lead to self-reliance, a development that comes from within, because "it is not possible to develop people; development is something people have to do themselves."[474]

The backdrop of agricultural dwarfishness is evidently lucid from the above discussed agricultural policies. Of course the effect of these revealed lopsided principles and failed political will to implement governmental policies were very harsh on the people at the margins of the society. Thus the location of Idah diocese as a rural one meant immense and conspicuous hardship to the average people. The different state's agricultural policies and programmes bore all the marks of failure, they came and passed without making any impact in the lives of the masses. DDS like other NGOs came in as humanitarian saviour to fill the humanitarian void created by these failed policies and the inability of the people to come out of these economic woes.

By 2003, all the past projects executed eventually evolved into four major structures: The Farmer Self Reliance Programme (FSRP), the Agricultural Innovation Programme (AIP), The Village Development Programme (VDP) and Water Development Programmes (WDP).[475] These structures are principally the synthesis of the protracted historical developmental projects/events of the DDS, notable among them are; the establishment of the Farmers council (FC), the influences of the state Ministry of Agriculture (MOA), the period of DDS joint work with the sponsored World Bank project called the Ayangba Agricultural Development Project (AADP), the period after, the many services the DDS

---

[473] Cf. Catherine Oguonu, The Diocesan Development Services (DDS), in: Ed., Pub./Hist. Sub-Committee of the Idah Diocesan Silver Jubilee celebration, Catholic Diocese of Idah at twenty five, Enugu 2003, Pp. 38-45, 36.
[474] G. Ehusani, The Social Gospel, 42.
[475] Cf. C. Oguonu, The Diocesan Development Services (DDS), 46-47.

offered and still offers. Another strong influence in the present DDS state of affairs comes from the many agencies who tirelessly supported the DDS, the Canadian High Commission in Lagos, the Irish Embassy Lagos and Abuja, the Dutch Embassy Lagos and Abuja, Development and Peace-Canada, the Department of Foreign Affairs Ireland and *Misereor*, furthermore the contributions of the IITA- collaborative jobs with DDS. These events, projects and organisations have together shaped and coalesced to produce the existing DDS structures; moreover they portray the DDS's scope of operation.

3.9.1 Farmers Self-Reliance Programme (FSRP)

The FSRP began with the introduction of the Farmers' Council (FC). The FC (like a co-operative) was one of the most productive programmes and the most eventful foundation laying structure in the history of DDS with the farmers. The impressive Latin American church model of reflection system became the facilitating mechanism towards building this fascinating foundational structure. Dialogue became a prerequisite to understanding the needs of the people and their milieu. An in-depth knowledge of their socio-cultural structures and organisation were paramount before kick-starting any development programme. DDS employed the diocesan wide network whose contacts cut across age, religious affiliations and other barriers within the diocese.[476] Its results were amazing, beginning from the farmers' complaints and insistence on lack of finances. However, it was going to be counterproductive to the maxim of self-reliance if DDS took the bait to offer money immediately to the peasant farmers. Moreover the DDS had no finance to offer, its basic objective was the development that would empower beneficiaries to be both the subject and the object of their own development. It was wise to understand how the local people function as a group, who runs things in the communities and to know the pattern and methods of communication. The findings of the DDS extended beyond the farmers' complaint of financial shortages for agricultural works; there was also the problem of huge cost of labour requirements especially for the clearing and cultivation of land, the problems of weeds, low fertility, poor quality of seeds and their planting materials.[477]

---

[476] Cf. N. McNamara, S. Morse, Developing Financial Services, 81.
[477] Cf. Ibid., 84.

Despite these mountainous problems, there was however the need to begin from somewhere. Through interaction with the people, the development team was able to ascertain and decipher some means to create a saving scheme among the people. This careful investigation into the existing local structure among the people resulted in the discovery of an informal economy generating revenue and contribution system called the *Oja*.[478] The adoption of the *oja*-system into a modern practice by the DDS makes DDS an emblem of solidarity. This is because solidarity brings about measures that modify or change the pre-modern understanding of the human person as a social and organic being into the network of the present modern and complex economic system; thereby producing a cooperative society for the common good of the human person.[479] This was the pragmatic role that the *Oja* system of contribution eventually played out in the history of FCs. It was the most profound system of financial management scheme that DDS utilized to collate the financial contributions of the farmers in order to meet their (farmers') needs. The DDS through this medium was bringing about subsidiarity too, by "supplementing, complementing or augmenting the efforts of the ...individual members or ... [the] smaller social units"[480] since they could no longer help themselves. Thus the duty of DDS was to accumulate the farmers' capitals and also to give the farmers the opportunity to express their thoughts about the idea. However, it had its own share of scepticism from the local farmers, but once these scepticisms were clarified through the dialogues, the FC idea emerged stronger. Due to the growing awareness of the need for savings, farmers in a consultation requested the DDS to convert the FC system into a financial pool, where they could withdraw their proceeds at the beginning of the planting season. For many reasons, finances were difficult among farmers during the planting season, (that is at the beginning of the raining season in March/April). Since all members would need their monies at the planting season, it was absurd to go the traditional rotational method in the *Oja* system; in addition the record keeping was quite poor thus raising suspicion of theft. But the problem of

---

[478] The *Oja* financial institution is known for different names in different parts of Nigeria. It involves routine cash deposits of all members either weekly or as the case may be. One person takes home the contribution at every meeting, this process continues till all members receive theirs. There are some other services like lending which attracts interests and the group may be operated as unisex one or otherwise.

[479] Cf. M. L. Lamb, Solidarity, 908.

[480] Matthew Ezea, The ILO concept of decent Work in the Light of the Social Teachings of the Church and its Relevance to Nigeria, Münster, 2011, 110.

record keeping was curtailed when experienced members of the Ministry of Co-Operatives and the Credit Union (CU) were invited to assist the FCs.[481]

The membership of the FC grew exponentially as farmers came to understand the advantages therein with the adopted *Oja* institution now called FC. Ejule for example had 400 members with a good number of women. The FC was different and larger than the regular *Oja* in the villages; also because of the increasing number and for proper administration, the FC was split into different FCs, for example: farmers who benefited only from this Financial Service (FS) of the FC and farmers who were also ready to key into the envisaged DDS programmes. A feasible structure was later set up by the DDS: thus an FC is made up of 25 members with a hierarchical organisational structure like the village *Oja* and is to be led by a chairman and secretary. A zone is made up of 16 FCs and each FC meets weekly while the executives meet at the level of the zones once a month.[482]

Two major developments were set in play through the FC: the savings and the credit scheme. Through the zonal structures the FCs adapted the *Oja* contribution system into a financial saving scheme so as to solve the seasonal ensuing problems of cash shortages at the beginning of the planting season. Each farmer was to make an agreed contribution weekly and the FCs were to withdraw these savings at the beginning of the planting season. The savings were collected by a DDS staff and kept in DDS custody since there was hardly any bank in the diocese then. But the people were confident they could always get their contributions when they needed it at the beginning of the rainy season. The second development that came with the FC was the credit scheme. This was more problematic as it affected the basis of self-reliance. The sum realised from the savings scheme was invariably too meagre for the farmers to effect any meaningful DDS oriented 'development'. There was consequently a need to augment the savings. After series of consultations with church authorities and the expatriate priests in the diocese, the DDS resorted to credit scheme arrangements.[483] The assistance of *Misereor*, through the CSN eased the idea of micro financing to fund these initiatives. The repayment took place for several years but was almost a 100% success.[484] Securing such finance was trouble-free but the

---

[481] Cf. N. McNamara, S. Morse, Developing Financial Services, 85.
[482] Cf. Ibid., 85-86.
[483] Cf. Ibid. 86.
[484] Cf. R. Goldstein Landwirtschaftliche Beratung, 237.

clarification of the complexities of this micro finance and its interest to the illiterate and semi-illiterate farmers was an uphill task. The FC's officials were charged with the responsibility to ensure members were credit-worthy and should pursue the repayment of loans at the end of the season; besides the rules penned down by DDS to ensure the return of capitals scared many farmers away. For many, the funds were meant to be gifts or a 'church largesse'. The FC members collectively agreed that loans be paid back through the chairmen and anyone who failed to pay back the loan before the next season ceased to be credit-worthy. Also because of the difficulty of lump-sum payments by farmers, instalment payments were granted.[485]

The FSRP was funded by many foreign agencies and local contribution. The payment of the consultants' salaries for example was first sponsored by some Canadian agencies and later by *Misereor* as well. The agricultural training of the consultants from the state was free of charge and the agency Voluntary Service Overseas (VSO) England provided two tropical farmers for this operation. The diocese was to foot bills like the pocket money and accommodation of these consultants. The local churches were responsible for the upkeep of the area managers and the miscellaneous cost was to be covered partly by the membership dues of the farmers and foreign assistance. Even though the initial arrangement was that consultants should finance their transport fares and administrative cost from the membership dues, the increasing rate of inflation thwarted this plan.[486]

The expatriate priests in the respective parishes assisted in the collation of FC's contribution and record precision. The advent of the Union Bank in Idah lessened the DDS burden, as monies were lodged into the FC's account and could even receive the little interest rate offered by the bank. As part of the monitoring strategies of the DDS, each FC owned a communal farm which in the long run became a condition for loan too. The need for donor and lender knowledge on loan usage made DDS officials to visit on a regular basis these farms so as to ascertain the use and benefits of the loans. This monitoring strategy increased the FC's participation. The monitoring strategy of the FC itself brought about very stringent rules: that members had to be active farmers, have common environment with the other FC members, the same cultural background and as well should belong to the same part of the village. This homogeneity later became the ethical line for loan

---

[485] Cf. N. McNamara, S. Morse, Developing Financial Services, 86-88.
[486] Cf. R. Goldstein Landwirtschaftliche Beratung, 246.

eligibility. As a result of this, interested people who never met up with these criteria were not eligible as FC members. Unfortunately, DDS despite her keenness to reach all had to respect this structure to be able to recoup her finances. The repayment system was hinged on the FCs and the zones and defaulters were not shortlisted for the loan benefits in the next season; a few cases ended in courts but were very minimal. Some cases were very critical but many defaulters had used the loan for medical treatments or school fees, whereas some were diverted for other private uses.[487] The continuation of the self reliance idea was prospectively carried out with the maintenance of the local institutional background of the FC as it did not promote foreign or imported knowledge in its management. Such resulted capabilities through this adopted structure is a potency en-route its maturation to a 'help to self help' group, that would transcend the parasitic art of benefactor/recipient relationship to an independent relationship.[488] Therefore the maintenance of this adapted structure stimulates the self help growth and that is one of the major constituents of the humanitarian objectives of this work.

The collaborative work of DDS with AADP (a project funded with a World Bank loan) beginning from 1977 marked another phase of DDS's experience. In June 1974, feasibility studies were carried out by recruited staff of World Bank and financed by the Federal Military administration. The cost of AADP was approximately $30 million, the World Bank was to provide $19,000, (to be spent in foreign currency) while the federal and state were to complete the remaining cost;[489] meanwhile, the World Bank's homepage on AADP gives the total project/commitment cost to be $35 million.[490] It was intended as a five year project 1978-82, but the 1977 was to mark the beginning of the project; however suffice to say the project ran 1977-1982. This huge project included:

> ...physical infrastructure, support services and farm inputs, including: 1,300 km of feeder roads; construction of 180 wells and an administrative center at Ayangba; establishment of a seed multiplication farm; expansion of a training center to provide for an expanded applied research capacity and a training program for project staff and farmers; establishment of an evaluation unit; and

---

[487] Cf. Ibid., 89-90.
[488] Cf. Aku Edmund, Solidarity, Subsidiarity and Common Good. Fundamental Principles for Community and Social Cohesion, Bloomington, 2011, 56.
[489] Cf. N. McNamara, S. Morse, Developing Financial Services, 100.
[490] Cf. Ayangba Agricultural Development project, The World Bank, http://www.worldbank.org/projects/P002032/ayangba-agricultural-development-project?lang=en (16.07.15)

construction of 30 Farmers' Service Centers to provide adequate input supply and credit facilities, and a market advisory service to farmers; the provision of veterinary services and improvement of local small livestock; establishment of about 1,000 ha of township fuelwood and pole plantations; establishment of 15 fishing lagoons and an improvement and expansion of the fishery extension and an expansion of the Agricultural Project Monitoring, Evaluation and Planning Unit financed under Loan 1092-UNI; and the purchase of an aircraft.[491]

The nature of these construction works made many to perceive the AADP as a construction company, besides AADP was a 'top-down' project.[492] These premonitions among many others made DDS hesitant to join the AADP crew; also, many church personnel did not welcome the idea of the World Bank, its philosophy was criticised as capitalistic and designed for the rich rather than the poor. Nonetheless, the AADP's objective was towards assisting the very poor; of course there were no rich farmers in this part of the nation then which certainly means AADP had only the option of the poor in mind.[493] The AADP period was both enriching and depressing to the DDS. It however became a major factor in the work of DDS and marked clearly the pre-AADP and post-AADP phase of DDS.[494]

Through the FSRP, the FC became so important and turned out to be one of the structures that played a crucial role in the DDS/AADP joint work from the mid 70s to the early 80s. By the arrival of AADP in the 70s, DDS through the FC structure had over 10,000 registered members, at least 30 members of staff and a couple of functioning programmes. The presence of the AADP brought in ample developmental opportunities. It was meant to create new agricultural initiatives in the present Kogi-East. The DDS with its strong structures on the ground before the coming of AADP was like opportunity meeting preparedness. Thus the FC's structure became one of the greatest beneficiaries of the AADP projects like the tractor services, seed multiplication and demonstration farms and so on. Besides the AADP too used these DDS structures to advance her many programmes, therefore the FC members became the most active contact members. The FCs were

---

[491] Ibid.
[492] It is a common characteristic and a tag when manufacturing establishments or companies are imported, built or handed down to the masses without local technical inputs.
[493] Cf. N. McNamara, S. Morse, Developing Financial Services, 104.
[494] Cf. Ibid. 106.

always ahead of the other farmers' cooperatives who just emerged with the birth of the AADP.[495]

The AADP like other World Bank projects in Africa was a debacle. The implementation rating, outcome rating, government performance were either without rating, unsatisfactory, or there were no available data to buttress the millions spent and the effort so far.[496] The problems of AADP were multiple beginning from the organisation; the local Farmers were never consulted before decisions were made. From the feasibility studies to the project itself, it was an expertise idea or an already-made venture transported to the people without the cultural/behavioural consideration and the current developmental status of the people in question. The AADP took too many things for granted like the failure to carry the local situation along, the short research period and so on. Many of the beneficiaries saw trickles of finances and agricultural services as handouts. To worsen the matter, AADP came in while Ayangba the seat of the project was under Kwara state; as new states were created in 1976, Ayangba was carved into Benue state; finally in 1991 Ayangba came under Kogi state. This movement from one state to the other, the implanting and incorporation of the AADP into the existing agro-offices in the new states were not without problems. The different ethnic composition within the states, local power struggle and internal politics undermined the already weakened AADP, which finally led to its collapse. Hence, the lopsided bureaucratic nature of the Nigerian state was a contributing factor for the paralysis of the AADP. Despite the fact that its expiration was extended severally, this last reason disillusioned the dreams of AADP and thus could not transcend into a state programme as envisaged at its expiration.[497]

The DDS/AADP collaboration was ambivalent as it widened the scope of DDS knowledge, popularity and prospects; however the DDS recorded a setback after the demise of AADP. It was a moment of second thoughts as the projects and the general attitude of farmers were critically affected. DDS had to adjust its approach, operations and FCs membership. Many of the farmers had taken other jobs that were less tedious or strenuous and less physically tasking as farm jobs; that consequently reduced the FCs

---

[495] Cf. Cf. Ibid., 146.
[496] Cf. Ayangba Agricultural Development project,
http://www.worldbank.org/projects/P002032/ayangba-agricultural-development-project?lang=en (16.07.2015)
[497] Cf. N. McNamara, S. Morse, Developing On-Farm Research, 30-32.

to about 250 councils. But by 1997 the FCs had increased to 1,907 active councils.[498] This subsequent growth of the FSRP programme encouraged the demand for the establishment of the FC in other parts of the diocese. The FC was attractive because of "its loan scheme and DDS was therefore invited to many areas in order to allow more farmers to benefit. Explanations had to be repeated regarding the whole philosophy of the movement, and many went away disappointed. They had hoped for a loan without strings attached and which did not require repayment."[499] The growing demands for the expansion of the FC from the nooks and crannies of the diocese presented a management crisis to the DDS as new workers had to be employed to train the new employed FC officials. This was the period of the 'Udoji Award' when the DDS had to come to terms with the nationwide sudden increase in remuneration.

Since the loans were to be paid back, it kept the hope that the FC would grow to depend solely on its contributions. For this reason there was primarily no need for external funding, moreover the FSRP was geared towards self-reliance. Self support would be the only tool to facilitate the credo of self-reliance. Obviously, the farmers' savings and credit schemes were managed under this programme by the appointed officials of the FCs. The farmers appoint the officials of their FCs and DDS assists in training them to be eligible and responsible to manage the savings/credit scheme in their respective communities. As at 2003, there were over 2,500 functioning FCs.[500] The success of the FCs, the background for this self reliance programme was very pronounced, but it was however difficult to present its success story through statistics, owing to the extensive informal economy of the nation and other reasons. Apart from few statistics gathered from the farmers, the assessments of the DDS management's team came from,

> ...listening to what people were not saying [too]. Farmers often refuse to reveal income and to enumerate positive benefits gained from FC membership. Though successful, it may not be helpful for them in many circumstances to be boastful as resentful neighbours could poison them or destroy their property. The society has its ways of dealing with ambitious people, and it may not augur well for future development if some became too conspicuous by their progress.[501]

---

[498] Cf. N. McNamara, S. Morse, Developing Financial Services, 146.
[499] Ibid., 91.
[500] Cf. C. Oguonu, The Diocesan Development Service, (DDS), 47.
[501] N. McNamara, S. Morse, Developing Financial Services, 145.

Also taxation was another factor or problem and as a result food producing communities have the tendency to maintain a low profile to avoid paying tax to the government.[502]

3.9.2 Agricultural Innovation Programme (AIP)

This initiative is the extension service arm of the DDS modelled to the global practice of agricultural extension. This extension programme is called: the 'On-Farm Research' (OFR) or Farming Systems Research and Extension (FSRE). It was initially executed by the extension agents, but later became the affairs of extension farmers. The DDS version of this programme is called: 'Farmers Level Agricultural Investigations and Response' (FLAIR).[503] The DDS kick-started this ongoing research programme to assist the growing challenges of food production as observed by the FCs and the poor storage/preservation methods in this part of the nation. The results of these researches were to generate new ideas and technologies that would consequently enhance sustainable agricultural production. Moreover, at the beginning of the OFR, the DDS and the farmers were not even in the know of the existing literatures of the OFR except the AADP experience. [504]

Many factors influenced the DDS idea of founding the OFR programme. The socio-economic backwardness and the absence of any agricultural development scheme in this vicinity necessitated this programme. However, other factors like the joint DDS/AADP programmes, the decline of the nation's economy between 1970 and 1990 and the eventual introduction of the Structural Adjustment Programme (SAP) were basic issues that prompted the need for a research body within the ambience of DDS. The most upsetting factor was the AADP's failures together with the oil boom that rendered the guiding principle of DDS, the self help; redundant and unpopular. This was because people "had become accustomed to cheap imports and salaries without work. Many farmers had left the land to take up salaried jobs, and this was particularly true around the Ayangba area."[505]

---

[502] Cf. Ibid. (See also Richards P., Indigenous Agricultural Revolution - Ecology and Food Production in West Africa, London, 1985).
[503] Cf. Diocesan Development Services, Functional Guidelines, 5.
[504] Cf. C. Oguonu, The Diocesan Development Service (DDS), 47.
[505] N. McNamara, S. Morse, Developing Financial Services, 105.

The collapse of the AADP in the early 1980s (an offshoot of development aids problem) and government's inability to pay back loans resulted in the introduction of harsh economic measures like the structural adjustment programmes (SAP).[506] SAP was one of neo-liberal economic doctrines that eventually gathered confidence from the 1970 poor world aimed at promoting economic stabilization through austerity measures. Indebted nations went on a loan seeking mission to the international financial institutions of Breton woods to cushion the economic catastrophe of failed economic policies. Critics have it that the neo-liberalist perception of SAP was a post-independence moral economy exerted upon governments in the new nations.[507] Because of the increased revenue from oil imports, Nigeria's case was exceptional as regards seeking for International Monetary Fund (IMF) loans. However, Nigeria's resort to IMF loan was the fallout of the gross mismanagement of oil proceeds and the absence of coherent policies, national priorities/interests to pursue sound developmental plans. Thus, SAP was aimed at restructuring the consumption and production pattern of the Nigerian economy in order to eliminate price distortions, discourage overdependence on crude oil export and over importation of technological and foreign goods. There was really nothing welfare about SAP.[508] Rather, its antecedence bespeaks an elitist compromise and crisis response to ameliorate a more complex problem than the political class could comprehend.[509] The serving Nigerian governments from 1973 were guilty of unscrupulous spending of oil revenue on white elephant projects that were corruption-ridden, leading consequently to the implementation of SAP as a remedy for the fallen economy.[510] SAP wiped away the middle class and visited the masses with excruciating pains. In the interiors like Eastern Kogi setting, where there was relatively less economic activity and government's presence, it made economic pains worse. It neither reduced unemployment nor stabilised the prices of goods and services; there was increase cost in the price of medical and educational services. Nevertheless, "its sole salutary effect is that it forced rural people to think in terms of self-reliance, especially in relation to agriculture. At micro-level the benefits of SAP were most obvious. Almost overnight the farmers began to benefit from higher prices in local markets, although of course their production costs also

---

[506] Cf. D. Moyo, Dead Aid, 17-22.
[507] Cf. Alex de Waal, Famine Crimes, 49.
[508] Cf. N. McNamara, S. Morse, Developing On-Farm Research, 22.
[509] Cf. Matthew Kukah, Democracy and Civil Society in Nigeria, Ibadan, 2007, 68.
[510] Cf. P. Collier, The Bottom Billion, 41.

increased."[511] The small scale farmers met this liberalisation and deregulation measures of the 80s unprepared and it thus weakened their access to global market. Unlike the super rich nations, the consequence of an inactive Nigerian government to provide basic facilities in the rural area retarded the competitiveness of the local farmers to the market demands.[512] Despite all these negative tendencies, its major thrust among the local farmers was the consequent return of the masses to the neglected agriculture. However difficult this return was, it thus boosted and encouraged the presence and relevance of DDS in the diocese.

Two DDS's evaluations in 1982 and 1983 showed that after a decade of development work, the problems remained unchanged despite the oil boom. It seemed even worse because of the knowledge of the better days gone down the drain.[513] How was DDS to breathe new life into her self-reliance programme? The collapse of AADP in the early 80s meant there was virtually no agricultural development programme in the present Kogi-East. Government's presence through the MOA and the local governments were very minimal, besides the state agricultural project: Benue Agricultural and Rural Development Authority (BNARDA) was very poor in performance. The misty federal system of Nigeria created a federal assisted project like the Lower Benue River Basin Development Authority (LBRBDA) that was running parallel and without collaboration with the state programme BNARDA. Some of the FC members too were carried away by the hurricane of handouts (for example the tractor services and the loans) offered by the fallen AADP and consequently turned away from the FCs. Thus DDS had to begin a new phase of development projects to salvage the humanitarian space created by AADP's exit. This factor led to the advent of the DDS version of the extension service called FLAIR, which was like a continuation of the status quo of the OFR programme of AADP; that is what basically constitutes the present AIP.[514] Among the many projects executed under this initiative was the seed multiplication, input services like fertilizers

[511] N. McNamara, S. Morse, Developing On-Farm Research, 22.
[512] Cf. Deutsche Bischofkenferenz, Den Hungern bekämpfen, Unsere gemeinsame Verantwortung für das Menschenrecht auf Nahrung, Studie der Sachverständigengruppe "Weltwirtschaft und Sozialethik", Bonn, Mai 2012, 39.
[513] Cf. N. McNamara, S. Morse, Developing Financial Services, 105.
[514] Cf. N. McNamara, S. Morse, Developing On-Farm Research, 33-35.

and seeds, the trainee farmer's programme, the follow-up service for the trainee farmers, soil testing and staff training.[515]

Between 1977 and 1980 the AADP and the DDS adopted some of the methods of the MOA by examining different crops on the demonstration farms. They were mini rotational gardens designed for crop rotation on small scale farms. Different groups were formed to represent and practise the crop rotation on a larger scale. The AADP provided the inputs while the DDS granted the credit through the FC loan scheme. Some of the groups were still functioning even after AADP's demise. This AADP's concept was meant to be integrated into the secondary schools so that young minds could be introduced to this process too. Despite the failures of AADP, it gave farmers the awareness of new technologies so that many eventually took to their farms; and since the DDS was in collaboration with AADP, the DDS could intervene in moments when there was shortfall of input. Also, this joint work gave the yardstick to measure farmer's performance.[516]

From 1983, through the AADP, DDS became familiar with the OFR literatures. From the example of FLAIR during the post-AADP period, it was clear that there was no other equivalent of OFR programme in Nigeria then. However, local farmers despite the frustration of the failed AADP were still ready to try new ideas within the spectrum of their cropping system. The AADP-package was far too complex, innovative and sophisticated for the local farmers to employ and only very few ideas were adopted by the farmers in the long run. DDS had some advantage as an NGO, because NGOs "generally operate on longer scales than many international or national projects; they generally have more extensive and robust linkages with the local population. This results in better ability to judge what is feasible and apply it. NGOs are typically more flexible, innovative and socially responsible than government even international institutions."[517] With the background experience of AADP, DDS began through dialogue to assist interested farmers to interpret and analyse their needs; these farmers would eventually be responsible to take decisions but in partnership with the DDS. The first farms were introduced 1983-85, a combination of New Crop Varieties (NCVs), with the expertise view on reduction of fertilizer and pesticides as provided by senior DDS scientists. The yields were so very

---

[515] Cf. Diocesan Development Services, Functional Guidelines, 5.

[516] Cf. N. McNamara, S. Morse, Developing On-Farm Research, 63.

[517] N. McNamara, S. Morse, Developing Financial Services, 25.

commendable that by 1985 many DDS extension farmers were already familiar with them and thus began to adopt these methods. Also, these farmers were permitted to retain a good proportion of the yield. The process of planting these new seeds gave opportunity for data and insight knowledge to the farmers. The new technologies learnt and the new seeds were frequently adopted into traditional cropping system. This also exposed the DDS to other available NCVs; IITA was very pleased with the feedbacks from the DDS experience.[518]

By 1986 DDS felt the need to extend the numbers of its beneficiaries and that consequently led to increase staffing of the DDS. The transfer of technology had to be taken with caution. DDS combined the AADPs ideas of 1970s: the Farming System Research (FSR), Adaptive Research (AR) and Farming Systems Research and Extension (FSRE) into a one system whereby there would be farmer's involvement and response with the researchers. The FLAIR trials concentrated mainly on the NCVs and the pre-harvest production process. It was only in 1993 that attention was given to post-harvest processes including marketing. Major NCVs that needed such attention were soya bean and groundnut. This was important because these two crops became very dominant in the DDS nutritional programme to prop up the prevalent dietary imbalance among the people. Later the frontiers of FLAIR were increased to include new cropping systems like alley cropping in Nigeria. There were other reasons for the people's participation in FLAIR programme: the AADP factor (that the DDS farmers were already accustomed to the AADP's demonstration farms), the ease of adapting NCVs to local agricultural systems, the ability of DDS and the farmers to multiply the NCVs, the independence of DDS on this programme and that it could supply what it needed became an added advantage, a morale booster and a vote of confidence in DDS from the masses. Above all, through the seed multiplication programme very many improved breeds of NCVs were introduced that proved very good yield over the time and were also prone to less insects and disease attacks. All these factors encouraged and increased the esteem of the FLAIR programme.[519]

There were basic principles that facilitated the success of the FLAIR programme; simplicity was crucial, since despite the fact that many of the extension farmers were experienced, many lacked basic education while

---

[518] Cf. N. McNamara, S. Morse, Developing On-Farm Research, 65-66.
[519] Cf. Ibid., 67-68.

others had very little educational background. There was a high demand of trials from the extension farmers on different farms, therefore serious considerations were given to variations in the cropping system. The yield was a very vital and observable fact to determine the technological performance of the crops. However, other factors like early maturity, resistance to pest and diseases, reduction in labour input and its palatability were essential too. Also it encouraged the introduction of Local Varieties (LVs) into the trial farms, the introduction of NCVs with the use of fertilizers and pesticides and how they fared on the different available soil types. Apart from the yield that could possibly determine the success rate of the crops at the end of the experimental process of a particular programme, the ensuing dialogue between the DDS management/staff and the farmers on the ground was crucial too. There was exchange of ideas and experience as regards the pre- and post planting observations of the women and farmers and these were possible due to the regular DDS farmer meetings in the villages. Furthermore, regular visits were made each year by contact farmers to the farms where technologies were adopted. This created opportunities for exchange of views and adjudication.[520]

Studies have proved the effect of the NCVs from the yields of the farmers. Sometimes the farmers have the tendency to hide their income for many local reasons, as stated above. However there are discrepancies between the yield level from the farmers and that of the women. The introduction of the women into the trial farms presented the DDS with extra information on the processing, food preparation and marketing. Contrary to some preconceived view that NCVs were labour intensive, studies have shown especially from the submission of many women that a lower level of labour requirement was experienced at weeding, harvesting and food processing.[521]

3.9.3 Village Development Programme (VDP)

The antecedents of the DDS like the medical relapse experienced in Igala/Bassaland and the contacts with people through farming created a need for a development scheme to assist some of the poor people, for example women's programmes (training of women apprentices), nutrition, rehabilitation of the handicapped, income generating activities (milling and

---

[520] Cf. Ibid., 68-71.
[521] Cf. Ibid., 141-144.

others), assisting motherless children, HIV/AIDS patients and provision of various small scale projects.[522]

By 1969 the missionaries on the ground were well aware of the educational backwardness of the female population; not many young women went to school and the few who eventually did, hardly exceeded the primary school level. Therefore a women's centre was established to provide some vocational skills to these underprivileged women. Such courses include crafts, child care, gardening, soap making, weaving, tailoring, cookery and household management. Through the acquisition of these skills that lasted up to two years, these women could become self-employed and consequently self-reliant. For others, such skills could serve as auxiliary-jobs to augment their income and to better their household plans. Like every beginning the women's centre had its own disappointments and challenges, there was lack of accommodation for the many prospective beneficiaries. This problem was later on resolved through the provision of hostels to interested apprentices; meanwhile the system was eventually integrated into the DDS scheme. The recruitment of the would-be candidates came through parishes, the village *Ojas* and women's general meetings.[523] At its beginning in the mid 80s the DDS Women Resource Centre (as is known today) had an average of 15 intakes. By 1991 after the completion of the permanent site, the intake had increased to 25 women at a time.[524]

The departure of AADP created a humanitarian vacuum that made DDS deeply saturated with an alley of fears. In addition, this AADP exit coincided with the oil bust, the SAP and the sudden disappearance of cheap imports of agricultural foods from the local market. The general effect was the consequent hardships in the rural areas. Besides, such fears made the DDS wary of the fate of the much advocated 'self-reliance' it was pursuing. As the subsidy of agricultural goods ceased, the ensuing economic decline resulted in the spread of diseases and malnutrition among these rural masses. Moreover the swift finances that came the way of these ordinary folks in the oil boom from 70s to 80s were transformed into increased family structures, which invariably meant increased number of wives, children, additional mouths to feed and above all increased responsibility. The abovementioned

---

[522] Cf. Diocesan Development Services, Functional Guidelines 5; Catherine Oguonu, The Diocesan Development Service (DDS) 47.
[523] Cf. N. McNamara, S. Morse, Developing Financial Services, 76.
[524] Cf. C. Oguonu, The Diocesan Development Services, (DDS), Functional Guidelines, 51.

fallen educational standard, unemployment, redundancy and the lack of new skills in the cities became worse in the rural areas and most importantly with harsh economic consequences. This tragic period was moreover precarious in the rural areas as government services were almost at a zero level. The DDS, aware of this economic handicap went into wide scale humanitarian relief to deserted wives, widows, orphans and people at the margins of the society.[525]

Despite these humanitarian engagements through different welfare services to the needy, DDS was still keen about preserving its principle and mantra of self-reliance. This brought about "special concession... to poorer people, especially women. Over 400 small-scale projects have been initiated in the 1988 to 1993 period, and between 1993 and 1996 a further 240. They include many off-farm activities, for example milling and food processing. These also have as an added objective, the reduction of physical labour especially for women."[526]

The poverty induced by SAP and other factors persuaded the DDS's intervention in the nutritional life of the people. This was another landmark created by the DDS. One of the major global sources of meat and dairy products is cattle farming for the provision of protein, which encourages proper growth and development especially among children. However, the Igala/Bassa People are not originally cattle-rearers.[527] Besides, the nutritional consciousness was very low in this part of the nation. Before the advent of DDS precisely in the 50s, the Holy Rosary Sisters already had a similar experience of nutritional imbalance among the people through contacts with the people in schools and hospitals. As they grew weary of this low nutritional consciousness, the missionaries as an interim remedy went sometimes on house visitations to teach interested people the essence of nutritional consciousness and also possible food supplements.[528] The arrival of the founder of the DDS, Sr. Nora McNamara in 1971 coincided with a

---

[525] Cf. N. McNamara, S. Morse, Developing Financial Services, 107.

[526] Ibid.

[527] There are many contestable reasons on this issue; it is stressed in the literatures that the presence of tsetse fly retards cattle rearing. But over the time, the nomadic Fulani herdsmen, whose primary occupation is cattle rearing have extended their presence in southern Nigeria today, they are thriving well and are grazing their cattle. Though the Tsetse fly factor may count, the absence of cattle farming in other parts of Nigeria is basically because the traditional people were not in the custom of cattle rearing.

[528] Cf. N. McNamara, S. Morse, Developing Financial Services. 76.

nutritional campaign in the Grimard Hospital Ayangba. This was evidently important as the nurses and the expatriate staff became exhausted of treating particular types of illness all the time. These were illnesses that could be avoided through improved nutrition, as malnutrition caused setback to the medical aspirations of the mission's work. That this nutritional deficiency was so rampart and yet never attracted government's initiative, funding or provision for research, baffled the founder and the foreign staff of DDS. Nevertheless, it tells the disconnection of governance from the people and how insulated the hinterlands are from state and governance. The DDS founder initiated an education programme every morning at the OPD, whereby out-patients were given a short orientation on nutrition, aimed at preventing some frequent diseases. This move was greeted with disapproval at the first instance, as many of the patients had developed a liking for only injections and nothing less. How could one reconcile malnutrition among an agriculturally oriented people who grew many crops and also owned palm trees that could provide a balanced diet?[529] They had almost all that was needed but the knowledge of the right input and the combination was lacking. It was this finding that propelled the DDS to carry out a more humanitarian gesture of looking inwardly, by assessing the many locally grown crops and the kind of food combination with the local staples that could bring about a balanced diet. One misunderstanding was the conflicting and sometimes unacceptable views proposed by the expatriates to the local people. Some of the suggested food combination, for example groundnut paste with local dishes, was never a practice the people were used to; hence it was greeted with mixed feelings. It was a sign that there was need to integrate the people into finding better and more acceptable alternatives.

One of such improvements was the introduction of soya bean as a food supplement to the local nutrition. This staple was not common among the local people and the few who planted it were for sales in Northern Nigeria. However, it was already a major source of cash and food crop production for over 30 years among the neighbouring ethnic groups, like the Tivs and Idomas in Benue state.[530] Soya bean belongs to the class of legumes, a class of rich protein foods and well known for its special characteristics to be "the most important source of plant protein. It is known as miracle seed which has saved a lot of deaths in many countries where malnutrition especially among children is rampant. The soya plant comes

---

[529] Cf. Ibid., 82.
[530] Cf. N. McNamara, S. Morse, Developing On-Farm Research, 105.

from the Far East, but different varieties have been successfully grown in different climates."[531] It was originally grown for the oil industries, however it was discovered that after the extraction of oil the residue still contained up to 50% of protein and could be used for other purposes. Soya bean is a rich protein food, with 40% protein, 21% fat, 34% carbohydrate and 5% ash. Moreover, it has other traces of nutrients like: calcium, phosphorus, iron, thiamine, riboflavin, niacin. For this reason soya bean is considered as a complete protein food and its combination with local dishes enhances nutritional value.[532]

The soya bean programme was introduced into the FLAIR programme in 1992, but had featured in the nutritional programme of the DDS since the 1980s. This interest came from two backgrounds: The people requested the DDS's expertise on how best to market the soya bean and its utility in the preparation of local nutrition, since it provides high quality protein. This request coincided with the government's campaign on the promotion of soya bean consumption as a substitute for protein; it could serve as substitutes for meat and dairy products that were not affordable by the people. However, this was one example of the SAP induced resourcefulness. Besides, the nearness of an oil mill in Taraku (that has folded up today) in the neighbouring state emphasised the importance of soya bean's supplement in the day to day nutrition of its neighbours.[533] Also, the incorporation of this challenging soya bean's experiment into FLAIR programme was informed by the nutritional imperative to provide alternatives to the people. Thus, DDS collected available varieties from IITA which were tested on the people's soil. Since it was first time on this soil, it had its own natural challenges. However, the DDS and the Extension Farmers were able to overcome many of such challenges through seed multiplication. The DDS arrived at many varieties but it finally adopted three main varieties. These three varieties mostly researched within these three years showed stability in its yield. Farmers over the time could affirm the methods that generated better yield, for example the sole cropping system of farming gave more yield than the inter-cropping system.[534]

---

[531] Diocesan Development Services, Functional Guidelines, 62.
[532] Cf. Ibid.
[533] Cf. N. McNamara, S. Morse, Developing On-Farm Research, 105.
[534] Cf. Ibid., 106.

The responses from the DDS's study on soya bean have been interesting. The general complaint was the cumbersome nature of the soya beans processing before consumption. But the ingenious research of IITA proffered another solution: the act of milling the beans was more efficient and a safer method of processing than the earlier method of long soaking and fermentation period to neutralise the toxins. This research gave a boost to the processing of the NCV soya bean in the DDS nutritional programme. This processing was well greeted by the people because the milling process was labour-light and it also enhanced an uncomplicated application of the soya bean into the nutritional make up, consequently creating the envisaged balanced diet. The milled flour could be used as milk for babies above 4 months old. With this, the aim of substitution for meat and other protein providers was guaranteed. The women found out that the remaining cakes after the milk processing could be used for soap-making and livestock feeds especially chickens. The study of 1993 to 1995 showed the keenness of both men and women regarding the dishes prepared with the soya bean flour; this could be combined with other local dishes to ensure a balanced diet especially for children. To this effect many households encouraged at least one person of her members to be acquainted with the knowledge of such food preparation.[535] The established PHCs and their different centres in the diocese became centres for nutritional classes to be run by the DDS team and the community health workers trained by DDS. Furthermore, curative and preventive methods were taught in these centres with nutritional demonstration classes, which is the combination of local foods and soya beans.[536]

The DDS through the principle of solidarity identifies with less privileged people and has subsequently executed humanitarian projects in areas that have often been neglected. The commonest among them is the provision of humanitarian assistance to the disabled. Before the advent of the DDS, the fate of the disabled in this part of the globe was linked to some superstitious belief, like witchcraft or sorcery.[537] Through the humanitarian interventions of DDS, aids and many opportunities are offered to the disabled as recognition of human rights and human dignity. Through the principle of solidarity, the DDS by way of compassion identifies with the fate of the disabled, in the spirit of shared responsibility and joy. In essence,

---

[535] Cf. Ibid., 107.
[536] Cf. C. Oguonu, The Diocesan Development Services, 52.
[537] Cf. Ibid., 51.

DDS does not shy away from sharing in the pains of the primordial corporate liability of the community.[538] Therefore, solidarity ought to be an attribute of a community, because "a community that does not join hands to strengthen the weaker ones is bound to break."[539] The DDS' action fosters the intimate relationship between community and solidarity; a link that is both intrinsic and inseparable. Through this support, DDS gives the disabled a societal recognition that consequently empowers and gives them the opportunities to contribute to the growth of their society. Another important aspect of DDS's contribution was in solidarity with the national slogan 'education for all by the year 2000'. Since the year 2000 the DDS has been involved in adult education class; the state literacy office Idah also assists the DDS in this programme.[540]

The United Nation's declaration of International Youth Year (IYY) in January 1985 emphasised the importance of youth participation and contribution in the implementation of the new economic order that is based on the principles of equity, justice and peace towards shaping the future of mankind.[541] The pastoral letter of John Paul II to the youths of the world on the occasion of the IYY titled *'Dilecti Amici',* reminded the church of her responsibility and care for the youths. The bishops in response to this letter devised some humanitarian approach in their respective dioceses. One of such was the DDS's response package: the training of 'youth farmers'; who in turn were to help the local farmers. The programme entailed a good number of young people to be trained for this purpose. The DDS conceptualized this programme under the 'Trainee Farmers Programme' which was like using a stone to kill two birds; youths were to be trained, in order to assist farmers. From the DDS perspective the training of the youths was a contribution towards the IYY objectives and on completion of the training, they were to be assisting-agents to the local farmers who were mostly peasant, aged and less educated people living in the villages. The DDS offered to train these young men in the various techniques of improved agriculture, but were not to be employed by DDS; rather they were to

---

[538] Cf. Alois Baumgartner, Solidarität, in: Ed., Marianne Heimbach-Steins, Christliche Sozialethik, Bd. I, Regensburg, 2004, Pp. 282-292, 283.

[539] E. Aku, Solidarity, Subsidiarity and Common Good, 7.

[540] Cf. C. Oguonu, The Diocesan Development Service (DDS), 51.

[541] Cf. United Nations, General Assembly, A/RES/39/22, 23, November 1984, http://www.un.org/documents/ga/res/39/a39r022.htm (12.04.2015).

channel their knowledge into agricultural endeavours in their communities.[542]

Training the youths was one step but getting access to land was another huge problem. The consequent 'land use act', the supposed panacea to land problems that has turned into one of the greatest hurdles of agriculture in modern Nigeria, makes the process of securing sizeable land for agro-business very cumbersome. Due to the obscure land tenure system, the communities where these DDS newly trained 'young farmers' came from were committed to guarantee that the trained youths got adequate land for farming after the courses.[543] The need to avoid this rivalry between landowners and tenants ought to be cleared from the onset to enable the DDS newly trained youths have a permanent farm, where the DDS could assist, monitor and invest in. It was left for the community either to alienate or provide the trained farmers with community land or with family land.

The DDS provided the trainees with the basics like, some kilos of improved seeds and planting materials, agro inputs like fertilizer, seed dressing and so on. A knapsack sprayer was also given partly on loan. In the end, many youths, at least over 40 of them benefited from this programme.[544]

3.9.4 Water Development Programmes (WDP)

From the inception of the DDS foundation in 1971, the appeal for a water project always took the centre stage whenever the founder came in contact with communities.[545] Even though agriculture was the main focus, concession was given to this request. This DDS's concession spells out one of the consequences of solidarity. Thus, through the DDS's solidarity gesture, it provoked chains of solidarity engagements which were not even envisaged as part of the DDS's programme in the first place. Consequently, miscellaneous projects were executed in the course of DDS's venture, like the building of culverts and bridges. It indicates the fact that every contact with the neighbour can lead not only to solidarity but to additional solidarity, thus DDS in her spontaneity was able to accommodate such emergencies. However, among these sundry projects, the water project was more prominent. Therefore, a society that lacks such prospects is devoid of true

---

[542] Cf. Diocesan Development Services, Functional Guidelines, 10.
[543] Cf. C. Oguonu, The Diocesan Development Service (DDS), 51.
[544] Cf. Diocesan Development Services, Functional Guidelines, 10.
[545] Cf. N. McNamara, S. Morse, Developing Financial Services, 84.

solidarity.[546] Nonetheless, agriculture still took precedence over other humanitarian issues in the operations of the DDS.

Even though Nigeria is known to possess ample water resources, its distribution has always been problematic. About 90% of the water usage in Nigeria is domestic inclined. The major source of water supply before colonialism was direct collection of rain water from roofs of buildings into containers and pots, or the fetching of water from the rivers, springs, ponds, streams and hand-dug wells. These water sources were irregular and unreliable and the likelihood of contamination with household waste and faeces was high; consequently posing hazardous health problems like water-borne diseases. Most times people travelled long distance especially during the months of dry season to collect water.[547] However communities dependent more on rain water than other sources of water faced a more precarious fate coupled with the seasonal variation of the Nigerian weather today that has at least 4-6 months of dry season pending the closeness to the coast.

The first major water project scheme in Nigeria was commissioned in Lagos in 1915 by the colonial administration. Since 1953 many other water projects have been constructed in other parts of the country up till the good days of the 80s. Despite the scanty nature of statistics in Nigeria, the 1976 water supply statistic is very shocking. The old Benue state, which was made up of the present Kogi-East, (together with at least three other ethnic groups) had pipe borne water services in 8 towns only. It highlights the disparity of water supply in the urban and rural areas; thus, water supply favours the urban population that comprises barely 30% population of the nation. From this statistic, only 4% of the population of Benue state was served with potable water. The rural areas are deprived of such services and the urban areas are likewise undersupplied. The majority of urban dwellers buy water from public standpipes or selling stations. From the population of those with access to pipe borne water in the urban areas, only about 10% are served through house connection; this depicts just a tiny section of the urban population.[548] Apart from the few water supplies in the major towns through pipe-borne waters in the 80s, other towns and villages in the present Kogi-East buy water from tankers. The water project in Kogi state is so poorly

---

[546] Cf. A. Baumgartner, Solidarität, 290.
[547] Cf. A. Onokerhoraye, Social Services in Nigeria, 199.
[548] Cf. Ibid., 200-202.

managed that even the state houses and establishments are supplied by water tankers; it tells the level of dislocation in government. Even though this statistic is over 40 years, the status quo has remained almost unchanged especially in the interiors. However, a 2002 statistics published in 2008 shows that "only 72 percent of urban residents and 49 percent of rural residents had access to safe drinking water."[549] In Kogi State about 70.1% of households have access to improved source of drinking water.[550] One could deduce from these facts the dysfunctional nature of the Nigerian state's structure and flawed federalism with very weak institutions. Even the above mentioned improvement over the past years is the effect of the many boreholes sunk by individual efforts especially in the cities and towns to supply potable water to the growing population.[551] Nonetheless, the question remains, what becomes of the larger population in the villages especially in Kogi-East where the population is mostly rural? It brings out the challenging humanitarian vacuum that NGOs like DDS and well meaning people have to cover up to encourage the common good of the people.

DDS carried out the provision of potable water to the people through boreholes, rain-harvesting and surface water utilisation. Many communities first went into the construction of boreholes, but maintenance cost and expertise have led to the breakdown of many over the years. This was succeeded by the rain harvesting projects. Some villages were assisted through the building of a reservoir that could collect about 20,000 to 30,000 litres of water in the rainy season. The DDS through aids, finances the labour and the materials, while the community contributes 10% of its cost.[552] This persevering and determining commitment of the DDS to assist the people is a mark of responsibility that furthers the common good of the beneficiaries of the aforementioned projects. Therefore, solidarity is a bond that welds human beings together, as it connects the DDS to the different beneficiaries of its projects.[553] The groundbreaking water project by DDS was the establishment of the 'pure water factory' in 2000. Despite the competition from other water factories today, the DDS water factory still enjoys good

---

[549] Library Congress, Federal Research Division, Country Profile, Nigeria July 2008, 9.

[550] Cf. National Human Development Report 2015, 49.

[551] Sometimes these private boreholes are dug arbitrarily without observing standard regulation, because there is a geological mandatory distance that must be maintained from one borehole to another to avoid the intermittent drying up of the water table.

[552] Cf. C. Oguonu, The Diocesan Development Service, 53.

[553] Cf. E. Aku, Solidarity, Subsidiarity and Common Good, 14 (See also E. Erhardt, Solidarity.).

patronage at Idah and its environs. Besides, many health practitioners have commended the quality of its water. Moreover, this water is used as source of irrigation on the DDS farms during the dry season.[554] The generated revenue from this water factory is a mark of self-reliance and brings about sustainability too. Therefore the proceeds could serve as a means for running the affairs of DDS and as well finance its many projects.

---

[554] Cf. C. Oguonu, The Diocesan Development Service, 53.

CHAPTER FOUR: THE IMPERATIVE OF A SELF RELIANT LOCAL CHURCH

4.   Self-reliance and the church today

Having dealt with the pre- and post-colonial background of the people in the last chapter, it is worth the task in this new chapter to approach and re-evaluate in detail the factor of self-reliance as the facilitator of humanitarian work for her beneficiaries. The basics of humanitarian work which include the alleviation of the sufferings of humanity, through assisting distant strangers that brings about a healthy international community is just one side of the story. On the other side, this beautiful agenda would remain a one-way-traffic if not embraced or directed towards self-reliance. The church in her *diakonein* task has consequently been careening from one humanitarian programme to another to cushion the effect of poverty especially in the developing nations. Coupled with the call for solidarity since the Vatican II Council, it has tremendously increased the tempo of the church's approach towards development. In spite of this incredible momentum, its corresponding effects have eluded human sight. The obvious scenario spells a degenerating poverty aggravated by the many global effects and above all the global village mechanism and the new world order, which undoubtedly is the product of the process of globalisation. Unfortunately these *diakonein*/humanitarian approaches of churches in the developing nations create a dependent syndrome and constantly raise concerns among critics and African minds that International Non-Governmental Organisations (INGOs), donor agencies and relief organisations are mere "channels for the flow of material resources to communities, rather than facilitators of development".[555] However, such a perplexed atmosphere is true of many NGOs, the early missions and even the local church today. It informs the irony of more help that consequently creates a giver/beggar relationship or a superiority/inferiority complex between the churches of the industrial nations and poor nations of the world respectively. At the governmental level too it has shaped an African policy that is merely saturated with the administration of aids relations. The obvious aftermath of such a system is the present aid fatigue in the humanitarian and development

---

[555] Ezra Mbogori, African Civil Society, coming to terms with Globalisation, in: Ed., Phoebe Griffith, Unbinding Africa, Making Globalisation work for Good Governance, London, 2003, Pp. 21-26, 22.

aid communities.[556] This failure calls for the use of intelligence and curiosity as to why the aid system is not working. Donors sometimes are able to trace even where their monies are being used like rehydrating some children, improving some lives and eventually avoiding consequent death. But what about a decent life, which is the ultimate goal, does it matter if their deaths have only been postponed for weeks, a year or a month?[557] Has the humanitarian really changed the world? Besides, what value have those donations and good gestures added to humanity? Is it another wasted effort or could it be one of the good intentions that are yet to be subjected to critical reasoning and evaluation? Therefore the humanitarian must go beyond avoiding physical death to a life-giving endeavour.

That is why the imperative of self-reliance becomes crucial to the people, which will consequently give the local church that anticipated autonomy. The axiom of self-reliance is bottom-up as opposed to the prevailing top-down development since the 70s; such emphasis is based on the premises of partnership and inclusion.[558] It is a catalyst to embolden local churches to relate as partners to churches in other parts of the world. It is a call for autonomy that animates the true spirit of oneness, equality, mutual respect and true appreciation because "no one branch can think it is superior to the others because: 'You do not support the root; it is the root that supports you'. The mission is only really complete when this equality is achieved."[559] The mission of the universal church in communion with the local church could be attained when the different parts are self-reliant. It is imperative that every local church reaches the height of self-reliance; such stature determines the true and complete universal mission of the church. Since the local church is immersed and rooted in her own culture, she is able to give a cultural expression to her faith by providing social answers to her people's plight through collaborative venture of the people with her ministers.[560] The onus therefore is on the local church in her collegial relationship with the universal church to strive in her little capacity towards complementing this desired fullness of the universal church.

---

[556] Cf. U. Engel, Africa Images and African Policy, Pleading for Realism, 19, 25.
[557] Cf. Kwame Anthony Appiah, Cosmopolitanism, 167.
[558] Cf. N. McNamara, S. Morse, Voices from the aid 'Chain': the personal Dynamics of Care, in; Social and Cultural Geography, Vol. 5, No. 2, June 2004, Reading, Pp. 253-270, 256.
[559] A. Shorter, Theology of Mission, 53.
[560] Cf. U. Obodoechina, The Imperative of Self-Reliance, 40.

The local church on this developmental odyssey is experiencing in recent times diminishing returns in the humanitarian attention granted her by foreign church NGOs, donors and financiers. This is partly due to the opening of the Eastern bloc since the end of the cold war in 1989.[561] Since the foreign churches are influenced by the actions of their respective governments and the global phenomena, there was a consequent change of humanitarian direction from their NGOs. The effect of the failed development era of 70s and some of these global factors did not only reduce development aids towards Africa, but have slowed down economic, political, intellectual development over the time. Moreover, poor planning, the overt poor governance and other local hurdles have crafted a lacklustre economy calling for humanitarian intervention. But to live on humanitarian or development aids should not be the practice of any sane government or church like the old adage say, 'he, who goes borrowing, also goes sorrowing.'

Societal disorganisation foments national poverty and one of the most strategic means to eradicate this poverty is not by acquiring foreign assistance and transfers but by societal change and reforms, like the resolve against over concentration of the nation's fortunes on the presence of mineral resources.[562] Like the state today, the Nigerian church too lives on the crumbs of the oil income. The proceeds of the oil revenue since the last four decades have only increased the Nigerian dependence on the oil economy. After the oil boom of 1973, another phase of exponential rise in the price of crude oil began in 1995 from $35 to $50 per barrel. Then after, it soared to $70 in 2010, $107 in 2011, $109 in 2012, falling slightly from $105 in 2013, to $ 96 in 2014 and falling sharply to $49 in 2015.[563] As an

---

[561] Cf. A. A. Agbali, The Catholic Church, Social Justice Teachings.., 62; Rolf Hoffmeier, Five decades of German- African relations: limited interests, low political profile and substantial aid donor, in: Eds., Ulf Engel, Robert Kappel, Germany's Africa Policy Revisited, Interests, images and incrementalism, Politics and Economics in Africa, Vol. IV, Münster, 2002, Pp. 39-62, 54. The end of the East -West Germany confrontation on the aids to African continent for example, ended with the cold war, thereby leading to the revision of the underlying principles of aids distribution. Despots were no longer favoured and with the new outlook in the development aids distribution, development aid to Africa was cut down in favour of the eastern bloc.

[562] Cf. Joachim Wiemeyer, Soziale Ungleichheit und Armut in Deutschland, Ursachen und aktuelle Entwicklung, Bewertung und Maßnahmen zur Begrenzung in: Ed., S. Lunte, Amosinternational Gesellschaft gerecht gestalten, 10Jg, 2016, Heft, Pp. 1, 3-10, 5.

[563] Cf. Statista, the Statistics Portal, http://www.statista.com/statistics/262858/change-in-opec-crude-oil-prices-since-1960/ (04.09.16)

import dependent nation, her foreign exchange from oil revenue funds virtually every aspect of the economy from the military to payment of salaries, pharmacy and food. The different media hypes about economic diversification have resulted in mere charade. This overt petro-dollar economy depicts Nigeria as a rudderless nation when it comes to issues of self-reliance. Norway as an oil producing nation for example operates an investment fund, where oil revenues are deposited to protect upcoming generations and only the interest of this fund is used for the common good. But the excess crude oil account in Nigeria accrued from the global price increase was lavished to compensate for the shortfalls in the oil revenue and for fiscal spending at the different levels. Besides, this surplus fund was shared indiscriminately between government at federal/state level and for the bogus salaries of government officials. It is clear that there is hardly any provision and political will to save even for the rainy days.[564] Such misguided economic plans not considering other generations spell a case of intergenerational injustice and betray the lack of concern for self-reliance on the part of the nation. The nation must think outside the box of oil revenue and so the church that exists within such a systemic frail state is bound to change her mode of operation as she inherently depends on this mono-economy. Therefore, she must make a purposeful movement to limit her dependency in order not to be consumed in the national dilemma and the consequent pool of poverty. This makes the call for self-reliance a *conditio sine qua non* and a fundamental issue to the Nigerian church, because "...Christian Africa will never be at home in the church of God until she stops being under a perpetual obligation, in a condition of beggary, in a state of eternal juniority."[565] It also corroborates the Swahili adage that: 'that which spoils friendship is borrowing and lending.' Therefore, the search for financial maturity on the part of the local church is the road to adulthood, responsibility, autonomy and mutual respect between the different local churches.[566]

The autonomy of the church for example is not to be mistaken with independence, since every local church even from its commencement is expected to be autonomous, which evidently, is a product of self-reliance.[567] The platform of self-reliance remains the most enviable means to gain

---

[564] Cf. M. Ezea, The ILO, 299.
[565] Ibid. (Quote from an African Priest, Fr. Meinrad Hegba)
[566] Cf. U. Obodoechina, The Imperative of Self-Reliance, 35.
[567] Cf. Paul VI, Ad gentes, 15.

candid access into global interactions. Hence, if the Nigerian church truly craves for sincere liberation, autonomy, respect and human dignity, she needs a new operational motive and strategy. To earn positive global attraction and respect, she needs to pay the price by standing up to global reality and to make the needed sacrifice amid threats and strings that may be tied to such moves; else she will still be eluded in the future by more global events and will continue to dance perpetually at the borderlines. Globalisation for example is factor for growth that 'serious minded' nations must tap into, therefore "blind opposition would be a mistaken and prejudiced attitude, [making the poor] incapable of recognizing the positive aspects of the process, with the consequent risk of missing the chance to take advantage of its many opportunities for development."[568] It is left for the local church to explore its positive angle so as to "enhance human communication, [to] improve human productivity, enhance our awareness of being inhabitants of a fragile planet and [to] facilitate empathy between societies across vast distances".[569] It is only when all hands are on deck to build the needed capacity towards self-reliance that the possible flaws of a ruthless/faceless economy could be checkmated. Consequently, it could lessen the growing tension between the rich and the poor and other global menace threatening the happiness of the human person today.

The Nigerian church is poor largely because Nigeria is poor.[570] Accordingly, Amartya Sen understands poverty as "capability failure, not just as shortage of commodities or even of income and wealth. Poverty involves heterogeneous failures of opportunity which are not always well correlated with income."[571] Moreover, the conversion of available resources into diverse use demands the presence of capability; this makes income and resources only a means to an end and capability is that end.[572] The clarity of this endemic poverty by the different global statistics, for example World Bank reports and Human Development Index (HDI), challenges a resolute response from the humanitarian church. For the church to make positive impact in the post modern Nigeria, she needs to champion a pathway to true autonomy, self respect and that desired dignity. Charity or aid no matter how

---

[568] Benedict XVI, Caritas in Veritatis, 42.
[569] A. Mazrui, Nkrumah's Legacy, 1
[570] Cf. E.E. Uzukwu, The Listening Church, 91.
[571] Martha Nussbaum, Creating Capabilities, The Human Development Approach, Cambridge, 2011, 143.
[572] Cf. Ibid, 144.

well organised cannot reduce poverty, the most central issue is the development agenda tailored down by humanitarians in a broadened developmental programme that would give the beneficiaries a sort of leverage to control their own lives. It thus makes them able to confront and control future humanitarian distortions without outside help.[573] Such a life can only be guaranteed by a self-reliance oriented thought pattern and a humanitarian follow-up. The proposed humanitarian work here is geared towards self-reliance from the following three paradigms of development:

- increasing the capacity to produce,

- education and re-education, and

- advocating for structural changes through the political *diakonia*.

This brings out the new era of humanitarianism, a humanitarian approach that is factored with self-reliance from its onset.

4.1   Increasing the capacity to produce

The innovation and cumulative hard work of a people over a period of time determine their capacity to produce as they change and upgrade the available means of production in the society to satisfy their desired and growing goods and services. Adam Smith, (1723-1790) a proponent of free market economy believed in the doctrine of natural law that every human person is the best judge of his or her self interest and should be left alone to pursue his or her advantage so as to achieve the common good. Therefore, if all are left free to seek and maximise wealth, it could maximize aggregate wealth. His views are geared towards maximising the wealth of the nations, but his overrated policy of *laissez-faire* and the invisible hand is not tenable in modern economics, since every government is supposed to set the control mechanism.[574] Nevertheless, it is the capacity to produce that consequently creates wealth, a factor that has been enhanced in the modern age through the effects of capitalism. The industrial revolution since the late 18th century to the mid 19th century made the western nations and Japan the global centre for wealth creation. This process ushered in many changes like improved standard of living in the life of the ordinary people within the aforementioned geographical confine. Recently other nations have joined the

---

[573] Cf. G. Bolton, Poor Story, 76.

[574] Cf. M.L. Jhingan, The Economics of Development and Planning, Delhi, 1997, 83.

ranks of these nations like, China, India, Brazil and others. China today earns international respect for the ability to pull millions of her population from the strings of poverty into prosperity and as such is now counted among the most progressive nations of the world. This is obviously from the yardstick of economic strides achieved through increased capacity to produce her needs and to export her surpluses. This advantage is undoubtedly through the principles of wealth creation; citizens of such nations have more benefits and welfare opportunities. Such citizens in the words of David Rieff are prosperous citizens because they belong to prosperous nations.[575]

One of the greatest plights of pre- and post-independent Nigeria is her inability to support almost all spheres of life in a modern state. This lack of required/qualified manpower coupled with the poor finances to cater for the immediate and basic social infrastructural needs of the new nation have crippled national development over time.[576] The failed capacity to meet local demands in modern times creates an economy dependent on the western nations. History has proven that the presence of war and strife anywhere on the globe retards the volume of production.[577] The slave trade period for example decreased African production; there is "...historical evidence [which] suggests that in the past much of this region was under cultivation, but as a result of slave-trading much of the land reverted to bush allowing the tsetse-fly to flourish. Furthermore the slave-raiding led some communities to migrate to relatively inhospitable areas of land."[578] In addition, it was a period that marked a direct investment of African resources in the procurement of firearms which consequently dislodged, eroded and shook African foundation of trade and humanity; possession of firearms meant power and the capability to raid other communities for slave trading. This undermined the socio-economic base of the collective Nigerian people as it led to the disruption in the production of agricultural goods.[579] At the

---

[575] Cf. D. Rieff, A Bed for the Night, 31.
[576] Cf. G. Bolton, Poor Story, 40.
[577] Cf. Wilfred Beckermann, A Poverty of Reason, Sustainable Development and Economic Growth, Oakland, California, 2003, 14. This is exemplified by the fact that "the great famines of the twentieth century, ...were caused not by failures of supply to keep up with demand but by civil wars or appalling government policies, such as the collectivization policies carried out by Stalin in pre-war period and China's 'Great Leap forward' after World War II."
[578] L. J. Lewis, Society, Schools and Progress in Nigeria, 7.
[579] Cf. W. Rodney, How Europe underdeveloped Africa, 129.

abolition in 1807 and beyond, many notorious communities were rendered economically powerless because of their dependence on this nefarious act.

Also the imperial politics of the gradual displacement of food crops for cash crops increased the trading mechanism and the expansion of the export sector for foreign goods. It thus created neglect in the local production sector and as a consequence, Nigeria "from 1955 to 1965 suffered a growing yearly deficit. Exports, though rising in quantity, held virtually steady in their earnings, while imports increased in both volume and cost."[580] Commodity trade is a fragile, feeble and non productive system of economy, which soon extended into the petroleum sector from the 1970s. It thus created a culture of laziness, corruption, narrow-mindedness and consequently diverted the private and public sector's attention towards rent and not on the much advocated manufacturing sector. This negative hindsight underpins the need for a return to the system of production, because it remains the only key to economic breakthrough and increased general welfare.

Based on the economic advantages of the western nations, their Catholic dioceses, western founded churches and agencies have become global ecclesiastical centre for appeals to the churches in the developing world; also are the governments of developed nations in relation to the governments of developing nations. As such, humanitarian actors interested in the growth of Nigerian churches for over a hundred years till today have been relating with agencies to canvass for funds to build and maintain structures. Virtually every Nigerian Catholic diocese has lived through the many years of her existence on the benevolence of such agencies.[581] It therefore, calls for a turnaround to look inwards, how to increase local production, which is the gateway to the humanitarian goal of improved standard of living and the general welfare of humanity. This responsibility calls for the empowerment and capacity building towards self reliance.

Capitalism has become undoubtedly the driving maxim in today's global economy and it is the most up-to-date engine of wealth creation, better than any other system that pre-existed it, because without wealth you

---

[580] Chinweizu, The West and rest of us, 264.
[581] Cf. U. Obodoechina, The Imperative of Self- Reliance, 41; (See also M. Mammi, The Financial Self-Reliance of the Church in Africa, 335-345.

cannot create schools, hospitals, build roads, provide security and so on.[582] One way to achieve this is through exploring the local opportunities and potentials that could prompt the ingenuities hidden in the local people to increase their capacity and capabilities to produce their ordinary needs and wants. Adam Smith admits that, "farmers, traders and producers [are] the three agents of growth ... [therefore they] can help in developing the economy, by raising productivity in their respective spheres. In the absence of a free market economy, state can induce them to produce more."[583] Because of the unwavering belief of the people in mission enterprise, the humanitarian church is called to fill this vacuum in a Nigerian society that experiences a poor leadership structure. The church is therefore challenged to proffer solutions to increase the capacity to produce from the available resources. She must be involved in teaching the people how they are "to organise themselves with fields and factories, schools and hospitals, places where citizens can work and produce goods useful for themselves and additional goods to be traded".[584] This will lead nations and people out of poverty.

4.1.1   Building sustainability from available resources

Even though the term sustainable development has been used in varied ways, it was first introduced into the international realm by the Brundtland report of the World Commission on Environment and Development (WCED) in 1987. It is termed "as a development that meets the needs of the present without compromising the ability of future generations to meet their own needs".[585] From this commission the foundation for sustainable development was laid and a new leitmotiv for environmental policies was born. Ever since then the principle of sustainable development has been recognised as a social principle among the existing social principles of human dignity, solidarity, subsidiarity and common good

---

[582] Cf. G. Bolton, Poor Story, 309.

[583] M.L. Jhingan, The Economics of Development and Planning, New Delhi, 2004, 87.

[584] Pippo Ranci, Economy and Finance for Everyone, Nairobi, 2012, 10.

[585] Peter Bartelmus, et.al, Translating Sustainable Development into Practice: a 'Patchwork' of some Concepts and an Introduction to Material Flows Analysis, in: Eds., Raimund Bleischwitz, Peter Hennicke, Eco-Efficiency, Regulation and sustainable Business, Towards a governance structure for sustainable development, Cheltenham, 2004, Pp. 1-32, 2. It is also called the Brundtland Commission, named after the former Norwegian Head of State Gro Harlem Brundtland. This commission prepared the UNCSD conference for the earth summit in Rio de Janeiro.

in the CST. Sustainable development therefore, refers to the general societal and global development in social ecological and economic development that considers present and future generations.[586]

Despite the widespread nature of the WCED report, it however failed to present a comprehensible image of what this terminology is in relation to the different disciplines where its usage was already commonplace.[587] Its perceptions and perspectives differ to the industrial and developing nations of the world. For the west, it is about the quality of life because of increased environmental consciousness and the effect of wasteful use of resources, whereas for the developing nations it is about sustaining the very existing population since she they are still confronted with the struggle for survival. Moreover, in the struggle to maintain these basic needs, they destroy the resources for the future. This approach brings the global fight for sustainable development on different fronts.[588] Nevertheless, Robert Allen defines sustainable development as the "development that is likely to achieve lasting satisfaction of human needs and improvement of quality of human life".[589] This could likely form a contextual definition of sustainable development from a perspective of a developing nation, because present quality will determine the future too. Another definition that fits this contextual meaning of sustainability is that of the 'International Union for the Conservation of Nature' (IUCN) in 1991. It defines sustainability as the "development that improves the quality of human life while living within the carrying capacity of supporting ecosystems".[590]

The Pre-colonial economy was primarily a subsistent agricultural production and the surplus was traded in exchange for a few goods with neighbours. Today the Nigerian state structure is the responsible agent to guarantee that local demands and supplies are met. Such a drive for sustainable development was the primary economic reason that led many western states from the 16th century in the exploration of other parts of the

---

[586] Cf. Werner Veith, Nachhaltigkeit, in: Ed., Marianne Heimbach-Stein, Christliche Sozialethik, Bd. I, Regensburg, 2004, 302.

[587] Cf. S. Michael, Undermining Development, The absence of Power among local NGOs in Africa, Bloomington, 2004, 131.

[588] Cf. Jennifer A. Elliot, An Introduction to Sustainable Development, the developing World, London, 1994, 1.

[589] Ibid. 3.

[590] Stephen Morse, et al., Visions of Sustainability, Stakeholders, Change and Indicators, Aldershot, 2000, 5.

world to maintain and sustain the growing population and industrial demands of their metropolis.[591] Its consequent political factor was the extensive attention towards export of goods from the colonies to the imperial nations. This political factor, the ensued preference of cash crops over food crops set the precedent for recurring famine in many sub-Saharan African nations. Nigerians therefore, became producers for export, that were never beneficial to her;[592] whereas any "...healthy economy, because of its right orientation, has as its first priority its domestic increase and integration. In a healthy economy, foreign trade, however vital to continued prosperity, is never allowed to dislocate, with detriment, the old patterns of prosperity."[593] This trade destroyed, wrecked and weakened the production capacity of many sub-Saharan communities over the time. Studies have proven that incidence of hunger and starvation in many parts of the world is "far more the result of political developments than of any technological limitations on the potential to supply food for the inhabitants".[594] Contrary to many nerve-racking claims about Africa as a den of hunger, some genetic studies have disproved pre-colonial Africans as an abode of hunger, malnutrition and starvation, albeit life was short, brutal and full of atrocities like other pre-civilised world. Pre-colonial African diets in many independent communities were varied, even though they did not meet present global standard. Besides, even the available nutritional consciousness in the developed world today is an evidence of the progress and development in technology, science and trade since after World War II. The menace of Nigerian and African stagnation in general over these years brings out the conspicuous difference between African nations as developing nations and other parts of the world as developed and emerging nations today. Most Africans who suffered specific nutritional deficit at the beginning of colonialism for example, were those brought into the colonial economy, especially the urban workers. A Brazilian scientist Josué de Castro (1908-1973) offers succinct studies of different African communities showing that primitive Africans in the tropics never showed any clinical sign of dietary deficiency.[595] Nigeria and many other African societies were launched unprepared into the global economy, because no matter how deplorable the site of the rural areas may look, "rural

---

[591] Cf. Fredrick D. Lugard, The Dual Mandate in British Tropical Africa, Edinburg, 1922, 613.
[592] Cf. U. Obodoechina, The imperative of Self-Reliance, 101.
[593] Chinweizu, The West and the Rest of us, 221.
[594] W. Bekermann, A Poverty of Reason, 15-16.
[595] Cf. W. Rodney, How Europe underdeveloped Africa, 259-261.

poverty is not ... [as] degrading and intractable as urban poverty. There is still a good chance for rural people to support and feed themselves."[596] It accounts for one of the reasons why urban dwellers often relocate to rural areas in moments of recession or prolonged periods of unemployment. Nevertheless, this problem goes in a circle because "disease, malnutrition and low productivity form in fact a vicious circle... the peasant, because of the multiplicity of diseases to which he is exposed [to] and which saps his energy, is often an inefficient agriculturalist."[597]

These findings are neither intended to discharge, acquit nor to condemn anyone but to serve as a gadfly to waken sensibilities towards past and contemporary failures. These findings echo the reoccurring negative role of past and present Africans in the history of humanity, who have left a void of production within the continent; otherwise predators would not have dared to fill the space in their own way. In addition, the essence of this background knowledge is to show that human community everywhere has this basic intent to sustain its population. It will be absurd, therefore to overlook that missing link in the case of Nigeria and sub-Saharan Africa in general. It is not a search for a scapegoat, but a soul-searching strategy to identify the collective faults of a people and about her present dependency syndrome; it is about a people asking questions to know why they are where they are today. This knowledge will help to fill the already created mental void, a means that will provoke new thoughts and ideas towards sustainability that has been failing in many years. Thus knowing how it was lost will help in the search to get back to the foundation, because "each generation must, out of relative obscurity discover its mission, fulfil it, or betray it."[598] Therefore, the proposed humanitarian job which is the basics of this work is not only to contain past and prospective failures alone but also a search for decisive measures to root out the dearth responsible for the humanitarian failure in the first place and to avoid a repetition in the future.

To fill this void created by the lack of production capacity will demand an arduous study of the available resources within every community. The adopted system of reflection by the DDS has revealed that

---

[596] A. Shorter, Religious Poverty in Africa, 6
[597] L. J. Lewis, Society, Schools and Progress in Nigeria, 8 (See also; A Brown, Land and People of Nigeria, University of London Press, London 1955)
[598] Chinweizu, The West and the Rest of us, 185; (See also Frantz Fanon, The Wretched of the Earth, New York, 2004, 145).

Nigerian communities were not only agrarian; they were into production but were stagnated over time. But if agriculture was the greatest pre-colonial economic mainstay of many Nigerian communities, how come there is a distortion in this development in the first place? Why has this factor of continuity eluded the entire region and many sub-Saharan African communities for long? Because humanity everywhere desires food, shelter and clothing, these basics form the fundamental duties of parents toward their offspring. It is these basics that set the difference between the human person made in the image and likeness of God from other animals.[599] It is a role that has been disproportionately disregarded in Nigeria and Africa at large. Moreover, why is hunger so prevalent in Nigeria and like a synonym with the name Africa? There are definitely many horrendous global reasons for hunger like the war induced hunger in the case of present South Sudan. However, some African nations like Ghana are today writing a new story altogether. The 2015 FAO reports opine that about 12 million Nigerians are undernourished, which is 7% of the population.[600] According to the principle of subsididarity, a middle income nation like Nigeria could avoid this hunger scenario through equitable distribution of local resources.[601] Nonetheless it is the "persistent accumulation of wealth among a few and the unequal distribution of the benefits of growth [that has] continue[d] to make development unsustainable."[602] For this reason, the local church with her age long humanitarian presence is called to take recourse in the divine mandate of Genesis creation account (cf. Gen 1-2; 23) that guarantees local demands and supply be met from the available resources. From this biblical creation account, the human person was the last being to be created after all other animals and vegetation were created and established. Therefore, it is necessary

> for the church to teach that God intended the earth and all that it contains for the use of all men so that all earthly goods flow fairly to all under the principle of justice, charity, and love. The urgency and importance of this principle [justice, charity and love] was stressed by St. Ambrose, who taught that when

---

[599] Cf. F. Nuscheler, Entwicklungspolitik, 230.

[600] Cf. Food and Agriculture Organisation of the United Nations, (FAO) International Fund for Agricultural Development, (IFAD) World Food Programme, (WFP) The State of food insecurity in the World, meeting the 2015 hunger targets: taking stock of uneven progress, 2015, Rome, 45.

[601] Cf. Joachim Wiemeyer, Globalisierung als Herausforderung der Christlichen Sozialethik, Beobachtungen und weiterführende Überlegungen, in: Ed., A. Fritzsche, M. Kwiran, Kirchen und Gesellschaft, Ökumenische Sozialethik, Vol. III, München, 2000, 1-12, 5.

[602] National Human Development Report, 2015, 11.

one complies with this Christian principle of universal purpose of earthly goods, by helping the poor, one is just performing an act of justice, not charity.[603]

This act of helping the poor should transcend the offering of a pittance for survival in favour of a holistic and welfare approach. Without this the principle of self-reliance will be jeopardised and humanitarian works will resort to going in circles. It suffices to say that humanity has been divinely placed to benefit from the fruits of the earth. It would also be adequate to say that every community is endowed with resources to sustain her, but it is the failing ingenuity on one hand and the abounding avarice on the other hand that encourages societal indecencies like subjugation, exploitation and other crimes against humanity. Moreover, many of the social encyclicals have communicated this relationship of the human person towards the goods of this earth in this principle: "The bounty of the earth has been given by God to all people equally- without exception and without preference."[604] This assertion is buttressed by the amnesty publication that "there is more than enough food produced in the world to feed everyone."[605] The statistics of malnourished people today has drastically reduced from 90% of the previous 1 billion world population in 1800 to 12% of present population of 7 billion, which is the lowest ever. However, Amnesty still reiterates the need for every state to ensure that the right to adequate food be guaranteed to her citizens and to tackle this menace so that men, women and children have access to food and the means to procure it.[606]

Since the second Vatican council, there has been a growing emphasis on the need for maturation of the mission churches to the status of local churches. As a result, more attention has been focused on the autonomy of the churches, funding and leadership. Many of the local churches therefore have invented several methods and the concept of self-reliance over the time.[607] Nevertheless, it has proved unsatisfactory to provide the

---

[603] Obioma Des Obi, Church's Role in Alleviation of Poverty in Contemporary Nigerian Society, in: Ed., Sasa Michael Sunday, West African Journal of Ecclesial Studies, (WAJES) Ibadan, 2009, 92.
[604] Charles K. Wilber, Catholics Spending and Acting Justly, A small- Group guide for Living Economic Stewardship, Indiana, 2009, 8. (See also Quadragesimo Anno, 46; Rerum Novarum,14; Centesimus annus, 6.)
[605] Amnesty International, Human Rights for Human Dignity, A Primer on Economic Social and Cultural Rights, Oxford, 2005, 17.
[606] Cf. Ibid.
[607] Cf. U. Obodoechina, The Imperative of Self-Reliance, 168.

innumerable demands of the local church because the church too lives within the borders of the state and as such is affected by the state's policy. Even though the church does not seek to interfere in state affairs, she carries the message of Christ through bearing witness to the truth to save and not to judge, to serve and not to be served.[608] The church's duty also is to share in "...the noblest aspirations of men and [in their] suffering when she sees [that] these aspirations [are] not satisfied, she wishes to help them attain their full realization. So she offers man her distinctive contribution: a global perspective on man and human realities."[609] If the church, saddled with the responsibility to care for the poor wishes to be relevant despite her dwindling capital, then she needs to build and develop a sustainability base as her contribution towards peace, bearing in mind the emphasis of the encyclical *Populorum progressio*, on the need for the development of the people as another name for peace.[610]

How is the church with her meagre resources to ensure this development of the people which is a consequent development of peace? In an expanded view on the meaning of peace, Michael Barnett also captions this peace evolving process from the perspective of development as a concept of the age of Liberal humanitarianism. After the cold war "humanitarianism and security collapsed under peace building, which became known as liberal peace building because of the emphasis on the importance of markets, democracy, and human rights for curing states of their ills and creating more peaceful and progressive societies."[611] To be part of the development process of this peace building age, the humanitarian church, an agent of change must come to terms with issues like the market relevance, democracy and human rights. Like the early missionaries, she must take additional steps to develop a broad base of sustainable development in the teaching and encouragement of entrepreneurial way of life in her people. Without such financial strength, she will resort to only cheap substitutes, like alms and sometimes at the mercy of societal miscreants, the very agents of injustice. The presence of such entrepreneurial force from both church and private is a first step towards meeting her aspirations and that of her many beleaguered faithful.

---

[608] Cf. Paul VI, Populorum Progressio, 13.
[609] Ibid.
[610] Cf. Paul VI, Populorum Progressio, 76.
[611] M. Barnett, The Empire of Humanity, 164.

4.1.2   Building entrepreneurial culture

There has been a positive changing attitude over the years in the concept of entrepreneurship in Nigeria. In the past, entrepreneurial culture was "largely defined by necessity driven entrepreneurship; that is entrepreneurship as a means of survival. [It was] viewed as a last resort, as opposed to the pursuit of an opportunity or aspiration."[612] What is clear today is that cultivating entrepreneurial skills is a key factor for economic sustainability. This culture involves the preparedness of a people towards undertaking risks through increased quest for creativity and inventions in their different walks of life. It forms the backbone of any thriving economy and is built on the foundation of indigenous industries. It is the manufacturing sector that enhances the production of such goods and services for the people's welfare. Today, its expansion, growth and development have become the yardstick for efficiency and success rating of any state. Industries are unceasingly subjected to the change and chance mechanism of the environment just like the factors of demand and supply; it is an impulse for continuous transformation and improvement in production. Accordingly, the people's needs and the available natural resources "determine the pattern of relevant skills developed and multiplied, the selection of technologies imported, adapted, and developed locally, the type of institutional services provided, and the domestic flows of financial and material resources."[613] William H. Lever (1851-1925) from 1885 began the Unilever soap-making firm in a swamp in Merseyside near Liverpool. It was an entrepreneurial spirit that emerged from the available resources and the need of his people. As the firm grew from strength to strength over the years the township of Port Sunlight emerged from the name of the soap firm 'sunlight'. Despite the competition from other similar industries and the later threat for merger with UAC, Unilever maintained its name and grandeur and from the little household production, it emerged as a multi- corporation.[614] Industries therefore, grow from little household firms to companies, to mega companies and sometimes to multinational corporations. This growth

---

[612] David McKenzie, Identifying and spurring High-Growth Entrepreneurship. Experiment Evidence from a Business Plan Competition, Policy Research Working Paper, World Bank Group, August 2015, 3 (See also Omidyar Network, 2013, p. 18).
[613] Adebayo Adedeji, The Monrovia Strategy and the Lagos Plan of Action, Five years after, in: Eds., Adebayo Adedeji, Timothy M. Shaw, Economic Crisis in Africa, African Perspectives on Development Problems and Potentials, Boulder Colorado, 1985, Pp. 9-34, 16.
[614] Cf. W. Rodney, How Europe underdeveloped Africa, 199-201.

includes the harmonization of the economic and technical evolution with the social adaptation of the people. The inability of such progression and coordination remains one major industrial hurdle in Nigeria.[615] This is partly because many industries still take the 'top-down' model like AADP, a model of industrialisation where the political class since the 60s 'lobby' multi-corporations from the industrialised nations to set up industries in Nigeria.

Definitely Nigeria needs the services of industrially developed firms, such that local workers can have technical skills to improve home production. It was through such skills that the Japanese and Germans after World War II were able to break into the global market in the 70s; thus breaking the monopoly of the American dominance in global economy. This was repeated 1970-1990 in South Korea, China, Taiwan and other nations today.[616] Unfortunately, the many foreign industries that are or have come and gone in Nigeria have delivered little or no technical know-how to the local workers. Because of this factor, even the purported oil sector, a supposedly natural gift to Nigeria, has suffered considerable setback. Nigeria remains a petrochemical Lilliput despite her active presence in the petro-business for decades. The inability of added value to the petroleum product stems from the fact that there are hardly any indigenous petrochemical and subsidiary industries. What appears on papers today as indigenous petro-industries are more or less companies of 'oil wells' and 'oil blocs' owned by 'big shots', to be sold out to foreign oil firms in return for royalties. Whereas the goal of every foreign investment is for the local staff to learn and perfect the know-how, it is mostly the reverse in the Nigerian industries. The Nigerian political elite has been criticised for being accomplices and in conspiracy with the foreign firms just for their pecuniary advantage. Their 'success' lies in 'scavenging' and lobbying for foreign industries and firms to be located in their communities so as to score cheap political points from their electorates as a mark of their contribution towards development and employment. It explains why communities would even encourage potentially dangerous industries with track records of unfriendly environmental policies

---

[615] Cf. Heinz-Dietrich Ortlieb, Entwicklungshilfe für Afrika, Bemerkungen zu den politischen und wirtschaftlichen Entwicklungsproblemen westafrikanischer Länder, in: Ed., Heinz-Dietrich Ortlieb, Hamburger Jahrbuch, Tübingen, 1961, Pp. 25-44, 30.

[616] Cf. Mahbub. Ul Haq, Reflection on human development, how the focus of development economics shifted from national income accounting to people centred policies, told by one of the architects of the new paradigm, Oxford, 1995, 31-32.

to be sited in their community, whereas in the developed world the reverse is the case.

Apart from the absence of sound industrial policies, the provision of a sound and broad based human capital development is a panacea to end this industrial anaemia. So long as these investments are not locally integrated, it means they lack the basic foundation and they are only Nigerian in name. What the community may benefit is mainly from the menial jobs offered to the peasants, while the expatriates and local experts (if any) take over the main jobs. Such firms do not guarantee employment sustainability. Besides, every manufacturing unit has a technological history with basic intelligence and techniques gathered over the years. They may release peripheral skills to the public, but key information and technologies are retained as top secret and no amount of money can buy them, because that is the strength, existence, the being and the *dasein* of the company. There is no human person, who after long years of intensive labour, toil with casualty records and research costs that will confer his innermost and hard-earned technological findings to a 'foreigner'. They are the product of "efficient accounting and business methods which... characterise[s] capitalist firms, [they] did not drop from the sky. They are the results of historical evolution..."[617] that cannot be given on a platter of gold. That was one of the greatest blunders of the Nigerian government especially from the oil boom era that money could buy technical intelligence. All over the world people crack and imitate technology, but the Nigerian successive governments have waited consistently on the mercies of expatriates.

The Monrovia strategy and the Lagos plan of action in 1980[618] for example emphasised the development of the indigenous factor as the most viable means of local industrialisation and consequent self-reliance. Without such strategies in view, local resources will remain perpetually in the hands of foreign companies who primarily pursue their own interests.[619] After 30 years the Lagos Plan of Action was succeeded by the Cotonou Partnership Agreement known as Africa, Caribbean, Pacific States - European Commission (ACP-EC) in 2000. It is sad enough to know that the many

---

[617] W. Rodney, How Europe underdeveloped Africa, 203.

[618] Cf. A. Adebayo, The Monrovia Strategy and the Lagos Plan of Action, 16. On the 29th April 1980, African leaders in an economic summit unanimously endorsed the Lagos Plan of Action for the Economic Development of Africa 1980-2000. This move was the first of its kind.

[619] Cf. Ibid.

predictions of the Lagos Plan of Action have come to pass. Nigeria today has become very much more economically dependent than she was in the 60s and 70s, with a very fragile economy and very much exposed to food imports and food aid to feed her growing population. Close to 90 percent of her capital requirements is imported and even Petroleum products and petroleum made goods, which ordinarily should be the preserve of Nigeria, are also imported.[620] These shameful and despicable traits are the problems of a politically dumb, fearful and ill informed public that has refused to take the bull by the horns. Despite the market size of Nigeria for her locally manufactured goods, the failed governmental policies and protection of local industries have warped the opportunity to create wealth and job opportunities; such that even petroleum products like fertilizers and other products have become scarce commodities today.

The Jonathan administration in 2011 did set up a business plan competition for young entrepreneurs in collaboration with different ministries: Finance, Communication, Technology and Youth Development with the support of DFID and World Bank. Its objective was basically to encourage innovation and the creation of new jobs by assisting the opening of new businesses and the expansion of existing ones. Many rigorous and stringent measures were put in place to determine the authenticity of the registered contestants; eligible winners were to receive the sum of 10 million Naira (US$64,000). Of the 23,844 applications, 3,614 were for existing business expansion while the rest were to set up new businesses. Contestants must be Nigerian citizens interested in entrepreneurship skill learning and should fall in the age bracket of 40 years old or less. Training was opened and offered in all the six geo-political zones. But one major problem of such programmes is that the greater population of attendants are usually urban dwellers mostly from Abuja and Lagos, such that the hinterlands are most times sparsely represented. There was the tendency to favour existing businesses rather than the new ones.[621] However, statistics proved that in the first three years the new businesses created more wealth and job opportunities than the already existing firms.[622] It was important too that the

---

[620] Cf. Ibid., 25-26.
[621] Cf. D. McKenzie, Identifying and spurring, 6-7.
[622] Cf. Ibid., 30.

programme should not be captured by individuals with political and ethnic ties.[623]

The creation of wealth in a society can trigger a chain of positive development like improved standard of living, quality of social services and so on. Despite the huge effort in the training of potential entrepreneurs, the presence of decayed infrastructures hinders the growth of entrepreneurial realization. Social institutions today are on the brink of final collapse and there is a systemic decay in all sectors of the economy. Good infrastructure connects firms to suppliers and customers and this enhances the use of modern technologies; whereas deficient infrastructure creates production barriers and increased cost of production. The acute shortcoming in electricity and water supply in Nigeria today mars the growth of the manufacturing sector terribly.[624] It is several years after the arrival of the 'Monrovia strategy and Lagos plan of action', yet her social predictions have come through. There is serious

> deterioration in the quality and quantity of social services. ...Access to education, health, potable water and electricity [today is only] available to a diminishing minority; cities [have] become overpopulated [with] ghettoes; and diseases, famine, riots and crimes [have] escalate[d]. In brief life [has become] short and brutish. Without doubt under the historical trends scenario, the 1960s seem[ed] like a golden age, and self-reliance and meaningful and effective political independence [seems] to the generation of 2008,... like slogans of the past...[625]

The stark difference between urban and rural bias makes these shortfalls very recurrent in the rural areas. Despite these, the deceptive publications of the United Nations Economic Commission for Africa sing gloriously that investment is replacing aid in Africa. The claim that investment has grown for example from US$9 billion in 2000 to US$62 billion in 2008 and according to IMF that GDP has grown annually at 5.7% seems like a political decoy by the ruling class. The truth remains that the peripheral people are not feeling this growth, because they are top-down investment. The GDP rise does not translate into improving the lives of the ordinary folks; instead it widens the gap of the mammoth poverty in the midst of

---

[623] Cf. Ibid., 10.

[624] Cf. International Finance Corporation, (IFC) World Bank Group, Nigeria Country Profile, 2014, Washington DC, 6.

[625] A. Adebayo, The Monrovia Strategy and the Lagos Plan of Action, 26.

plenty.[626]Agreed, there are few fiscal structures in the cities, but development is not just the presence of skyscrapers. Unfortunately the tendency to mistake fiscal development for human development is one of the commonest features of underdevelopment in developing world.[627] Development rating therefore should not be restricted to GDP; rather it should be concentrated on the volume of physical goods produced with local expertise and domestic resources. What also matters is the level of diversification and how these developments spread to the length and breadth of the nation and are not restricted to the major cities alone.[628]

Modern government protects indigenous firms and in return firms owe some 'loyalty' to the mother nation. Though firms are driven by profit motives, they still need the protective base of the state to thrive. Such state protection makes a nation a lucrative and investment friendly environment to local firms and to would-be entrepreneurs; this in turn discourages to a great extent the kind of corruption between entrepreneurs and government officials since the terms of relationship are constitutionally protected. Though it is not the entire solution to corruption, because issues of corruption are multifaceted, it could serve as a contribution. Nevertheless, corrupt practices of public officials create administrative and financial burdens on firms. The demand for unofficial payments and bribes for operating licenses and permits have distressed the growth of entrepreneurial ambition in Nigeria.[629] New firms and young entrepreneurs are sometimes subjected to clandestine demands, which consequently scare them away from the production scene. Whereas multinationals like Shell for example are able to stay put and play along despite the corruption tide, by flexing their financial muscles to mend broken walls that are created by this institutional vacuum.[630] It consequently affirms the grip of the manufacturing sector in the hands of expatriates and the few Nigerians who 'understand'

---

[626] Cf. Joseph Ogbonnaya, Religion and Sustainable Development on Africa, in: African Catholicism and Hermeneutics of culture, Essays in the Light of African Synod II, Eugene, 2014, Pp. 55-74, 62-64, (See also Commission for Africa our common interest 76.)
[627] Cf. James Shikwati, Redefined Governance – Key to Africa's Development, in: Ed., Johannes Michael Nebe, Herausforderung Afrika, Baden Baden, 2011, 176-172, 167.
[628] Cf. A. Adebayo, The Monrovia Strategy and the Lagos Plan of Action, 26.
[629] Cf. International Finance Corporation, World Bank Group, 9.
[630] Cf. Andy Rowell, James Marriott, Leone Stockman, The next Gulf, London, Washington and oil Conflict in Nigeria, London, 2005, 14.

the shady politics of Nigeria.[631] Because of this backdrop, the manufacturing sector of Nigeria since independence is commandeered by the expatriates and mischievous Nigerians that perpetually hoodwink the nation. For example, the misdemeanours of oil boom experience produced an industrial impasse that "even as Nigerians and foreigners were galloping Nigeria on into the industrial age, it was clear the country was never going to make the jump."[632] Since independence, the Nigerian government has squandered enormous resources on this wild goose chases. It is imperative for a robust governmental regulatory and supervisory body to checkmate such a flaw. Hence, the informal sector thrives arbitrarily, because it mainly survives by cutting through the red tape and bottlenecks but also poses "unfair competition for [the] formal units".[633] Of all the drafted development plans since independence, one thing is clear today that development has a lot more to do with the people than money.[634] It is about offering research opportunities, improving, adapting, adopting, upgrading and modernising the traditional mode of production but not only by attracting foreign firms to do them. The present political structure is in a development deadlock and Chinua Achebe (1930-2013) describes this scenario as the "commonest manifestations of underdevelopment... tendency among the ruling elite... liv[ing] in a world of make-believe and unrealistic expectations"[635]. This inclination plunges the nation daily into the abyss of poverty and economic stagnation. Even though the nation is caught up today in this dependence syndrome, the humanitarian church must take practical steps towards human capacity development programmes to teach entrepreneurial culture in order to arrest this stalemate.

One of the greatest predicaments of a people is the inability to believe in her own selves and her discoveries. There are countless discoveries made by Nigerians that have ended up in the workshops of foreign firms, because of government's naivety, short-sightedness, greed, indecisions and the lack of political will to go beyond this status. The production of palm oil in Nigeria for example, one of the past outstanding sources of revenue, has remained on the primitive level of production to

---

[631] Cf. Julius O. Ihonvbere, Timothy Shaw, Illusions of Power, Nigeria in Transition, Trenton, 1998, 28.
[632] M. Peel, A Swamp full of Dollars, 60.
[633] International Finance Corporation, World Bank Group, 10.
[634] Cf. J. O. Ihonvbere, T. Shaw, Illusions of Power, 84.
[635] Chinua Achebe, An Image of Africa, London, 1983, 29.

date. Malaysia in the 80s collected palm seedlings from Nigeria and today accounts for the highest producer of palm oil. Nigeria can learn from the Malaysian experience, the cost of labour in Nigeria is cheap which means reduced cost of production. Obiora Ike of CIDJAP (Catholic Institute of development justice and peace Enugu) advises governments and NGOs not to go in search of new policies but to put in place practical methods to actualise what exists already. Development does not come from the air but through visible transformation. Efforts must be made to tap from the existing structures otherwise the social status may remain unchanged.[636] The humanitarian church is challenged to tap into the present Nigerian structure to invest in such projects like Palm oil farms, firms and sales. It is not too bogus a business venture for churches and religious houses, after all monasteries and nunneries in Europe in the Middle-Ages were centres of such creative production. If dioceses and religious bodies are involved in such projects, it will go a long way towards changing the face of the economy.

The Catholic Laity Council of Nigeria, CLCN made a suggestion in 1987 that parishes "could embark small scale industries, operating grinding machines, buying and selling of agricultural products and establishing a printing press."[637] Also the CLCN was challenged from within to think and plan towards active participation in the economic and especially industrial life of the nation. The CLCN came out with robust plans to "establish a reputable company with major branches in all the dioceses of the country and minor branches in parishes. The diocese could be made to subscribe the shares of the company according to their usual categories."[638] This idea carries the humanitarian message of building an exemplary church that emphasises and teaches entrepreneurial culture. Even though it is profit oriented the service aspect is very important to the humanitarian mantra of being a vanguard of change to assist humanity. The primary intention is not profit-making like every other contemporary business but to bring the Christian values to the forefront. Just as dioceses and parishes play a spiritual central role for all within their jurisdiction, they could as well serve

---

[636] Cf. Obiora Ike, Human capital development, panacea to national growth, http://www.cidjap.org/invest-in-human-capital-development-don-urges-ngos-government.php (08.03.16)
[637] Gabriel Afolabi Ojo, Catholic Laity in Nigeria, Yesterday, Today, Tomorrow, Ibadan, 2004, 272.
[638] Ibid.

as the hub of socio-economic activities for the socio-economic transformation and emancipation.

It is on this ground that humanitarians are meant to serve as a gadfly in the issues of development in developing nations. Because, humanitarian work is not only about sharing relief materials but also engaging average minds into innovative thinking. However, this step is not meant to discredit humanitarian achievements on one hand and on the other hand it is not to exaggerate the work of humanitarians and development workers. It is meant to motivate the humanitarian to offer the right impulse for such a societal animated progressive process; because the growth of indigenous industries gives the people industrial foundation, self-reliance and the needed self esteem to make other global exploits.

4.2 The education and re-educational strategy

The manner and mode of education says it all about a people and their future, because "the good health of a nation is largely dependent on the quality of education of her citizens."[639] The herculean task of overhauling an educational system will require first of all a cursory glance at the broad meaning of education and its conceptual meaning in Nigeria. Many scholars have varying opinions about education, however, Andrew A. Onokerhoraye defines education as "the process by which every society attempts to reserve and upgrade the accumulated knowledge, skills and attitudes in its cultural setting and heritage in order to foster continuously the well-being of mankind and guarantee its survival against the unpredictable and at times hostile and destructive elements and forces of man and nature".[640] The pre-colonial nations in Nigeria had varying informal educational systems in their empires, kingdoms and chiefdoms; they were the oldest and indigenous educational systems. The advent of Islamic education especially in northern Nigeria dates back to the 1803 jihadist conquest. Thus, Islamic education pre-existed western education in many parts of Nigeria, while Christianity the harbinger of western education had its roots since 1842. The customary educational system in many of these pre-colonial states was oral and informal, also its collective objectives were to conform the child to societal

---

[639] Catholic Bishops' Conference of Nigeria (CBCN), Church and State Partnership in the Provision of Quality Education, Communiqué at the end of the First Plenary Meeting of the Catholic Bishops' Conference of Nigeria (CBCN) at the Divine Love Retreat and Conference Centre Sabon Lugbe, Abuja, 8th -14th March, 2014, 3.

[640] A. A. Onokerhoraye, Social Services in Nigeria, 11.

accepted norms, that he or she belonged to the society, was part and a product of the society; it was a very strong factor and the child was thereby taught to respect elders of the society. Unlike western education, indigenous education was a makeshift of fables, stories, folklores, names of trees, and these were compulsory intellectual exercises. Besides, the promotion of skills was held in high esteem, which leads eventually to the choice of a later vocation. While the boys were limited to the choice of their father's occupation, the girls were to become good housewives.[641]

The literal learning style of colonial education era aimed at providing a working class of clerks and other minor jobs for the colonial administrative and missionary working force encouraged 'bookishness'. It is a book learning rather than practical skill learning process,[642] thereby encouraging later a white collar job dominated economy to the detriment of blue collar jobs. This system unfortunately survived through the educational landscape even after the independence. Despite the criticisms of educational experts in several forums, subsequent adopted reforms and evolved educational methods have not plausibly effected meaningful change in contemporary Nigeria. Whereas what Nigeria like any other sub-Saharan country needs today is a future economic and political independence that is engrossed in a pragmatic educational system; a sort of system that is built on the foundation of a technical, scientific, technological and political training.[643] The educational system needs to be clear on what it intends to instil in the young minds because ideas rule the world. Besides every nation has a right to conceive and develop an educational system that is relevant to its history, people, antecedence and that which can withstand the contemporary and universal challenges of what globalisation entails.[644] The nation must take into consideration her underlying problems: the socio-economic and political development, so that men and women could be trained in a satisfactory manner to acquire the necessary skills to be able to exploit the natural resources of the nation for the benefit of all and not the self. Also, they are to be imbued with the spirit of co-operation with all people to enhance the development of the nation.[645] The innumerable problems and challenges bewildering the nation, like armed robbery,

---

[641] Cf. Ibid. 12.
[642] Cf. L.J. Lewis, School Society and Progress in Nigeria, 26.
[643] Cf. H. D. Ortlieb, Entwicklungshilfe für Afrika, 30.
[644] Cf. J. Wiemeyer, Keine Freiheit ohne Gerechtigkeit, 199.
[645] Cf. L.J. Lewis, Society, Schools and Progress in Nigeria, 3.

corruption, poverty, abuse of power, discrimination and so on can only be confronted by investing in quality education.[646] President Obasanjo in Dakar Senegal on the 27th April 2000 buttressed this point that for Nigeria to be reckoned as a global force in the 21st century, her human capital must be empowered to play for the required socio-political and economic emancipation.[647]

The application of the see judge and act could help to bare the facade covering the epileptic educational system over the years. Thus, the ideal society which humanitarians ought to conceive would remain unattainable if the application of the ideals of education into contemporary Nigerian situation is not implemented. The Nigerian society today is facing a hydra of perplexing, weak and ignorant scenarios from a failed educational system that has contributed abysmally to her corporate entity and as a sovereign nation. Through comparison with the present global standards, one is able to judge the vagueness of the present educational system. What is the plausible act to avoid further pitfalls? If truly new results are intended then the mould of education must be broken, otherwise it shall keep yielding the same end results. This informs the need for a change in the orientation and the need to cultivate a new attitude of looking inwardly, building and developing on the human capabilities and to jettison overt dependence on the fortunes of natural resources. Such dependence only brings out the poverty of the mind of a people, like the great philosopher Hegel (1770-1831) will say that the environment is the reflection of the mind, therefore what is obvious today is a true picture and an existent reflection of the minds.[648] The next question is, how is the mind to be redesigned to see its shortfall and to conceive new thoughts?

Julius Nyerere (1922-1999) proposes a very new first step which includes the re-education of the African to "regain our former attitude of mind. In our traditional African society we were individuals within a community, and the community took care of us. We neither needed nor wished to exploit our fellow men,"[649] but today those tenets have been eroded with modern principles, not because modernity is itself bad but Africa's method of adaptation into the global space is totally out of touch

---

[646] Cf. CBCN, Church and State Partnership in the Provision of quality Education, 3.
[647] Cf. G. A. Ojo, Catholic Laity of Nigeria, 298.
[648] Cf. David Rose, Hegel's Philosophy of Right, London, 2007, 12
[649] A. Shorter, Theology of Mission 49, (See also Julius Nyerere, Ujaama, Oxford, 1968, 6-7.)

with the African culture. Every culture is dynamic, modifies, changes and improves through contacts, however, the vacuum and the void created by this inability to connect the African worldview and western methods for over five hundred years makes the retracing task very cumbersome. The Nigerian people "will have to rediscover and promote a concept of a person and his or her relationship with reality [and] that is the fruit of a profound spiritual renewal".[650] It is worthwhile in the spirit of this renewal to be acquainted with national/local antecedence and like the Igalas would say, 'even if you fail to know your destination, know your background.'[651] Though the retracing process of past steps may be an uphill task, it is necessary and will help to straighten the path to the Promised Land. On this retracing and rediscovery mission, the Nigerian is called to learn the new ways of doing things. The new ways do not undermine the aboriginal but are called to mature in a rational growth to develop the individual nature that was inherent but seemingly unaddressed in the different cultural milieu; through this he or she grapples with the expected responsibility to face the future.[652]

Since the church was the initiator of western education, she could still play this *diakonein* role at this critical period of educational underdevelopment to set the nation in a new development motion, to decolonise the mind and engage the young minds in critical thinking, to ask questions, be inquisitive and above all to be proactive. The presence of churches and private hands in the affairs of school in the 80s because of the liberal policy of states was a right step in the right direction. The next step should be to improve on the contents of learning, since the schools have the liberty of its contents. It should be a well accentuated step to decolonise the mind, to restore the failed self worth, to be aware of global realities, the perceptions of the world about Nigeria and Africa at large, to walk away from a stereotyped worldview of culture and people and to embrace a new and modified African thought pattern that will create new and original African dynamism. The European church has been heavily involved in charting ways to solve the social malaise of her time. It is high time the church in Africa taught "the continent [on how it] should be self-centred and work for its own interest instead of responding simply to the interests of others. This involves a re-education of African youth: a re-education in self confidence, hard work, self reliance, self sacrifice, virtue, and uprightness; a

---

[650] Benedict XVI, Africae Munus, 11.
[651] Ẹma chaka m ugbo k ẹlon, ẹ mugbo kẹ kwo.
[652] Cf. H. D. Ortlieb, Entwicklungshilfe für Afrika, 30.

re-education of the masses of Africa to consume less in order to invest in the future–the future of their youth."[653]

Self-centredness is not to be mistaken with selfishness, because for centuries national interests have been sacrificed on the altar of betrayal and naivety. The idea of self-centredness includes the re-positioning of any nation even before the self. The volumes of information humans receive and digest determine their power of inquisition. The answers are there in the universe but the human person needs to be critical to unlock the secrets of the universe. These are traits that have been haphazardly developed in Nigeria and sub-Saharan Africa in general. Thus, the right to a full scale education is a doorway towards attaining professional heights in the society. The pool of such professionals would create the bulwark against exploitation of the nation (both from external and internal agents) and enhance the struggle for emancipation. This foundation creates the basis for a better and fulfilled life. It gives the masses the opportunity to stand against injustice and other social problems.[654]

For centuries, the economic landscape of Nigeria like many other African nations has been subjected to unspeakable exploitation from external forces. It is a void created by the lack of locally grown capacity to build, invent and upgrade the minimum standard of living for her people and as a result encourages outright dependency. These are the effect of failed and nonexistent educational objectives and ideologies, the greatest sham and the bane of the nation's woe today. This tendency will keep rearing its ugly head until the tools are acquired or invented to truly understand the universe. The inability to possess this mental tool which is proper education also means the failure to understand and to resist exploitation.[655] Moreover, education is far deeper than mere passing through the four walls of the classrooms or passing examinations. The impression one gets even today from the educational landscape of Nigeria still seems like a set of "pupils [in a classroom] just sponges, imbibing knowledge not understood or digested, [but just] for the sole purpose of regurgitating it for examination".[656] Albeit there are a few changes in some parameters today, the overt book-learning is still very

---

[653] E.E. Uzukwu, The Listening Church, 72.
[654] Cf. Internationale Politik und Gesellschaft, IGP, der ausblutende Kontinent, http://www.ipg-journal.de/kolumne/artikel/der-ausblutende-kontinent-942/ (03.06.15)
[655] Cf. Chimamanda Ngozi Adichie, Half of a Yellow Sun, New York, 2006, 13. "How can we resist exploitation, if we don't have the tools to understand exploitation"
[656] L.J. Lewis, Society, Schools and Progress in Nigeria, 78.

dominant in the Nigerian educational system. Therefore, passing examinations or 'coming out in flying colours' is not a determinant factor of possessing the educational tools to unlock the secrets of the universe, to match the tide of globalisation for example, to be innovative in the world of science and technology, respect for human life and dignity and to be able to break the prevailing chains of poverty. These qualities will guarantee a balanced human development concept for future progressive generation. One of the economic emphases of President Obama was the place of mathematics in the schools. To make a headway in the present world, children must be given a strong foundation in mathematics, easy access to information, competent use of the internet, proper funding of schools, creating an enabling environment for learning, avoiding overcrowded classrooms, creating opportunities for research and contacts studies, libraries and workshops.[657]

4.2.1 Situating the relevance of human development

The conceptual use of human development by disciplines like biology and psychology vary with the contextual connotation of human development. It refers to the offshoot of the developmental approach from the criticisms against the then established concept of human development in the 80s that presumed a link between national economic growth and the expansion of individual human choices. The works of Amartya Sen in 1988 was foundational to this development; the contributions of the Pakistani Economist Mahbub Ul Haq (1934-1998) in 1990 under the auspices of the United Nations Development Projects (UNDP) formulated the existing parameters for determining human development index today. Human development in this respect is about developing human capabilities; it thus includes ecological economy, the wellbeing of humans, economic growth, sustainable development, welfare economy, human capital and how these fall into the concept and standard of globalisation today.[658] His first Human development reports in 1990 spelt out clearly that "the real wealth of a nation is its people. And the purpose of development is to create an enabling environment for people to enjoy long, healthy and creative lives. This simple but powerful truth is too often forgotten in the pursuit of material and financial wealth."[659] Therefore "people are both the means and the end of

---

[657] Cf. J. Wiemeyer, Keine Freiheit ohne Gerechtigkeit, 195.
[658] Cf. Human Development Reports, http://hdr.undp.org/en/humandev/ (06/05/2010)
[659] M. Nussbaum, Creating Capabilities, 1.

economic development."[660] The church's view on human development comes from the fact of human dignity reflected in each person's humanity, intellect, freedom and conscience. Since humans are created in the image and likeness of God, they share in the dignity of God and if the gift of the intellect is accompanied with wisdom, humans are able to conquer their environment.[661] This makes humans the subject matter of every development; by implication anything short of this should be relegated from human development.

The hitherto overrated Gross National Product GNP reports most times disregarded the welfare of the poor in many societies because despite the rise of GNP the quality of human life still depreciates. This has created the maxim that human welfare is the true end of development and not the GNP. Human development teaches that economic planning must be geared towards integrating people into the production and distribution of wealth. The people must become the means and the end of such development.[662] This can be achieved through the humanitarian maxim of self-reliance by assisting humanity to conquer the root cause of her problems. The requisite policies to accelerate this people centred development in order to attain the human development threshold would encompass diverse factors that influence human life. It highlights such sensitive issues about the perception of the human person vis-à-vis other humans. Does a person really mean a person because of societal achievements or is the belief in shared humanity upheld?[663] For the humanitarian church to judiciously pursue a coherent human development, she must be well informed about social facts and therefore must take into cognisance some basic questions of humanity like:

> what kind of human resources exist in the country? How educated are its people? What is the inventory of skills? What is the profile of relative income distribution and absolute poverty? How much unemployment and underemployment are there? What are the urban-rural distribution and the level of human development in various regions? Has the country undergone a rapid demographic transition? What are the cultural social attitudes and the aspirations of the people? In other words how does the society live and breathe?[664]

---

[660] M. U. Haq, Reflection on Human Development, 3.
[661] Cf. Gaudium et Spes, 15.
[662] Cf. M. U. Haq, Reflections on Human Development, 4-5.
[663] Cf. M. Nussbaum, Creating Capabilities, 14.
[664] M. U. Haq, Reflection on Human Development, 5.

However the minimum requirements of human development for the masses is sound and average nutrition, education, health care, housing and transport.[665] These factors sum up the roadmap of the capability journey, as they determine what a person is, able to do and to be. Amartya Sen describes them as substantial freedom; it is their functional combinations that give rise to opportunities which are the combined capabilities.[666] Capabilities "are not just abilities residing in a person but also the freedoms or opportunities created by a combination of personal abilities and the political, social and economic environment."[667] This combination is meant to serve the human person because the human person "is the source, the centre, and the purpose of all economic and social life".[668]

As the Aristotelian views of human good expatiate the need for a social arrangement that reflects the social good of humanity, so does Immanuel Kant agree to treating humans as the end of all actions. Basically, philosophers even up to John Stuart Mill are united in the view of human development perspective that unfolds powers of humans towards self realisation and human flourishing.[669] For a society to discharge this duty, it must create the enabling environment for human development perspectives. Much of the political, social and economic landscape of African nations for centuries has been dominated by external control and in this manner it opens a parlous atmosphere that deters the development of potentials and capabilities. Apart from the combined capabilities, Martha Nussbaum describes the internal capabilities which are not innate but "...are trained or developed traits and abilities, developed, in most cases, in interaction with the social, economic, familial and political environment".[670] The educational system remains one of the best avenues to bring about these monumental changes, but for many years the many proposed human development concepts in Nigeria have never seen fruition. However, I believe that the three development strategies proposed by Adebayo Adedeji, five years after the adoption of the Lagos plan of action, if rooted deep in the new form of human development, could uplift the masses from the colossal humanitarian

---

[665] Cf. Ibid., 5.
[666] Cf. M. Nussbaum, Creating Capabilities, 20
[667] Ibid.
[668] Gaudium et Spes, 63.
[669] Cf. M. U. Haq, Reflection of Human Development, 13; Martha Nussbaum, Creating Capabilities, 23.
[670] M. Nussbaum, Creating Capabilities, 21.

failure over the decades. It should include such pragmatic steps that will promote "self reliance and self sustaining process of development...[through the] ... (1) rediscovering of self confidence; (2) mastering sovereignty over natural resources [and] (3) strengthening the leadership role of government in socio-economic engineering."[671] These three-steps encompass the social, political, economic and familial human development package towards arresting failed human development. Nevertheless, the first step may seem absurd but it calls for objective enquiry, because in the history of development there is hardly any

> ...mention of discovery or rediscovery of self confidence as a factor in development. Yet nothing could be more important a determinant of development and social change than this, particularly in Africa where for centuries it has been drummed into African's ears that they belong to an inferior race and are therefore incapable of attaining the heights that others have reached. If the slave trade dehumanized the black man for a long time, colonialism consistently undermined his self confidence. Africans were made to believe --and indeed for a long time did believe -- that the colonial masters were near supernatural, while Africans belonged to the lowest caste of homo sapiens.[672]

These complex problems were almost non-existent in all the years of European exploration in Africa in the 15th and 16th century as Afro-Euro trade flourished with no colour bias or inferiority complex. But the mutual respect diminished to a great extent as Africans did not only consent to the supply and demand of labour to the new world, but also offered slaves.[673] Its pains and the memories are well articulated by Benedict XVI in the *Africae Munus* as the memories of Africa that is not only scarred with internal violence but also by colonialism, slave trade and new forms of enslavement.[674] Such domination over Africa according to Walter Rodney creates a negative subconscious feeling because "...no people can enslave another for centuries without coming out with a notion of superiority."[675] However, one of the groundbreaking moves that began to crack this undue superiority myth was the African soldiers who fought on the side of their colonies during the World War II. On their return they joined in the national

---

[671] A. Adedeji, The Monrovia Strategy and the Lagos Plan of action, 17.
[672] Ibid.
[673] Cf. Francis Shagbaor Wegh, Neo-Colonialism and the Plight of African Identity, in: Ed., Chudi C. Mbanusi, The Aquinas Journal, Volume 1, Number 1, Makurdi, 2008. Pp. 58-69, 59.
[674] Cf. Benedict XVI, Africae Munus, 9.
[675] W. Rodney, How Europe underdeveloped Africa, 99.

movements for self-rule because of the obvious quest for freedom, which they experienced in Europe and among Europeans; whereas the colonial administration was the citadel of repugnant power and oppression in Africa.[676] Despite the remarkable improvement over time, the lingering tendencies and presence of such stigma of inferiority, the distorted history of Africa and African people worldwide, a disenchanted people with historical bankruptcy, calls for the need for the decolonisation of the African mind. The new lessons of human development should include the teaching of the young minds to be proud of Africa's glorious past and to stand for a self-esteemed Africa. Besides, human societies are the creation of humans; despite the dark and dreary history a new society can be re-created: a society that is built on equity, love and peace. The example of St. Josephine Bakhita, (1868-1947) the slave girl sold into slavery in Sudan who had an encounter with the God of hope serves as a vantage point for the spirit of Christian love and hope.[677] Charity as the saying goes begins at home; Africans and Nigerians in particular, must begin to practise true love and charity among themselves. It is a gateway to re-create that lost self-esteem and like Bakhita, Africa can emerge from economic and political slavery to greatness. St. Bakhita passed on this experienced love and hope from her encounter with Jesus to all she came in contact with in her mission; she gave them this received hope and liberation from Jesus. Just as the missions factored the deliverance of the African people from slavery as a major objective; the humanitarian church is called to further the steps of African deliverance and rediscovery of lost self-confidence through a socio-cultural engineering and spiritual renaissance in her human development endeavour.

One of the church's teaching that could stress the engineering and spiritual renaissance mission is the views of the church fathers articulated in the 'Decree on the Apostolate of lay People', the Conciliar and post Conciliar documents of the second Vatican council promulgated in 1965. It fervently created a new phase of inspiration in the activities of the laity in Nigeria and has animated the laity to be involved in the emancipation of God's people from socio-economic distress. It also provoked other teachings like the 'Apostolic exhortation *Christifidelis Laici*' of John Paul II, the vocation and the mission of the lay faithful in the church and in the world'. This teaching encompassed the synod on the laity in 1987 'the vocation and mission of the Lay faithful in the church and the world' and as such became

---

[676] Cf. Chinweizu, The West and the rest of us, 103.
[677] Cf. Benedict XVI, Spe Salvi, 3.

a charter for the lay faithful worldwide. The message was broken into two: proclaiming the gospel and living the gospel.[678] It follows simply that "proclaiming the gospel calls [for the] re-evangelisation of the self and going into the world. Also to live in the gospel involves promoting the dignity of the person, respecting the inviolable rights of life, to sustain the family and to place in the centre socio-economic life, among others."[679] It motivated the CLCN nationwide on the role of the laity in the emancipation of the nation. This is a God-given task, moreover that the exhortation of John Paul II together with the Conciliar and post Conciliar documents were all centred on the restoration of human dignity, were pointers to the need for re-discovery of the self confidence lost in the new nations long ago. It is an infusion of spiritual energy and psychological vitality to counter the effect of the backlog of negative experiences over the last two to three centuries.

The church's role in the propping up of the human dignity to encourage self esteem in young minds should include encouraging the teaching in homes and schools about unity, cooperation, adopting the global image of what a person is. It is a giving and receiving (Cf. Lk 6, 38), because the way fellow Nigerians and Africans treat one another will influence and determine the treatment and perception given to them by other nations and races. Young minds should engage in critical thinking to separate the truth from lies, realities from propagandas and stereotyped analysis from sound judgements. Besides, it is through their positive contributions to humanity that socio-economic crisis would be eliminated; it is about turning weakness into strength.[680] These humanitarian goals of the church are geared to arrest this societal retrograde. It is a psychological journey to decolonise the unconscious inferior tendency of the African mind, so as to avoid complex problems that cripple creativity.[681] The strong global Jewish unity that humiliation and the anti-Semitic tendencies have helped to galvanise among the Jews is a lesson for African descent.

---

[678] Cf. G. A. Ojo, The Laity in Nigeria, 261-262.

[679] Ibid. 262.

[680] Cf. Joseph Ogbonnaya, Critical Culture for integral Development in Africa and responsible Governance in Sub-Saharan Africa, in: African Catholicism and Hermeneutics of Culture, Essays in the Light of African Synod II, Eugene, 2014, Pp. 37-54, 46. (See also Appiah Kwame Anthony, Cosmopolitanism: Ethics in a World of Strangers, issues of Our Time, 6-7, New York, Norton, 2007.)

[681] Cf. Ibid. 47.

Though self-rule and independence became common phenomena in many African nations since after the World War II, there is outright need to emphasise the decolonisation of the mind, because African minds are still very much anchored in the West. It is geared towards regaining African originality and identity. So long as decolonisation is not attained Africans will fester in the travails to develop in a genuine, authentic and unique way. Inasmuch as western contact with Africa has introduced considerable improvements, in her emulation, she is to imbibe only that which will boost her ego and wherewithal. Some African intelligentsias disagree with the mental inducement to catch up with the rest of the world, thus what is paramount is a personal model of human development and when that is achieved, catching up becomes effortless. It is the path towards authenticity and uniqueness, therefore the catching up mentality without a feasible human development path is like the proverbial cart before the horse.[682] For that reason mental decolonisation is a positive step in the new human development process, as it paves the way for autonomy, self-reliance and African-oriented results to the looming social questions that cut across the length and breadth of Africa. Thus, Africans must desist from being always a receiver from outside.[683] This is because the hindsight of African's development portrays a continent that is quick in the habit of imbibing negative tendencies of the developed world rather than the positive. Consequently "we have imitated... [every aspect of life] and whatever else we saw was fashionable in Europe or America. Hence we are, on the whole, drowning in European culture more deeply than 50 years ago."[684] But how come the positive sides of the western world has always been overlooked, like the culture of discipline, hard work, diligence, welfare-oriented thinking, dedication, sacrifice, trust, the effective administrative system, social security, effective police institution and the judiciary? In such an efficient state management every one gains (a win-win constellation not a zero-game). Despite the commitments to adapt other views in this new human development journey, a people must be wary of their negative influence and application in her environment, so that it would not end up like a square peg in a round hole. Apart from the alien nature of these developments a people must bear in mind that every evolved human system is not exempted from

---

[682] Cf. F. Fanon, The Wretched of the Earth, 238.

[683] Cf. A. Shorter, Theology of Mission, 71.

[684] Chinweizu, Education for Liberation of Black Africa, Paper presented at the Codesria Conference on 50 years of African independence, Legon, September 2010, Pdf, Pp. 1-10, 3.

flaws as every human, economic and social system is influenced by the history of the people in question.

A people need to redefine their problems and mark out strategies for eliminating them, because the "social, political and economic challenges... are really symptoms of deeper spiritual, cultural and moral crises... [as they] explain the deep divisions, conflicts, corruption, injustice, and retarded human development that undermine the environment."[685] The use and the fusion of the term spiritual, cultural and moral refer to how a people look at themselves, their fellow human beings, environment and God. It explains their emotional intelligence and social imagination, which is their sense of identity and their emotional relationship to God, others and the creature of the earth. This influences their political, economic, institutional and organisational perspectives. It is a synthesis of the spiritual and the ethical assumptions of the society that forms a value system, which consequently informs the political, economic and social struggles. But when politics and economics threaten these values, they weaken the very ethical foundation of the society. Even Adam Smith the father of capitalist free-market economy recognises that the market will remain unproductive if it fails to recognise certain values as the ethical basis of a society. Ethical values that motivated the success of Pan-African movements for example ceased to be successful in many independent African nations, because successive regimes hijacked this medium to oppress and to hold on to power.[686] It did not transcend into a permanent ethical system that could galvanise concrete development to happen. Thus "a general comprehensive ethical/spiritual framework appropriate for the post-colonial modern society and sensitive to the traditional African imagination simply does not exist. It is this required framework that CST can help to develop."[687] Whatever human development process is to be adopted, it "must encompass [the] spiritual, health and self-reliance as well as material wellbeing. The perspective... [must be] naturally African-centric."[688] It must be related to Nigeria and Nigerians through well outlined teachings of the church in the spirit of human development. The CST should stress the process of human development that is "reasonable

---

[685] David kaulemu, Building Solidarity for Social Transformation through the Church's Social Teaching, in: Ed., Daniel McDonald, Catholic Social Teaching in Global Perspective, Maryknoll, 2010. Pp. 37-80, 41-42.

[686] Cf. Ibid. 42

[687] Ibid.

[688] A. Adedeji, The Monrovia Strategy and the Lagos Plan of Action, 26.

and... human..., aimed at creating a happy, human community, a community in which men/women are free to be themselves and to live the fullest possible human lives. This in turn, requires that there be an ideology, or system of values to give purpose and meaning to the process of socio-economic development."[689] Such a Nigerian flair in the light of the CST presents amazing advantages; besides, its advantages far outweigh its disadvantages or flaws, as it is consciously geared towards capacity building, capability and self-reliance. Also, such teachings should be wary of repeating the humanitarian distortions of the developed world. It must enhance a development that creates wealth, but abhor failure to guarantee human happiness, it must be a development that creates leisure but detests unnecessary use and profit of these resources, it must promote development that can lengthen life, but despise what denies the dignity of life, it should also encourage an education that can turn humans into efficient tools of development, but detest what makes humans forfeit the worth of humanity.[690]

The second and third strategies proposed by Adebayo Adedeji could be linked to the case of developing the human factor and capabilities. The ethical basis of any community that controls the political, economic and social life, as observed above, is in the view of Senyo Adjibolosoo, the human factor. They form a wide range of personality characteristics and other dimensions that influence the social, political and economic life and are to be kept functional. They are the "rule of law, political harmony, disciplined labour force, just legal systems, respect for human dignity and the sanctity of life social welfare".[691] Even though its political undertone shall be addressed in the political *diakonia*, the essence of having these attributes wired into the concept of human development will breed in the future credible leaders; leaders with a sense of purpose who become the product of human resource development and human capital that is to be acquired through education and training.[692]

---

[689] A. Shorter, Theology of Mission, 38.

[690] Cf. Ibid.

[691] Senyo Adjibolosoo, The Human Factor and the Failure of Economic Development and Policies in Africa, in: Eds., Fidelis Ezeala-Harrison, Senyo B-S.K. Adjibolosoo, Perspectives on Economic Development in Africa, Westport, 1994, Pp. 25-38, 26.

[692] Cf. Ibid.

Africans must jettison the humanitarian tendency of 'crisis management attitude' to life management; thus the idea of 'fire brigade' action should be discouraged to move towards a holistic approach of development. The envisaged concept of human development training should encompass an extended view and effects of the human factor in the course of this new development viewpoint. Furthermore, Senyo Adjibolosoo distinguishes the primary and secondary factors, the former includes: honest and law abiding nationals, self discipline, vision, dedication to duty and development, while the later comprises of natural resources, human resources, capital and infrastructure. The fruit of vast development among developed nations of the world is a consequent presence of the primary factors, while poor nations of the world seem to remain only at the level of the secondary factors which is the sale of domestic goods or raw materials in the international market. They suffer enormous capital flight and brain drain because of the absence of the primary factor to harness these human and natural resources. Nigeria and other African development plan/policies and projects need to emphasize the primary factors as the availability of the primary portends effective use of the secondary factors.[693]

Unlike other African states with less population, which invariably means small national markets, Nigeria's overwhelming population is a prospect for developing a huge internal market for economic activities. She can substitute import products with her production, produce her goods within the same price range as the Chinese and Indian counterparts and with good quality. But for Nigeria to really launch herself into this community of industrialised nations, the teaching and the preservation of the primary factors must be sacrosanct at all levels of education, beginning from the homes to the highest level of education. Nations with primary factors are always several steps ahead of others with only secondary factors, because their stronghold, the manufacturing sector is a product of self-discipline, diligence and honesty, whereas nations with abundant secondary qualities especially raw materials are like the cesspool of corruption. It accounts for the overdependence of nations with secondary factors on the technologies of nations with the primary factors. Though anyone can acquire science and technology from any good university in the world, the quintessential qualities to break the jinx of industrialisation, to carve a national

---

[693] Cf. Senyo Adjibolosoo, The political Economy of Development in Africa: Reflections on Orthodox Thinking and Policy, in: Eds., Fidelis Ezeala-Harrison, Senyo B-S.K. Adjibolosoo, Perspectives on Economic Development in Africa, Westport, 1994, Pp. 205-218, 215.

manufacturing niche, will demand abundance of the primary factors. It is a long term development process that could rarely be learnt from any university manuals.[694] This also accounts for why nations like Germany rose from the rubble after the World War II to become the engine room of Europe today. It was basically the profuse presence of the primary factors for development while the Marshall plan was only a secondary factor. I believe that is why the likes of Adebayo Adedeji in 1985 questioned the economic idea of a takeoff grant for African nations. The takeoff was meant for the recovery of self confidence, to identify and solve the existing socio-economic problems and to salvage the welfare of the people. Since the 1950s African nations have been on the voyage of re-discovery of self-confidence.[695] However, the erratic changes of adopting wrong developmental patterns and plans after independence also changed this status quo. Since the last fifty years bad governance has been the synonym of African backwardness. To avert this fateful twist will demand a well tailored ethical base of socio-politico-economic integrated teaching in all facets of life that will generate the needed impetus for creative thinking. Such a significant mental orientation and discipline can alter an unconscious mentality of dependence to a proactive mentality of self-reliance. This required working zeal is attainable through purposeful training, teaching and development that "...will produce the kind of people and institutions required to attain such economic progress".[696] This can take the state to that El-Dorado, a self-reliant and self-sustaining nation. The church is therefore called in this onerous task to a new form of human development that transforms humans to greater heights. Her human development strategy with the teachings of CST must strive to cultivate a concept of development that would give the masses a sense of purpose.[697] Her teachings should penetrate the different facets of human life, to interiorise man's experience, to humanise the world, to probe and understand every angle of his environment, to develop his talents and the use of the resources of nature.[698]

---

[694] Cf. Senyo Adjibolosoo, The Human Factor, 27.
[695] Cf. A. Adedeji, The Monrovia Strategy and the Lagos Plan of Action, 18.
[696] S. Adjibolosoo, The Political Economy of Development in Africa, 215.
[697] Cf. A. Shorter, Theology of Mission, 16-17.
[698] Cf. Ibid., 37.

4.2.2 Change in the mentality and cultivating a culture of development

A people's mentality is one of the most difficult obstacles in human development as it forms their upbringing. There are adaptive features of failed human capabilities that consequently create a mentality of dependency.[699] That is why the place of proper education to overcome such natural indolence is important towards the realisation of their full capabilities.[700] Hence, both those at the brink of trans-generational and transitional poverty will remain perpetually at that borderline.[701] Humanity is predisposed to change, improve, transform and attain perfection through science and technology in order to increase its standard of living. The divine mandate to multiply and subdue the earth (cf. Gen 1, 28) for example lends credence to this foundational change, resourcefulness and development. From population progression, Nigeria like many African nations has been more committed to the former than the later and thanks to improved medicine that has encouraged rapid population increase. Nevertheless, this inability to subdue the earth retards the quality of life in Nigeria and many African nations beyond the global standards of human dignity. Despite the abundant oil revenue of the Nigerian mono-economy, many Nigerians seemed poorer than they were at independence in 1960.[702] This shock stems from subsequent World Bank reports and other sources. The reports of the National Bureau of Statistics (NBS) in February 2012 for example observe that "the percentage of Nigerians living in absolute poverty rose to 60.9 percent in 2010 from 54.7 in 2004."[703]

These statistics are reminders of the failed capabilities and the inability to subdue the earth for man's own use. The ex-president of France, Nicholas Sarkozy in Dakar Senegal in July 2007 reminded Africans in very

---

[699] Cf. M. Nussbaum, Creating Capabilities, 83.

[700] CF. C. K. Wilber, Catholics spending and acting justly, 24.

[701] Cf. Ibid., 42. Trans-generational poverty develops among children who grow up in poverty and as such lack the basic education or have poor educational quality, poor health care, improper nutrition and the absence of other social benefits. It is different from transitional poverty, which is temporary poverty when an individual suddenly falls below the poverty margin because of unemployment, divorce, death, illness of bread winner and so on.

[702] Cf. J. Campbell, Nigeria, Dancing on the Brink, Wisconsin, 2007, 11,

[703] Ibid., 128. According to the US Dollar-a-day poverty measuring scale, poverty rose to 71, 5%, in the Northeast and Northwest, which are the poorest geo-political zones. The measuring scale today is $1.50C per day.

painful but frank language that "Africans have never really entered history. They have never really launched themselves into the future. In a world where nature controls everything, man has remained immobile in the middle of an unshakable order where everything is determined. There is no room either for human endeavour, or for the idea of progress."[704] This statement was like stirring the hornets' nest, as it opened up lots of pro and contra arguments. However, as bitter as this Sarkozy pill may sound, it opened up some truths; thus, a critical look at Africa since five hundred years illustrates a continent that has been too passive in global affairs. Africa's response to the labour demands of the new world gave rise to the inhuman transatlantic slave trade, the largest ever in global history. Despite the abolitionism many African kingdoms were still interested in the trade, until the machine age that brought an abrupt end to the trade. African people had no input to whatever reasons, terms and agreement of the imperial nations in 1884 as regards the fate of Africa. Thus the map of Africa was drawn and through military subjugation the many inorganic and artificial boundaries were implemented and established. Despite the nationalistic movements and activities, African independent process was sped up by the effect of World War II. Diseases, human and natural catastrophes in Africa are never really conquered by Africans until the West begins or anoints the process. Most of the commodity goods that account for Africa's 2% contribution to the global market were discoveries and by implication are still operations of foreign firms today. Besides, the opening of the little economic window today is a credit to the Asian giants' access to the global market. Despite some of its occasional duplicity, it has increased African nations bargaining chip and chances of survival. In a *resumé*, the accident of history is most times responsible for African development and progress. Thabo Mbeki the one time President of South Africa in response to the Sarkozy pill said "...what you have said in Dakar Mr. President, has indicated to me we are fortunate to count you as a citizen of Africa, as a partner in the long struggle for a true African renaissance, in a context of European renaissance."[705] It calls for a time to really wake up from the long slumber of passiveness to activeness in every ramification of life. Africans need to enter history; the Nigerian state, church and establishments must learn to take their destinies in their hands. The need for regional unity is very important so that ideas and breakthroughs can flow the length and breadth of Africa, it is high time to get past this

---

[704] A. Adebajo, The Curse of Berlin, 185.
[705] Ibid.

unproductive but euphoric community life that Africa is often embellished with. Therefore the real community life is where the 'greater community' comes first and not my 'ethnic group' or the 'I' before the community.

This inability to access nature has deluded many Africans into believing the recurring economic depreciation as a common state of affairs. In the midst of this disaster, neighbouring regions are experiencing abundant growth in science and technology. This non-inquisitive tendency is encouraged by a mentality creation that such expertise is peculiar to a particular people and not all of humanity, just like the mentality that elders know it all. The humanitarian must be ready to counter such existing structures of mental creation. A change from blind to critical followership must be cultivated towards 'alleged elders' and those in authority. This has developed a numb culture where people hardly question leaders and the 'perceived elders'. Besides, they even expect their leaders to loot from the coffers of the government. This encourages the demand for largesse, a factor that takes over hard work, competence, merit and responsibility. Also, as negative as the perceptions of neighbours and early explorers may be, a critical evaluation and second-thoughts may give new disposition towards life. It is substantiated by the Socratic saying that 'an unexamined life is not worth living'. Also it is worth knowing that 'no one sees himself very well except with the aid of a mirror or through the help of another person'. There is a need for a total change from the waiting, naive and expecting mentality, like Mahatma Ghandi (1869-1942), to a mentality of being part of the change and solution itself. The humanitarian church is called to challenge every mentality towards underdevelopment and to encourage every mentality that spurs development. There is need to cultivate the passion for critical thinking, to be inquisitive for true change, not superficial or artificial change, not to be carried away by consolatory offers like largesse, handouts and bribes as they fall short of welfare; besides they maintain the very system that keeps the poor perpetually hopeless.

Africans, according to John Mbiti are notoriously religious.[706] This religiosity has crafted an overriding and dependent spirit of miracle expectation in the average Nigerian psyche today. The Christian religion for

---

[706] Cf. J. Mbiti African Religions and Philosophy, 1-3. The African's whole life is entirely saturated with religion and the sense of divine and as such places great emphasis on religion. Religion has very strong influence in his thinking and actions and thus finds it difficult to exist without religion.

example ushered tremendous social changes and growth in Europe and America. The church was the advent and the foundation of the working ethics of many European nations. Their economic institutions thrived on the principles, ethos and values of Christianity, like the works of St. Benedict the patron of Europe and the Protestant ethics, thus leading to the development of their different institutions. Japan was the only exception whose breakthrough was founded on a societal oriented ethics.[707] Other Asian giants consequently emulated a similar pattern of growth and "for the first time in modern history, Asia is now richer than Europe in terms of accumulated private wealth."[708] Even though religion has improved some aspects of life in Nigeria and was meant to change the failed concepts of life, it is partially responsible for the economic woes today. A judge once commented that in Nigeria, religion, politics and ethnicity are frequently intertwined and habitually beclouded by the forces of corruption, poverty and insecurity.[709] Politicians for example use religion to advance their ulterior motives; Islam has slowed down the growth of education in the north and has created a reservoir of street urchins, the foot soldiers for religious riots and Islamic extremism. Today, some shrewd Pentecostals have found a niche in prosperous gospel, thus creating and marketing "a new religious culture that preaches wealth and health, and have brainwashed people into believing that prosperity, miracles and giving of multiple offerings to the men of God are the surest visa to heaven".[710] Through this medium, the poor are consequently exploited, a culture that is fast spreading into the fabrics of other denominations too. The standpoint here is against the excesses of religion in the daily rhetoric that; "only God can save Nigeria. But the question is: will he save Nigeria without Nigerians?"[711] Aesop the ancient Greek story teller will say 'heaven helps those who help themselves.' The humanitarian church against all odds of this time must be able to teach the truth that "...inventions do not [just] come from heaven, nor through dreams - well, sometimes a dream can give you an idea, but not often. To invent something you need to be curious. You need to think, study and experiment. The progress of humanity has been marked by interventions, new knowledge

---

[707] Cf. S. Adjiboloso, The Human Factor, 31-33.
[708] Graham Allison, Destined for War, Can America and China escape Thucydides's Trap? Melbourne, 2017, 15.
[709] Cf. J. Campbell, Nigeria, Dancing on the Brink, 23.
[710] Kenneth Enang, The Nigerian Catholics and the Independent Churches, 358, A Call to Authentic Faith, Nairobi, 2012, (See also Ezeoniya, Pentecostalism, 4).
[711] George Ehusani, Years eaten by the Locust, Ibadan, 2002, 34,

[and] new ways of doing things."[712] So long as religion becomes the altar of deception and manipulations for criminal minded ministers, the gullible, less educated and uncritical minds will fall prey of evil machinations and the vicious circle of poverty.

The political landscape of Nigeria has been beleaguered by the evil of corruption, a monster that deters productivity and creates a dependant mentality. Many factors are interlocked in this maelstrom of poverty: the glaring case of "social ills... [from] armed robbery, violent crimes, unemployment, official corruption, deteriorating infrastructure... falling standards of education and health care, have continued unabated to such an extent that the quality of life of most Nigerians has degenerated to a level that is below human dignity."[713] The CBCN made this call in 1997 and twelve years later, these social ills were still as real as yesteryear's and of course they still persist today. In a communiqué issued, the CBCN gives a detailed view of how corruption cuts across the fabric of Nigerian society. Thus Corruption:

> ...is not only found among the big men and women in government, it is also found at the lower levels of our life: from the filling station attendant who tampers with the dispensing machines, the messenger or clerk who hides files, the stockbroker who manipulates the markets, the policeman or woman who extorts money from the citizen, the banker who defrauds shareholders and customers of his bank, the judge who fiddles with justice, the lawyer who sells out his client, the politician who rigs elections, the teacher who solicits favours from students, the student who cheats while writing an examination, the religious leader or preacher who manipulates the people in the place of worship for his own purpose, the farmer or seller of farm produce who hides rotten foodstuffs under fresh ones, the hawker in traffic who runs away with your change.[714]

Another tendency that could fan the embers of corruption and some state of indecision is the extended family structure. Sometimes it is so overstretched that a well-to-do entrepreneur or a government official is put to task with too many dependants.[715] Indeed the society expects and

---

[712] P. Ranci, Economy and Finance, 13.

[713] Cf. Catholic Bishops' Conference of Nigeria (CBCN), Conversion for Justice and Reconciliation, Communiqué at the end of the Second Plenary Meeting of the Catholic Bishops' Conference of Nigeria (CBCN) at the Centre of Transfiguration Kafanchan, 7th - 12th, September 2009, 15.

[714] Ibid., 17.

[715] Cf. D. McKenzie, Identifying and spurring, 17,

sometimes compels the rich and of course the 'seemingly rich' to share with the less privileged among the extended family, friends and acquaintances. Inasmuch as poverty is the root cause, it could encourage the coast of corruption and sometimes deter these dependants from taking responsibility in life. The culture of corruption destroys the zeal for hard work and encourages laziness, cutting corners and the use of 'connection' in all spheres of life. Such a mentality does not encourage the spirit of self-reliance and the culture of diligence and industriousness, whereas these are the real values that modern societies are built upon. To this effect the CBCN called for a change of heart among Nigerians, because the whole distress is anchored on the dearth of a nation's relationship with God and amongst fellow humans. When the right relationship is missing, injustice prevails and injustice marks the beginning of conflicts. The absence of right relationship is according to the CBCN the action of sin. Therefore, the incurable social ills are symptoms of a deeper and more chronic sickness, which is sin. Sin has turned Nigeria into a sick nation and her people are wounded from the action of this sin.[716] The collective goodness of a people (cf. 1s. 3, 10) makes a nation righteous and it is the righteousness of a nation that exalts a nation to her aspired greatness (cf. Prov. 14, 34). Beautifully, the CBCN captions this in a communiqué that: 'good families make good nations. Because,

> ...a nation is itself a family of families, a community of persons who share common core values, and the family is the nucleus of a community of persons that a nation is. Every nation needs effective institutions and leaders of intellectual, and moral and technical competence to administer these institutions. The family, as vital cell of the society, is where such leaders are born and nurtured. Hence, both the effectiveness of such institutions and the emergence of good leaders in the nation largely depend on the family. The family, as a community of persons, gives birth to and nourishes the nation and every other institution critical to the life of that nation. Nations are built on and secured by values, and the family is the first place of acquisition of values. That is why the state of a nation is a reflection of the state of its families.[717]

The CLCN issued a call to holiness and it is only those who respond positively to this call that can truly engage in the socio-economic

---

[716] Cf. Catholic Bishops' Conference of Nigeria (CBCN), Conversion for Justice and Reconciliation, 18.

[717] Catholic Bishops' Conference of Nigeria, (CBCN), Good Families make Good Nations, Communiqué at the end of the First Plenary Meeting of the Catholic Bishops' Conference of Nigeria (CBCN) at the Daughters of Divine Love Retreat and Conference Centre Lugbe, Abuja, 20th – 26th, February 2015, 5.

emancipation of the nation that is today weighed down with many evil forces.[718]

The humanitarian church is called to step into this arena besieged with utmost bewilderment so as to save humanity, by offering a holistic approach through the teaching of Christian values to provoke a change of mentality and to cultivate the culture of development. Because "the World we have created," according to Albert Einstein "is a product of our thinking. It cannot be changed without changing our thinking;" Therefore, "...what various African communities imagine and feel about themselves is critical to how they relate to themselves and to others in the political, economic, and social spheres."[719] The need to change the corporate thinking of the people to welfare and society minded must be embedded in the new system. The Aristotelian philosophy of continuous practice of virtuous act offers a pragmatic example that could entrench practised virtues into the minds and hearts. The CST, the instrument of such human development could stress the need for unity, collaborative spirit and oneness. However, "unification [in this sense] does not mean forcing uniformity, reducing everything to a single blueprint or common denominator. Unification is not a conquest, it means spreading the mentality of co-operation, mutual understanding, optimism, justice and the desire for peace."[720] Stripping off this unwanted mentality will create a new mentality for development and a culture of self-reliance that leads to true independence. This could serve the contextual hallmark of a CST approach towards human development in Nigeria and Africa at large.

4.2.3 The culture of true independence and self-reliance

Many have opined over and over in development literatures that Africans are best to solve African problems. To narrow it down: it is only Nigerians who are best to solve the Nigerian problems. Regardless of the external support, the job of economic breakthrough and increased life standards lie in the hands of the Nigerian masses. Despite how widespread these views are some development experts still hold contrary views that it "is not because Africans have some deep understanding of the mysteries of Africa that is denied to outsiders or that foreign ideas are irredeemably alien

---

[718] Cf. G. A. Ojo, Catholic Laity in Nigeria, 266.
[719] D. Kaulemu, Building Solidarity for Social Transformation... 37.
[720] A. Shorter, Theology of Mission, 35.

or inappropriate."[721] Such views probably emphasise that Africans are not the sole solution finder of her numerous social problems. I strongly believe that inasmuch as charity or aid workers, humanitarians and development aid workers have good intentions, they basically fill the social void created by failed political will/process, reckless economic attitudes and missed developmental opportunities. I still reiterate that development must come from within and must be a people's development (chapter. 3.5) and that is why the duty of humanitarian agents is to prepare the enabling ground for such changes to occur. Besides, good intentions are not enough and according to Giles Bolton "would you ask a farmer from rural Mozambique to tell you where to build a school in, say downtown Detroit or Dublin, how big it should be or what books the students most need? So why presume it works the other way round."[722] It is true that the monumental losses in the humanitarian and development aid industry are creating donor fatigue and eccentric feelings among donors and western governments as it threatens the continuation of further aids.[723] However, the bone of contention is about creating a true culture of independence which will provoke sound reasoning and innovation because "what works here can fail there."[724] The new orientation to be imparted to the people must stress that development becomes people-oriented and indigenous by consciously avoiding the top-down syndrome of development or an obscure foreign development to, if I may say a 'down-top' development blueprint.

Anthropological poverty is another salient point. For example even though slave trade was abolished, the psychological negative thrust from the history of slavery, colonialism and the weakness of the states by African rulers weaken the worth of the African, who is locked perpetually in both material and anthropological poverty.[725] Therefore it creates

> ...even [a] bigger problem... [since]... the people of Africa and other parts of the colonised world have gone through a cultural and psychological crisis and have accepted at least partially the European version of things. That means that the African himself has doubts about his capacity to transform and develop his natural environment. With such doubts he even challenges those

---

[721] Alex de Waal, African Famine, 214.
[722] G. Bolton, Poor Story, 90.
[723] Cf. Alex de Waal, African Famine, 216.
[724] F. Nuscheler Entwicklungspolitik, 222, (translation is mine).
[725] Cf. E.E. Uzukwu, The Listening Church, 80.

of his brothers who say that Africa can and will develop through the efforts of its own people.[726]

Even those who may aspire for true independence are caught up in the imitative life-styles, borrowed foreign concepts and ideologies, as if foreign ideas and concepts are a 'one-size-fit-all' solution. On this social and economic transformation for example, "instead of finding an authentic path to social and economic development, our governments and leaders seek an identity for our respective countries and societies in the image of others. ...We give the impression that we want to create little Frances, little Britains, little Americas, little USSRs and little Chinas all over Africa."[727] Though there is need to learn from other people's concept and progress stories, the need for authenticity and independence must not be forgotten. This begins with instilling and installing conscious independent thoughts in the collective minds, a task that the humanitarian church is called to play.

Self reliance has a lot to do with the perceptions of the people, because languages are products of thinking, communication, culture and imagination.[728] The 'survival' vocabulary is weightily conspicuous in this milieu. Such profuse use and its consequent syndrome coupled with the culture of dependence over the years create a mental dislocation that unconsciously encourages the frenzy and hectic atmosphere of the fight for survival. It is the current picture of the economic landscape and standard of living. Like the Hegelian philosophy of rights puts it: a people are the children of her time.[729] But a people must deliberately move away from the use of such language of SURVIVAL to a language of LIVING. Consequently, the state and her people "require self esteem and a healthy self awareness that one can make a head way through self-effort".[730] These elements must be embedded in a new school structure to impart a progressive thinking pattern to young minds.

---

[726] W. Rodney, How Europe underdeveloped Africa, 30.
[727] A. Adedeji, The Monrovia Strategy and Lagos Plan of Action, 14.
[728] Cf. Ngũgĩ Wa Thiong'O, Decolonising the Mind, The Politics of Language in African Literature, Portsmouth, 2005, 13.
[729] Cf. D. Rose, Hegel's Philosophy of Right, 12.
[730] J. Wiemeyer, Soziale Ungleichheit, 5 (translation is mine)

4.2.4   Encouraging change/improvement of school curriculum

Proper education is a relevant factor for future growth and development of any nation. This explains why progressive nations today are very keen on the contents of their educational system. J.S. Mott's statement (Ch.2.1.3) during the WMC in 1910 validates the consequence of sound education as a positive energy towards future national development. Besides, it substantiates the established fact that ideas rule the world, thus an unfocussed educational system impedes national development. Since the introduction of the MDG in 2000 the Nigerian government has vigorously pursued the 'goal 2', to "ensure that, by 2015, children everywhere, boys and girls alike, will be able to complete a full course of primary schooling."[731] Accordingly, many programmes and projects were designed to achieve this millennium goal, they include raising the enrolment, boosting the retention and completion rate of children in schools, providing improved teaching and learning environment and by upgrading educational infrastructure at both primary and secondary levels. Government at all levels were tasked with these commitments and to ensure that all children irrespective of religion, ethnicity, class or gender were given access to primary and junior secondary education. From all indications Nigeria was on track in the pursuit of the MDG goals with an enrolment rate of 95% in 2000, but was subsequently slowed down by the insurgency in the north to 84% in 2004 and 80% in 2007.[732]

The perennial problems of educational backwardness in Nigeria have been stressed in many literatures from the woeful failure in the implementation of governmental policies to poor funding, corruption, unpaid wages of teachers, strikes, poor staffing, poor learning facilitates and a litany of other causes. Today the rising abuse of examination malpractice, bribery and indecency between lecturers and students are new factors that impede educational growth. These shortfalls distort the flow of values, norms and the responsible traits meant to be delivered by teachers/lecturers to their pupils/students. Even the international statistics at present have shown that the Nigerian educational system is very weak. According to the recent World ranking of universities 2015-16, the University of Ibadan is rated among the

---

[731] Millennium Development Goal, End-point Reports 2015, Nigeria, Abuja, 38,
[732] Cf. Ibid., 38-39.

601 to 800th universities in the world.[733] As important as the benchmark for the pursuit of the MDG goals to the Nigerian educational system, they are still the minimum standards required of any nation. The consequent failure of government to keep abreast with this minimum standard has crafted a longing for private schools at all levels. While the children of the rich aspire for overseas schools, private classes are organised for children of middle class families and the poor are left in the public schools where learning is almost infinitesimal. The school a child attends today depicts the financial status of the family. There is no 'compulsory educational policy' in Nigeria unlike in developed nations; however the status quo of educational awareness differs from place to place. In Kogi-East for example, the society expects that children on or before the age of five should be enrolled in a school. Therefore parents who fail in such duties could become an object of mockery in the society. Such expectation obviously puts a subtle pressure on parents to step up their responsibility.

The local input and the national relevance is another side of the coin regarding a school's curriculum. Such a feature is not determined by the UN or by any international body but by the affected people. This brings about the importance of ideologies for a change in the mechanism of thinking and approach of life of a people towards global realities. Such issues have been haphazardly treated within the educational landscape since the 60s. A humanitarian interested in groundbreaking facts towards implanting a coherent human development programme in the curriculum, would ask the question, what kind of ideology has been common in the Nigerian curriculum to date? Because every nation has a set of ideologies it intends to impart to its generation. But the obvious fact is that the Nigerian educational system has been a merry-go-round. The vision here includes a pragmatic concept of national development to be enshrined in schools and this must embrace a development culture, mentality change and the true spirit of independence and self-reliance. Like Malcolm X will say, "A man who stands for nothing will fall for anything." Often, many mistake education for mere transmission of information, whereas "education... needs to be

---

[733] The World University rankings, Young Rankings 2016, https://www.timeshighereducation.com/world-university-rankings/2016/world ranking#!/page/0/length/25/country/159/sort_by/rank_label/sort_order/asc/cols/rank_only (19.09.16)

focussed on the formation of the human person in its totality."[734] There are lots of Catholic schools in the European nations like Netherlands, France, Belgium and so on. The Catholic schools in Germany for example are given 90% support by the state for personnel cost, which consequently enhances state control of schools. Also, since the pupils/students sit the same final examinations, factors like uniform curriculum, textbooks and other similar matters automatically become the prerogatives of the state. However, in the USA for example, the Catholic institutions enjoy the freedom to build in their own ideologies.[735] Nigeria and Nigerians have the tendency to tilt towards the US system. Since the nation lacks a clear driving national ideology, the church has the leeway to introduce her inputs like a Christian driven ideology that is packed with pragmatic teachings to arrest this obvious ethical backwardness and move towards economic and political changes. According to the CBCN, to grow a new Nigeria through education would require that knowledge be communicated along with societal and religious values and also that truths be discovered in the course of learning.[736] Nevertheless, the crux of the matter too lies in the teachers, the very agents of this change, who are to make the difference. They need to be transformed as well so as to bring about this anticipated change.

The encyclical *Populorum progressio* raises a salient issue that a person could be "hindered by his teachers and those around him".[737] How has the environment influenced underdeveloped people to think backwardly and how could these negative tendencies be supplanted by proactive, humanitarian and progressive thoughts? Like the biblical phrase (Matt. 13, 30), the church must assist to separate the chaff from the grain by scrutinizing the traditional values of her people. Therefore to avoid casting in the same mould, agents of change and development must work hand in hand with the school teachers who are the human actors in situ and the bridge between the agents of transformation and the children to be

---

[734] Wojciech Gierych, The Common Good and the Diakonia-Service of the Church in Society (Forms of Cooperation, Education and Culture, in: Ed., Second Catholic Orthodox Forum, Church and State Relations: From historical and theological Perspectives, Rhodes Greece, 22 October 2010, Pp. 165-183, 173.

[735] Cf. Ibid., 175.

[736] Cf. Catholic Bishops' Conference of Nigeria, (CBCN), Promoting authentic development in Nigeria, Communiqué issued at the End of the Second Plenary Meeting of the Catholic Bishops' Conference of Nigeria (CBCN) at the Bishop Anthony Nwedo Pastoral Centre, Umuahia, Abia State, 8th – 14th September, 2012, 8.

[737] Paul VI, Populorum Progressio, 15.

230

transformed. Their ensuing collaborative solutions must aim to uproot the seeming causes of underdevelopment around the people. It follows that a people must jettison the negative human tendencies that are anti-human and anti-development and inculcate her good traditional values into her education.

The educational system in Nigeria in her different phases has adopted too many foreign systems that lacked the requisite factor to stir national and economic development. The church therefore must resort to implement her meticulously evolved humanitarian plans and strategies in her schools and homes. Since learning is an ongoing process she must also be ready to learn from other progressive minded forums too to update her data. It is a task and a roadmap towards self-reliance, true independence and sustainability so as to improve the mental and fiscal production. The CBCN reiterates the need for a return to the authentic Catholic education system that offers the integral formation of the human person for the optimal service to God, the society and humanity. To this effect the bishops recommended that all Catholic institutions should draw lessons from the Catholic policy of education so as to improve the quality of education offered by these institutions. In addition, the CBCN recommends these policies to other institutions that are interested in integral growth and the development of the human person.[738] This recommendation comes from the fact that "Catholic schools [worldwide] have the distinction of guaranteeing healthy, cultural and educational pluralism which makes them welcoming to all."[739]

The humanitarian church must address in the new curriculum the basic issues that today threaten national coexistence like religious and ethnic divide, corruption, violence, bad governance and so on. The action of God sending His son to reinstate humanity after the fall of man marks the dawn of new humanity. It thus redeemed and remade humanity in God's image. Whenever this consequent human dignity is violated there is a rebellion against divine sovereignty.[740] This human dignity that makes everyone share in the image and likeness of God represents the Christian values that the humanitarian church must teach the young minds. It "is not dependent on

---

[738] Cf. CBCN, Promoting authentic development in Nigeria, 8.
[739] Ibid.
[740] Cf. Catholic Bishops' Conference of Nigeria (CBCN), Faith and the Dignity of The Human Person, Communiqué at the End of the First Plenary Meeting of the Catholic Bishops' Conference of Nigeria (CBCN) at the Daughters of Divine Love Retreat and Conference Centre Lugbe, Abuja, 16th –22nd February, 2013, 8.

race, ethnic affiliation, gender, age, nationality, physical ability, talents, religion, or economic status. It can neither be conferred nor withdrawn by anyone. It simply belongs to human nature given by Almighty God."[741] The church resents ethnic chauvinism and religious bigotry but thrives on the solidarity of all people and in the defence of faith and human solidarity. The CBCN emphasises the teachings of *Lumen Gentium* on love and that the grace of God moves the Christian to live in harmony with God and all human beings. This faith is exemplified in charity, which is the love of God and neighbour.[742] The church is that instrument of faith "which takes the form of charity, [this church's faith] is the basis of her mission ... to bear witness to the Good News that God loves every human person [and] that his love invites every human person to live in communion with God and in unity with all human beings... Therefore, to be true worshippers of the one true God is to be respecters of the dignity of every human person."[743]

Even though parents, family, media and peer groups form the agents of orientation and the training of children, the school still remains one of the mediums for humanitarian change. It is a vehicle for conveying these wonderful humanitarian concepts, ideas and also the culture of hard work, diligence and productiveness towards sustainable development. The humanitarian church is called to emulate the examples of some western nations, where such ideologies have taken root and consequently produced fruits. These are the fruits of integral education, where "the human person is formed to be loving and caring, [which empowers him] ...to actualize his or her potential, [to] contribute to the attainment of the common good and [also to] fulfil his or her aspiration."[744] Therefore, if the Nigerian church applies these contents in the light of the CST in the school curriculum, it could serve as a background for ethical changes and national transformation. Such quality education carries both "religious and moral content. Education, in the final analysis, is a means of cooperating with God to overcome evil and to bring out the best in the human person."[745] The church having passed through the decays and flames of many global incidents has much enriched her Social Teachings. This gives her strong and deep roots of institutional development, which are the evidences of its ability to have survived through

---

[741] Ibid.
[742] Cf. Lumen Gentium 1.
[743] CBCN, Faith and the Dignity of the Human Person, 8.
[744] CBCN, Church and State Partnership in the Provision of Quality Education, 3.
[745] Ibid.

the political and economic upheavals of the ancient times, the Middle Ages to the present age. The successes of such ethical practises by the Nigerian church would draw the attention of the Nigerian public and stake holders to these rich Catholic teachings. Moreover, if the church could attract the state to adopt such a global, historical and evolutionary metamorphosis that is embedded in the CST into the national ethos, it could ignite the needed flare for change in the society. The CST could help to build average and young growing minds to see the world differently from past generations.[746]

This may raise arguments as to what becomes of the non-Catholics within the Catholic schools, when eventually such lessons are impressed in the general curriculum of the mission schools? The answer probably is, even in the colonial and post colonial educational era, mission schools enjoyed patronage of non-Catholics because of the church's insistence "that there exists an objective moral order that is the foundation of society",[747] which she factors into the syllabus of her schools. Among these was discipline, for which she is lauded by many non-Catholics who attended Catholic schools. I believe that if the church today teaches conscientiously her fundamental ethical principles of 'human dignity, solidarity, subsidiarity, common good and sustainable development' for example, it will go a long way to bring out good traits over the years, because the duty of the church is not just to design systematic social teachings but developing minds to be social critics.[748] It will wake positive sensibilities, draw consciousness and credibility to Catholic schools. Besides, that the existence of this objective moral order even pre-existed Christianity for example the days of Cicero (106-43BC) the philosopher, makes it a human objective and moral order that should consequently cut across humanity. Thus, its end goal is the application of such principles in every sphere of life, most especially if it permeates the legislative citadel of the nation; it could influence the stability of the state and provoke other developments as well.[749] Therefore CST is not just ethics for instituting order but ethics that provoke changes.[750]

---

[746] Cf. J. Ogbonanya, The Role of African Catholicism in the Light of Africae Munus, African Catholicism and Hermeneutics of culture, Essays in the Light of African Synod II, Eugene, 2014, Pp 75-112, 56.
[747] W. Gierych, The Common Good and the Diakonia-Service of the Church in Society, 166.
[748] Cf. J.B. Metz, Zum Begriff, 21.
[749] Cf. W. Gierych, The Common Good, 166.
[750] Cf. J.B. Metz, Zum Begriff, 45.

Even though the quest to instil new ethical teachings in the new curriculum is important to energize the required zeal for productivity, such a human development pattern will be incomplete if the background of a people is obscure to them; because education in Nigeria has suffered history-aridity over the time. Most curriculums are totally devoid of local, national, continental and global antecedence. For example, despite the fact that the entire world experienced two cruel world wars, there is hardly any curriculum that teaches about the place of Africa in respect to these two global events in Nigeria, from the primary to the tertiary institution. It is as if Nigeria or Africa at large is not part of the world. It exposes the self-made disservice, the profound historical emptiness in the intellectual circle today and the consequent poverty depth of the Nigerian educational system. It is only under obligations in the course of extra studies that many are constrained to find the place of Africa in such global events. These issues hardly appear in the school curriculum and when they appear in history books they are more or less treated like one of the folklores. The worst case scenario is the Nigerian Civil war; despite the bloodbath that claimed millions of lives the underlying issues have never been nationally addressed. They are not even given the chance in the school curriculum for critical thinking and brainstorming. Every attempt has always been to undermine and discredit its effect in contemporary Nigeria, hence missing the chances of nation building and tolerance.[751] The true wish to understand the past of humanity, its diversity and complexities makes the study of history indispensable.[752] Nigerians over the years, in terms of national life, are well-known for very short memories. Even though this short memory may have earned Nigerians and Africans in general the virtue of possessing low hate retention tendency;[753] a factor that sounds very Christian and worthy of emulation indeed, but must one forget his/her history? A people must recognize history because it connects the past and the present. According to George Santayana "the one who does not remember history is bound to live through it again" and Africans, precisely Nigerians have missed this connection and are consequently living through the same history on and on again. The Chinese military adage from Sun Tzu succinctly hints that "if you know the enemy and you know yourself, you need not fear the results of a

---

[751] Cf. E. Ayebome. The Nigeria- Biafra War and the negotiating role, 70.
[752] Cf. Finn Fuglestad, How to write African History in the Post-modern era. And how to integrate African history into the mainstream of history, a personal view, in: Eds., Hans Peter, Gerd Splitter, Afrika und die Globalisierung, Vol. 18, Hamburg, 1999, Pp. 258-268, 267,
[753] A. Mazrui, Nkrumah's Legacy, 31.

hundred battles. If you know yourself but not the enemy, for every victory gained you will also suffer a defeat. If you know neither the enemy nor yourself, you will succumb in every battle."[754] How much do Africans know about Africa and her enemies of growth? How much do Nigerians know about Nigeria? Besides, who and what are her possible enemies? I rate all these as failed battles of life. It is high time these events were given a place in the national curriculum so that her people cease to be historically passive and spectators of global interactions. Kwame Nkrumah (1909-1972) maintains that "...our youth from the primary schools, through the secondary schools to the universities and higher institutions of learning ... must be taught to know the workings of neo-colonialism and trained to recognize it wherever it may rear its head. They must not only know the trappings of colonialism and imperialism, but they must also be able to smell out the hide-outs of neo-colonialism."[755] This statement is borne out of the colonial challenges of his time as one of the founding fathers of independent African movement, Pan-Africanism and the subjugation of his time coupled with the psychological undertones of such machinations even in the present age. It calls for the re-education of the African to self worth and self esteem. It is not a hate broadcast, not a propagation of violent motives, not terrorism, but redemptive measures to relieve the African, in this context the Nigerian, from the global shadows and yoke of psychological oppression.

Such teachings could make citizens "cultivate a loyal and generous spirit of patriotism."[756] It is a patriotism that is not narrow-minded but directed towards the good of humanity and can douse, dissolve and bind up all the possible divides of humanity.[757] I believe these were part of the elements of change suggested by the very first pastoral letter of the CBCN in 1960 in the independent Nigeria. It thus made the clarion call for the revision of the school system that would fit into the Nigerian circumstances. Because,

> ...for too long, our ideal has been based on models hastily imported from abroad. We have no wish to reject much of what has been imported. Modern Nigeria bears far too deeply the impress of Western ideology and technology to have that impress ignored or despised. But there is a great difference between accepting in our own way what the West has to give and accepting it

---

[754] G. Allison, Destined for War, 236, (See also Sun Tzu, the Art of War 84).
[755] Chinweizu, Education for Liberation of Black Africa, 1. (Extract from Revolutionary Path).
[756] Second Vatican Council, Gaudium et Spes, 75.
[757] Cf. Ibid. 75.

without adequately assimilating and adapting it. A genuine effort to formulate a policy of Nigerian education that nonetheless meets the requirements of scholarship in any country will help to found a proper national self-respect. In building up an educational system that is properly adapted to the way our people think and feel and that meets the technical and commercial requirements of our own situation we shall also heal any injuries that the period of colonization has caused.[758]

The failure of the government over the many years to stir an academic path for the nation challenges the humanitarian church in this respect to champion this struggle to enhance and to upgrade the quality of education; an educational system that will imbue in young minds the pride and love of the nation and the responsibility of an individual towards his society. Utmost attention should be channelled towards national development, to make it as a people not as individuals, because it gives a unity of purpose and national strength. The church through advocacy and a support base to the masses must be ready to put pressure on the government to invest in human resources, as the "quality of human capital changes the destiny of a nation."[759] At the moment in Nigeria, even the inherited but unsatisfactory colonial system dwindles in its former quality because of decay at all levels of government. The NGO 'Exam Ethics International' observes that Nigerians in the search for stable environment for learning outside Nigeria today is costing the nation a whopping sum of 1.5 trillion Naira annually.[760] Therefore, there is a double task to uphold the good from the old and to invent something pragmatic that becomes the priority of a people.

The CBCN lamented the exceeding cost of education that many parents are burdened with in Nigeria, because the visit of the plague of corruption in the educational sector as well. The CBCN reiterated the need for funding and that the present laws impede the smooth atmosphere for public-private partnership. The Bishops therefore asked for an urgent look at the regulatory framework of the educational sector. They are aware of

---

[758] Catholic Bishops' Conference of Nigeria, (CBCN), The Catholic Church in an independent Nigeria, joint pastoral letter of the Nigerian hierarchy, 1st October 1960, in: Ed., Peter Schineller, The Voice of the voiceless, Pastoral letters and Communiqués of the Catholic Bishops' Conference of Nigeria, 1960-2002, Ibadan, 2002, Pp. 1-46, 11.
[759] M. U. Haq, Reflections on Human Development, 102.
[760] Cf. The Exam Ethics International, ITV Radio Nigeria, http://itvradionigeria.com/news/nigeria-spends-n1-5-trn-annually-on-students-studying-abroad-says-ngo/(10.09.14)

parents who cannot fund their children's education and it is not plausible for government's takeover in all respect today; nonetheless they plead for a synergy in education funding, so that parents are able to choose what kind of education they want for their children. In the light of subsidiarity the government is encouraged to assist in the co-funding of schools. The different stakeholders like government, parents, religious organisations and other corporate bodies are actors in the pursuit of quality education. Together all must fight against discrimination of Nigerian children in private and mission schools, because they have equal rights and their parents are tax payers too. The CBCN tasked the government in the provision of infrastructure and tax reduction for parents whose children are in private schools. Other requests include minimal charges on land where private and mission institutions are built, the reinstatement of grant in aids for mission and private schools and finally the return of schools to their rightful owners.[761]

4.2.5 Vocational institutions of learning

One of the principal economic successes of many developed nations today is the presence of well developed systems of skill learning and acquisition. It will be absolutely difficult to grow any modern economy if it is not anchored on technical schools for skill acquisition. Notwithstanding its cost effect, private investors and government/private institutions are called to this economic drawing board, otherwise the impetus to drive a modern economy will continue to elude the nation. Unfortunately, Nigeria unlike the developed nations lacks such prevailing industrial culture and skill-learning process. In Western Europe for example and precisely Germany, where an organised skilled learning process prevails, the apprentices in the different institutions and companies for skilled jobs are granted certificates at the end of a training period, which makes them eligible for employment in the society. The fruit of South Korea's investment in technical and vocational education as well as in scientific and technological research gives her at least 46 scientists per thousand people.[762] It is not every child who has the capability for university degrees, yet such professions which form the blue collar jobs play a very fundamental economic role in the society.

---

[761] Cf. CBCN, Church and State partnership in the Provision of Quality Education, 5-6.
[762] Cf. M. U. Haq, Reflections of Human Development, 94.

One of the strengths of the powerful southern NGOs mentioned above is capacity building projects among the local people. The humanitarian church would gain credibility if she is able to launch capacity building courses so as to increase people's disposition to production, which also means increase in the acquired rights of the faithful. Apart from their inalienable fundamental rights which the state must respect, they possess acquired rights through their economic contribution to the state. Therefore the church through capacity building and vocational institutions could integrate the people at the borderlines into the economic heart of the society, which makes them

> a part of the society by contributing to the accumulated good of [the] society. [Such] individuals acquire the right to profit from the services offered by that society through the state structure. [Therefore] ...access to public health care, education, civil protection and social security are rights that individuals acquire through their or their family's personal participation in production, in the paying of taxes, in engaging in military services etc.[763]

There is scarcely any rudimentary format for skill learning in the Nigerian economic activities. Many school systems have been borrowed and adapted to factor in the technical aspect of the economy, but have remained inefficient. The 6-3-3-4 system since the 90s for example envisioned such skilled learning, but is a shadow of itself today with no technical structure. The enabling environment for skill learning has remained a mirage, such that apprenticeship period for skilled jobs like trading, mechanics, electrical and other domestic jobs requiring artisans is often informal, irregular and most times abused.[764] The humanitarian church can learn from the example of the *Kolpingsfamilie*[765] that specialises in skill training and acquisition. Lucky enough the Kolping Society of Nigeria (KSN) already exists in Nigeria. She was founded in 1989 by Bishop Lucius Ugorji of Umuahia diocese in Umuahia, the present seat of KSN. Since then she has spread into twelve dioceses within Nigeria.[766] She is into computer training and maintenance,

---

[763] W. Gierych, The Common Good and the Diakonia-Service of the Church in Society, 169.
[764] Cf. K. Meagher, Identity Economics, 64-66.
[765] The *Kolpingsfamilie* is an international Catholic social organisation founded in 1846 in Cologne Germany and named after Adolph Kolping (1813- 1865), According to Bishop Emmanuel von Ketteler, the *Kolpingsfamilie* is a Catholic contribution to the solution of unskilled labour question in Germany.
[766] Cf. Kolping Society of Nigeria, (KSN) http://www.kolpingsocietyofnigeria.org/history.php (09.03.16). As a priest student in Münster Germany, he was an active member of the KSN, which he later founded in his hometown Umuahia in Nigeria on his return. With the help of

film making, video production, video editing and photography, media studies, bread making, tiling, alumaco glass fitting work, pottery, fashion dressing, hair dressing, welding metal works and catering.[767] Apart from skill acquisition she is into many social issues.[768]

Different Catholic professional guilds like the 'Catholic entrepreneurs' and so on could independently or in collaboration with the KSN operate corporative institutions of learning. Such corporations could serve the need for skilled workers, where different skilled jobs are registered by different corporations and interested people could apply directly to. It therefore moves the informal to the formal sector, where rights and duties of master/apprentice are legally fine tuned. Apart from the statutory rights of fairness, justice and equity in the apprentice/master relationship, it provides its Christian ethical foundational teachings that would encourage an additional environment of Christian charity. In essence, any apprentice could receive an agreed and well articulated format of training from any of the members of the guild. At the end of the training period, the trainee receives a certificate from the guild, thereby creating a level playing ground, anonymity, transparency, effectiveness and professionalism. It automatically reduces master/apprentice friction and the excesses of masters over apprentices. It helps to formalise the informal system of skill acquisition, given that "no country grows on informal trade alone."[769]

4.2.6   The church, reaching the unreached

One of the principal tasks of the church from the *Lumen Gentiun* documents like the great commission too is to spread the message of faith and Christian charity to the ends of the earth. This invigorating exhortation of John Paul II on the duties of the laity gave the CLCN the impetus for new proposals to spread the message of faith for the socio-economic emancipation of God's people. In this respect the CLCN adopted the *Lumen*

---

many good people he was able to carry the idea through. Between 1992 and 1994, KSN was eventually recognised by the international *kolpingsfamilie* in Cologne Germany.
[767] Cf. Kolping Society of Nigeria (CSN) http://www.kolpingsocietyofnigeria.org/skills.php (09.03.16).
[768] Cf. Kolping Society of Nigeria (CSN) http://www.kolpingsocietyofnigeria.org/edu.php (09.03.16). She is actively involved in promoting the CST, workshop on leadership training, primary health care, civic and political educational programmes, poverty alleviation and many other societal relevant social issues.
[769] J. O. Ihonvbere, T. Shaw, Illusions of Power, 117.

Gentium definition of the laity as "part of the people of God, who by virtue of their baptismal state are members of the common priesthood entitled and qualified to participate in the priestly, prophetic and kingly mission of Christ".[770] The CLCN was engaged in many synodal activities, pilgrimages, conferences and workshops at the different levels, national, provincial, diocesan, deanery, parish and church-station level to communicate the message of faith and the socio-economic emancipation. The most important topics in all the forums were the call to holiness and the promotion of human dignity at all levels. To achieve the socio- economic emancipation of the nation,

> the laity should appreciate, promote and protect the human rights of the inhabitants of the nation in their various group-formations, such as family, women, children, youth, elderly, and in terms of their aspiration for work, welfare justice and freedom in all their dimensions. Most importantly, the inviolable rights to life of everybody should be protected and promoted. Through their determination to promote the Gospel message in the world, the laity must be thoroughly conversant with the all the fundamental human rights as prescribed and promulgated by the United Nations and its agencies and in the African Charter on Human Rights in addition to the fundamental rights enshrined in the nation's constitution.[771]

The CLCN calls on all Nigerians as stakeholders of this vanguard of change and emancipation. Since the church is made up of educated, semi-educated and illiterate people, those who possess the knowledge are the instruments to assist in passing such information of change to the poor and those at the borderlines of the nation. Otherwise they shall remain perpetually unreached, fully or partially neglected.[772] It is imperative to reach the poor and those at the margins of the society because they are major losers in the economy, which makes them the primary benefactors of humanitarian work in every diocese. Every Catholic diocese ought to design a strategy to reach them. Inasmuch as the emphasis on improved school curriculum is important, the aged and middle aged, who have passed the school age must be factored in as a people requiring a humanitarian touch. This crop of people is the target audience for the envisaged humanitarian mass enlightenment campaigns at parish levels. They are product of a weak systemic social society who need radical humanitarian encounter to experience the real world. What is imperative is a confrontational package

---

[770] G. A. Ojo, The Catholic Laity in Nigeria, 265.
[771] Ibid.
[772] Cf., Ibid. 264.

that consists of progress designed humanitarian teachings of the church, to engage and provoke complacent minds into productive and proactive thinking. That is the needed ingredients for self-reliance and not the concept of providing material benefits always, because permanent charity is the worst policy prescription for any poor.[773] The best bet is to engage their minds towards self-reliance orientation to understand better the universe, statehood and politics, because

> the gospel is a living reality, not a book, and it is understood less by reading books and listening to sermons and exhortations than by communion among and between people. The Gospel is a way of life - a sharing, a mutual fulfilment, a *koinonia*. Because of this, no one who accepts it can keep it to himself. Living the Gospel means accepting the mission and accepting to be missionary. To refuse to share it is to betray the Gospel.[774]

The JDPC for example could also serve as a good umbrella for this message of change, transformation and emancipation. It is geared towards sharing this message of hope and love with the poor, underprivileged, ignorant and the oppressed people of the society; it is about the promised liberation from political and economic repression and how they could take their destinies into their hands. The lower echelon of the society today suffers enormous oppression from the state securities and personnel. Many have no share at all in the dividends of governance and for those entitled to meagre salaries, they are sometimes held indefinitely; arbitrary deductions are also made from workers' wages, pensions, gratuities and sometimes workers are denied their allowances without question and impunity. The CBCN urged successive governments and governments at all level to pay up such remunerations without further delay and she characterises this as an act of grave injustice.[775] The possibility of these vices is the results of the absence of rule of law, security and the weak judiciary. Subsequently the average Nigerian who lacks fame, money and 'connection' with the 'haves' faces persistent oppression, neglect, deprivation and no institution to appeal to. Making them to see economic options could also inform them of other economic opportunities outside the already overloaded civil service of the state. It could further their psychological and mental strength to defend their

---

[773] Cf. M. U. Haq, Reflections of Human Development, 20.

[774] A. Shorter, Theology of Mission, 33.

[775] Cf. Catholic Bishops Conference of Nigeria, Seeking the way of peace, Communiqué issued at the end of the first plenary meeting of the Catholic Bishops Conference of Nigeria (CBCN) for the year 2003, held at the Pope John Paul II Catholic Centre Abuja, from 10th to 14th March 2003, 5.

rights. The fruit of such engagements will strengthen the political *diakonia*, which shall be discussed below. The great commission to reach all men and women is also a humanitarian consequence, where the experience of the faith challenges and confronts their poverty and ignorance. Through these media, humanitarian actors could recognise the new face of Christ in others.[776]

4.3   The church and the political *Diakonia*

The mission to increase capacity for production and the need for a sound and coherent orientation in education will remain incomplete if the political angle is not addressed. This is because even within the economic and educational sectors, the policies that determine the place, pace and the actualisation of these economic and educational capabilities of humans are the prerogatives of the politics. Man according to Aristotle (4 BC) is by nature a political being. He is either a political animal (the natural state) or a natural outcast like a bird that flies alone.[777] Economic activities are basically pursued for the welfare of the society and they must be defined in a politically agreed legal order in a nation-state. It is only a functioning state economic system that is capable of providing such a platform for the production units to operate responsibly for the societal welfare. Thus, systemic or weak political, administrative and unjust institutions cannot be compensated by the presence of companies.[778] The political body of a nation bears this responsibility and it serves as the security base of the capabilities from "the whims of the market or from power politics".[779] This makes the political consciousness a *conditio sine qua non* in the new human development and political humanitarian task of the church, as she offers *diakonein* services to the political machinery of the state she lives in. This political obligation stems also from the fact that the church is universal. Besides, that she pre-existed nation states and will still continue to exist even if nation states were to disappear, makes her conscious of her *diakonein* role

---

[776] Cf. A. Shorter, Theology of Mission, 33.
[777] Cf. The Works of Aristotle, Vol. II, in: Ed., Mortimer J. Adler, Great Books of the Western World, 8, Aristotle II, translated by Benjamin Jowett, Chicago, 2005, Pp. 445- 552, 446; Joseph Omoregbe, A simplified History of Western Philosophy, Vol.I, Ancient and Medieval Philosophy, Lagos, 1990, 65.
[778] Cf. Joachim Wiemeyer, Business Ethics from Christian socio-ethical perspective, in: Kirche und Gesellschaft, Nr. 403, 2013, Pp. 1-12, 12.
[779] M. Nussbaum, Creating Capabilities, 43.

to contribute towards the progress of the state.[780] In doing this political *diakonia*, the church respects the political sector and refrains from creating a parallel society; however the state's emergence and its antecedence are of paramount importance to the church. Such knowledge gives her the understanding to make her inputs.

A swift exploration of state formation in African political history will expose the depth of present statelessness of Nigeria and the many states in Africa. There is hardly any continent in the world with many straight lines like in Africa.[781] This was the cartographic interpretation reflecting the agreement of the powers-that-be during the Berlin conference in 1884-85. It marked the beginning of

> a hectic journey for the modern state in Africa from imposed invention through joyful liberation to today's unfulfilled expectation. It is impossible to understand Africa's present plight, and especially the failure of Africa's governments to perform better, without a whistle-stop tour through this unconventional and engaging recent past. Yet as far too much non-African writing continues to overlook, African history goes far beyond colonial interference.[782]

There were pre-colonial conquests, compromises, some level of self-determination and nation-building in Africa, but these new nations hurriedly put together by cartographers lacked self-determination, a factor that still haunts the development of these nations today. They were more or less a geographical expression, a statement echoed by Obafemi Awolowo (1909-1987); one of the founding fathers of Nigerian independence. In essence the name Nigeria was more or less a terminology that referred to a particular people living in a certain geographical zone of the globe,[783] such that the birth of Nigeria like other African nations was artificial and "a sort of [an] immaculate conception, lacking ...the usual passions of creation;"[784] so that even though Nigeria was an independent state it was a nation only in name

---

[780] Cf. W. Gierych, The Common Good and the Diakonia-Service of the Church in Society, 185.

[781] Cf. G. Bolton, Poor Story, 31.

[782] Ibid.

[783] Cf. Femi Ajayi, The question of mental dislocation of some Nigerian leaders as Nigeria clocks 51, Nigeriaworld, http://nigeriaworld.com/columnist/ajayi/100911.html. (9.10.2011); Count Metternich, Europe's leading diplomat in 1814 first made this statement in reference to Italy. What is Italy today was made up of fragmented principalities on the Peninsula until 1870 when the idea of a truly sovereign Italy was realised.

[784] G. Bolton, Poor Story, 33.

and a Pandora box.[785] Also "the emphasis of [decolonisation] after the second World War was increasingly on political reform, but not self-rule. There was a new concern with the creation of a political class of administrators which could rule within the framework of 'trusteeship'."[786] The shared heritage of Nigerians and Africans today is a collection of traditional aristocrats and political elites who form the nouveaux riches.[787] They are the political/economic custodians of Nigeria and other African states since the departure of colonial administration. The political parties in Nigeria for example constitute a recycling of the patrons and clients of the nouveaux riches, such that even when acronyms of political parties change, substance still remains.[788] The whole thing goes in circles, a drought-national ideologically propelled educational system gives birth to a mediocre political class that is totally devoid of ideological principles; that is the pictorial nature of Nigerian politics today.

The post-independent Nigeria comprised poor state of infrastructure, inefficient political/economic institutions and manpower coupled with the absence of national identity to bind these hitherto different nations together to face the onerous challenges ahead; these were the roadblocks and bottleneck to future development. Besides, the nouveaux riches inherited the plush environment, like large houses, lush garden, servants, swimming pools used by the colonial administration to lure minor officials from London and Paris to Africa; they were part of the inherited legacy of trusteeship.[789] How were these African elites to renounce or sacrifice such pleasures in the face of an abject and compounding poverty of the masses? It thus encouraged the ubiquitous patron-client relationship such that loyalty and allegiance were directed not to states but to primordial ethnic lines. It became the elite price of running a modern Nigerian state, a very steep price and an unsustainable informal system that is today very widespread in the political landscape of Nigeria most especially because of the oil revenue. Thus, the continued survival of Nigeria hangs so much on the pecuniary interest of these shrewd oligarchic elite and their political network.[790] In a situation where so many vested interests prevail, how does the nation stand as one entity? How does she as a nation face cases of external conspiracy since the average mind is

---

[785] Cf. Ibid., 38.
[786] J. Healey, M. Robinson, Democracy, Governance and Economic Policy, 22.
[787] Cf. J. O. Ihonvbere, T. Shaw, Illusions of Power, xxiv.
[788] Cf. Ibid, xxv.
[789] Cf. G. Bolton, Poor Story, 39.
[790] Cf. J. Campbell Nigeria Dancing on the Brink, 31-32.

preoccupied with greed and personal gain? The 2006 Wikileaks publications exposed how deep the multinational Shell Corporation for example had infiltrated the Nigerian politics and thus have direct influence in all the ministries. It portrays the level of greed and the absence of national consciousness and patriotism,[791] because educational and developmental ideologies are designs of patriotic sentiments and national consciousness. This void affirms the poverty of the developmental scenario of a people and the nation. These factors make some development experts argue that African independence came perhaps too quickly.[792] But considering the divide and rule mechanism employed in the lumping up of hitherto enemy nations together, even a hundred years after 1885, African nations like they are today especially Nigeria would still not have been ready for independence. If imperial states had respected primordial ethnic lines in the formation of nations that probably would have been the greatest good of colonialism to modern Africa. Definitely the minority nations would need alliance but it should be out of volition and not compulsion and like the Igala adage will say that the burden of such a self-willed errand is easier to bear.[793] So that if in the future these nations for whatever reason decide to unite as one nation, it would be on the ground of mutual consent based on the principles of liberty, egalitarianism and fraternity as envisioned and envisaged by the French Revolution.

Nigerian political history since the period of self rule down to the independence and today still portrays a people of different nations. Since the 60s many constitutional conferences have been held to harness and unite the Nigerian people, so that the phrase 'unity in diversity' could become a reality. Even though "this diversity may be enriching, it is also the source of ongoing conflict, largely revolving around the distribution of power and state resources."[794] The last constitutional conference from March to August 2014 was composed of stakeholders from the different ethnic-, religious groups, traditional ruling councils, state-, local governments and political parties. This singular action meant a national gesture and the readiness of the people to address in a holistic approach the fundamental problems that are weighing

---

[791] Cf. Caroline Lange, Der Fluch des Öls in Nigeria, Ein Land zwischen Reichtum und bitterer Armut, Norderstedt, 2013, 14.
[792] Cf. H. D. Ortlieb, Entwicklungshilfe für Afrika, 30.
[793] Uchẹ k' onẹ kp' ọla nwu, ya w'ọlan.
[794] Mathias Kemp, The Governability of the Multinational State of Nigeria, Is Decentralisation the Solution or Part of the Problem? In: Ed, Gerhard Wahlers, Konrad Adenauer Stiftung International Reports, 6/14, Vol. 30, Berlin, 2014, Pp.7-30, 6.

down on Nigeria. Although the implementation of the constitutional conference is still a mirage, that the Nigerian people were and are ready to talk about the 'Nigerian Project' portends consensus on the general political interests and the common road towards nation building.[795] The church as an institution breaks through all barriers of humanity, the rich and the poor, the educated and uneducated, peoples of different ethnic groups. This makes her an agent of union and a platform for national unity and common interests. In spite of the shared flaws and the political upheavals since the 1960s and irrespective of the religious and ethnic affinities, one can infer that Nigerians are still concerned about their joint wellbeing and common good. Therefore living together must be constitutionally revisited. Every political altercation and disintegration move has been as a result of political imbalance coming from a lopsided constitutional frame. Every right-thinking being desires peace, law and order, but these qualities do not fall from heaven; humans have to strive to achieve such a constitutional concession. But it gets uglier by the day since politicians, the supposed custodians of the law use such a vicious medium like sectionalism to advance their political interests and not the people's intentions. Today "politics in Nigeria is still [very much] perceived by many in authority more as a self-serving pursuit, opportunity for easy money and prestige, than as genuine service for the good of all."[796] It is a people's fight to conquer this vice. The church must stand on the side of the people and teach the people how to demand the account of stewardship of public officials.

The delegates and observers of the national conference were clear on one issue "that changes must be made to Nigeria's systems in order to guarantee stability and cohesion in the face of the country's many challenges, especially if the oft-touted 'unity in diversity' is to become a reality."[797] Therefore institutions are indispensable to chart this way forward. If the humanitarian church must make impact in development, she must address the political imbalance as it affects the ordinary people. She must offer some political service and a political humanitarian approach to correct and improve the existing lopsided political status quo that seems "like a stick

---

[795] Cf. Catholic Bishop' Conference of Nigeria, (CBCN) The Lord comforts his People, Communiqué at the end of the second plenary meeting of the Nigerian Catholic Bishops conference of Nigeria, CBCN, at the Diocesan Conference Centre, Bishops Court, Effurun, Delta State, 11-19 September, 2014, 11.

[796] CBCN, Promoting Authentic Development in Nigeria, 6.

[797] M. Kemp, The Governability of the Multinational State of Nigeria, 12.

of dynamite waiting to be detonated".[798] She neither takes to political battle nor replaces the state, but must not be silent over injustice. Through rational reasoning she reawakens the desired spiritual energy, which demands sacrifice for justice; thus she has a responsibility to remind the state of her duty.[799] That is why some powerful southern NGOs maintain that "we not only want a piece of the pie, we also want to choose the flavour, and know how to make it ourselves."[800] Therefore, the humanitarian church through her ethical arguments "is duty-bound to offer, through the purification of reason and through ethical formation, her own specific contribution towards understanding the requirements of justice and achieving them politically".[801] Because, take it or leave it, "development cannot be separated from obvious and clear issues of governance."[802]

Beginning from 1990s, humanitarian agencies like Oxfam, Save the Children and Cooperative for Assistance and Relief Everywhere (CARE) began to adopt and replace humanitarian programmes with issues of rights. This was to replace the perceived 'third worldism'; a process that could return some optimism of revolutionary liberation in Africa and Latin America. They were not interested in collective ownership and a government led economic development, but were focussed on the essential liberal notion of individual rights. They were determined in response to the global political changes to effect transformation among the people; it was another form of political humanitarianism.[803] Issues like good governance, democracy, transparency, strong and credible institutions, rule of law and corruption free economy became the humanitarian mantra among the agencies, lending organisations and many governments in the West.[804]

The question is: how does good governance have a place in a clientele society like Nigeria? Where "in the absence of effective political institutions, personal rulers have played... important [but often mischievous] role in maintaining political order,"[805] since weak institutional presence

---

[798] Max Siollun, Oil, Politics and Violence, Nigeria's Military Coup Culture, (1966-1976), New York, 2009, 15.
[799] Cf. Benedict XVI Deus Caritas est, 28.
[800] S. Michael, Undermining Development, 33.
[801] Benedict XVI, Deus Caritas est, 28.
[802] S. Michael, Undermining Development, 34.
[803] Cf. C. Foley, The thin Blue Line, How Humanitarianism went to War, 28-29.
[804] Cf. D. Moyo, Dead Aid, 27.
[805] J. Healey, M. Robinson, Democracy, Governance and Economic Policy 32.

prevails nationwide; thereby filling such a political vacuum with 'strong men'.[806] These 'strong men' and 'strong hands', a contrast to strong institutions, are the conventional, eventual and underlining political institutions and rallying point in Nigeria today. Consequently, only people who do their bidding and clandestine activities are given opportunities to operate uninterruptedly in the political landscape. Institutions produce "solidity and impartiality that people often don't have and they will outlast momentary swings of sentiment".[807] These human institutions are ironically the same rent seekers who are profiting from the overt economic shift to neo-liberalism and as such constitute the nouveaux riches.[808] They are political 'kingmakers' who anoint and select who leads so much so that the electoral votes command less effect. According to Pat Utomi, elections are merely ceremonial; a few power brokers whom he referred to as the 'club of capture' actually control and determine the state of art.[809] Their interest ridicules governance with corrupt practices thereby exhibiting a do or dies affair, such that it is hard sometimes to understand where their interest begins and ends.

How does the church, the humanitarian face of the common man, the supposed societal last resort and the voice of the voiceless challenge this existing status quo? Does she dine with the nouveaux riches or oppose them? The quest for financial sustainability seems to be tearing the church apart and consequently foot-dragging the cooperative spirit that is needed to pursue a coherent political *diakonia*. The Pentecostal system of fund raising coupled with endemic poverty opens the church today to greed and avarice in the pursuit of wealth for maintenance of church structures and for individual advantages. For the church to be truly humanitarian, which is to assist humanity, she must be sensitive about what means she has and how she comes about them. The humanitarian target audience are the immediate parishioners who are mostly under a diocesan priest. This special ministry and context gives the diocesan priest a distinct function, role and spirituality. His spirituality nurtures and supports him to carry out his mission of

---

[806] Cf. A. Adebajo, The Curse of Berlin, 289. President Obama in his visit to Ghana made this statement that African nations need strong institutions and not strong men.

[807] M. Nussbaum, Creating Capabilities, 181.

[808] Cf. Alex de Waal, The African State and global Governance, in: Ed., Phoebe Griffith, Unbinding Africa, Making Globalisation work for Good Governance, London, 2003, Pp. 11-19, 10.

[809] Cf. Pat Utomi, Nigeria is bleeding, needs healing, http://www.vanguardngr.com/2017/08/nigeria-bleeding-needs-healing-utomi/ (12.08.17)

evangelisation. Without this inner orientation he simply becomes preoccupied with the self and a mere functionary, rather than one who should stand for the faithful. Moreover, not only would the faithful be starved of his services but would find it difficult to rise above such sentiments, because of the primal meaning attached to the priesthood by the lay people is men of God or people in touch with God.[810]

The church is made up of the bishops, priests, religious men/women, monks/nuns and the lay faithful. Despite their differences in apostolate and hierarchy on one hand and sometimes the misconceptions and misunderstanding on the other hand, they are meant to work hand in hand to bring about successful political *diakonia*. The ministers of the word and sacraments "should be looking for Christ in many places: ...in faithful meditation on God's word, in active communion with the most holy mysteries of the Church, especially in the Eucharist and the Divine Office, in the bishop who sends them and in the people to whom they are sent, especially the poor, the young, the sick, the sinful and the unbelieving".[811] It is only in the name and the love of Christ and when the church ministers place the apostolate and the service to humanity first that humanitarian works may yield sustainability. Therefore "the priesthood must never be seen as a means for improving one's lot in life or in terms of gaining prestige,"[812] but for the service of the faithful and humanity in general.

Pope Benedict XVI succinctly encourages the church that one of her principal duties "is to assist in forming upright consciences [that are] receptive to the demands of justice, so as to produce men and women willing and able to build this just social order by their responsible conduct".[813] Nevertheless, in forming these minds the church must be wary of the growing spirit of clerical arrogance and materialism in the priesthood, which also breeds anti-clericalism.[814] In addition, the lay faithful today is witnessing an increasing number of adults, more educated people, critical and better informed people among whom the priest exercised his ministry in the past. Besides, many are driven by different ideological settings of this

---

[810] Cf. Catholic Bishops' Conference of Nigeria, (CBCN), I chose you, The Nigerian Priest in the Third Millennium, September 2004, 24-25.
[811] Ibid., 25.
[812] Ibid., 26.
[813] Benedict XVI, Africae Munus, 22.
[814] Cf. CBCN, I chose you, 26.

pluralistic and humanistic world.[815] Thus, the message of justice must begin from the inside and this is very fundamental towards the development of a people, it is a movement from the inside to the outside. If justice then prevails in public and private, economic and social life, it will stimulate the growth of endowed potentials and God-given talents of the faithful into the service of the nation and her people. This has to be sustained by solidarity and subsidiarity and inspired by the spirit of charity. The church therefore has this mission to bear this truth to the society.

This humanitarian journey to impart values to young minds will remain at a crossroads if a people fail to conceptualise her intended values to be passed down to other generations. The members of CLCN are pre-eminently the group that carries this message of faith into the political realm of the Nigerian state. Sad enough, politics in Nigeria over the time has been branded as a 'dirty game' and as a consequence lacks emulation and is very much resented.[816] The games and pranks exhibited sometimes by political figures could be contained if the political awareness of the masses is guaranteed, but the grave issue is in the angle of religion and politics. Politics in Nigeria is mostly dreaded as inseparable from occultism and this widespread contention construes politics as an aberration. Even though these claims are neither empirical nor scientifically verifiable, the Nigerian movie industry for example, the supposed conscience of the nation has made such footage very extensive. The approach of the different religions to such tendencies varies. The kind of Islam introduced into Igalaland for example in the 17th century and in many parts of Nigeria by extension, "tolerated traditional beliefs and practices. As a result, there existed in both religions (Islam and Traditional Religion) beliefs in spirits, magic, medicines, divination and sorcery."[817] This propels a different attitudinal background towards political practice. While Christianity has strong aversion towards occultism, Islam and the ATR are very much indisposed towards such ethical questions. Due to this discord in Christianity, the Nigerian Christian must come to terms with the moral question of dining from the table of the Lord and that of the demons (1 Cor.10; 21). These assertions and the proclivity for differing religious practices sometimes create the ground for a negative attitude towards politics.

---

[815] Cf. Ibid., 31.
[816] Cf. G. A. Ojo, Catholic Laity in Nigeria, 42.
[817] P.E. Okwoli, Introduction to Igala Traditional Religion, 76.

Max Weber (1864-1920) gives a critical and best-selling approach geared towards finding a foundational consensus on the implications of Christian faith as regards ethics and politics. He underscores the importance of *Gesinnungsethik* the ethics of conviction and *Verantwortungsethik* the ethic of responsibility in the call or vocation to politics *Politik als Beruf*. There is a tension between the Christian conviction and the political responsibility of a person in question who as a citizen is both a politician and a Christian. Max Weber hints exclusively on the need to acquire power and his ethical approach is towards the use of legitimate violence to achieve ultimate good. Therefore he attempts to narrow the gulf between the two kingdoms: the absolute ethics and the Sermon on the Mount. But when he agrees that every state is founded on the use of force or violence, it sounds like euphemism for political practice being at par with getting one's hands dirty.[818] His arguments may have faced contrasting opinions and other suggestions, but Aristotle's observations that the state is a creation of nature, also man by birth is a political being reiterate the being of man as intrinsically inseparable from politics. Therefore anyone who turns his or her back on politics, because of its inherent violence turns his or her back on the society, his goal of life and happiness.[819] However, the *Sitz im Leben* was a post World War I experience to disagree with young pacifists who wanted political powers. The contemporary problem in Igala/Bassaland and in Nigeria is the 'efficacy' of occult powers for politics. Despite its unscientific status as it may sound to the average Westerner, its presence is a widespread belief. Leaning on the resolve of Max Weber, Politics is not just a mental activity but includes issues of the heart and power; though it is not an end itself. Politics therefore "demands loyalty, commitment and an element of faith".[820] The consequence of political actions must find communication with the conviction and the responsibility of the politician in question. The harmony and the communion of these two elements is the real image of a true emergent politician.[821] His responsibility and conviction gives him the audacity "to stick his hands into the spokes of the wheel of history".[822]

---

[818] Cf. Johann Verstraeten, The Tension between 'Gesinnungsethik' and 'Verantwortungsethik'. A Critical Interpretation of the Position of Max Weber in '*Politik als Beruf*', Pp.180-187, 180-181.

[819] Cf. The Works of Aristotle, 446; J. Omoregbe, A simplified History, 65. Therefore it is not self-sufficing for an individual to live in isolation, that is without political involvement. Such an individual is either a beast or a god.

[820] J. Verstraeten, The Tension, 182.

[821] Cf. Ibid.

[822] Ibid.

Anyone who falls short of this quality does not deserve the name and vocation 'politician'. Therefore, political membership, religious affiliation or social group link forms the pedagogical impetus that accompany a person not just to offer guidance and discernment but also to assist in forming formidable, true, responsible, convincing and lasting politicians.[823]

As a humanitarian church her fundamental role is not only to teach but also to take these political convictions to the outside world so as to clean up the system, beginning from the laity who represents the church in public life together with the Bishops and priests. For that reason, "until Nigerians focus more on the considerable influence of leadership on political behaviour at all levels, [she] may be pursuing the shadow and leaving aside the substance as [the masses] condemn one type of political party or the other as being unworkable and unsuitable."[824] For a long time overemphasis has been laid on the role of the leaders in both religious and political sectors of the nation. But the ills of the society are consequent effects of leadership and followership both from the political and religious angle. Thus, every leader, be it religious or political must recognise his or her roles and limits; and it extends to the followers as well. For the one who doubles as religious and political leader, he or she must not pursue his or her religious convictions against the will, dignity and freedom of his or her subjects, because the world is quite pluralistic.[825] What the CLCN advocates as basic and just is a nation of "religious and political freedom and tolerance, all of which can promote justice, love of one another, honesty and diligence".[826]

Even though corruption has eaten deep into every sector of the nation including the church, a people must set a benchmark to eradicate such social ills. The church begins with a soul searching journey into herself by disregarding religious and ethnic affinities and ties in her relationship with political actors. One of the humanitarian duties and service of the church is the commitment to confront structural injustice in the society. Donal Dorr proposes four stages of the church's approach to politics that could be adopted as a political *diakonein* strategy: the analytical stage, the stage of collusion, the period to challenge and proffering alternatives. The humanitarian church as first step is to carefully analyse and understand the

---

[823] Cf. Ibid. 184.
[824] G. A. Ojo, Catholic Laity in Nigeria, 42.
[825] Cf. Ibid., 43.
[826] Ibid.

underlying political sources of such injustices. Doing such will conserve political energies for structural changes and so avoid an artificial approach and superficial changes. Proper diagnosis is important to get to the root causes so as to avoid a symptomatic approach because symptoms are only indicators of the fundamental issues. The second stage is the action of distancing oneself from the agents of injustice; it is a vital step as many church leaders today have crossed such Rubicon through reception of gifts, favours and invitations from the agents of injustice, which may be construed as subtle support for injustice.[827] Besides, utmost care must be taken to avoid internal sabotage among the political *diakonein* actors because it is another subtle tactic of 'divide and rule'.[828] The third stage is a "carefully planned and concerted action at the political level to challenge the injustice".[829] It may begin with private protest, a press statement, public protest march, but all must be done within the legal national framework as provided by the constitution with appropriate permission of the security agents. Finally, the humanitarian church is to offer some alternatives to the fundamental unjust social issues she stands against, in order to be a good example to the state.[830]

The churches political service to humanity occasions the action of the incarnation message; it is an evidence of God's solidarity with the fallen human race through the raising of the human standard to a Godly one. Thus, it brings out the theological dimension of the term Solidarity as "a theology... [that] indicates how the ontological unity of the human species is redeemed as a 'new creation' in Christ. Political and liberation theologians insist on the theological truth and reality of the identification of God with the least of the human species in Christ Jesus (Mt 25;31-46)."[831] Solidarity is the feeling and the readiness to share in the pains, afflictions, fate, underdevelopment, misery, destitution of the neighbour, the plight of wars among communities and the social malaise suffered by any human person both distant or near, through employing every available resource for the betterment of humanity. Besides, by entering the world of deprived people

---

[827] Cf. Donal Dorr, The Social Justice Agenda; Justice, Ecology, Power and the Church, Dublin, 1994. 111.

[828] Cf. Karl Meier, This house has fallen, Nigeria in Crisis, London 2000, 104. One of Ken Saro Wiwa's Strategy for the Ogoni struggle in the 90s was to avoid internal sabotage. However this was broken as internal rift was created leading to different factions, even bribes were offered to chiefs and other covert attacks were employed.

[829] Ibid.

[830] Cf. D. Dorr, Social Justice Agenda, 111.

[831] M. L. Lamb, Solidarity, 911.

one experiences their hopes and their joys,[832] such access and communion with the poor succinctly offers assistance that "...is not just makeshift assistance but sustainable change of the present difficulties and the correction of the structural deficit, that gave rise to such actions in the first place."[833] The *logos* at the incarnation became flesh and the church bears this *logos* that transforms the world. As the *logos* breathed life into man at creation so should the incarnational message of the church bear such fruits by breathing in a new kind of air to re-create a transformed political class and society.

4.3.1 Towards building democratic culture

One of the most recommended and widespread strategies to influence people's political development since the age of political humanitarianism is through active grassroots participation. It is a major ingredient of democracy that envisages and encourages the pursuit of good governance. When local communities participate in governance they have a say in their destinies. The effect and memories of the once predominant monarchical system that still lingers in the subconscious of many Nigerians consequently retard grassroots participation in many communities today. Accordingly, governance since the 1960s portrays a replica of this pre-colonial system, for example the one party system and the subsequent military regimes; where every opposition was perceived as enemy and eventually crushed out of the political scene. These factors have construed politics and governance as the affairs of the 'strong' in the society. This poor understanding creates a complacency that sends negative signals about governance and statehood and has therefore reduced election in Nigeria to selection. The JDPC since the political dispensation in 1999 has been actively involved in election monitoring side by side with many international NGOs. However the reports of human rights watch has characterised the Nigerian political system as criminal politics.[834] The obvious reason for this manipulation comes from the lack of democratic culture since the ordinary people both rural and urban are ignorant of their civil rights and democratic duties. Even the reports of international observers are confined to the cities where they have their hotel accommodations and 'safety nets', while the rural areas are the den and centres for manipulative or rigged results. The

---

[832] Cf. D. Dorr, Social Justice Agenda, 108.
[833] A. Baumgartner, Solidarität, 287 (Translation is mine).
[834] Cf. J. Campbell, Nigeria Dancing on the Brink, 32.

capital territory Abuja, the supposed centre of unity, is "viewed as a symbol of arrogance and parasitic character of Nigerian elite politics".[835] Governance and government presence are felt mostly in Abuja and the 36 states capitals; every further movement into the hinterlands comes with depreciating governmental presence.

Over 60-70% of Nigerians live outside the 36 states and the federal capital but some statistics are drawn mainly from this spurious 30%. That accounts for the fraudulent GDP reports made yearly that conflicts with the principles of HDI. The truth is that "HDI reveal much more about the socio-economic progress of a country than GNP [or GDP] does."[836] These are issues of human development realities that the humanitarian church must address. She must teach her people at the periphery to understand how a democratic state functions by demanding good governance from the elected. This would assuage the helplessness of the masses and assist them to articulate better the clandestine and political intrigues built on their collective ignorance.

The church and the political community are two very autonomous and independent bodies, yet they are dedicated to the service of humanity and their cooperation serves the social good of humanity.[837] Even though the church lacks the finance to provide for the people she is called on one hand to the service of advocacy and on the other hand to conceive a political theory that fits into the Christian message. Such a call includes organising laymen and women in different forums so that they become conversant with the CST and be sound in their understanding of human rights. The church also is encouraged to organise seminars for politicians, trade union leaders, chairmen of NGOs and leaders of pressure groups. These opinion leaders need the CST orientation and the requisite qualification to stir their groups. As a result they could guide and direct their different opinion groups by finding compromises, respect for the rule of law, holding political speeches/rhetoric, using the modern internet media like facebook for their political interests and creating advertisements for those who represent their common ideas. Also it is important that they are knowledgeable in economics, law and other organisational aspect to judiciously represent the common interests of the group they stand for. Such teachings are a stimulus

---

[835] Ibid., 40.
[836] M. U. Haq, Reflection on Human Development, 61.
[837] Cf. Paul VI, Gaudium et Spes, 76.

to wake up political consciousness and sentiments for questioning government and government officials representing their society. One example of political organisation in Nigeria today that teaches political and leadership consciousness is Lux-Terra Leadership foundation.

The CLCN in her annual meeting in December 1982 inferred three common concerns about the Nigerian laity in the field of religion and politics: the secular status of Nigeria from the constitution, politics being regarded as a dirty job and the interrelationship between religion and politics, which ought to be cooperation and collaboration. These three findings led to resolutions, which were akin to a roadmap for building a sustainable democratic culture.[838]

1   Organised bodies like CLCN shall refrain from political partisanship. But Catholics with political abilities must not reject politics. Even Jesus was involved in the religious and political life of his time. Therefore, the church calls Catholics to invest their God-given talents in their different capacities to represent the church in political matters.[839]

2   Every effort must be made to choose credible men and women of integrity irrespective of ethnicity and creed, but who can stand the test of corruption and the abuse of office. It is the presence of such people in all levels of government offices and parastatals that may change the fate of a nation.[840] A good example is that of Prophet Jethro who advised Moses (Ex 18, 21) that those to be chosen must be people of proven character.

3   Catholics should be led by their religious values and principles in the pursuit of politics, so as to bring about justice, equity and peace. Their exemplary life could transform society such that the politics could be guided by moral order to encourage the growth of the common good.

4   All Catholics vying for political offices must refrain from secret cults and any 'oath taking' to avoid mortgaging their consciences and political lives.

---

[838] Cf. G. A. Ojo, Catholic Laity, 44-45.
[839] Cf. Paul VI, Gaudium et Spes, 75
[840] Cf. Francis, Laudato Si, 179.

5   They should strive for equal opportunities for all political aspirants regardless of religion and ethnic difference. Their watchword should be the choice of candidates with integrity and those who put the fear of God before politics.

6   All Catholic parents and guardians are to be keen on the religious contents of their children in schools. They ought to choose schools with good religious instructions for their children or wards, where they could learn those accepted fundamental ethics.

7   In the defence of the fundamental human rights of parents and children, CLCN calls on religious bodies in Nigeria and the government to recognise each other as partners of educational development. Like the CBCN, the CLCN also calls for the return of schools to voluntary agencies and appeals for private and interested hands to set up schools that will carry the needed impetus for corporate change in a modern Nigeria.

8   All Catholics are asked to join hands with the government at all levels for effective change in the education that will bring about fundamental changes. That is why they must ensure that only political leaders with religious ideas and fundamental ethical character are given access to such offices to effect change through exemplary living.[841]

Such political strategies with religious values and humanistic undertones could equip the lay faithful with the requisite mental capability to stand politically to defend the people's interests. Adherence to these strategies could give a leeway to sustainable democratic culture.

As much as these strategies are important for the planting of democratic culture the ripple effects of ubiquitous corruption must be unearthed and fought conscientiously. Otherwise, present political/economic quagmire will persist; this is akin to the ethical question of the prisoner's dilemma.[842] The structure of this dilemma is such that in a given concrete

---

[841] Cf. G. A. Ojo, Catholic Laity, 45-47.

[842] Cf. J. Wiemeyer, Keine Freiheit ohne Gerechtigkeit, 150. It is an ethical lesson drawn from the American jurisprudent thinking of criminal law and leniency on why two rational individuals may best not cooperate even if it is in their best interest. Two suspects of a gang are arrested for a criminal act that is punishable by fifteen years imprisonment. As reward for cooperating with the system, they could be given a lighter prosecution e.g. on illegal possession of weapon, which meant one year imprisonment, if they confess and admit their crime. However, they will be separated from each other when giving their confessions, which

situation, every stakeholder is bound to take a different decision while everyone becomes ignorant of the actions of the other participants. Such a dilemma structure could exist in the case of two importers for example, where one bribes to obtain his goods from the customs, while the ethical minded stakeholder refuses to bribe. The likely outcome is that the former experiences a business turnover despite the ethical question behind his actions, whereas the latter becomes a culprit of failed shrewdness. How do you explain a situation of two competing contractors, when a better one is rejected and the less qualified one is awarded a government contract just for oiling the wheels of government officials? The end result is an inferior job. Therefore, the greatest plight is that the reactions and behaviour of these several stakeholders as regards the issue in question cannot even be determined or predicted. Accordingly, despite the different efforts to remove the monster corruption in contemporary Nigeria, a constellation of minorities has remained the kingpins and major perpetrators of such surreptitious activities. Though the populace may well understand the values of justice, the dilemma of this powerful minority immersed in day to day crafty corrupt practices, reduces the national pace of economic development. It thus creates infighting and misplacement of values among the masses. To strengthen the individuals' values so as to evade the asymmetry of the prisoner's dilemma structures and the shabby structure responsible for corruption will demand good control measures to be put in place.[843] The issue about corruption is unending, but how a nation or a people go about to curb it by reducing it to the minimum level is very important.

One of the strongest elements of control and supervision is transparency which involves the use of modern technology today. The details of expenses of all monies approved and released by government for building schools, roads and other projects must be published on all media including, twitters and facebook for the common man's access, to be able to checkmate fraudulent actions of politicians.[844] It is also important to employ

---

would determine the weight of the leniency. The four possibilities are: If both of them deny, each gets one year imprisonment, if both confesses, they get eight years imprisonment each. If A confesses and B denies, A goes free and B gets fifteen years imprisonment and when B confesses and A denies, A gets fifteen years imprisonment and B is set free. The end analysis shows that isolated actions of two individuals can lead to their utter destruction.

[843] Cf. Ibid.

[844] Cf. P. Collier, The Bottom Billion, 150. The governor of Ugandan Central Bank Emmanuel Tumusiime-Mutebile began such a heroic move in the mid 90s to publish budgets of the nation. The Nigerian Finance Minister Ngozi Okonjo Iweala adopted this same

the 'four eyes principles' where at least two different individuals approve something before it is implemented. It is also referred to as 'two-man rule' or 'two-person rule'. This system adds to the security of any decision process because it is expected that the two individuals are dealing with an issue; however it all depends on the ability, integrity and diligence of the individuals concerned.[845] Also, a sense of professional bureaucracy must be raised to meet global standards coupled with a reasonable remuneration for staff so as to avoid any act of financial misconduct. There must be constant rotation of workers to counteract unhealthy familiarity that breeds laxity for misconduct. Whistleblowers must also be protected by government authorities otherwise the fear of the 'strong men' may retard such good gestures. There is need for an independent financial control and supervision system. Also, the supervision of staff members must be strictly adhered to so that officials are paid only when they work. Therefore the ministry of labour must roll out stringent control measures for teachers and civil servants to avoid complacency, idleness and *laissez-faire* attitude towards work. With the use of modern technology card reading system today, workers will have to prove they came for work. In moments of doubts, reputable but independent firms could be called to read the machines to avoid internal fraud.

Inasmuch as these positive changes within the system are very important, they only emanate from a politically conscious people and a people who are ready to demand change. Such development meets the aspiration for sustainable democratic culture that can consequently lead to sustainable political reforms. History has shown that these are the product of structural reforms championed by the casualties of injustice or the peripheral people like in the French Revolution. Therefore, the local support and the momentum of a politically informed society aspiring for structural reforms can change the underlying structure of injustice, which is a composite of relationships between individuals and society developed over the time. Freedom as Martin Luther King Jnr. says, is never voluntarily given by oppressors, it must be demanded by the oppressed. Change therefore must come from within and such readiness to oppose existing structures of injustice encourages critical examination of its primary causes. Every

---

example in 2003, which began to raise public consciousness. The many death treats she received made her understand that she was on the right track.
[845] Cf. Powered by WhatIs.com, http://whatis.techtarget.com/definition/four-eyes-principle (04.07.2016)

structure needs to be challenged to grow and it must be in reference to the people's wellbeing and welfare, it must create the freedom for reasoning and the opportunity for amendment.[846]

Many have berated the political imbalance in the structure of Nigeria, which remains a major hurdle for human development. Aliyi Ekineh observes that "more than half the population [of Nigerians] do not even know the name of the country. They learn it at school. If they do not go to school, there is no way they could comprehend they are Nigerians... thus ethnic division and distrust are more obnoxious in Nigeria than racism is in some other countries."[847] The political difficulty to satisfy the wishes of the multitude of ethnic groups in this political package constitutes a major hurdle to human development. On the contrary, Botswana with lesser ethnic diversity and fewer resources has been able to integrate herself into the global market through her democratic consistencies as the basis of agreements between her fewer ethnic groups is easier.[848] Even after the 1957 conference in London for self rule, the Sir Henry Willink Commission of the same year admitted the problems of minority ethnic groups. From its several tours this commission came up with proposals to address the minority question, but they were never implemented;[849] thereby provoking persistent agitations since the 1960s for political restructuring of Nigeria and for a true or fiscal federalism. Albeit it has appeared severally on the pages of magazines, newspapers and through several constitutional conferences, it has remained like a circus. Though politics is a game of numbers, it is only through constitutional reform that judicial protection can be granted to the capabilities and entitlements of minorities; because minorities remain at a disadvantage in a political process dominated by majorities.[850] If political understanding and participation at the grassroots were in existence, true federalism, the minimum requirements for a Nigerian project would have been implemented long ago. The commitment towards the realisation of a federal structure marks the "struggle against injustice... [through] changing the structures of society so that there is a better distribution of power. The aim is to give effective power to those who have been left out on the margins. This involves reducing the excessive and unchecked power of those

---

[846] Cf. A. Shorter, Theology of Mission, 49.
[847] Nigeria's new Dawn, Last Chance for the Patchwork State? 17, an extract from: Foundations for Disintegration.
[848] Cf. P. Collier, The Bottom Billion, 50.
[849] Cf. J. O. Ihonvbere, T. Shaw, Illusions of power, 50
[850] Cf. M. Nussbaum, Creating Capabilities, 177.

in the centres of power in the various sectors of the society."[851] It is akin to the article 20 of the German constitution that power emanates from the people. It was such constitutional changes that encouraged the likes of Bishop Emmanuel von Ketteler to participate in the constitutional reforms of his time. Unfortunately, the Nigerian public is yet to understand this power dimension. Instead her political language is saturated with such frivolous statements as: 'power comes from God' but forgetting the political injunction that *Vox Populi Vox Dei*. Such a shallow mindset has perpetrated a corporate political complacency that prefers a cosmetic approach of governance that carries no constitutional weight.

A human development that is stirred by political factors must bear these four essential paradigms: equity, sustainability, productivity and empowerment. Equity is the basic human right that gives all humans equal access to political and economic opportunities, whereas sustainability maintains that no option should supersede human opportunities. Productivity emphasises that people are central because productivity is only an aspect of human development and finally empowerment substantiates the need for people to have the power to exercise choices.[852] These paradigms are untouchable principles of political humanitarian service that the humanitarian church is called to stand for, to recreate and create the political momentum and democratic culture for the societal lower-class. The absence of such democratic impetus makes the task of teaching democratic culture and awareness an imperative for the humanitarian church. Therefore, teaching such democratic culture from the grassroots will move the complacent spirit of obvious monarchical and one party system's viewpoint from the sub-conscious to a democratic system. This is a system where reason and active participation in governance prevails, not power, influence or connection but where equal opportunities abound, people know their rights, they can ask questions and leaders are held responsible for their stewardship. This failed understanding of state's functions, has persuaded many into euphoric suggestions for a military comeback, 'strong hand' and all sorts of totalitarian traits of leadership. This is a task of the political *diakonia* to educate the masses on state consciousness, democracy, good governance, functioning institutions and fundamental human rights.

---

[851] D. Dorr, The Social Justice Agenda, 108.
[852] Cf. M. U. Haq, Reflection on Human Development, 16-20.

Democracy is the most up-to-date representative system of governance and whatever disadvantage it posits, even the worst of democracy is still better than the best of military. The military regimes is known to revert the think-tank democratic system to the primitive African totalitarian setting, where the opinion of one man or a tiny group of loyalists triumph and institutions are not given opportunity to grow. The CLCN describes military rule as "the worst form of aberration in governance through which the rights of the electorate are ruthlessly set aside by the military who steal their way to power through the barrel of the gun".[853] The first military rule in 1966 was preoccupied with eliminating "corruption, nepotism, ethnicity, inefficiency and waste rather than a fundamental socio-economic and political restructuring of the Nigerian social formation".[854] This has been the rhetoric of subsequent military administrations and military men turned into civilian leaders, but in reality "the advent of military governments has provided new and unequalled opportunities for people with little or no education, expertise or experience to climb the social and political ladder and become prominent and affluent overnight."[855] Unlike many Asian nations who despite their trying times were spared from military interruptions and could mature within their space and time politically, Nigeria's political history has been truncated by too many coup d'états. Consequently, it has created an infatuation and a hangover of military rule or the leadership through strong men and strong hands even in this democratic era.

The building of credible institutions is the gateway to a strong state. Individuals may influence decisions today, but global politics and economy are driven by institutions. Without credible internal democracy that will prop up healthy national institutions, Nigeria for example and like many African states may never be integrated into the global politics and market.[856] Therefore, the impasse and the parade of strong men and strong hands masked as statesmen/democrats must permit the growth of institutional capacity for the emergence of strong states; otherwise such states remain preoccupied with survival issues and consumed by domestic hegemony. Right now the global economy needs Africa for her raw materials which she

---

[853] G. A. Ojo, Catholic Laity of Nigeria, 262.
[854] J. I. Ihonvbere, T. Shaw, Illusions of Power, 51.
[855] Ibid., 153.
[856] Cf. Marvin Nii Ankrah, Regionalism and Political Instability in West Africa: Development, Challenges and Prospects, Hamburg, 2013, 100.

already has access to.[857] Nations of other continents are on steady growth in different ramifications and will never wait for Africa. The global community has already integrated Africa into the global realm. But integration is not a one-way affair, which makes it imperative for each African nation to integrate herself politically and economically into the global reality.[858] Also, this "new global economy has not generated a new scramble for Africa, as the expansion of international society did in the past. Rather it is African countries that need to scramble to integrate economically and politically, and that requires stable states and capable governments."[859] The humanitarian church, the hope of the common man is charged with this political duty to teach and instil democratic awareness that will become a culture among her people, in her very local milieu, so that "the new name for culture becomes politics."[860]

4.3.2   Creating democratic awareness from the grassroots

The greatest political assets of any community is the ability to organise herself into a political quorum within the context of the state and thus is able to bend her government to popular will within a democratic setting. This can easily attract the attention of politicians because they are always sensitive to such shifts in public opinion.[861] The first clarion call of Ken Saro Wiwa to his Ogoni people was, "no matter the system of government, unless a people take a destiny into their own hands, no improvement will come to them."[862] The result of such political awareness made Ogoni people stand against every further attempt of reckless petroleum extraction in their community unless grievances were addressed; besides basic human dignity, mutual respect and orderliness in company-host relationship must be adhered to. The community rejected every cosmetic attempt of reconciliation offered by the government and the multinational Shell Company.[863] This is the kind of democratic awareness that is

---

[857] Cf. M. Ottaway, The State before Democracy, 9.
[858] Cf. Jean Francois Bayart, Stephen Ellis, Beatrice Hibou, From Kleptocracy to the Felonious State, in: Ed., Jean Francois Bayart, The Criminalization of the State in Africa, Oxford, 1999, Pp 1-31, 3.
[859] M. Ottaway, The State before Democracy, 9.
[860] J.B. Metz, Zum Begriff, 39. (Translation is mine)
[861] Cf. M. U. Haq, Reflections of Human Development, 38.
[862] A. Rowell, et al., The next Gulf, London, 77. (See also K. Saro Wiwa, A month and a day, Penguin, 53.)
[863] Cf. Ibid., 221-224.

encouraged in every community and that is the aim of political humanitarianism, to make each community politically vigilant, where her inputs count in the policies and the daily politics that affect her.

The church as an institution and her long historic presence represents that solidity and impartial character of a prototype institution to correct these social anomalies. With her local network she is called to teach democratic cultures, to create such awareness and sensitivity of the people towards their rights and duties. Its fruits are so amazing because "...politicians are often afraid when the church actually takes her prophetic role seriously, when she begins to educate the citizens on their political and social rights."[864] Such a confrontation comes with its own challenges, because "...challenging conventional wisdom is a potentially politically volatile undertaking: it can backfire and become counterproductive, particularly in view of vested interests involved."[865] But 'come what may', a people must be ready to stand as one indivisible union and to hold on to her resolute political objectives. Although external vested interest may pounce on such a people like wounded lions, the ability to hold on will guarantee success. It recalls the statements of Tertullian about the blood of Martyrs as the seed of the faith in the church's history.[866] The average Nigerian is too fearful to stand and pay a political price. The cry of Niger/Delta being heard partially today is the consequence of the blood of Ken Saro Wiwa and the Ogoni eight. The humanitarian church must not shy away from her duties, because the present world has a growing tendency to create relative truths and not authentic truths about cultural and social issues. It is at this point that the practice of charity to teach the truth comes in strongest to uproot the illicit and relative truths of the society (John 8, 32). Therefore, adhering to Christian values is not only important but a medium towards building a humane, sustainable society and a true integral human development.[867] This envisaged humane society built on the effort of the church would serve as a foundation and a heritage that could be passed from generations to generations, thus "the Church in Africa [could] draw... her life from this heritage. For the sake of Christ and in fidelity to the lesson of life which he taught us, she feels the duty to be present wherever human suffering exists and to make heard the

---

[864] J. Ogbonnaya The Role of African Catholicism in the Light of Africae Munus, 108
[865] A. Adedeji, The Monrovia Strategy and the Lagos Plan of Action, 14.
[866] Cf. Karl Baus, Von der Urgemeinde zur frühchristlichen Großkirche, in: Ed., Hubert Jedin, Handbuch der Kirchengeschichte, Vol. I, Freiburg, 1985, 286.
[867] Cf. Benedict XVI, Caritas in Veritate, 4.

silent cry of the innocents who suffer persecution, or of peoples whose governments mortgage the present and the future for personal interests."[868] The action of the church teaching political awareness must be accompanied by political practice. The laity cannot exist all by herself; she must carry the message of change to the outside wall of the church. She is the salt and the light of the earth (cf. Matt. 5, 13-16), the leaven of the society (cf. 1Kor 5, 1). It is the responsibility of the laity to be part of the governance at local, state and federal government level.[869] Catholic men and women must be given the opportunity to exercise the wonderful and beautiful Christian values learnt in and from the church, in the practice of active politics so as to clean up the system. Therefore, the support of these good Christian and Catholic politicians who are ready to stand for the masses is important; as a church "we must learn to push our people to the decision-making stages of politics so that nobody is allowed to set aside the decisions and will of the electorate."[870]

Even though civil societies have ventured enormously in the creation of democratic awareness, together with humanitarian organisations they play political service to humanity. Their duties as a group of political actors and animators in this task of political service include building, encouraging and growing the rural communities as inclusive and integrated societies into the political mainstream of the nation.[871] Without such political growth, the dream to achieve desired economic emancipation and regional sustainability shall remain a mirage. It is the momentum that can power poor nations out of the global periphery. The church is called to be a sentinel, to reject every trace of dehumanization among people and every development that excludes the interest of the people.[872] The humanitarian church that champions the option of the poor must serve as the meeting point for social, economic and political attention for the poor.

In this journey of political service to entrench political awareness, the humanitarian church must factor an African democratic development as

---

[868] Benedict XVI, Africae Munus, 30.
[869] Cf. G. A. Ojo, Catholic Laity of Nigeria, 270, 279
[870] Ibid., 271.
[871] Cf. Obiora Ike, The Church and Civil Society, the Case of Nigeria, in; Eds., Gerhard Kruip, Helmut Reifeld, Church and Civil Society, The Role of Christian Churches in the Emerging Countries of Argentina, Mexico, Nigeria and South Africa, Bornheim, 2007, 111-126, 123.
[872] Cf. Benedict XVI, Africae Munus, 30.

it suits Nigeria and her interests. Democracy as it sounds has variations in many nations of the world, thus the democratic structure of USA differs from that of Germany, France and Japan; despite their occasional limitations, they are still referred to as democratic nations. The question is what results do they bring to the table and what is their level of transparency? These are fundamental issues that need to be dealt with. But since independence, Nigeria as copycat has been on a borrowing spree of different models of governance and democratic practices. Consequently,

> ...our laws, our customs, our cities, everything bears the characteristics of European colonizers. Our administrative, judicial, military, educational institutions and procedures have not significantly deviated from those implanted by the colonizers. We have followed the European fashion in every aspect of life. When they sponsored military government, we went along. When they changed their mind and demanded electocracy, we went along, and dutifully imported constitutions and legislative institutions that imitated those in Paris, London, and Washington.[873]

Nigeria from the first republic practised the British parliamentary system of government, the second and third republic have been dominated by the flamboyant and expensive American presidential system of government. From every indication Nigeria lacks originality and authenticity in leadership and the fact remains that what is borrowed lacks Nigerian antecedence and as such is ever foreign to the Nigerian people; they do not take care of the leadership loopholes and the perennial problems and they practically make the political system a mere smokescreen. What is needed are governing structures that will adapt African history and corporate thinking, such that will recognise and rediscover the African way of transparency and responsible leadership. Despite the different democratic designs proposed in many deliberations by credible and progressive Nigerian political stakeholders, the love of foreign concepts has hampered such application. The Nigerian Church represents the voice of the voiceless and is challenged rationally to keep reminding the state of her authentic duties towards her citizens.

---

[873] Chinweizu, Education for Liberation of Black Africa, 3.

CHAPTER FIVE: HUMANITARIAN ENGAGEMENT IN IDAH DIOCESE: PROBLEMS SETBACKS AND PROSPECTS.

5.   New strategies of humanitarian action

The fruit of every organised humanitarian engagement ends with prospective developmental plans that could be translated through well thought out adaptive features for local transformation. In the last chapter, the premise of prospective humanitarian development hinged overwhelmingly on the triangle of education, production and political consciousness. The different humanitarian engagements, suggestions and prospects in the literature would demand an adaptive mode among the local people, which warrants the expertise of the humanitarian. A successful humanitarian endeavour entails that the humanitarian must go beyond the present modification of the people in question.

Having studied the historical background of the pre-modern Igala, (chapter 3) what are the necessary impulses to prop up the present educational, economical and political awareness? How have the past structures made or marred the people's social development? Such evaluations are geared towards discovering the strengths and weaknesses of the structure to pave way for rejection, adoption, improvement or reformation of the historical elements that are embedded in the culture. No matter the ambivalence of such conclusions in the different fields of life, the major concern here is about an experimentation of humanitarian development which is a people's task and must be people-centred and people-oriented. Such rational exercise could connect the dots of the primitive lifestyles to the present age, its effects, the need and kind of change to deal with the glaring poverty and towards resolving issues of self-reliance and sustainability.

The new task of the humanitarian church includes the drive for sustainability in every Igala/Bassa village, so as to produce and sustain its population and to avoid the waiting for oil money or handouts. There must be a conscious move away from the trauma and shackles of the economic and political destabilization of the colonial and post colonial era. The question is how does Igala/Basaland reconnect with the rest of the world? Though the traditional people had their own ways of transferring knowledge, such oral transfer was not sustainable and could not rival the sophisticated and effective record of production that is of global practices today. This inability to document the art of production distorted the flow of production skills and strategies and has invariably contributed to the loss of some traditional knowledge of production. But the worst was the failure to understand the politics of the modern market economy, thus a new market strategy must be cultivated and invented to protect national interests for self-reliance, -sustenance and -sufficiency.

The proposed concept of development here must engender a conscious voice of a people ready for freedom, because true development comes with personal freedom and liberation. There must be a change of language to 'we can', 'we want' and 'we must overcome our problems'.[874] Taking into cognizance the sustainable livelihood agenda of the UK's Department for International Development DFID, development must be holistic so that humans take responsibility for their lives. They must be able to deal with stress and shocks and must also grow the capability to recover from them. It also provides the platform that betters their assets and capabilities, so as to produce for the next generation and above all to be integrated into the global economy by supplying both at the local and international levels.[875] How is Igala/Bassaland to be integrated into the present global economy to better her chances of production, to meet her immediate needs and to supply the excesses? Also, how many of these questions for example can the DDS answer?

5.1   Globalisation and the growing state of poverty

One of the strongest factors of growth in modern times that has pulled nations from the bottom of poverty to affluence today is globalisation. How come globalisation has so eluded Nigeria despite her stupendous human and natural resources, her population which means a good market and unlike other African nations, she is not landlocked? This question becomes more relevant as over 70% of Nigerians live below the poverty margin today whereas other nations profit exceedingly from the gains of globalisation. Poor agro-policies are among the greatest undoing of the nation and other factors like the long effects of the depression in Kogi-East associated with the civil war and the effect of the oil bust on the general economy. NGOs presence has become a global response to issues of poverty

---

[874] Cf. Nora McNamara, Nigeria, Diocesan Development Service, (DDS) of Idah, Source: Trocaire, 13th April 2006, 1-8, 7.
[875] Cf. Stephen Morse, et al., Sustainable Livelihood Approach, 4.

and since the oil recession in Nigeria, NGOs presence has become inevitable to offset the looming poverty and to cushion the pains of the masses. Globalisation is a strong phenomenon of the present age, but has it made or marred the efforts of Nigeria and how is it in relation to the local people?

Even though the term globalisation has been very much around, it has made headlines in the media and massively dominated the literatures in the last two decades. Globalisation has pulled humanity from its primordial background into a modern society. Therefore, humanity that was preoccupied with its immediate environment from antiquity has gradually evolved into unified scenery, thereby bringing about positive and negative changes to the affairs of humans and their respective sovereign states. Despite the distance of the local people from the mega cities of the world today, regardless of the differences between the nations of the world and notwithstanding the boundaries, vast oceans and seas that demarcate the various continents from the other, they have all been synchronised into one economic pool through the effect and process of globalisation. It represents the much spoken 'global village' and the 'new world order' in the media. How does this global phenomenon affect the African? How does globalisation affect the once 'estranged' Nigerian people? How does globalisation affect the rural people of Kogi-East? Does globalisation further or hinder the advocated humanitarian force that ought to be the springboard and the imperative of self-reliance?

There are varying definitions of globalisation, as economists believe it is the internationalisation of products and the breaking down of world trade boundaries, while social scientists agree to the proliferation, the contraction of transnational social relations and the emergence of a global society. For political scientist it is the tendency of breaking state's consciousness and the loss of the meaning of their national borders, constitutional- and international law, the wearing down of sovereignty and the emergence of a global domestic law. From the viewpoint of cultural experts it is the emergence of a world culture, or a culture that cuts across all people. These aforementioned concepts of globalisation are mostly from the developed nations; nevertheless there are other views from critics of globalisation and from the developing world.[876]

---

[876] Cf. F. Nuscheler, Entwicklungspolitik, 52.

The term globalisation in a simple term is the act of creating "the world as a single entity, a world without borders [and] a free society without boundaries".[877] It is the act of uniting the world for the common good of all humans. It is believed that this act can lead to the greater happiness of humans and above all that humans can consequently enjoy a fuller humanity. Globalisation encourages capital flow at the transnational level as it brings about the standardization of consumer goods. Another name for globalisation is capitalistic or economic globalisation since globalisation is anchored on capitalism. It also means the global extension of the principles and practice of capitalism. The prominent agents of globalisation are the rich nations of the world together with the financial institutions of Breton woods, the World Bank and IMF.[878]

The impact of globalisation in Africa began from the annexation of its different parts by the colonial administration. The establishment of colonial rule from 1900 in the greater part of Nigeria for example, saw the expansion of the effect of globalisation, beginning from the penetration of the British chamber of commerce into the hinterlands, British West Africa. It was a punitive expedition that was tenaciously pursued under the policy of free trade by the many companies that eventually galvanised as a British multinational, the UAC. Also, other measures like customs regulations/rules were put in place to checkmate the export-import trade.[879] As these changes took place in the far Niger Delta for example, it subsequently affected trade relations along the Niger for example Idah and the nation at large. Besides, the presence of an office stationed at Idah by these firms to control imports and other towns along the Lower Niger River brought about the subjugation of the people and the implementation of the free market enterprise. Moreover, the shift in the production of food crops to cash crops for export points to the early effect of globalisation. The displacement of the traditional

---

[877] Bisong Kekong, The African Quest for Self-Determination within Postmodern Globalization and Civilization, in: Ed., S. Nnoruka, The Nigerian journal of Theology, Vol. 21, Ikot-Ekpene, 2004. Pp. 101-120, 101.
[878] Cf. Tissa Balasuriya Globalisation, in: Eds., Virginia Fabella, M. M; R.S Sugirtarajah, Dictionary of the Third World Theologies, New York 2000, Pp. 91-94, 91.
[879] Cf. W. Wariboko, The CMS Mission, 45-46. This included punitive measures with bloody consequences exerted on native middlemen, who for the imperialists constituted obstacles to the establishment of British mercantilism. In the Niger Delta for example, it eventually led to the overthrow and deportation of King Jaja of Opodo to the Caribbean Island of St. Vincent between 1879 -1887. Others suffered this fate up till the 1900 after the eventual establishment of colonial rule.

trading system through the introduction of the British currency and other economic measures subsequently increased the globalization borders of the colonial states and thus established the principles of free market enterprise. This enforced free market enterprise arm twisted the local traders leaving the European merchants as the major dealers and brokers of the trans-Atlantic commerce between Africa and Europe.

The principles of free trade and the colonial trade treaties crippled the African trade even till after her political independence. The lingering effect of her devastating collapse lies clearly in her exports of primary commodities (raw materials) to the international market whereas the affluent nations of the world deal extensively in the export of superior and manufactured goods. As a consequence, the African net weight trade to the world market today is just a staggering sum of 2%.[880] The Nigerian trade performance in respect of this 2% comes basically from oil and from all indications the entire Kogi-East like many other parts of Nigeria portend a zero decimal contribution.[881] In essence, all of its economic activities however minute fall into the informal economy. That is why, "Africa's gross continental product is about $540billion, more or less the same as that of Spain, and only five times the size of Exxon Mobile."[882] This is because other nations like China or India for example have grown from commodity to industrial market whereas African nations have remained perpetually at the level of commodity sales. Another striking factor where African nations miss out on the positive angle of globalisation is the lack of capability to add value to their commodity goods. Despite the global increase in the fortunes of the oil sector in the last decade, Nigeria's oil dependent economy has remained economically stagnant. With this fair share of global proceeds she still failed to break into the global market due to pockets of violence, myriad issues of corruption at all levels, nepotism, failed governmental policies and the lack of political vision and will.

---

[880] Cf. Greg Mills and Jonathan Oppenheimer, From Spectator to Player: Strategies for globalising African Trade, in: Ed., Phoebe Griffith, Unbinding Africa, Making Globalisation work for Good Governance, London, 2003, 32-44, 32.

[881] Cf. Odumakin Yimka, Confab: the complete story of the conspiracies, Vanguard Nigerian Newspaper, http://www.vanguardngr.com/2014/08/confab-complete-story-conspiracies-odumakin/(16.09.14).

[882] Phoebe Griffith, Introduction, Unbinding Africa, in: Ed., Phoebe Griffith, Unbinding Africa, Making Globalisation work for Good Governance, London, 2003, ix-xvii, ix.

The inability of the poor nations to access the global market has been likened to historical trade agreements because most of the global trade agreements began after the World War II; for example, the General Agreement on tariffs and Trade (GATT) in 1947, which was concluded before the 60s when many African nations were still in the colonial age.[883] Thus "when African and [other] poor countries began to join the GATT negotiations in the 1960s and 1970s, in the aftermath of post-colonial independence, they had to sign up to the rules already agreed in previous rounds."[884] This institutionalised status quo since colonial times expanded into unfair terms of trade in an established free market enterprise today as it constitutes one of the most negative effects of globalisation towards the poor nations of the world today. Pope Paul VI in his encyclical *Populorum Progressio* bemoans the evil of colonialism, its legacy of unfair terms of trade and the general economic imbalance created through different neo-colonial policies as they create injustices in trade relations.[885] The pontiff proposes social justice as he admonishes the unfair terms of trade practised under the guise of free market economy. Thus "trade relations can no longer be based solely on the principle of free, unchecked competition, for it very often creates an economic dictatorship. Free trade can be called just only when it conforms to the demands of social justice."[886]

These and many other factors crafted a dependence syndrome that soon created a catch-up mentality among the African people. Therefore, African societies on finding themselves for whatever reason to be technologically trailing behind others, have had to apply a catch up mentality not only by independent inventions but also by borrowing skills.[887] Moreover the improved media presence today heightens this catch-up mentality as people are able to compare and contrast even from the comfort of their homes, thereby breeding public outrage. Surely the rest of the world cannot afford to wait for the poor nations, nonetheless many African societies from the primitive times and till today still lack the technical know-how to advance their interests. The impending solution is not just the invention and borrowing of skills but also the ability to adopt these skills and synchronise them with local skills and conditions which the process of

---

[883] Cf. G. Bolton, Poor Story, 173.
[884] Ibid.
[885] Cf. Donal Dorr, Option for the Poor, A hundred Years of Vatican Social Teaching, Dublin 1983, 140.
[886] Paul VI, Populorum Progressio, 59.
[887] Cf. W. Rodney, How Europe underdeveloped Africa, 115.

globalisation permits.[888] These are the positive sides of globalisation. Thus, if borders are truly broken as globalisation dictates, then the act of adoption should be problem-free; again, this process even from primitive African history was truncated by many factors because

> ...very few of man's major scientific discoveries have been separately discovered in different places by different people. Once a principle or a tool is known, it spreads or diffuses to other peoples. Why then did European technology fail to make its way into Africa during the many centuries of contact between the two centuries? The basic reason is that the very nature of Afro-European trade was highly unfavourable to the movement of positive ideas and techniques from the European capitalist system to the African pre-capitalist (communal, feudal, and pre-feudal) system of production.[889]

There are major factors that make up the forces of globalisation like religion, technology, economy and territory. They act not only separately but over time have reinforced one another.[890] Nevertheless, the major areas of globalisation that mostly affect underdeveloped nations are trade, movement of capital, the migration of people and the media. These factors as a matter of fact are very distinct factors, pending which of them one intends to address in the global market. In terms of capital flows and migration for example, the developing nations were better globalised a hundred years ago than today.[891] The media factor is wielding stronger influence at present. Telecommunication service prior to 1990 was very poor, inefficient, epileptic, insufficient and expensive in many parts of Africa; however mobile telephones made Nigerians bypass the fixed lines.[892] The presence of the Global System of Mobile Communication (GSM) since 2001 has recorded immense success through providing services to over 140 million subscribers by connecting families, friends and businesses today; it is one of the fastest growing industries and the largest job provider in Nigeria.[893]

---

[888] Cf. Benjamin Ofori-Amoah, Technological Change Strategy for Economic Development in Africa, in: Eds., Fidelis Ezeala-Harrison, Senyo B-S-K. Adjibolosoo, London, 1994, Pp. 85-103, 93.

[889] W. Rodney, How Europe underdeveloped Africa, 115-116.

[890] Cf. K. Bisong, The African Quest for Self Determination, 102; Ali Mazrui, Nkrumah's Legacy, and Africa's Triple Heritage between Globalization and Counter Terrorism, Accra, 2004, 1. Here the author substitutes territory for empire.

[891] Cf. P. Collier, The Bottom Billion, 80.

[892] Cf. G. Bolton, Poor Story, 195.

[893] Cf. Nigeria - Mobile Infrastructure, Operators and Broadband - Statistics and Analyses, http://www.budde.com.au/Research/Nigeria-Mobile-Market-Insights-and-Statistics.html (21.08.15)

However the cities are the major beneficiaries of this service and internet service is still almost a thing of luxury.[894] The total output of the industry is less than the public demand to the extent that it distorts the quality of service and thus brings about arbitrary price increase. This is due to the long military presence and its ensuing hangover in the democratic dispensation coupled with the patron-client economy that has slowed the productivity and the needed competition to drive the telecommunication industry farther than what it is today. Globalisation has increased access to television services beginning from the 80s when television sets were introduced into many homes in this part of the nation. Over the last decade, the quality and quantity of services have increased tremendously. On one hand this gives more homes access to global realities while on the other hand it brews unnecessary comparison, discontentment and resentment.

Since we live in a global village, virtually every economic decision made by the affluent nations has effects on the poor nations of the world; like the Swahili adage puts it that when two elephants fight, the grass suffers and when they make love too the same grass still suffers. Therefore, "whatever the west does... has an impact, from Cold War loans to trade policies. The simple reality is that since Africa is very poor what the rich west does matters."[895] Today the flattening of the borders encourages multinationals to 'pick and choose' from the cheapest of markets, a fact that creates bumper profits for these multinationals. Because of this factor, the European Union (EU) for example subsidizes the European farmers annually to avoid economic relapse, so that farmers are able to produce and sell in the world market even below the production cost. This politics of subvention makes the EU the second largest agro-market after the US and together they account for 40% of global agricultural production, which makes them the topmost exporter of agricultural goods.[896] But on the contrary, agricultural subsidies in Nigeria for example have been scraped off as one of the conditions for IMF loans, consequently, its results is a very pathetic agricultural scenario.

Today the urban areas in Nigeria determine the economic activities of such rural areas like Kogi-East, since they are given more prerogatives in

---

[894] Cf. Marina Ottaway, The state before democracy, in; Ed., Phoebe Griffith, Unbinding Africa, Making Globalisation work for Good Governance, London, 2003, Pp. 1-9, 5.
[895] G. Bolton, Poor Story, 49.
[896] Cf. Deutsche Bischofkonferenz, Den Hunger bekämpfen, 28.

governmental policies than rural areas. Urban-rural disparity has been one dominant factor on the political and economic landscape of Nigeria. The different wage commissions over time (the Adebo Commission in 1970 and the Udoji Commission 1975) have raised mainly the urban wage scheme, thus creating a sharp contrast in urban/rural income gap.[897] The different salary scales in Nigeria from federal to state and to the local governments portrays the economic backwardness of such a rural area, where the majority of the civil servants are staff of the third tier of government (the local government) that has the least resources. Because of the clumsy administrative system riddled with all sorts of corruptions traces, what falls into the third tier of government equals the biblical crumbs from the master's table (Cf. Lk 16:21). The average home take of some workers is less than 100 Dollars monthly whereas their state counterparts take almost twice and their colleagues at the federal level about thrice that same amount. The imbalance in the different tiers of government increases dissatisfaction in the rural areas where the small scale farmers and peasants are mostly resident. Such disparity fuels of course more hunger and starvation and consequently affects the national life.[898] Although the cities may be better off, they are still caught in the web of increased cost of food items. Furthermore, that Nigeria records very low in the Human Development ranking, for example as 152nd nation out of 187 countries in the annual World Human Development publication of 2013 for example, portends the harsh effect of poverty in this age of globalisation, where many industrialised and emerging nations are becoming very welfare conscious and oriented.

According to Michael Barnet globalisation is a consequent factor of the age of liberal humanitarianism, a factor that is overtly tied with a yardstick for measuring success and failures. As globalisation blossomed at the end of the cold war it led to heated debate on its definition and measurement and how to assess its accrued benefits and consequences, because whether one likes it or not, the world was in the process of globalisation. Thus globalisation, in the words of Thomas Friedman's, was flattening the world and creating winners and losers.[899] This fact unfortunately echoes mixed feeling between affluent and poor nations of the

---

[897] Cf. Fidelis Ezeala-Harrison, What Ails African Economies: Lessons from Over-stretched Underdevelopment, in: Eds., Fidelis Ezeala-Harrison, Senyo B-S.K. Adjibolosoo, Perspectives on Economic Development in Africa, Westport, 1994, Pp. 3-24, 16.

[898] Cf. Deutsche Bischofskonferenz, Den Hungern bekämpfen, 10.

[899] Cf. M. Barnett, Empire of Humanity, 165.

world. In spite of the wonderful opportunities globalisation has created in the western world and the Tiger nations and some modern economic strides made by some poor nations of the world, the "sad reality is that although globalisation has powered the majority of developing countries toward prosperity, it is now making things harder for these latecomers."[900] Therefore, for the poor nations of the world, who despite their committed economic policies to escape economic woes but are still locked down with the chains of poverty and economic traps, they would definitely have a negative perception of that concept of globalisation that says it is a "new development model of a globally integrated market economy."[901] This failed access into the fortunes of the global world economy robs them of the fortunes of globalisation. According to Paul Collier, these are nations, who may have missed the global train of economic success.[902] Such inability to access the global market makes poor nations of the world develop cold feet towards globalisation.[903] However, this inability also shows the level of unpreparedness of many of these poor nations, a factor that keeps them at the borderlands today. Nonetheless, the wise counsel of Pope Benedict XVI reconciles the fact that globalisation on its own is not a bad development, it is rather what humanity makes out of it that is bad.[904] The example of China experiencing immense reduction in hunger and destitution through the effect of globalisation is a lesson for developing nations that globalisation is not a mirage. It is the hope that successive governments of developing nations like Nigeria for example would in the future take the bull by the horns to grapple with the problem of poverty like the Chinese have done. At the moment most efforts are still questionable and that is what comprehensive humanitarian action intends to pursue, to decipher a roadmap that could catapult humanity from the margins to the heart of the society.

---

[900] P. Collier, The Bottom Billion, 80.

[901] T. Balasuriya Globalisation, 91.

[902] Cf. P. Collier, The Bottom Billion, 80.

[903] Cf. T. Balasuriya, Globalisation, 92. Such discontenting feeling in the developing world makes the principles of globalisation a bad omen for these nations. It increases the dependency of the poorer nations on the rich nations of the world since the economic productions of the poor nations are determined by the needs of the rich nations, because globalisation commercialises almost every aspect of life, sports, transport, communication, education and so on. Because of the media superiority of the rich nations, it expands, promotes and dictates alien cultural ideas, which diminishes the local cultural ideas of the poor world. These factors make many in the third world to feel globalisation is another name for neo-colonialism.

[904] Cf. Benedict XVI, Caritas in Veritatis, 42.

Inasmuch as globalisation through improved medicine has kept many mothers and children alive today, it has added to the population index of the people in Kogi-East, Nigeria and Africa at large.[905] Albeit Africa still has enough land for the teeming population,[906] the scarcity of resources for this teeming population and the lack of planning on the part of the ill-prepared government make matters worse. The average West African nation in a 2014 forecast is said to be experiencing a 2.7% growth in population, while the economy grows at 7.2%, which cannot sustain the growing population.[907] Nigeria from the 1960s with barely 100 million populations is en-route 200 million today. One of the many reasons for increased population is the inefficient and poor education, because good education is a strong factor for birth control.[908] Increased population creates massive unemployment both in the cities and rural areas. It incessantly multiplies the number of people at the margins of the society who eventually overstretch the scanty infrastructures, thereby encouraging the growth of slums and very dehumanising conditions of living that pose health hazards.

The beauty and the gains of globalisation are enormous, therefore the ability to develop potentials and be a force in the global market is like a mass of water collected over time; its ability to overflow will leave no option for partakers to recognise its presence and thus create a path, else the water creates its own path. The Asian nations have something to offer in the global market today; that is why nations all over the world are eager to do business with them. From all political and economic indications, the readiness of Nigeria and many African nations to key into the global market is still very shallow. I believe that when African nations are ready, they will have their way. The Asians have found a way and are consolidating their presence; until African nations find theirs in a corporate, unique and sustainable manner to break into the global market, they shall remain spectators and not partakers in global affairs. It is a humanitarian call to get to the root of the matter. NGOs like DDS for example are called to invent coherent plans so as to halt this dependant spirit, to act from the angle of service to humanity, the appreciation of humanity and not from convenience, so that humanity

---

[905] Cf. G. Bolton, The Poor Story, 195.

[906] Cf. Ibid. 23.

[907] Cf. Maja Augustinović, Demographie und Entwicklung in Westafrika, in: Ed., Hans Seidel-Stiftung e.V., Politischer Hintergrundbericht Westafrika, August 2014, Pp. 1-7, 1.

[908] Cf. Ibid., 6. The population increase today comes basically from the illiterate and semi-illiterate citizens. Thus Education will go a long way to give people opportunity to determine the size of the family they can sustain.

everywhere could access this global economic river. NGOs on this new humanitarian journey are not only to be reactive in containing past and prospective failures but to be proactive to the future.

5.2 The DDS and the onerous challenges, impact and lessons of globalisation

Under colonial dispensation, organisations like DDS and its likes that are founded to ease the rising poverty in the developing nation would have been categorised as voluntary agencies. Such agencies were committed principally towards the building of social institutions and performing several humanitarian tasks.[909] They are the humanitarian agents and the custodians of this new humanitarian era that were inspired by the global aid development from 1950 to the 70s. Consequently they influenced the founding of the DDS that came with some robust universal humanitarian programmes. Besides, the humanitarian modification between 1970s and 1980s that occasioned the gradual move of foreign aids into poverty alleviation opened NGOs like DDS to the humanitarian funding from the secular world.[910]

Another global effect on the DDS was the impact of the neo-liberal policy of structural adjustment programme as the DDS had to alter her programmes in order to address the declining standard of living among the local people. Nevertheless, donor nations too were not left out of this trend;[911] so much so that by the early 1980s development aids had come under severe attack for example from both conservative and liberals in the UK. The fallout was the heavy outburst of criticisms against many western governments as the masses began to demand for more private participation and less government participation in development aids. It consequently provoked a shift of humanitarian activity from government institutions to

---

[909] Cf. C. Lancaster, Aid to Africa, 25.

[910] Cf. D. Moyo, Dead Aid, 14-17.

[911] Cf. Ibid., 17-22. Even though the 1980s was fondly referred to as the golden age of humanitarian aid vocation, it only portrayed the experience of an aid saturated Africa that had no corresponding development; thus the 1980s was another lost age of development as harsh economic measures were exerted by lending agencies like IMF upon borrowing nations. The much dreaded neo-liberal policy of structural adjustment programmes (SAP) and other terrible measures like free market, reduction of government stakes in public corporations became the fallouts to debtor nations. It only encouraged the recycling of poverty and furthered the aids dependency syndrome and by implication more debt.

private, which the church agencies were part of.[912] Therefore "private agencies were thought to be more efficient, more accountable and more appropriate conduits for the west's largesse."[913] Accordingly, the American and Dutch governments from 1999 began to shift a greater proportion of funds for aid development in Africa through the NGOs. Such policies were sooner or later adopted by other western governments, donors and financial institutions. It was a general boycott of the many corrupt African administrations that were in the first place responsible for this economic decline.[914] It however, consolidated the presence of these agencies both secular and religious organisations. This

> ...combination of neo-liberalism and advocacy of a 'human face' has created a new role for international NGOs as subcontractors in large-scale delivery of basic services such as health, agricultural extension and food rations. They have found both an institutional opportunity and an ideological opening. Often the larger service-delivery NGOs (CARE, Catholic Relief Services, Save the Children Fund) have been drawn in when there has been a crisis such as famine or institutional collapse, and have stayed on afterwards.[915]

This background of NGO's advent basically reveals the contemporary image of humanitarian NGOs' structure and practices as organs of poverty alleviation and not poverty extermination. If NGOs in their humanitarian tasks really intend to solve problems, it becomes imperative to examine the root causes of poverty and accordingly be proactive. In consequence, NGO's duty extends beyond the habitual dispensing of charitable goods for immediate use. Even though the NGOs cannot replace the state (the sole agent of infrastructure, the rule of law and welfare) NGOs are like a harbinger, who pioneers a major change, who

---

[912] Cf. D. Rieff, A Bed for the Night, 103. Among the U.S agencies, it took another development; a few agencies consented to privatization, while some others stuck to their former ideas and practices.

[913] Ibid., 104. In the UK and USA, where humanitarianism was a commonplace, (that was the era of Margaret Thatcher and Ronald Reagan respectively on the seat of power) these governments incurred criticisms from the masses that were coming in at the period of demand for more private participation in the economy. It became a challenge towards many western governments to reconsider the issue of aids. Government presence in dispensing bilateral aids for development constituted *Thatcherism*, which was another name for bureaucratic ineptitude, poor planning, paternalism, financial mismanagement, lack of accountability system and a smug, self-regarding, and self-perpetuating culture, which by then had become a mark of third worldism.

[914] Cf. S. Michael, Undermining Development, 8.

[915] Alex de Waal, Famine Crimes, 53.

foretells where the pain is most, like the example of Caritas, (chapter 1.5) as it most times recognises the pains of the people first before the state. She is called to partner with the state to effect meaningful change and development. Since NGOs are not parallel organisations, they work hand in hand with states to bring about positive transformation. Such a co-operative and proactive failure makes NGO's presence today merely symbolic.

The DDS, awash with myriad factors beyond her control, like the demands of donors and agencies, the erratic nature of the Nigerian government policies and the privatisation demands of the IMF conditions threatened the quality of her practices. The Nigerian government in a haste to meet the deadline for the privatisation of government corporations created more disaster than economic restoration. The DDS was forced to relieve the foreign expatriates and hand over her affairs to the Nigerian citizens who managerially were still ill equipped for this task. Due to the rural nature of Idah diocese, it was difficult to keep qualified staff. Though it was the era of massive retrenchment, the affected workers perpetually looked up for greener pastures in the cities.[916]

Globalisation opens up institutions to the others and they influence one another; such that no one agency can afford to stay aloof to face the multitude of NGOs presence and growth today. Owing to the Catholic/western humanitarian background of neutrality, the DDS was practising such a humanitarian quality in a society dominated by the contrary (chapter 2.3.6). This was the result of the global move from the religious to humanistic viewpoint of humanitarianism (chapter 1.4). Even though it raised eyebrows among the many Catholics because of the existing contrast among some of the non-Catholic agencies, it however portrayed a DDS that was ahead of the zeitgeist of her people in her humanitarian practice.

Since the barometer of globalisation has created two different groups of nations: the successful and the less successful nations, the obvious fight to be successful at all costs became central to many nations. Winning therefore became the in-thing for every state.[917] Nigeria today is a loser for her many bouts of economic waste, long military presence, non cohesive developmental plan, non functional institutions, deficient rule of law and protracted violence. Besides, the present political scenario portends a

---

[916] Cf. N. McNamara, S. Morse, Developing Financial Services, 109-110.
[917] Cf. M. Barnett, Empire of Humanity, 165.

political class with a deep sense of unpreparedness towards leadership and good governance coupled with the failure to understand the complexities of the global market economy. What can the church do to remedy this vacuum? What element of winning attitude should the NGOs like DDS bring on board to step up a new winning mentality among her beneficiaries? Asian nations for example that once had lower or the same per capita income as Nigeria have massively increased their margin today. Some of the NGOs played a vital role in this development.

Because there are winners and losers, winning states became supersized after five decades of excesses and have therefore envisioned humanitarian practice to address the other side of globalisation; it was like states wanting to become lean and fit after five decades of accumulation. Therefore Humanitarianism became another induced solidarity through the process of global capitalism known also as globalisation.[918] However, the success of this trait goes back to the political struggles of citizens for increase welfare rights. It has made states today to concede that "basic protections and services were properly the purview of, and more efficiently delivered by, NGOs, faith based agencies and even the private sector."[919] This makes humanitarianism sometimes an arm of state's charity and has captioned humanitarianism as a major instrument of foreign policy of the wealthy nations today especially in the USA.[920] Such a wanting economic stand of Nigeria made NGOs like DDS a conduit of the resources of such wealthy states.

The expansion of global capitalism has come under criticisms as another name for globalisation. Marxists generally believe it is the unquenchable desire of capitalism to expand beyond it bounds. It feeds its insatiable quest to conquer, govern and integrate those at the margins or as some authors will call it those at the borderlands. It argues further that for capitalism to survive in a world where all may not enjoy its benefits, capitalism has to cushion the pains of the poor to curtail the likely causes of frustrations that may result in rebellion. This consequently makes humanitarianism a global welfare institution where aid workers and social workers work akin to emancipators but are more or less agents of a social control. Such controversies affect the forms and functions of humanitarian

---

[918] Cf. Ibid.
[919] Ibid.
[920] Cf. Alex de Waal, Famine Crimes, 67.

engagements. Therefore, global capitalism needs humanitarianism as a vehicle for public pacification.[921] This concept conflicts with the projected image of true humanitarianism, the appreciation of humanity and not actions by convenience. Nevertheless, to prove humanitarianism as a vehicle for change and innovation, humanitarian works should be structured as a takeoff measure for the local people. Humanitarian and development aid should not be reduced to mere alms, charity or handouts of the rich towards the poor, so that the poor can live temporarily but should be geared to create a roadmap for sustainable development. Humanitarians are meant to assist others to find their own lasting means of survival.[922] Unfortunately, this is always the rhetoric but the practice most times reflects the Marxist's criticism. It is in the light of this mistaken approach that NGOs like DDS are admonished to be pathfinders, to accommodate new designs and develop new methods in assisting the people in this age of globalisation, where the emphasis of 'help to self help' is paramount.

Since humanitarian international are mostly western dominated, there is the tendency for transportation of all readymade solutions into the developing nations.[923] Even though the rich nations of the world passed through social malaise after the World War I and II for example, it was however a different age, people and culture. The strategies for success after 1918 and 1945 may not be adequately fitting for the present age and for the present developing world in a globalised age. How could a competitive spirit be induced into these communities to match the tide of this global age? It demands real ingenuity to undo this trauma of underdevelopment among the local people. It is not just the act of increasing temporal welfare opportunities and support programmes. Because, projects of the NGOs all have a lifespan, what happens when the duration period is over like the case of DDS who lived only on projects? The DDS has the imperative in this new humanitarian dispensation to create a winning mentality among its beneficiaries. Cultivating the idea of winning is paramount to a self-reliant spirit, where beneficiaries are taught the self-confidence, zest and dynamics for economic productivity. It is about envisaging a programme that carries an antidote to neutralising the present loser and helpless mentality inherent among the people. If humanitarianism does not conceive such a practice, it

---

[921] Cf. M. Barnett, Empire of Humanity, 24.
[922] Cf. H. D. Ortlieb, Entwicklungshilfe für Afrika, 27.
[923] Cf. S. A. Garret, Doing Good and Doing Well, 52.

will continue to be at a crossroads, delivering the same results as it has always done.

Regardless of the welcome stance given to welfare opportunities as they cushion the crunching effect of poverty in the poor communities, beneficiaries should be given the awareness that such assistances are temporary and only a stepping-stone towards self reliance. Otherwise these beneficiaries risk an unconscious but dependent mindset towards NGOs' resources like the unproductive way the largesse of miscreants and opportunists are treated. NGOs like DDS should avoid such pitfalls and tragedies in the rural areas, where government presence, state institutions and economic activities are negligible. That is probably why some elites share the opinion that humanitarian international today is like the human face of the neo-liberal economy, as it presents a charity with less accountability. It is a human face in an economic system posing with SAP as if it were the arbiter and masterpiece solution to the developing world's economic problems. This questions one of the weird definitions of humanitarianism as the duty of the rich towards the poor. But the question remains: how should humanitarianism be pursued to avoid this inacceptable definition? If this feeling has become a global concern, then NGOs like DDS would be walking into a big mistake of a charity adventure that impairs self-reliance. Based on this assertion, some critics of humanitarianism consider both humanitarian international and neo-liberal economy as suggestive tendencies and justifications for foreign institutional intrusion in the internal politics of poor nations.[924]

Despite the fact that DDS is a church NGO and operates on Christian charity motives and other humanitarian reasons, its influences, methods and mode of operations from global antecedents were not immune to problems and challenges. When institutions grow bigger, they are vulnerable to institutional problems. The quest to increase the frontier of operations, new skills, new employees, additional funding and requisite professional inputs came along with enormous institutional and professional challenges to the humanitarian practices of the DDS.

---

[924] Cf. Alex De Waal Famine Crimes, 66.

5.3 Professionalism among humanitarian agencies and the case of DDS.

The pursuit of precision in humanitarian actions and the maximisation of humanitarian achievements in a globalised world have conversely led agencies to employ and adopt administrative skills and some ideologies in the training of their field workers. This trend has also led to undue global expectations from humanitarians' performances and the agencies in general. The presence of professionals is to guarantee greater output and it also depicts the quality of standard set by such an agency. It is like the proverbial 'use of one stone to kill two or more birds' at a time. This expected standard from trained professionals on humanitarian fields has become overrated by the presence of humanitarian vacuums perpetrated by incessant global crises today. Besides it creates a crisis of identity on the part of the agencies to deliver so as to establish their raison d'être. Professionalization is like a synergy, the administrative combination of adequate, desired and effective skills toward maximum humanitarian achievements. It was this precision and professionalization that propelled Henry Dunant in 1859 into the idea and founding of ICRC in 1863. Thus professional craving which was a factor of organised help predicated the founding of the ICRC. In addition, resolutions arising from administrative rancour among the aid industry and humanitarian agencies have made calls for improved performance and consequent increase in the quest for professionalization. The seven defining principles of humanitarian rules by Jean Pictet of ICRC, the neutrality failures of the ICRC and the eventual creation of the Red Crescent Society in 1919, the two UN constitutional amendments after the Nigeria/Biafra War are consequent examples of increased quest for professionalization among the many humanitarian agencies. Inasmuch as these factors were eye-openers to humanitarian realities and improvements, they constituted professional problems in the pursuit of humanitarian objectives. Besides they triggered the multiplication and the proliferation of agencies and other humanitarian ideologies, as new principles and additional staff found their ways into the humanitarian circle. A study by the London School of Economics in 2003 reports that there existed 39,729 branches of international charities across Africa; most of them have their headquarters in the North Pole thousands of miles away from their point of operation.[925]

---

[925] Cf. G. Bolton, Poor Story, 93.

Before the 1980s, governments, UN agencies and NGOs were more conspicuous in the humanitarian landscape. What is obvious today according to Alex de Waal is the humanitarian international that constitutes a good number of international elite and professionals ranging from the staff of international relief agencies, academicians, consultants, lobbyists, specialist journalists, specialists in conflict resolution and human rights; thereby creating another sub group of the humanitarian international. It becomes a puzzle why humanitarianism has underperformed despite the array of these available professionals with good intentions and occupying the humanitarian staff cadre in different institutions.[926] Instead of these qualities increasing humanitarian achievements, they are sometimes the very grounds for administrative negligence and failures. Since this humanitarian shift of the 80s to the private agencies, the rules of the game have changed, such that "as donor governments began to channel emergency funds through NGOs, [they were] deliberately circumventing African governments [and that]... radically changed the nature of institutional humanitarianism."[927] The humanitarian landscape today began to experience systemic flaws with "lack of enforceable professional standards and the absence of formal barriers of entry"[928] into the humanitarian field.

It is expected that NGOs improve their operations, gain more confidence in the course of time and establish themselves sometimes as drivers of civil societies. But in the case of the African NGOs like the DDS, they hardly reach this maturity stage, since they find it difficult to let go the supports of the INGOs, financiers, protectors and donors. Most times they become an extension of northern NGOs primarily to deliver development and aid programmes.[929] One of the major questions that run through this work is, whether humanitarianism is based on the appreciation of humanity or from convenience. If humanitarianism is truly the appreciation of humanity and not an emblem of failure, some level of independence on the part of donors towards the humanitarian agencies should be guaranteed. This invariably means donor agencies ought to reduce overbearing control on their benefactors. Albeit the joy of donors is to be acquainted with the progress reports of the NGOs they sponsor, "the fundamental question [still remains]..., have they the right to decide what is best for a field-based NGO

---

[926] Cf. Alex de Waal, Famine Crimes, 65.
[927] Ibid., 79.
[928] Ibid.
[929] Cf. E. Mbogori, African Civil Society, coming to terms with Globalisation, 21.

many thousand miles away from the scene without any involvement in the nuts and bolts and daily pressures that determine the efficacy and worthwhileness of the NGO?"[930] The case of NGOS and donors having opposing intentions is commonplace in the humanitarian scene; nevertheless, "donors do not just exert their power over local NGOs by getting them to do something they would not otherwise do, but by influencing them to the extent that the NGO itself willingly rethinks its priorities to fit the mould provided by its donors."[931] Despite the effect of such influence, many aid workers still believe that dialogue with the donors has helped to clarify where and how productive their funds could best be channelled into; nevertheless there are donors for example who would wish that the site of demonstration farm be close to the road for ease of access when they come on supervision. But the truth is, you put things where the people work and live and not just on the road, otherwise food security would be compromised. Many development experts believe that donors have learnt over time, therefore it is a sharing. That is why such experts disbelieve the tendency that the donor is always right and you take a risk when you challenge him or her.[932] This insider's view emphasises the effect of dialogue and that despite the administrative hiccups in the lifetime of the DDS, the DDS team benefitted from the dialogue approach and process.

It consequently follows that donors do promote the partnership between home grown NGOs like DDS and their international counterparts (INGO, the donor agencies), but the decision sometimes to exert these stringent controls stems from the international donor system. These conditions are the outcome of accusations on the ground of opportunism, corruption and mismanagement levelled against past governments.[933] They were the custodians of developmental aids in collaboration with the foreign agencies before the overt shift to private agencies in the 70s and 80s. When nations and international organisations give assistance, such aids are meant to transform the receiving side into an independent, self help group not to sycophants and parasites. Therefore, every action towards self help should be committed towards alleviating and also the eventual defeat of poverty; a sort of economic emancipation, which invariably strengthens the dignity of the human person. Every solidarity therefore should be accompanied by a

---

[930] N. McNamara, S. Morse, Developing Financial Services, 110.
[931] S. Michael, Undermining Development, 21.
[932] Cf. Interview with Sr. Nora McNamara.
[933] Cf. E. Mbogori, African Civil Society coming to Terms with Globalization, 24.

corresponding level of subsidiarity, because "the principle of subsidiarity must remain closely linked to the principle of solidarity and vice versa, since the former without the latter gives way to social privatism, while the latter without the former gives way to paternalist social assistance that is demeaning to those in need."[934]

Even though NGOs are sometimes eager to do good, utmost carefulness must be taken to scrutinize sponsorship. Some NGOs take up very questionable assistances either for lack of bargaining chips or overestimating their own potential powers. Therefore, jumping at every funding may be foolhardy, besides rejecting every aid may be cowardice too. Nevertheless the Aristotelian principle of the virtue that lies in the middle encourages the virtuous act of 'caution' to weigh the effects and the 'courage' to take the most plausible decision. Consequently NGOs must bear in mind that behind every humanitarian support, there may be the danger of playing to the dictates of donors and agencies. It is admirable for NGOs to be committed to accountability; this determines the level of their productivity and its end results, which are their organisational level and the principle of subsidiarity. Unfortunately many local NGOs lack this rudimentary financial monitoring system and this makes accounting problematic. The idea that small is beautiful may not always be realistic as the absence of a control mechanism can lead from self-employment to self-enrichment.[935] Also the mindset that indigenous NGOs are "borne out of local problems and [must use] local skills and resources to solve them"[936] can lead to this vicious circle of self-enrichment. Nevertheless, every aspiration to extend the frontiers of these NGOs means serious pecuniary commitments, which are mostly attainable from foreign donors, INGOs and sponsors. It is true on one hand that "northern donors have an enormous amount of power, [on the other hand] they are able to shape the lives of the organisations they support, not simply because they fund them, but also because of the processes and disciplines they require the organisations to become involved in."[937] But expecting a meticulous accounting system according to western standard may be sometimes unrealistic, because "if African systems were so perfectly efficient, well staffed and robustly

---

[934] Caritas in Veritate, 58.
[935] Cf. Georg Cremer, Corruption and Development Aid, Confronting the Challenges, Colorado, 2008, 81.
[936] S. Michael, Undermining Development, 4. (from Paul Wangoola)
[937] Ibid., 21.

accountable, they doubtless wouldn't need anyone's help anyway."[938] It is the same factor of poverty and weak financial system of local NGOs like DDS that makes them excessively vulnerable and dependent on donors. Moreover, sponsors do have a right to know the affairs of the NGOs, like the proverbial German adage that accepts trust as a good factor but ascribes its comparative with supervision.[939] It is therefore good to trust but it is absolutely better to monitor or checkmate the NGOs. Nevertheless, because of the local periphery of these NGOs, their activities are murky to the average western donor who is used to scientific reports and precision. Regardless that these donors may be wary about the nitty-gritty of the NGOs on the ground, "a line must be drawn between 'participation' and 'control'. NGO ought to have the greatest respect for the intentions of benefactors who, in turn, provide funds to donors who diligently ensure efficient and effective usage. Donors may have a vision of what they would like, but only those in situ really know the difficulties and limitations inherent in each situation."[940]

The many demands of donors and sponsors have marred the success of many humanitarian projects in the developing world, because the threat to withdraw, reduce or the promise to increase funding can dictate pace and direction of NGOs interests.[941] Since the historical yearning of the masses for more private participation in humanitarian projects, governments, donors and organisations who bankroll these agencies have not only played a great role from behind, but most times have had to call the shots even from a distance through their control mechanism. According to Graham Hancock, such people constitute "a group of rich and powerful bureaucracies that have hijacked our kindness".[942]

The drive for funds to sustain the professional requirements, run programmes and projects since the 1980 humanitarian change of government to private agencies' participation has increased the dependency and marketing nature of the agencies towards,

---

[938] G. Bolton, Poor Story, 107.

[939] Vertrauen ist gut, aber Kontrolle ist besser. (Trust is good but supervision is better).

[940] N. McNamara, S. Morse, Developing Financial Services, 110.

[941] Cf. Sarah Michael, Undermining Development, 21; Nora McNamara, Stephen Morse, Voices from the Aid 'Chain, 260. In all the ups and downs with the NGOs my best guess is that the DDS kept it under the radar. Most times the names of the donor agencies were only figuratively written or totally eclipsed from the understanding of the outsider.

[942] D. Rieff, A Bed for the Night, 102.

...governments, private donors, and individuals;... [since these agencies have] no special legal status in the sense that say, the ICRC did by virtue of its having been recognized by international treaty as the custodian of the Geneva Conventions; and their success or failure in what was after all, a world competing humanitarian organisation would depend largely on the degree of public recognition they managed to secure—in other words, on the way they marketed themselves both to the public and to the donors. Relief organizations were not business in the sense that IBM, Siemens, and Alcatel are businesses, but they struggled for market share and attention much as conventional businesses did.[943]

There is no gainsaying that professionalism does not enhance the learning process and the success of humanitarian endeavours; however, excessive professional pursuits have sometimes turned humanitarian works into some form of business today and as such have lost spontaneity over the time. Agencies are today where their donors have interests and humanitarian agents do everything possible to keep their jobs and their offices running.[944] The fact is 'either you grow or you die', therefore getting more donor and funds becomes more imperative than the normative principles of humanitarianism.[945] It consequently wipes away the supposed humanitarian regulations between donors and agencies, thereby making donors to cash in on NGOs' desperation. This guarantees the tool to exercise power over the NGOs, like the old saying that 'he who pays the piper, calls the tune.'[946] Also, even the financial monopoly enjoyed by ICRC too has been compromised through competition and rivalry with other agencies today.[947]

Excessive financial drive generates conflict between the 'soft' and 'hard' humanitarian interest of agencies today.[948] Due to these hard humanitarian interests today, virtually every humanitarian agency is submerged in the marketing strategy for survival; because marketing strategy consequently fashions a modern leeway for the desired productivity and

---

[943] Ibid. 108.
[944] Cf. Ibid. 299.
[945] Cf. Ibid. 296.
[946] Cf. Alex de Waal, Famine Crimes, 81.
[947] Cf. D. Rieff, A Bed for the Night, 295.
[948] Cf. Alex de Waal, Famine Crimes, 66. The soft interests are the fundamental principles of the humanitarian institution like the provision of succour to the poor and vulnerable, relief in war torn areas, issues of human rights and so on; while the hard interests includes the institutional challenges, the demands of the agencies and their workers like the question of institutional expansion, the security of workers and their careers, the sense of job satisfaction and others. Conflicts arising from hard interests could mare the effect of humanitarian practice of agencies, such that only financially robust agencies could tackle over the time.

relevance of humanitarian pursuit. This intermittently brings back a new form of government's presence into humanitarian and aid development projects that was hitherto discredited by the masses. The agencies involved in this marketing-strategy (mostly western agencies) are the very agencies that DDS and many NGOs in Africa depended and still depend on to execute their humanitarian programmes. To support these African NGOs, these foreign agencies are financially dependent on their home governments; a fact that often makes it difficult for example to know where the interests of an NGO or an agency end and where those of the donor agency or their mother nations begin.[949] The CRS's example (chapter 1.4.5) highlights how CRS got huge supports from the US government between 1943 and 1946 in the hope to create contacts for military intelligence through the CRS in Europe.[950] This same support from the US government and the fight against communism turned CRS into an arm of the US government in Vietnam. These were the negative sides of government support to humanitarian organizations, sending wrong and ambivalent messages to the beneficiaries. It undermines the church agencies and whatever they stand for.[951] Besides, the admonitions of Pope Benedict XVI from the Motu Proprio document of 2012 (Chapter 1.3) confirms these threats and abuse of financial support. As a result of this, many foreign governments and private donors have become the sustaining power of agencies and by implication are privy to the day to day running of these agencies. It unfortunately induces agencies and their proxies (the African NGOs) with undue professionalism like over bloated bureaucracy. Sometimes this exists in a well crafted control mechanism on the financial system to checkmate whether donors' and governments' ideologies are implemented or not. Humanitarian agencies from this period henceforth became susceptible to a new professional pressure to deliver according to the demands of their donors. This factor creates immense pressure on African NGOs like DDS. DDS for example took pre-emptive decisions in the course of her lifetime over particular projects, so as to manage the position and demands of the donors and also the local situation at hand; thus,

> ...the DDS experience with its donors during the mid to late 1980s... [was] both sobering and frustrating, especially given that DDS tried continuously to communicate the limitations experienced over the preceding decade. Personnel within DDS were beginning to question the value of producing so

---

[949] Cf. D. Rieff, A Bed for the Night, 263.
[950] Cf. M. Barnett, Empire of Humanity, 109.
[951] Cf. Ibid., 127.

many reports and documents as well as participating in meetings both in Nigeria and overseas if the messages were 'lost'. Current dogma appeared to be the driving force, taking precedence over all that had been written and discussed.[952]

The DDS, as a nongovernmental agency and dependent on free will donations from agencies in the western world had to cave in to the demands of the donor agencies. The resultant effect was increased pressure and a strong bureaucratic approach towards its many projects. In contrast most field agents "would prefer open, frank dialogue between the beneficiaries, donors and NGO in situ. This would nurture that atmosphere of trust, understanding and care required for development to succeed. Finance is important but one would question if it gives the right to rule by remote control."[953] The DDS had two angles to contend with in her struggles, the facts on the ground and the hasty demands of the donor agency. Thus donors' pressure to achieve sustainability in the shortest period was frowned on by the DDS officials, who felt the FCs were already en-route to self-reliance, therefore additional pressure was unsubstantial and it was better to let the FC-system grow at its pace.[954] Such tension generated by the donor agencies heightens the NGO's struggle to strike a balance between the people and the donors. NGOs could consequently be forced to come to terms with the donor's view, which may be perceived as international standard so as to secure its sinecure, but it may eventually conflict with the local needs and the priorities identified by the local NGO.[955] Many agencies supported the DDS course, but the tendency to play by the book, to satisfy these donor agencies and their donors coupled with the dependence syndrome of DDS over time and the internal rancour, made DDS to fold up.

The example of DDS was a case that an overbearing control on the part of the sponsors, the over bloated cost from the several journeys, the uphill task of keeping up with the ideologies of the agencies and their donors were economically not acceptable especially to the beneficiaries. Such finances could be converted into other purpose; instead they were constituted into overblown administrative costs that eventually undermined the original intention of the NGO to assist humanity. The overt informal economy in Nigeria plays a very strong role and as such undermines accountability, a

---

[952] N. McNamara, S. Morse, Developing Financial Services, 110.
[953] Ibid.
[954] Cf. Ibid., 109.
[955] Cf. E. Mbogori, African Civil Society, coming to Terms with Globalisation, 25.

fact that necessarily underpins the need for trust. Too much attention was given to paper work, the ideology and the intentions of the donors. These and many other factors eventually crumbled the DDS that was so much sung on the lips of the people.

Today, the craze for professionalism has encouraged new operational imperatives; since 1990 academic degrees in humanitarian assistance are being offered at important American, British and Swiss universities today[956], a fact that brings about the institutionalisation of compassion.[957] Despite such professionalization tendencies, the Faith based humanitarian Organisation like DDS has a *diakonein* perspective to be prophetic.

5.4   The prophetic role of the church

In spite of the myriad problems that humanitarian practices are confronted with today, the church still commands a special position in humanitarian practice; she bears the picture of change in her humanitarian/*diakonein* perspective and also a healing feature through her prophetic approach. Unlike secular humanitarian organisations, she becomes a different emblem of change, because of her double approach to solving the problems of the peripheral people. Her teachings and humanitarian works connect the daily life of the people to the faith. This humanitarian-faith connection gives the beneficiaries a positive view of Christian life and its commitment to common good. Such dynamics could create the enabling environment for full realisation of human potentials and as well expose them to the reality of the kingdom of God here on earth.[958] Even though professionalism enhances the progress of humanitarian works, it represents a considerable setback to the success of the humanitarian and *diakonein* perspective of the church. How is the church to continue with her prophetic role in the midst of such controversies?

The care of the poor from the inception of the church has been part of the church's *kerygmatic* mission. The church in the modern age, determined to continue with this important role in her mission, is confronted by many global chains of events that invariably undermine her chances of

---

[956] Cf. D. Rieff, A Bed for the Night, 308.
[957] Cf. Ibid., 301.
[958] Cf. Joseph Ogbonnaya, The Role of African Catholicism in the Light of Africae Munus, 106.

maintaining this heroic mission: 'the care of souls'. Despite her many shortcomings, she still remains a strong humanitarian partner in this age. Thus, in the pursuit of these humanitarian actions among the poorest of the poor in the world she finds herself financially and morally incapacitated to attend to the needs of her followers and the masses in general. The hallmark of the church's *diakonein* principle is the ability to offer unfettered humanitarian access to humanity especially to the poor and handicapped in the marginalised and broken societies. These humanitarian endeavours have subsequently made her the hope of the hopeless, which corresponds to the opening statement of *Gaudium et spes*, that the church shares in the joys and sorrows of the people of God. This *diakonein* calling of the church makes the care of the faithful sacrosanct to the church, albeit she may have failed to deliver humanitarian and *diakonein* answers in very unbearable cases of human need. The probable question is how is the church to react in the midst of such handicaps bearing in mind the global and local phenomena that may have impeded her humanitarian engagements, which over time mar or sometimes totally cripple her aspiration to stand for the masses?

One could borrow a leaf from the second general conference of the Latin American Bishops held in Medellin Colombia in 1968, where it proposed a new strategy as an option for the poor. However, the Medellin documents were not conclusive on the mode of political changes it intends to create, besides, critics questioned the long Catholic monopoly in Latin America that ultimately stirred the wide gap between the poor and the rich. Moreover, from the Catholic Church the idea of liberation was too Marxist. Regardless of these criticisms, the anticipated approach and the initiative against poverty could be interpreted as *diakonein* perspective and a response to the second Vatican council motive of sharing in the joy and sorrows of the people. A prophetic church therefore, needs a major shift from the language of assistance/development to the language of freedom from political blindness and ignorance, thus it is a consequent change of focus from economic to political language.[959] The relevance of faith and liberation could be compared to the western struggle to synthesise faith and reason. It is absolutely difficult for an African church to speak about faith without addressing the issues of economic bondage and poverty.[960] Liberation in the

---

[959] Cf. G. Ehusani, Social Gospel, 46-47.
[960] Cf. Jean-Marc Éla, The Church-Sacrament of Liberation, in: The Church-Sacrament of Liberation, in: Ed., Maura Browne, The African Synod, Documents, Reflections, Perspectives, Maryknoll, 1996, 131- 138, 138.

African sense implies "decolonization, development, social justice [and] respect for the inalienable and fundamental liberty of each person".[961] The church's relevance in the modern age would be better appreciated if she transcends the attitude of proffering a piecemeal solution to a holistic one by cracking the enigmatic causes of poverty. It is a sort of groundbreaking foundational thrust that could lead to the eradication of the root causes of poverty, because poverty according to the Medellin documents "is not just something that happens; it is caused by human action of a kind that does violence to great masses of people".[962] Therefore, institutional reforms are imperative to bringing about a conclusive fight against poverty. This role includes "courageous and prophetic stands in the face of corruption of political or economic power".[963] The time has come for the church to reflect its original message, its prophetic vision of setting people free from the chains of poverty (Lk.4; 16). The horror and violence upon the people must be met with a critical-liberating task, which includes "a new language of justice in truth and a language that proclaims the peace of God among His people and the coming of the kingdom".[964] If there was anything insightful about the era of the second Vatican council, it was the universal trait that the church is open to all, a Diaspora church that lives not for herself but lives like Jesus, who lives for others.[965] It is implied that, "a man is baptized not for his own salvation alone but for the mission to the world since it is only through that mission that he can be one with Christ whose mission it is. His likeness to Christ consists in being 'a man for others'."[966] It is likened to the old saying of 'one for all, all for one',[967] a sort of solidarity statement where everyone works for the good of the other. Therefore, the collective duty of Christians is to make the society a better place and that is the kind of prophetic church the present Nigeria needs. A church that many scholars describe as the

> incarnational discipleship on the part of the Christians – a discipleship whose passion for justice, equity, well being, liberation and salvation will provoke not only powerful statements, but also concrete prophetic action towards realising the liberation of the oppressed, the conversion of the oppressor, the

---

[961] Ibid., 137.
[962] G. Ehusani, The Social Gospel, 47.
[963] John Paul II, Redemptoris Missio, 43.
[964] J.B. Metz, Zum Begriff, 15. (Translation is mine)
[965] Cf. Aylward Shorter, Theology of Mission, London, 1972, 14.
[966] Ibid.
[967] Cf. A. Baumgartner, Solidarität, 284,. „Einer für alle und alle für eine"

empowerment of the poor, the practice of authentic religion, and ultimately the salvation of all.[968]

A prophet is called by God to play a vital role in the evolution of God's people. God inspires the message in the prophet, who in most cases despite all odds accomplishes the mission even though it may seem as failure. In every sphere of life he proclaims God's plans; he denounces sin, oppression and evil ways and reminds the people of their commitments and the impending wrath.[969] For this reason, one of the outstanding features of the prophets was their timely intervention in the life of the nation of Israel to put the people (cf. Is; 3, 14) and their leaders (cf. 1 Sam; 15, 28) to right; the prophetic role of the church is not to be economical with the truth. Hence, the mission of the church in every age is to confront human society for positive changes, she cannot shy away from confronting the world and mankind as long as they exist. This makes her mission ongoing; moreover, her mission begins when she becomes a positive and relevant factor that can influence considerable and meaningful changes in the human society.[970]

One of the five principles of solidarity proposed by Alois Baumgartner is that solidarity insists on continuous improvement and changes and never gives up on short term improvement. In essence, solidarity prefers to invest in that which is reliable and not to depend on alms and contributions continuously.[971] It is an ongoing task of promoting the freedom of humans from all forms of bondage and captivity, be it spiritual, social, economic, political and intellectual. This should be factored into her *kerygmatic* approach, which also brings out the beautiful Christian message of this good news; a good news that guarantees a good life here on earth and the life after.[972] Thus, the proclamation of the message of salvation is the mission of the church in every age; a mission that encompasses and connects humanity to the corresponding historical situation of its time. That is why the pastoral constitution of the second Vatican council *Gaudium et spes* calls on the church to constantly analyse the signs of the times in the light of the

---

[968] G. Ehusani, The Prophetic Church, 71.
[969] Cf. Pierre Lèfebvre, Ministries and Community, For a Church as a family, Nairobi 1998, 9.
[970] Cf. A. Shorter, Theology of Mission, 15.
[971] Cf. A. Baumgartner, Solidarität, 291.
[972] Cf. G. Ehusani, The Prophetic Church, 81.

gospel, so that she can interpret the message of salvation in a changing world of global interdependence.[973]

The church's financial strength in the diocese has bedevilled her stance in the face of social crisis, a factor that necessitates the need and the imperative of self-reliance and a church that must factor the movement and actualisation of self-reliance. This dilemma to sustain the existing status quo has driven many churches and ministers into undue financial pressure, questionable methods and inordinate relationship with individuals deemed to be of questionable characters and intent. The persistent relationship of state and church for economic gains sometimes undermines the prophetic message of the church. The church's state of destitution is sometimes hijacked by political hoodlums as church officials are sometimes caught in the web of unwarranted relationships with state officials for economic gains. This encourages the coast of corruption in Nigeria, since being in power today becomes the most lucrative business. It calls for a time of independence of churches from the same forces that oppress her faithful, so as to credibly preach the message of faith and be the voice of the voiceless, because association with the villains of the society amounts to subtle support for kleptocracy and injustice. It is tantamount to maintaining the same system that oppresses the poor just for little and temporary gains. Besides, what this does to the church is, it creates distance and rift between the church officials and the good people of God.

Moreover, there is the need to stimulate, sustain and to further the independence in the socio-political paradigm of a nation in order to address the issue of poverty. The church needs to be innovative in her humanitarian perspective, so that she does not remain vulnerable to the demands of agencies, foreign and local donors, but is a partner. She becomes a partner who feels the pulse of her people, who could rationally and practically tell the fate and the real demands of the people. At the close of the last millennium and in connection with the African synod of 1994, many African Theologians like Jean-Marc Éla re-tasked the church on her role as the sacrament of justice and liberation. It proposed renewal of the teaching ministry of theologians towards the growing number and size of the African church that is wallowing in abundant poverty in a new world order; a system that is centred on the mechanism of money where most African nations are on the receiving end of its fallout. The local church must concede the

---

[973] Cf. J. Wiemeyer, Keine Freiheit ohne Gerechtigkeit, 47.

powerlessness of the socio-political projects that have delivered more or less nothing in many African communities and the many fruitless developmental approaches in many communities too. Consequently this growing poverty makes Africans risk more exclusion from the global activities and being less involved in the initiatives and decisions concerning her future and even that of the so much applauded growing faith.[974] Since each local church feels the impact of this social enigma that beclouds her people, she is encouraged like the evolved reflection system to "study how to take up the challenge, knowing that Africa calls upon the Christian conscience at a time when we are witnessing a renewal of structures of domination, and knowing that in spite of several declarations in principle for democracy, there is within our societies a return to dictatorships and a programmed re-colonization of the continent."[975] The inability of many African nations to understand the above reality and as well to manage their economies led to the invitation of IMF into their politico-economic mainstream. Despite the many brilliant and sometimes ambivalent reasons economists may give as the cause, I believe, a people bear corporate responsibility for whatever economic mess she is immersed in. Nevertheless, it remains an established fact among the people of the developing world that this global phenomenon through IMF is a synonym for imperialism, misery and famine.[976] Since information is power and knowing the truth sets one free (cf. John. 8; 32), the prophetic church leads by teaching her people the truth and the need to rely on themselves, of course with the support of other churches, but to look inwardly, to avoid the dependant mentality, to develop and activate their ingenuities as a way out of this miserable status.

The prophetic church is called to build an 'alternative society', a church that creates the ingredients that are lacking in the society so as to fill the void; a church that is able to invent and craft her teachings with the missing elements in the society so as to sensitize and electrify the darkness of the common mind.[977] In the words of J. B. Metz, she is to serve as institutions of second order, the bearer and guarantor of critical freedom.[978] The prophetic church is the church that teaches unity among different races, bearing in mind that the major democratic setbacks for African development

---

[974] Cf, Jean-Marc Éla, The Church-Sacrament of Liberation, 131-132.
[975] Ibid. 133.
[976] Cf. Ibid.
[977] Cf. E.E. Uzukwu, The Listening Church, 77.
[978] Cf. J.B. Metz, Zum Begriff, 19.

have been no doubt because of the millions of ethnic differences in Africa. The prophetic church aspires to increase the democratic sensibilities among the different ethnic groups; a situation where my nation comes before me, my family, ethnic groups, a teaching that roots out divisiveness and fosters unity, by stressing the win-win situation from the fact that 'together we are strong'.[979] The *Christi Fidelis* are this prophetic church and in the words of the African Bishops, "there must be prophets in our times and the whole church must become prophetic."[980] As long as African nations lag behind in internal democratic awareness and practice of unity, they shall remain blind and deaf towards advancing national interests and understanding the external/real world and its machinations, intrigues and the antics of the present age. Progressive Africans and the local churches on this 'catch-up journey' will only survive when they truly understand these perspectives, that 'to truly survive in the jungle, the prey needs to understand the antics of the predator'.

I believe in transformational humanitarianism, a church that is into such humanitarian works as she transforms her own people from within, a church that builds the necessary bulwark for a spiritual and material breakthrough, through her humanitarian works and teaching ministry. It is a type of humanitarian practice that truly partners, owns up, is realistic, truthful, altruistic and truly develops pragmatic strategies for radical change and development. If truly "humanitarianism represents itself as acting in the name of the international community as it crosses existing boundaries to transform societies in order to try to remove the causes of poverty",[981] then humanitarian agents have to partner with the local force on ground, in which the church is certainly a remarkable one; to truly remove the causes of poverty through combined efforts. This local church is called to serve as a partner agent of this social transformation that becomes a gateway and foundation towards autonomy and self-reliance. This partnership quality strips away paternalism from the practice of humanitarianism and curbs the indecisiveness on the part of the local church; a prophetic church becomes a self-conscious church, able to determine her interests and that of her people.

---

[979] Gemeinsam sind wir stark.

[980] P. Lèfebvre, Ministries and Community, 15.

[981] Michael Barnett, Humanitarianism as a scholarly Vocation, in: Eds., Michael Barnett, Thomas G. Weiss, Humanitarianism in Question, Politics, Power, Ethics, Ithaca, 2008, 235-264, 241.

5.5.   The DDS: A Revisit

The pioneers of DDS were primarily concerned with raising awareness of their assistance to people and to places that needed help. Therefore a resurgent DDS is meant to reach the poor as much as possible in a new but formidable and cooperative spirit to encourage local production. Despite the negligible Catholic population of 12%, the DDS has earned outstanding remarks from all the different divides of Kogi-East and beyond because of her many humanitarian and developmental practices. Also, the Catholic Church over the years has enjoyed an amazing and cordial social network of relationships with the traditional royal family. So far the social reality among the different religious groups does not spell doom but their understanding of humanitarian and development benefits differs from the perspective of the Catholics (Ch. 3.6) and some orthodox churches.[982] They basically maintain denomination and religious lines in the distribution of their services.[983] One of the observations of DDS was the infighting among the people despite the social reality of the Igala nation within the context of one Nigeria that is very much homogeneous. The new start however must cut across all the possible factions, because unnecessary rivalry and competition among the different religious groups, traditional divisions and factions will slow down economic and political maturation, potencies and process. It calls for a sense of unity among the different units of faith and the hitherto mini Igala states to enhance a smooth humanitarian and development takeoff.

---

[982] Cf. Weekly Progress Report no. 8, 13/10/69 to 20/10/69, 4. During the Nigerian Civil War for example, the Eastern region experienced this lopsided humanitarian services, as some other denominations were only interested in the welfare of their church members, whereas, the *Caritas* and the *Diakonie* were into the service of all irrespective of faith.

[983] In the midst of a thriving Pentecostal spirituality in Nigeria today, assistance if ever available is mostly directed towards its members likewise among the Muslims. The western orientation of humanitarianism in the Catholic Church has created a difference in the Catholic Church's approach towards humanity and not towards her members alone. Though ecumenical concerns exist on furthering the common interests of Christianity today, it is partly because of the rising Islamic aggression and extremism from northern Nigeria. However the social questions are hardly addressed and there is barely any common effort for development issues among these different denominations and the other faiths like the ATR and Islam. Apart from the non-religious oriented NGOs and the DDS example, other denominations have the propensity to employ only their members in religious controlled NGOs.

Since the traditional industry in Igala/Bassa land is agriculture, then revamping and rebranding the DDS may serve as the production pedestal for the local people. The advent of the DDS was heavily informed by the post-civil war depression in 1970; today the lingering decline in production calls for development works. However two key issues must be addressed accordingly: getting development workers who would cope with the low wage setting in Kogi-East and the readiness of a people for a development that is short of external funds from foreign, secular or church NGOs and state's help. It must be anchored on self-help, dependent on the subsidiarity level of the people and their ability to cope with such trends in the future. Even though such factors may seem untenable at the moment, the church must picture a new start that carries the antidote to neutralise the over dependent system of the previous development works. Also, it has to be drummed in consistently that the potential of humanitarian engagement is not to contain failures but to be proactive. It is about envisaging a new frame of DDS that will factor such objectives into a new structure of operation to accelerate sustainability and self reliance in Igala/Bassaland.

5.5.1 Sustainability and self reliance from the perspective of DDS

Unlike the WCED of 1987, (chapter 4.1.1) the 'Earth Summit' of 1992 in Rio gave a different approach to the meaning of sustainability in respect to the developing nations. The background of this preference and new understanding was basically because agriculture provides income and sustenance to the greater population of rural and urban dwellers in the developing nations. Sustainable agriculture is a modern term and was a reaction to the accelerated change of industrial agriculture in Europe and North America. Its concern was the loss of woodland, hedgerows, increased size of land for farming, increased use of pesticides, inorganic fertilizers and gene manipulations and so on. Though some of these features are potential threats in the developing world, the scope of agricultural sustainability in Idah diocese is about the rural livelihood based on crop production and yield.[984]

The major agent of sustainability and self reliance in the diocese till today was the example of the DDS. Despite its collapse, there are still lessons from the DDS experience. But to truly understand the context of the DDS in the light of sustainability will require a meticulous scrutiny of the

---

[984] Cf. S. Morse et al., Visions of Sustainability, 6.

successes and failures of the DDS's projects. Giles Bolton approach gives a three conceptual method of measuring development work: ownership, capacity and sustainability. This method could serve as a model and a guide to analyse the DDS *modus operandi* and her success story, because they are the anticipated and indispensable qualities for the success of any charity, aid or development project. The 'ownership' quality takes into cognisance what the people want and the best method is by asking questions. The DDS began wonderfully well with the keen study of the environment through the reflection method of inquiring what people really wanted. Many issues came up but agriculture, the local industry, became the mainstream. Secondly, the issue of 'capacity' is important because the beneficiaries must have the capacity to use it and build on the project. It is also the ability for such projects to fit people's expectation, experience and the cultural habits. Besides, the case of capacity challenges the people in new perspectives that they may never have been used to. The use of the Financial Scheme, the *Oja* system through the reflection-system paved the way for ownership and capacity. The third factor 'sustainability' is so important that development experts term it as the 'holy grail of development work'. It is meant to act as a catalyst for wider progress that would outlive the expiration of such projects, a rare issue that hardly takes place among charity and development aid industry. In all likelihood, the DDS like many charity and development aid projects did not deliver on sustainability.[985] One thing is to develop the people and another thing is the sustainability of the institution itself. Without this factor how does the NGO live on with successive programmes? It amounts to bringing people to a crossroad; therefore humanitarian work should be powered with sustainability to effectively create a lasting effect on her beneficiaries.

The lack of sustainability from the onset of the DDS for example was a consequent factor of its demise, thus dwindling supply of aids to NGOs can choke an NGO to death. This and other numerous factors determine the fate of many local NGOs in sub-Saharan Africa today who are into development works. It has created a mindset that "undertaking development work can itself be inherently unsustainable."[986] The DDS like many other African NGOs lacking power of sustainability was affected by government's new but hasty development principle of privatisation.[987] Also

---

[985] Cf. G. Bolton, Poor Story, 84-86.
[986] S. Michael, Undermining Development, 131.
[987] Cf. N. McNamara, S. Morse, Developing Financial Services, 110.

the Nigerian politically mischievous and questionable census motives worsened the DDS inability to project the real demographic picture of the concerned areas in Kogi-East. Besides, the rigorous but sometimes difficult demands of the donors and the departure of many staff over time became reasons for the failure of DDS to gain the desired power to pursue her objectives. All these emanated from a DDS that was heavily built on foreign finances, thus on the expiration of the projects everything returned to a standstill.[988] The survival of an NGO at its early stage could depend a lot on a charismatic pioneer who sets the ball rolling,[989] that is the first step in the establishment of its raison d'être. As second step, just like in a business environment the institution must outgrow the personality and the vision of the founder. That means, the less the name of the founder the more the NGO triumphs and this may include: openness, transparency, having a wider vision, possessing a sense of focus and maintaining the objectives of the NGO. Even though the DDS thrived it was marred by the inability to figure out a vision for the future and to prioritise its spending. Subsequently, many issues and offices were lumped together in the name of DDS.[990] There are dissenting opinions as regards the downfall of DDS, for example the possible issues of internal rancour within the DDS structure, which I think exceeds the scope of this work.

Soliciting for support and canvassing for funds have become today a synonym of NGOs' existence; such contemporary thoughts make one to believe that NGOs cannot exist without external funds. But the essence and the goal of humanitarian activities is self-help, which brings about self-esteem and self-determination in a democratic organisation and it is characterised by the ability to look inwards. Like the failed development years, NGOs too have taken the top-down development process which is antithetic to development since they merely qualify to be called conduits of largesse from both the west and from corrupt leaders. To satisfy such a humanitarian quest will demand a close and through examination of the prospects of development from within. The example of the German Cooperatives in the 19th century could be likened to the existence of NGOs in contemporary developing world perspective. It was a concise example of developmental ideas illustrated by the liberal position of Hermann Schulze-

---

[988] Cf. S. Michael, Undermining Development, 131.

[989] Cf. Ibid. 32.

[990] Cf. Aleta van der Woude, The church as partner in development in: Ed., Stenger Fritz, Africa is not a dark continent, Tangaza occasional papers, Nairobi, 2005, Pp. 80-85, 84.

Delitzsch (1808-1883) and the Protestant Friedrick Wilhelm Raiffeisen (1818-1888). The former believed only in self-help as the answer to the economic straits suffered by farmers and small crafts business people, while the latter advocated for external funds from the state. From this duo a development from within was ignited which was the true spirit of searching for the inherent possibilities around a people.[991] Nearly every village had a *Raiffeisen* cooperative and parish priests and teachers became the predominant initiators of these cooperatives. They held sensitive positions like management and supervision but offered free services to these cooperatives.[992] The proposed humanitarian progression in this study could lean on the pattern of the present cooperative system in Germany; a system that has been able to synchronise both the objectives of state support and self-help methods. Therefore even if NGOs were to live on donations and alms, in the interim they should also grow some sustainable features to stem their request for funds to be able to maintain some independence and to truly have an extensive and pragmatic effect on people's lives. Moreover, this should be geared towards a total independence in the future. Albeit such sustainable features may bear the traits of modern day business, they are not profit oriented in the strict sense. It is about building an Internal Generating Revenue system (IGR), a sort of integrated income generating project that powers the NGO itself. Therefore sustainability is indispensable for a resurgent and thriving DDS.

This contextual sustainable development is about the unearthing of existing indigenous means of production of the available resources by furthering, perfecting and improving their growth. It will primarily assist in the maintenance of the objectives and the overhead cost of the NGO without having to live on alms and donations alone. It is geared towards a self

---

[991] Cf. DGRV, die Genossenschaften, https://www.dgrv.de/weben.nsf/web/historyofcooperatives (03.07.2016). Hermann Schulze-Delitzsch's campaign of aid was to bring about sustainable improvement of economic conditions by bringing together weak individual traders. The consequence of this plan was to deter heteronomy. Therefore his principles of self-help, self-administration and self-responsibility became the first "raw materials association" for carpenters and shoemakers in 1847 and the first "thrift and loan association". He is the forerunner of today's Volksbank, 1850. The ideas of Friedrich Wilhelm *Raiffeisen* eventually gave birth to the *Raiffeisen* tradition through the provision of loans to crafts men and farmers. It thus became the first cooperative of the *Raiffeisen* tradition. He is the originator of the Raiffeisenbank today.

[992] Cf. Ibid. In 1920 for example, the chairman of the Bavarian cooperative organisation with over 5000 local cooperatives was prelate Kaiser. He was nicknamed as the *Raiffesisen Kaiser* (Emperor).

financing NGO, so that the DDS becomes even an emblem and a custodian of self -reliance, because 'no one gives what he/she does not have' -*Nemo dat quod non habet*. Therefore, "NGOs are... both an object of sustainability and a transmitter of sustainability."[993] The failure of the DDS stemmed also from the fact that it became a transmitter of sustainability but was never an object of sustainability itself. Unlike the DDS, some NGOs from central Asia and Latin America over the last four decades have recorded tremendous successes in the field of sustainable development that have warranted them a household name among rival NGOs, the international community and the circle of INGOs. Prominent among them is the case study of Bangladesh Rural Advancement Committee (BRAC). BRAC has proven a succinct example of sustainable development from available resources; although it absorbs a large pool of donors, these finances account for only 25 per cent of its budgetary expenditures. BRAC therefore funds the remaining 75 per cent of its budgetary expenditure through its several sources of revenues from programmes and commercial activities.[994] Other famous examples are the Self Employed Women Association, India (SEWA) and Proshika,[995] in Bangladesh, who through their credit and financial services make a lot of revenue from interest and service payments on loans. With this income, they are able to cover the administrative costs of the NGO and Proshika has consequently planned to achieve a 100 percent self-sufficiency. From its 1999-2004 slated credit programme plan of 400 million US Dollars, Proshika was to self-fund half of the programme. The *Institutio Brasileiro de Análises Socialis e Econêmicus*, in Brazil, (IBASE) owns an internet node that runs in 35 nations of the world. From these prospects it funds at least 44 percent of its budget. Also *Madres de Plaza de Mayo*, in Argentina is into commercial waters, bookshops and printing. The *Centro de Estudios y Promocion del Desarrollo*, in Peru (DESCO) has a reputation for a high quality research wing, capacity building and training services for local and international organisations, with a record of 70 consultancies annually.[996] Even though all the above mentioned NGOs are secular NGOs, the example of *Federaçao de Orgãoes para Assistência Social e Educational* (FASE) in

---

[993] S. Michael, Undermining Development, 132.
[994] Cf. Ibid.
[995] Proshika is an acronym from three Bangla words which stands for training, education and action.
[996] Cf. S. Michael, Undermining Development, 28-29.

Brazil[997] is one church NGO or FBO that has shown a case of self-reliance and self-sufficiency from the use of the available resources in its environment; thus, it is a task that church NGOs can venture into as well. These NGOs were established in the 70s like the DDS, but have grown to the status of powerful NGOs. Each of them has singlehandedly moved from the traditional dependent status of NGOs to wealth creating NGOs, a determinant factor of power, survival, sustenance, independence and recognition within the global NGO circle today.

From the many thousand NGOs in Nigeria, there are a few local NGOs among them that do not rely on foreign aid, but they still depend on the generous gestures of opulent families and cronies in government to assist people. At the end of the day they all end up in the same donor spectacle. But the issue remains that the obvious underdevelopment of some nations in a fast developing world and the uncertainty and stagnancy they experience despite the global social consciousness makes the idea of NGOs a real sign of deeper consequences than what the NGOs can solve. It does not matter how one dresses them, at the moment they do not seem to solve for example the fundamental issues like the German cooperatives did.

The DDS in her self-sustaining drive did establish a few mechanisms, like the water project[998] in the case of *Madres de Plaza de Mayo*. However, from all indications they were stunted from growth and lacked the needed impulse to grow into a self-generating DDS programme. This could be another source of a wealth generating scheme to carry the weight of the DDS's overhead costs. Whenever such projects thrive, it amounts to a move-away from the traditional mode of church- based humanitarian agencies (living perpetually on overseas funds,) to an NGO independence; so as to be free from the strings and pulls of the donor agencies. Such moves will enhance a DDS free from external control, able to assert her authority, assist the local people and to step up her humanitarian spirit. Another advantage this independence gives to powerful NGOs is that, such NGOs are able to choose which donor to work with, because donors

---

[997] Cf. Ibid., 38. FASE was a product of the CRS as the Catholic Church in Brazil took the leading role in the fight for human rights and democratisation during the age of authoritarian role. Today FASE works in the area of community development as well.

[998] Such a DDS project needs to be given priority. Though there is competition from other bottled water companies today, their distribution is still limited within their immediate place of establishment. Because of the diocesan network, DDS water has an added advantage of a good patronage.

and INGOs too are eager to be part of these success stories; it is about NGOs being able to turn the tables.

There are basics for a thriving sustainable development project; to this effect, Jennifer Elliot adopts a suggestion of five areas that could help to elucidate the practices of an NGO, which is into sustainability projects. They include:

1.   Assisting the very poor with self-help projects else they destroy their environment in the search for survival.

2   Self reliance should stem from the constraints of the natural resources within their immediate environment;

3   Apply cost-effective economic and development measures by employing modern and fitting criteria other than the traditional approach; these will upgrade traditional methods and environmental quality and will consequently increase productivity in the long run;

4   Taking cognisance of health issues, applying different control measures, ability to adapt appropriate technologies to the local situation, to ensure food self-reliance, clean water and finding means towards improving shelter for all;

5   Also that the development remains people-centred initiatives, whereby human beings become the resources.[999]

From the aforementioned steps and strategies, this is like a resumé of the four structures and activities that made up the DDS before it went moribund; one of the reasons for this decline was the apparent lack of finance to oil the wheels of the DDS. Thus, if continuity is factored into such an agency then the idea of building a sustainable developmental base becomes obligatory. One preeminent factor of wealth creation is that when humans learn to create wealth, they learn to distribute it judiciously. The DDS is to represent the model of wealth creation among the people, through the participation of the local people, respecting their freedoms and choices.[1000] Also this mechanism of wealth creation will help to equip the

---

[999] Cf. J.A. Elliot, An Introduction to Sustainable Development, 3. (See also Mustafa Tolba, Sustainable Development: Constraints and opportunities, London, Butterworth, 1987)
[1000] Cf. P. Ranci, Economy and Finance, 12.

DDS with the true knowledge and understanding of wealth creation and distribution towards the benefits of all. The sustainability of DDS will only be enhanced by harnessing the available resources. It is an independence that will cut short overbearing external control. Thus for DDS to truly

> achieve financial independence, [it] must also be able to survive without donor funds, either by tapping into alternative sources of funding or generating its own funds. In local development where governments rarely fund the work of NGOs and the donating publics are rare, few alternative sources of NGO funding exist. To survive without donor funds is often, therefore, to be able to generate your own funds. [To be] a powerful local African NGO, [DDS] would be expected to generate revenue internally, through its involvement in economic projects or commercial enterprises.[1001]

Therefore the question of using available resources to mature into a powerful NGO is a very crucial factor if the DDS must re-emerge.

5.5.2   Re-investing in Agriculture and other relevant areas

The different successful NGOs like BRAC, SEWA, IBASE, DESCO, *Madres de Plaza de Mayo* and Proshika above, give a lucid picture of NGOs that now wield power because of their network of investments. From the available resources and the funds from donors, they have been able to carve a niche for themselves and as such are labelled as powerful NGOs.[1002] Sarah Michael offers an articulate picture of what power means in the context of the NGOs as "the ability of an NGO to set down its own priorities, define its own agenda and exert influence over others to achieve its ends".[1003] Notwithstanding that DDS hit the wall in her operations, the dreams at its foundation were not devoid of investment plans. Its many goals highlight an integrated investment plan; accordingly, DDS was intended to go through

> a coherent programme..., [where] all projects [would be] 'knitting' and 'weaving' together overtime, [such that] people [would infer in the long run]... that improved agriculture, with increased yield etc. makes no sense unless nutrition improves; that profits must be re-invested in projects that further ensure progress and good health, for example a water project. This type of

---

[1001] S. Michael Undermining Development, 44.
[1002] Cf. Ibid., 147.
[1003] Ibid. 1.

'COHESION' shows us that though only a single improvement may be possible at a time, one innovation has to lead to another... [1004]

Since one development prompts and propels another, improved yield for example would create better opportunities for nutritional balance in the people's meals. Again profits from the DDS sales would create other projects like the water project and lastly, it would also create some humanitarian goal like improved sanitation and better health among the DDS's beneficiaries.[1005] From the above, one can imagine a DDS that was laden with proactive programmes of development from its commencement to provoke positive chain reactions of other developments. This agricultural programme, the backbone of DDS operation was to enhance sustainable agricultural production in Igala/Bassaland, a factor that envisaged the introduction of life-stock farming in the future as well.[1006]

One very remarkable benefit attributed to the DDS was the enormity of changes it steered through the agricultural landscape of Kogi-East with new ideas, new varieties and breeds of crops, which made it a people oriented programme. Despite its accomplishments, subsequent financial and managerial hurdles crippled the DDS, all because it lacked the wit for sustainability. For DDS to be sustainable, according to the definition of Sarah Michael, it has to achieve a space and create a secure position for itself. This will consequently endow the DDS with the power to set its own priorities even before donors and to face other rival opinions too. Nevertheless DDS till in the early 90s secured such a space and a name but did not gain the desired power because of a deficient sustainable approach. The DDS could not maintain the space because of its overt dependence on external funds. For this reason, the issue of dwindling funding opportunities from the INGO and donors vis-à-vis African NGOs calls for local fundraising. But then the thought of fundraising was out of the question for DDS because of the pronounced poverty status and the poor giving attitude in Idah diocese. In addition, the DDS could not have reckoned with assistance from Diaspora, which would amount to a drop of water in the ocean.[1007] At the end of the tale, DDS was confronted with the onerous task of paying her staff and financing its many projects without foreign means. Despite the DDS's death throes, many behind the scenes still believed in a

---

[1004] Diocesan Development Services, Functional Guidelines, Vol. I, 6.
[1005] Cf. Ibid.
[1006] Cf. Ibid., 9.
[1007] Cf. S. Michael, Undermining Development, 150.

DDS that had it all; it was like the proverbial biblical tree planted by the side of the river, that never goes dry. Also the presence of the local church Idah, the supposed agent of this *diakonein* action through the works of DDS was minimally represented. This church's *diakonein* picture was so negligible to the extent that many of the workers and aid recipients perceived the DDS as a 'European venture' or a channel of 'Western largesse'. The connection of DDS as the development arm of the diocese as stated in the guidelines was and is still very minimal and consequently faint in the minds of many of its workers and beneficiaries. Nonetheless a church NGO like every other NGO really needs some administrative independence to judiciously deal with its development issues and projects. If such platforms are distorted with undue bishopric control, the consequence of a stillborn NGO is imminent. Independence is a positive ingredient of development, however the NGO cannot exist as a parallel organisation to the diocese since it is a development arm of the diocese. There are many concessions among the clergy that at a point in time the DDS became too independent of the diocese. There must be rules guiding the NGO's relationship with the diocese, because overbearing diocesan control brings about abysmal failure and too much independence could create unnecessary arrogance and misconception. There must be a balance where both parties are called to respect each other and to recognise where the rights and privileges of each one begins and ends. Each party must bear in mind the primary interests and the ultimate goals of development. Every other interest, be it diocesan, congregational or individual must be relegated.[1008]

Self reliance is the true roadmap to independence; hence a self-reliant and powerful DDS will be emboldened to convincingly pursue capacity building among its beneficiaries so as to truly inculcate the genuine

---

[1008] The major controversies in the relationship of church NGOs and their Bishops lie undoubtedly in the financial control. Usually donor agencies request the signature of the sitting Bishop before a project is approved. In a financially constraint terrain for example, it can raise the bishop's attention and thus bring about increase interference in the affairs of the NGO. However one cannot rule out explicitly the abuse of office on the part of the NGO's head, be it a priest, lay man/woman or a male/female religious. At the long run, the question remains, who controls and takes responsibility of the finances? Is it the Bishop and to what level must the bishop be privy to financial records? Or is such piece of information restricted to the one in-charge of the NGO alone? These are fundamental and open ended issues. So long as these issues are not nipped in the bud, church NGOs will suffer major administrative bottleneck and undue twist. Nevertheless, the interests of the Bishop, diocese and whoever is the head must be jettisoned for the smooth running of the NGO or simply put: beneficiaries' interest must come first.

culture of self-reliance. For that reason, the onus lies with the DDS, the prospective banner of self reliance to seek for financial means of independence. A revamped DDS must factor self-reliance and such a journey would demand a careful examination of its past and failures, like the perception of its workers and beneficiaries mentioned above. Thus the lessons could turn a new page in the life of DDS and could consequently aid to avoid a repetition of such past mistakes. The emerged powerful southern NGOs today had their technical hitches at the beginning; however, they rose up to the challenges and have conquered this past burdensome state of affairs. Through their inventions and astuteness, they have discovered economic gaps and loopholes in their different localities and have subsequently exploited them to rise to the top. The ability of DDS to generate such meaningful and sustainable means of income will mean the pursuit of enterprises and opportunities that the DDS has good knowledge, capabilities and body of contacts to execute.[1009] Agricultural production for now remains unquestionably the best option where both the DDS and its beneficiaries would have common advantage.

The DDS occupies farm land that is approximately 12 hectares and used for seed multiplication exercise; if well harnessed with the recent development in yam setts, it could create additional opportunity for a little revenue to the DDS. Likewise the economic trees for example palm trees and cashew trees could serve also as new means of wealth creation.[1010] Moreover the many redundant tools, facilities, equipments and the expertise learnt over the time could still be of use today; despite the fact that they may have ceased production, a pocket of workers are still hoping for a revived DDS. It is therefore not a blank start, because the foundational head start had been laid. In-between the 70s and 80s when DDS was at its prime, it contributed massively to the production rate of this part of the nation and thus made DDS a household name in this interior. This return to agriculture therefore, offers a means towards ending the long drought of agricultural systemic productiveness in Kogi-East, to provide for the growing population. In Economics, the presence of one sector attracts another and triggers the growth of other subsidiary firms, therefore increased agricultural production in this non-government present locality could serve as a catalyst towards other developments. Thus, "...when agricultural surplus arises as a result of

---

[1009] Cf. S. Michael, Undermining Development, 151.

[1010] Cf. Diocesan Development Services, Functional Guidelines, Vol.I, 8; Interview with Sr. Nora McNamara.

economic development, the demand for commercial services and manufactured articles rises. This leads to commercial progress and the establishment of manufacturing industries."[1011]

In spite of the fabulous strategies of agricultural investment one may intend, there is also the need for the said NGO to do feasibility studies on the level of governmental loopholes in the affairs of agriculture. Governmental role in the success of a thriving agro-economy must include the issue of infrastructure, providing energy, accessible roads to the farms, protecting the agricultural industry through effective application of policies. So long as this is not feasible, the effect of NGO's presence would be too negligible for self-reliance and sustainability.

5.5.3 Building modern agricultural industry

Even though agricultural practice remains as one of the most prevailing modes of production from olden times, it has experienced changes and improvement in the methods and manner of operation. It has graduated from the use of crude tools to industrial agriculture and also imbibes new forms of management today. In spite of these tremendous changes in the modern age, the Igala/Bassa people like many other parts of the nation have remained at the level of traditional technologies, which involve the use of hand tools. The neglect of agriculture nationwide and the predominant use of hand tools results in weak and ineffective capability.[1012] Since the introduction of modern machines is still at snail-speed, the peasant farmers reckoned with the use of crude-, old tools and old system of agricultural practice bear the brunt of the lack of efficiency. It is even bitter enough to know that over 80% of foods produced in Nigeria for example come from these local farmers. Even after the return to land in the days of SAP, it was still the peripheral people for example, who grew the best crops and other food products, [1013] a status quo that has remained unchanged up to today. The neglect of farming during the oil boom and the continuous disregard for agriculture have relegated agricultural practice among the unfortunate, poor and less advantaged people. Therefore, the supply of food for the teeming population today is mainly from the inhabitants of the rural areas, a few industrial agriculturists and through imports. The Federal ministry of

[1011] M.L. Jhingan, The Economics of Development and Planning, 85.
[1012] Cf. B. Ofori-Amoah, Technological Change Strategy for Economic Development in Africa, 85.
[1013] Cf. Interview with Sr. Nora McNamara.

agriculture reports that between 2007 and 2010, Nigeria imported $628 billion worth of foodstuffs like wheat, sugar, rice and fish. It is incredible that a nation whose agricultural sector in the 70s accounted for over 60% global supply of palm oil, 30% of groundnut, 20 to 30% of groundnut oil and 15% supply of cocoa is lampooned with such a degenerated production. Such an economy is not sustainable and only portrays a state of inconsistent and failed agro-policies. This prior wealth from agro-business was generated by farmers from the North to the South. The present dependence from this depressing development undermines local production and creates fiscal challenges and according to the reports: 'Nigeria is eating beyond her means.'[1014]

Since agricultural occupation is very common among the people of Kogi-East coupled with the successes of DDS over the years, additional effort to put this as a banner of new development will consequently help to increase the net weight production of the people and by implication the nation. If such agricultural programmes are vehemently pursued, it could enhance the NGO's relevance, institutional sustainability and stability of DDS as a local NGO. In the words of Brinkerhoff and Goldsmith, a sustainable institutional NGO "depends upon maintaining: responsive output flows (high quality and valued goods and services); cost-effective goods and services, delivery mechanisms (organisation and management); and resource flows (recurrent costs, capital investments, human resources)."[1015] The collective and joint task of the local church and DDS could create an agricultural environment in the region, offering cost effective food products because of her *diakonein* standpoint and still maintaining a business friendly environment. Since the private sector drives the economy, the church and her NGOs could play a major role by increasing the level of agricultural production which will bring down food price and could create more access to food supply. The church through her years of effective management will be creating jobs which consequently mean wealth creation through capital flows. The task to establish industrial farms is a challenge to the churches in Nigeria to provide for the teeming population especially in this era of 'church boom'. If the present vigour and spirit of pecuniary aggressiveness and ingenuity of milking the poor, in the name of fundraising by the clergy and church body is channelled into running modern agricultural practices, it

---

[1014] Cf. Nigeria: Food Imports and the Struggle to Eat, http://allafrica.com/stories/201108100162.html (29.09.15)
[1015] S. Michael, Undermining Development, 132.

will go a long way to assist humanity, increase job opportunities and improve the standard of living of the people. The church has a divine duty towards the poor whom she ministers to; it is not by "seeking her own glory and material wealth; [but] by using her resources to serve the poorest of the poor and by imitating Christ's own simplicity of life".[1016]

That agricultural practices have gone scientific today makes the use of modern machineries inevitable. Nevertheless the glaring poverty on the part of the farmers makes it difficult for them to afford even the minimum machinery for agro-business, much more purchasing heavy agricultural machineries to enhance large scale farming. It calls for the need of a sort of hiring service from these NGOs and church owned agricultural centres, who could in the light of subsidiarity serve as centres for agricultural management, for hiring out agricultural tools and machines to the local farmers to enhance their production. In the developed world today, even farms that employed hundreds of people in the past are today managed by almost one man because of mechanised farming. Agro-firms are contracted from the tilling of the earth till the harvest. Even though it has displaced labour, which of course is the overwhelming consequence since the machine age, it increases yield, efficiency and less labour. What could be adopted from the developed world is the use of minimum tools to reduce the use of manual labour. The introduction of such minimum machine input will not lead to labour displacement, because farm business in this part of the world is more or less a family affair as almost every family engages its members in the onerous task of tilling and loosening the earth.[1017] This is the most cumbersome job of the farmers at the beginning of the planting season today. If tractors are provided, post-tilling jobs are less strenuous and there are enough labourers for such jobs.[1018] The establishment of agro-firms is one area the church could be offering technical and resolute social answers to unemployment, hunger, undernourishment and starvation. I want to believe there is no Catholic diocese in Nigeria that is too poor to operate such an

---

[1016] John Paul II, Redemptoris Missio, 43.
[1017] It is an organised labour force among group of relatives or friends. Such members work together on designated days on the different farms of its members. Among the Igalas this system is called *Adakwo*.
[1018] Like the Innoson Motor Company in Nnewi, it has employers who do works that robots do in Europe and America. The advantage is that, since humans can do this job and we still have a pool of labourers why import machines to do them. Likewise, what the machines do in Europe after tilling the earth may wait in the interim since we still have an army of unemployed all around.

agricultural undertaking and it is a matter of will power, organisation and interest. This call extends also to the Protestant and Pentecostal churches whose revenues are visibly channelled into ostentatious lifestyles like the purchase and maintenance of private jets for 'evangelism'. Considering the cost effect of such projects, it would suffice to say that an agro-project for the benefit of the masses or at least for their adherents should ordinarily not be a problem.

During the AADP days when the hiring of tractors and other modern machineries was at the people's doorstep, there were cases of consistent breakdown of the machine, because of the lack of manpower and organisation. There were grave problems as many of the farmers wanted to plough before the rains, while the soil was still hard and dry. Besides, the soil types could have strong iron pan close to the surface and consequently very close to the disc plough and sometimes there are stones, termite nests, strong roots and tree stumps left behind in the earth. All these posed a hazard to the disc plough in motion as they constitute one of the setbacks of modern agricultural management in Kogi-East today.[1019] To undergo tractor hiring services for example, the NGO or the church agro-venture must factor in the need to emphasise stumping of roots, clearing away stones so that the land is plough-ready. Such organisations could assist to lecture farmers by employing the services of agricultural experts and engineers to teach the farmers about landscaping their farms and how to do this onerous task with less labour and if possible provide the machines at affordable rate. It also includes the planting of trees at the edges of the farms to avoid erosion from water and wind. The church through her contacts with state personnel could use advocacy as a means to lobby for such machines, personnel and assistance from the state, thereby playing the role of the voice of the voiceless.

To be able to operate such agro-services, the soil type needs to be surveyed and appropriate measures be put in place. The different soil types in Igala/Bassaland for example determine the crop types and their yield. There are two major soil regions in Kogi-East: the riverine (alluvial) region along the banks of the river Niger and Benue and the plateau (upland) region, inland from the rivers. The Niger alluvial region receives a lot of deposition from the floodwaters. It is relatively flat with some undulation. Their kind of soil texture brings about varying yield and problem of

---

[1019] Cf. N. McNamara, S. Morse, Developing Financial Services, 102.

cultivation; the lower areas are heavy textured soils and are usually most fertile but have very hard soil texture that proves difficult to cultivate.[1020] Despite the high rate of flooding in this milieu, the high yield tendency has encouraged human settlement.[1021] The areas prone to flooding in the Niger alluvial are used as rice farms (upland and lowland) while the less flooding-prone areas are used as yam farms. The light sandy soil usually at higher elevation is easier to cultivate but has a poor fertility rate. The Benue alluvial flooded by the Benue River and its tributaries shares the same characteristics almost like the Niger alluvial, but could be used for a wide range of agricultural goods and horticultural crops. The soils of the upland region are well drained, deep, with variable texture and mostly yellowish-red and red colours. There are a few variations between the north-west and the south-east; however they are not as fertile as the alluvial and they lose their fertility when cultivated over time, which makes the farmers resort to shifting cultivation. There are many local systems of farming, but they are predominantly arable farmers who keep livestock as secondary activity and are usually left to free range system except during the cultivation period when the animals could be kept within a fenced environment to avoid damage on newly planted crops.[1022] Both soil types are today faced with serious environmental challenges. Just as settlement by the alluvial soil is intermittently under the threat of flood from the effect of global warming, so also are both the plains and the alluvial soils experiencing acute shortage of rainfalls and late rainfalls today. These are contemporary challenges that necessitate appropriate reaction from an agro-based NGO today.

To invest in agriculture, the NGO has to be certain of the value goods it intends to specialise in and the soil types; for example, the intended crop determines the location of the farm. Besides, increased investment in research and development as counselled by the International Food Policy

---

[1020] Cf. N. McNamara, S. Morse, Developing On-Farm Research, 23.

[1021] Cf. Olaide M. Aderoju, et al., Geospatial Assessment of 2012 Flood Disaster in Kogi State, Nigeria, in: IOSR Journal Of Environmental Science, Toxicology And Food Technology (IOSR-JESTFT) e-ISSN: 2319-2402,p- ISSN: 2319-2399.Volume 8, Issue 2 Ver. IV (Mar-Apr. 2014), www.iosrjournals.org, Pp. 74-84, 75, 84. In 2014 Kogi State experienced immense flood in 2012 and it was the worst ever. Some parts of the Kogi-East were heavily inundated and agricultural production was adversely affected resulting also in the loss of lives and property. Its causes were basically lack of functioning and buffer dams, lack of orientation on flooding, excessive deforestation and no visible afforestation programme.

[1022] Cf. N. McNamara, S. Morse, Developing On-Farm Research, 24.

Research Institute suggests that it will lift additional millions out of poverty, a task for the church NGOs like DDS.[1023] Increased research works on the possibility and the use of the soil through the use of improved seeds is another area where the NGOs could further their presence. The issue of land tenure has been problematic in Igala/Bassaland like every other part of Nigeria too. In the primitive times, shifting cultivation was possible; today the increase in population has opened farmlands into residential areas. Also the lands are overused and yield consequently depreciates over time. DDS for example has been into teamwork with IITA where huge discoveries and researches have been done over time. The resurgence of DDS could midwife such knowledge to the peasant farmers who have no contacts with IITA or with such sophisticated institutes.

Food processing is one area of agriculture that is rarely being assessed in Kogi-East. The local rice farmers from the Ibaji area have been exposed to immense and unfavourable competition from Asian markets since the days of the oil boom. The high valued Naira encouraged import and discouraged export because imports were cheaper and exports became invariably too expensive. Despite the aftermath of the oil boom and the years of dwindling economy, the preference of imported rice has encouraged importation and smuggling of rice into the nation. Accordingly, rice processing has remained at local production because subsequent governmental agricultural policies have not strived enough to change the status quo. Though several examples of Asian wonders were incorporated into different agricultural policies, they were never implemented and have thus become a figment of the imagination and mere state babbles (Ch. 3.4). Despite the increased consumption of rice today the "Nigerian rice farmers [still] cry as the imports undermine domestic production. We must accelerate domestic rice production and improve on processing to meet quality standards. We must tap into all the resources of our farmers across our nation and deliver a green revolution for rice that will make Nigeria self-sufficient in rice production."[1024] This point underscores the importance of the political *diakonia*; inasmuch as the onerous task of food security is state's duty, the advocacy's contribution of any agricultural-minded NGO includes making the government realise and deliver on her agricultural

---

[1023] Cf. Akinwumi Adesina, Growing Nigeria's Agriculture IITA, speech by the Minister of Agriculture and Rural Development (Nigeria) at the Cassava Forum held in IITA, Ibadan between 11 and 12 August 2011, Pdf,1.

[1024] Ibid., 2.

promises. The report of the Ministry of Agriculture suggests that Nigeria spends about 1 billion Naira (ca. $6 Million) daily on imported rice.[1025] There are some exceptionally established rice processing plants in some parts of the nation like Makurdi, Benue State, Abakaliki, Ebonyi state and so on, but their national output still remains insignificant to compete with the force of the imports and the smuggled Asian rice into the nation.

The increased yield and surplus from the introduction of machines could create a buffer economy through job creation in the agro-processing firms and in the marketing of agricultural goods. Food processing guarantees the reduction of post-harvest losses and also transforms agricultural, fishery and forestry products into more suitable forms.[1026] Today, a great percentage of local fruit and food crops are wasted all over the length and breadth of Kogi-East and many other parts of the nation annually because of the obvious lack of preservative and processing methods into economic products for sales and future use. This calls for a need for resourcefulness through food processing firms and other agro-firms to harness these God-given resources into modern, sumptuous and attractive commercial products.

The traditional industry was into processing of the cereals, grains, legumes, tubers and crops into different preservation forms for immediate use and for sales. Although it was prone to waste because of the meagre infrastructure and inadequate capability; food processing was still in place. However, its geometrical growth and progression does not tally with the speed of the globalised world today. There is an overwhelming absence of industrial culture, because agriculture and industry to date have remained like separate entities. Agricultural industry through food processing is another way of adding significant value to existing raw materials and it is a move away from being predominantly commodity goods oriented to a manufacturing status. Such productive strategy will enhance the shift and understanding from Agriculture to industry and such a secured status brings

---

[1025] Cf. Nigeria: Food imports and the struggle to eat, Daily Champion, Cf. http://allafrica.com/stories/201108100162.html (31.08.15)
[1026] Cf. Ruth O Oniang´, Agroprocessing: Adding Value to Food Production, in: Ed., Steven A. Brett, Food Security in a Changing Africa, Proceedings of the Workshop on Africa Food Security in a Changing Environment: Sharing Good Practices and Experiences held in Kampala, Uganda, June 6-9, 2001, Geneva 2002, Pp. 141-162, 141-142.

about the attributes of an industrial economy and its dynamism into play like technology, marketing, consumer preferences and so on.[1027]

5.5.4 Parishes as humanitarian and agricultural centres

Spreading the message of development could be another tool to spread enlightenment at the grassroots. The poor educational system and the poverty in Idah diocesan terrain make enlightenment programmes very important as catch-up strategies. Here the JDPC, DDS and other credible and interested NGOs could draft several humanitarian programmes to reach the disadvantaged in many villages. They could include different lectures, awareness programmes and teachings of health education (the example of ORT Ch.3.2.3) to spread the message to these disadvantaged. With the help of CRS, the Diocesan Health has been doing a wonderful job of HIV/AIDS awareness and assisting infected people in all the corners of the diocese. Nevertheless, there is the need to move away from the 'fire brigade' solution to a holistic one. It is about delivering a humanitarian proactive touch that includes proper and preventive education. Such education should be holistic like issues of health, diets, care of the aged, care/training of children, human rights, human relationship, parental responsibility, the social ethical principles and their application, their political rights/duties, self-esteem and so on. I am not denying the traces of such practices/teaching in the history of the diocese. Nevertheless my suggestion is they should be concretised, formalised and institutionalised, so that a diocesan framework and priority are given to such exercise. It is about exposing the disadvantaged to the real world, to a humane understanding of the world and the true idea of welfare and common good.

Another principal action of development as established by the DDS was that the local project or programme revolves round the beneficiaries, so that they become both the object and subject of the programme. Likewise investment, wealth creation and capacity building must be centred on the ordinary things that surround the people. The participation of the local people will create a deep socio-cultural transformation which will gradually change their attitude and behaviour over time.[1028] Like the example of CLCN, the parishes become the spiritual base as well as the agricultural

---

[1027] Cf. Ibid., 142.
[1028] Cf. Deutsche Bischofskonferenz, Partnerschaft mit den Armen, Wechselseitige Verpflichtungen in der entwicklungspolitischen Zusammenarbeit Eine Studie der Sachverständigengruppe „Weltwirtschaft und Sozialethik", Bonn, März 2004, 23.

centre. Thus, every parish could serve as an agricultural base. The essence of this grand development base is about running a 'development from below' which brings about the effect of subsidiarity into action. The priority of such development programme is to assist the locals by tapping their initiatives and cooperation, since they lack the voice and the contacts with state authorities, which makes their cases hardly heard. It will assist them to find a way-out of their predicaments. The church in her advocacy liaises with the civil societies to make the voices of the poor farmers heard by the appropriate authorities.[1029] Through this medium the church re-awakens government's attention towards the poor. The poor who were hitherto unheard could tap into the state's machineries and structures. Creating such an agricultural scheme in parishes in Idah diocese could invent new ways of doing things and re-activate the extension services that were practised in the DDS days. This will encourage the spreading of the message of development and the good news about development to the grassroots.

The potential and visible function of this agricultural centre is to assist in arresting agricultural backwardness among the locals. Although agriculture is the predominant occupation of the locals, their practice is obsolete and not in touch with modern technology; the NGOs can bridge this gap by bringing these technologies to the people's doorstep. The DDS at its prime recorded such progress in Eroke near Ankpa,[1030] and the case study of Ekwuloko and Odeke in Idah axis[1031] where both micro financing and modern technologies were brought down to the people. In this new era a holistic approach could be given whereby the agro-centre becomes integrated into the parish structure to reach more beneficiaries. The issue of land acquisition (Ch.3.8), which is a major headache in agricultural effectiveness, could be relieved too by working with the locals through these agricultural centres; because improved relationship through the parishes could create a relaxed atmosphere to negotiate land issues for interested farmers.[1032] Tractor services for example could be organised in such a

---

[1029] Cf. Deutsche Bischofkonferenz, Den Hungern bekämpfen, 42-42.
[1030] Cf. N. McNamara, S. Morse, Developing on-Farm Research, 138-150; Stephen Morse, et al., Visions of Sustainability, 77-143.
[1031] Cf. Stephen Morse, et al., Sustainable Livelihood Approach, 17.
[1032] Since land acquisition is by inheritance or shared inheritance especially in the rural areas, most lands have to be given out on the relationships. Even churches' access to land acquisition has been through such process. I believe that if such issues are raised within the context of the agro-centres, it could relax the tensions inherent in land acquisition. It may not

manner that everyone interested gets access to tractor services at the beginning of the planting season. This could be arranged through the FCs or through other means within the parish structure. But it must be transparent and all interested parties must be in the know of the financial implications of purchase, support from whichever donor(s), technical repairs and the requirements expected of any person to get such services. It is a humble beginning and definitely not the sole answer to the question of tilling the earth, which for now is in the most complicated stage that demands the use of modern machines.

One of the greatest dreams of DDS which was never achieved but was remarkably stated in her guidelines was the marketing strategy by controlling the sales of their products.[1033] The market strategy must be factored, otherwise middlemen could hijack the market and consequently become the greatest beneficiaries of the excess agricultural products. In most parts of the nation middlemen profit exceptionally more than the farmers who do the actual production. The Agro-centres too could be used as a medium to effectively market their products. Besides such centres could own storage houses or lease one and like the Canadian fishermen's example, such a controlled market by the farmers themselves could change their perspectives and economic positions.

5.6   Economic vacuum as stepping stone for production base

There are some FBOs and churches today that embark on economic institutions like bookshops, hotels, banks, insurance and ICT companies. Though some have recorded failures, others have thrived over time. But one major thrust from some of the successful church institutions is the initiative to partner with a competent private sector, whose responsibility includes the

---

erode all the fears but if dealt with within the context of the agro-centres it offers better room for trust.

[1033] Cf. Diocesan Development Services, Functional Guidelines, Vol. I, 79. It was a true story of a certain fishing community in Canada, whose fish harvest were being controlled by big traders with transport and cooling facilities. These traders made exorbitant profits while the fishermen groaned under continuous poverty. The fishermen had to sacrifice by organising themselves to buy a truck. It was thus a combined effort to ensure a united fight against this exploitation. This was the fruit of dedication, honesty, unity and discipline. They also worked out the modalities for profit sharing, which was based on invested shares. Also a certain sum was kept back for maintenance and for other issues. It was a proof that through unity, they could overcome the threats and market monopoly of the big traders.

provision of the requisite business acumen.[1034] Also some Catholic dioceses in the West invest in property holdings and ventures that create wealth, self-sustenance and –sufficiency that the diocese can fall back on in moments of difficulties or to augment the wellbeing and welfare of its workers. Evidence of failures by some of such organisations is obviously as a result of the fact that the building of firms and means of production has always been a reserve of the private sector. It is a probable reason why the church generally is found wanting in this area. That notwithstanding, the church has made huge landmark in the running of social institutions, which she could extend and thereby consolidate her presence.

One of the keys to economic success is the ability to explore economic loopholes with the aim towards filling such vacuums. One of such vacuums today is the deplorable state of health institutions. Though there are 30,098 primary-, 3992 secondary- and 84 tertiary medical institutions, public and private, published by the Federal Ministry of Health (FMH) in 2011,[1035] there is hardly any world-class hospital in Nigeria. In contrast, "before the discovery of oil in commercial quantities, the Saudi Royal Family [for example] received medical treatment from the University College Hospital, Ibadan. More than 50 years after the discovery of oil in commercial quantities our own leaders now depend on others for their healthcare. Why has this happened? In my opinion, it is because we got drunk on oil."[1036] The health sector is in shambles today and so neglected that one of the coup d'état plotters in 1983 described the Nigerian health institutions "as mere consulting clinics".[1037] As part of the church's *diakonein* duty, the church must think of building world-standard hospitals with modern facilities to provide for the numerous medical needs of her people. Nigerians in the search for medical treatment overseas spend billions of Naira yearly. Almost every retired or serving member of the political echelon, eminent and well-

---

[1034] Cf. J. Ogbonnaya, The Role of African Catholicism in the Light of Africae Munus, 66, (See also Olarinmoye Faith Based organisation in Nigeria, 15)

[1035] Cf. National Human Development Report, Human Security and Human Development in Nigeria, December 2015, 62.

[1036] Abubakar Atiku, Restructuring goes beyond resource control, http://www.vanguardngr.com/2017/07/restructuring-goes-beyond-resource-control-atiku/ (30.06.17).

[1037] A. A. Agbali, Ritualizing Communal Wellbeing, 324; Israel A. Ademiluyi, Sunday O. Aluko-Arowolo, Infrastructural distribution of healthcare services in Nigeria, an Overview, in: Journal of Geography and Regional Planning Vol. 2(5), pp. 104-110, May, 2009, Available online at http://www.academicjournals.org/JGRP ISSN 2070-1845 © 2009 Academic Journals, 109.

to-do Nigerians, receive medical treatment in the developed world. So much so that it has become a thing of 'class' for people to go overseas for treatment. The emerging nations like Malaysia, Singapore and India have joined the ranks of medical tourism and destination, where Nigerian patronage is recorded as very high. In 2012 for example over 18,000 Nigerians visited India and 47% of them were on health grounds, which sums up an estimated capital flight of this 'medical tourism' to N41.6 billion ($260 Million). The ministry of Finance in Nigeria lamented that if Nigerians were provided with health institutions locally, the nation could save over N30 billion ($200 million) per annum, which was 20% of the budgetary allocation of the health sector for 2011.[1038] This is even a conservative figure owing to poor statistics records; moreover this percentage represents the supposed middle-class who sometimes cannot make it to Europe or North America. This capital flight portrays the loss of opportunity for medical development, breakthrough and investment in Nigeria. All over the western world, dioceses and congregations own modern and technically befitting hospitals; though the Nigerian church has made an extraordinary contribution in this field, it is still negligible, not to be recorded as outstanding hospitals. It is a call for the Nigerian church to explore this economic vacuum. It will be absurd and false to complain about lack of funds because many local budgets run in billions of naira for building of gigantic churches and other questionable projects. The church should be more concerned about building human beings than raising magnificent structures, which invariably add nothing to human development.

It is a challenge in Idah diocese to upgrade the Grimard hospital today with specialist, consultative and referral possibilities. The 2011 statistics of FMH that Kogi state has just one public tertiary medical institution makes this project vital. Despite the 823 public and 45 private primary health institutions and over three-quarters of the 203 secondary institutions belonging to the private sector, the shortfall of medical ratio is a case of one health facility for 3044 people.[1039] It also calls for a change of management strategy. Therefore the church must move out of the box of inefficient and incompetent priests and nuns in the management of hospital affairs. She

---

[1038] Cf. 47% of outbound medical tourism in Nigeria go to India, http://www.hatman2010.org/index.php/newsletter/28-47-of-outbound-medical-tourism-in-nigeria-go-to-india. (19.03.2016).
[1039] Cf. National Human Development Report, Human Security and Human Development in Nigeria, December 2015, 62.

must engage the services of managers with requisite professional, business and managerial skills to give superlative treatment. Small dioceses could go into merger-projects with other dioceses. Besides the church needs some partnership and it is not just the transfer of material wealth from wealthy nations, but to employ the services of renowned health managing firms with Catholic orientation that specialise in the running of hospitals today. Because of the fall in vocations in Germany for example, there are such firms that manage hospital administrations for dioceses and congregations. Fortunately Idah diocese like other Nigerian dioceses has enough vocation but lacks professional and managerial skill. This sort of partnership and negotiation brings out the true humanitarian character of partnership as equals. A successful demonstration of such hospital administration can halt the capital flight and the loss of revenue that permeates every nook and cranny of the nation. Apart from its supplementary revenue to the church's coffer, it will be of assistance to humanity, to avoid some untimely deaths, to arrest emergencies and unnecessary casualty circumstances. As a humanitarian church, such services must include the humanitarian message of caring for the poor of the society. She must learn from her sister churches in the West to care for the health problems of those at the borderlines in her society. Though the functionality of health insurance scheme is still very negligible in Nigeria, the church must carve out avenues to care for the disadvantaged, bearing in mind the message of Pope Francis that the church belongs to the poor. The pontiff appealed passionately for the "inclusion of the poor in society"[1040] in every project and endeavour; he thus qualifies this as the vitality and enthusiasm of the new phase of evangelisation.[1041] The efficiency of church health services in the West has proven very successful and sometimes rival that of the state. Why should Idah diocesan context be different? These economic/humanitarian loopholes are potential strengths of the church, which every Nigerian diocese can tap into.

The only visible and substantial investment by the Catholic diocese of Idah was the Diocesan Works, which for long has folded up. Today there is no substantial investment by the diocese and this makes the growing dependency on the people's generosity very conspicuous and a matter of concern. The Works Department at its peak engaged in a number of projects (Chapter 3.6.5) and thus acted as a trustee in the exercise of these projects. There were no visible secular building-firms around the vicinity of Idah

---

[1040] Francis, Evangelii Guadium, 17.
[1041] Cf. Ibid.

diocese, besides most building projects (even within Nigeria) are exercised informally through direct labour. For that reason, whenever Igala/Bassa sons and daughters in distant cities were interested in erecting structures in their home land, they needed a partner, a contact or a trustee to execute such projects. Most times the services of close family members were recruited and this being an informal arrangement, the recruited family members/relatives were sometimes accused of mismanagement of funds. One can understand such tension between the rural and city dwellers because of the general attitude that urban dwellers have pecuniary advantage over the rural people; a factor that could result in mutual suspicion. That was how the Works Department with statutory rights and the trust of a church-based establishment became the contact partner and the trustee to many private contracts. This was an economic window and a vacuum that the Works Department explored by formalising the informal. Even though the Works Department ceased for many reasons, the diocese could still go back into harnessing such hidden opportunities in the society, because there are still countless persons who suffer such fraud today. To revive the Works Department effectively, the diocese must learn from the mistakes of the past and be ready to imbibe modern managerial skills. She must also conceive a new understanding of remuneration that the 'mission workers' reward is not only in heaven but begins from this earth and receives fulfilment in heaven. It is akin to the iron law of wages. Therefore it must be based on fairness and justice, which could bring out the true character of competitiveness and dedicated services from the workers.

One of the factors of developed nations is that virtually every village or city is integrated into the global economy and as such contributes to the nation's economy. Whether small or big firms, they are linked up in some international trade; this is an attribute that rarely exists in the developing world. Igala/Bassaland could integrate herself into the global economy by accessing the agricultural loopholes today. It is about selecting those economic activities that have the potentials to induce and provoke further progress within the community and the nation. The closeness to raw materials should be an added advantage for small enterprises to rival big ones. Local producers could utilize this advantage by giving value added processing to their products, since their products which are merely commodity goods would run the risk of market fluctuations caused by the forces of demand and supply, either induced by manufacturers or they could suffer intrusion and monopoly of the middlemen. When local producers begin to take the bull by the horns through adding values to their goods, it comes with appreciable advantages, as it reduces the importation of such hitherto finished goods. This value added processing would definitely increase local nutrition, income to the farmers and also encourage food exports to other African nations. It would consequently enhance continental trade, which can trigger African autonomy and self-reliance.[1042]

Such processing could boost local independence; for example there is too much importation of wheat at the moment. (Ch.5.5.2). This could be substituted by other flours like cassava, sorghum, rice, millet and maize flours, which for example have been proven to be of good quality for bread processing. [1043] Also it is time to extend tentacles and presence in other continents and this involves "taking an existing food product a step further".[1044] To tap into the exports of the competitive West for example Africans must "incorporate local products that do not exist in the countries of the north that are considered a thing of curiosity, a special delicacy, or an exotic and exceptional product".[1045] Today the wealthy nations "desire natural or organic foods. Here, it is not so much the product that is new, but the method of production. There is now considerable demand for agricultural products free of additives, pesticides, and fertilizers and Africa is as good a breeding ground as others."[1046] All these are prospects for the future and will also demand a meticulous implementation of the import regulations by FAO. Therefore it is a call to improve on the reservations made about a few African imports over time "that food products from Africa are being rejected due to food quality and safety issues. Products rejected range from fruits and vegetables to fish products. Among the reasons for rejection are contamination with pathogenic bacteria and pesticide residues, failure to meet safety regulations for low-acid canned foods, and presence of non permitted food additives."[1047] The varying climatic conditions of import and export nations must be clearly observed in the packaging of consumable goods.[1048] Nevertheless, the creative design of probable delicacies to be

---

[1042] Cf. R. Oniang O., Agroprocessing, 144-148.

[1043] During the Jonathan administration, there were cases of such substitutes with cassava, but the Nigerian government is notorious for lack of continuation with policies of past administrations.

[1044] R. Oniang O., Agroprocessing, 149.

[1045] Ibid., 151.

[1046] Ibid.

[1047] Ibid., 159.

[1048] Cf. Weekly Progress Report no 13, 16/11/69 to 22/11/69. A controversy arose from the stockfish supplied to the Biafrans from Norway by the JCA during the civil war. The fish got

packaged and sold elsewhere is a step towards industrial culture. It is a resonance of the need to integrate and teach the cultures of education, industry and democracy, which forms the backbone of this proposed humanitarian task towards uplifting humanity and the environment. It is the hybridization of the different local economies in Nigeria that can galvanise and initiate the kind of regional autonomy needed for social and economic emancipation of Nigeria in the long run.[1049] Such a development is capable of uplifting the next generation into economic breakthrough and the desired autonomy in both the secular and ecclesial world.

By and large, since the humanitarian church is not very business inclined and lacks the skills and spirit of the private sector, she must continue her role of advocacy, education and capacity building, because the wealth of the people determines the financial status of the church (Ch.4.). Through capacity building the humanitarian church should encourage and animate her faithful on the need to build an industrial culture through risk taking, to develop great thinkers with the foresight to unlock hidden opportunities, to be productive-minded and resourceful in their environment, to do things different from past generations and above all to be proactive; because they are the ones to change the society. God has endowed every human person from birth with talents to change the human environment for good, thus

> God's plan, [is that] every man is born to seek self-fulfilment, for every human life is called to some task by God. At birth a human being possesses certain aptitudes and abilities in germinal form, and these qualities are to be cultivated so that they may bear fruit. By developing these traits through formal education or personal effort, the individual works his way toward the goal set for him by the Creator.[1050]

That God bestows on humans with intellect and freewill, it is a consequent divine task and responsibility of humans towards self-fulfilment and salvation. Although the environment and other factors may delude the human person to the wrong path, yet he bears the responsibility for his success and failures. Here the church is encouraged to midwife the required humanitarian development, the skills and the requisite zeal that will lead such persons to an amiable goal of life, because the right use of willpower

---

rotten because they were processed under European regulation where 6% of salt was enough to preserve the fish, whereas the minimum of 18% was required for a tropical climate.
[1049] Cf. A. Adedeji, The Monrovia Strategy and the Lagos Plan of Action, 28.
[1050] Paul VI, Populorum progressio, 15.

and talent would enhance his humanity, perfect the self, the personal worth and self-esteem.[1051] These qualities are meant to be cultivated and as they bear fruits, God's plan of self- fulfilment for the human person comes into existence. That is when the relevance of faith comes into play as it rejuvenates and engenders positive change that is very essential in all strata of life.

[1051] Cf. Ibid.

CONCLUSION

Humanitarian works exercised by secular, church driven and private agencies over time have not erased the sufferings and decays of humanity. But one fact is certain that without such humanitarian gestures, the world today would have been poorer and more confronted by unprecedented misery. Despite their occasional ambivalence and interests even in the midst of this credit, they have assisted to reduce the level of poverty, ignorance, the abuse of human rights and above all the infringement of the interests of the societal less privileged. Also their media outcry has not only brought places of humanitarian crisis into the limelight but has also impeded the tendency of the growth of oppression and injustice in the world. Nevertheless the proliferation of NGOs after the oil bust that has clichéd the term NGO by synchronising foundations, civil societies, self-help groups and social organisations of towns, women, age-grades and so on as NGOs, has set a bad precedent. For some of the NGOs having their roots in the west, their jobs today are very promising because their workers are mostly paid in foreign currencies or according to foreign standards. It re-echoes the notion of humanitarian and developmental works wangling within the illusion of hope and the reality of the conduits of western or government largesse. But the fundamental question is, can these 'self-styled NGOs' really aspire for true distribution of wealth? Can they create wealth from the immediate environment? Is their concept of wealth creation and distribution a synonym of collecting from the rich for the poor? Is it for personal gains? The commonest scenario is a handful of NGOs translating the ideas of some western donor NGOs. Many contemporary studies have shown that most NGOs at present are make-shift houses seeking for survival and relevance; would new NGOs today take rival stance to alter this false perception of NGOs?

The design of this work is centred on the fundamental questions of NGO formation and humanitarian actions propelled by the appreciation of humanity and not by convenience. Inasmuch as humanitarians are products of time and space, their humanitarian actions must be driven by the appreciation of humanity and not by the present global convergent spirit of convenience. There are humanitarian challenges that provoke the establishment of NGOs, but should those NGOs fade away as soon as the problems are over? No matter the period of their longevity, NGOs must transcend the contemporary ethos of business to service for humanity. Such services must bear a positive energy for self-reliance. Any NGO that fails to reach such humanitarian heights should be relegated into networks other than to bear the name humanitarian. Most of what is called NGO in Nigeria these days has not really made any mark on humanity to warrant the name NGO. Local NGOs must have a clear vision and sound knowledge of the people they intend to assist; besides they must conceive a well defined remedy from commencement. That means the establishment of any NGO must be directed towards the eradication of whatever is grotesque about humanity that purposely and perpetually keeps humanity below the threshold of human development. Such a realistic humanitarian approach must aspire to position the local people in a way that their self-worth through the quest for sustainability and self-reliance becomes central. It is to assist the local people in the vital choices they make and the battles of life they are meant to embrace for their renaissance. The operations of such NGOs and humanitarian practices can truly galvanise what it takes to uplift the people in the long run.

Humanitarian concerns basically serve as ingredients that could prop up the needed zeal and enthusiasm for the envisaged changes but not the whole job of saving humanity in Idah diocese and in Nigeria as a whole. The primary job of humanitarians could be likened to the example of UNO, which despite its shortcomings of global insecurity and double/triple standards, was formed originally to reduce global misunderstandings and misgivings. Given the conclusions of Hammarskjöld Dag (1905-1961) the erstwhile Secretary General of UN, it is expected that the UN should be able to take humanity to some kind of heaven on earth; in retrospect the UN has only been able to save humanity from the pit of hell.[1052] Likewise, humanitarian work was originally designed to arrest failed human capabilities but remains incapable of solving all global problems of injustice and underdevelopment. At best it could serve at least to reduce the impact of that hell by creating an enabling environment for the needed change to occur. This includes doing all that the humanitarian can to ensure the respect and recognition of the rights and dignity of the human person, created in the image and likeness of God. Such a service to humanity rules out convenience but reinstates the service to humanity.

[1052] Cf. Adekeye Adebayo, The Curse of Berlin, 74, "the UN was not created to take humanity to heaven but to save it from hell."

BIBLIOGRAPHY

Books

Achebe Chinua, An Image of Africa, London, 1983.

Achebe Chinua, There was a Country, New York, 2012.

Achimugu Lawrence, History of Education in Igalaland, Lagos, 2005.

Abdulkadir Mohamed Sanni, A Political and Economic History of Igalaland, Central Nigeria: 1896-1939, Saarbrucken, 2011.

Adebajo Adekeye, The Curse of Berlin, Africa after the cold War, London, 2010.

Adichie Chimamanda Ngozi, Half of a yellow Sun, New York, 2006.

Aku Edmund, Solidarity, Subsidiarity and common good. Fundamental Principles for Community and Social Cohesion, Bloomington, 2011.

Allison Graham, Destined for War, Can America and China escape Thucydides's Trap? Melbourne, 2017.

Ankrah Marvin Nii, Regionalism and Political Instability in West Africa: Development, Challenges and Prospects, Hamburg, 2013.

Aneke Luke Nnaemeka, The Untold Story of the Nigeria-Biafra War, New York, 2007.

Appiah Kwame Anthony, Cosmopolitanism, Ethics in a World of Strangers, London, 2007.

Ayandele E. A., The Missionary Impact on Modern Nigeria, 1842-1914, A Political and Social Analysis, London, 1971.

Ayebome Emmanuel, The Nigeria-Biafra War and the negotiation Role of Carlo Bayer, (unpublished Master Thesis), Freiburg, 2013.

Barnett Michael, Empire of humanity, A History of Humanitarianism, New Delhi, 2012.

Baur John, 2000 Years of Christianity in Africa, an African Church History, Nairobi, 2005.

Beckerman Wilfred, A Poverty of Reason, Sustainable Development and Economic Growth, Oakland California, 2003.

Bolton Giles, Poor Story, An Insider uncovers how Globalisation and good Intentions have failed the World's poor, London, 2007.

Boston John S., The Igala Kingdom, Ibadan, 1968.

Campbell John, Nigeria: Dancing on the Brink, Wisconsin, 2013.

Chinweizu, The West and the rest of us, New York, 1975.

Collier Paul, The Bottom Billion, Why the Poorest Countries are Falling and what can be done about it, Oxford, 2008.

Cremer Georg, Corruption and Development Aid, Confronting the Challenges, Colorado, 2008.

Daly John A., Saville Anthony G., The History of Jointchurchaid, Vol 1-III, Copenhagen, 1971.

de Waal Alex, Famine Crimes, Politics &the Disaster Relief Industry in Africa, Bloomington, Indianapolis, 2011.

Dim O. Innocent, Reception of Vatican II in Nigeria/Igbo Church with Reference to Awka Diocese, Frankfurt am Main, 2004.

Diocesan Development Services, Functional Guidelines, Vol. I and II, Ayangba, 1984.

Dorr Donal, Option for the Poor and for the Earth, Catholic Social Teaching, Maryknoll, 2012.

Dorr Donal, Option for the Poor, A hundred Years of Vatican Social Teaching, Dublin, 1983.

Dorr Donal, The Social Justice Agenda, Justice Ecology Power and the Church, Ibadan, 1994.

Egbunu Fidelis Eleojo, Chieftaincy Titles among Igala, Problems and Prospects for Christians, Idah, 2001.

Egbunu Fidelis Eleojo, Igala traditional Values versus Modernity, Nsukka, 2009.

Ehusani George Omaku, A Prophetic Church, Ibadan, 2003.

Ehusani George Omaku, An Afro-Christian Vision "Ozovehe": Toward a more humanized World, Lanham, 1991.

Ehusani George Omaku, Nigeria: Years eaten by the Locust, Ibadan, 2002.

Ehusani George Omaku, The Social Gospel: An Outline of the Church's Current Teaching on Human Development, Ibadan, 1992.

Elliot A. Jennifer, An Introduction to Sustainable Development, the developing World, London, 1994.

Enang Kenneth, The Nigerian Catholics and the Independent Churches, A Call to Authentic Faith, Nairobi, 2012.

Ezea Matthew Irunnaya, The ILO's Concept of Decent Work in the Light of the Social Teaching of the Church and its Relevance to Nigeria, Münster, 2011.

Falola Toyin, Heaton Matthew, M., A History of Nigeria, Cambridge, 2008.

Falola Toyin, The History of Nigeria, London, 1999.

Fanon Frantz, The Wretched of the Earth, New York, 2004.

Foley Conor, The thin Blue Line, How Humanitarianism went to War, London, 2008.

Forsyth Frederick, The Making of an African Legend: The Biafra Story, New York, 1978.

Garrett A Stephen, Doing Good and doing well, an Examination of Humanitarian Intervention. Westport CT., 1999.

Haq Ul Mahbub, Reflection on Human Development, How the focus of development economics shifted from national income accounting to people centred policies, told by one of the architects of the new paradigm, Oxford, 1995.

Harmon E. Daniel, Nigeria, 1880 to the Present: The Struggle, the Tragedy, the Promise, London, 2000.

Healey John and Robinson Mark Democracy, Governance and Economic Policy, Sub-Saharan Africa in Comparative Perspective, Nottingham, 1992.

Heidrich Christian, Carlo Bayer, Ein Römer aus Schlesien und Pionier Caritas Internationalis, Arbeiten zur schlesischen Kirchengeschichte, Bd. VI, Sigmaringen, 1992.

Heilbroner L. Robert, The Worldly Philosophers, the Lives, Times and Ideas of the great Economic Thinkers, New York, 1992.

Human rights for human dignity, A Primer on Economic, Social and Cultural Rights, (amnesty international) London, 2005.

Hunt J. Timothy, The Politics of Bones, Dr. Owens Wiwa, The Struggle for Nigeria's Oil, Toronto, 2005.

Ihonvbere O. Julius, Shaw Timothy, Illusions of Power, Nigeria in Transition, Trenton, 1998.

Jhingan M.L. The Economics of Development and Planning, New Delhi, 2014.

Kukah Matthew, Democracy and Civil Society in Nigeria, Ibadan, 2007.

Lancaster Carol, Aid to Africa, So much so to do so little done, Chicago, 1999.

Lange Caroline, Der Fluch des Öls in Nigeria, Ein Land zwischen Reichtum und bitterer Armut, Norderstedt, 2013.

Lèfebvre Pierre, Ministries and Community, For a Church as a family, Nairobi, 1998.

Lewis L. J., Society Schools and Progress in Nigeria, Oxford, 1965.

Lugard F.D. The Dual Mandate in British Tropical Africa, Edinburgh 1922.

Lynch Irene Christina, Beyond Faith and Adventure, Irish Missionaries in Nigeria tell their extraordinary Story, Wicklow, 2006.

Macpherson C.B., The Political Theory of Possessive Individualism, Hobbes to Locke, Oxford, 1962.

Maier Karl, This House has fallen, Nigeria in Crisis, London, 2000.

Marx Reinhard, Christ sein heißt politisch sein, Wilhelm Emmanuel von Ketteler für heute gelesen, Freiburg, 2011.

Mazrui Ali, Nkrumah's Legacy and Africa's triple Heritage between Globalization and Counter Terrorism, Accra, 2004.

Mazrui Ali, The African Condition. The Reith Lectures, London, 1981.

Mbiti John, African Religions and Philosophy, London, 1971.

McNamara Nora, Morse Stephen, Developing financial Services, A case against Sustainability, County Cork, 1998.

McNamara Nora, Morse Stephen, Developing On-Farm Research, The Broad Picture, County Cork, 1996.

Metz Johann Baptist, Zum Begriff der politischen Theologie, 1967-1997, Mainz, 1997.

Stephen Morse, Nora McNamara, Moses Acholo, Benjamin Okwoli, Visions of Sustainability, Stakeholders, Change and Indicators, Aldershot, 2000.

Meagher Kate, Identity Economics, Social Networks & the informal Economy in Nigeria, New York, 2010.

Michael Sarah, Undermining Development, The absence of Power among local NGOs in Africa, Bloomington, 2004.

Moyo Dambisa, Dead Aid, Why Aid is not working and how there is another way for Africa, London, 2009.

Neher William, Nigeria: Change and Tradition in an African State, Massachusetts, 1999.

Nuscheler Franz, Lern- und Arbeitsbuch Entwicklungspolitik, Bonn, 2005.

Nussbaum C. Martha, Creating Capabilities, The human Development Approach, Cambridge, 2011.

Obodoechina Uchechukwu, The Imperative of Self-Reliance for the Churches in Africa, Frankfurt Am Main, 2006.

Ojo Gabriel Afolabi, Catholic Laity in Nigeria, Yesterday, Today, Tomorrow, Ibadan, 2004.

Okpanachi Blaise, Nigeria- Vatican Diplomatic Relations, Würzburg, 2011.

Okwoli P.E., An outline history of Idah diocese, Nsukka, 1984.

Okwoli P.E., Introduction to Igala Traditional Religion, Idah, 1966.

Okwoli P.E., Short History of Igala, Illorin, 1973.

Omoregbe I. Joseph, A simplified History of Western Philosophy, Vol.I, Ancient and Medieval philosophy, Lagos, 1990.

Onokerhoraye Andrew G., Social Services in Nigeria, An Introduction, London, 1984.

Oxford Advanced Learner's Dictionary, Ed., Joanna Turnbull, Oxford, 2010.

Peel Michael, A Swamp full of Dollars, Pipelines and paramilitaries at Nigeria's Oil frontier, New York, 2009.

Ranci Pippo, Economy and Finance for Everyone, Nairobi, 2012.

Rieff David, A Bed for the Night, Humanitarianism in Crisis, Frankfurt Am Main, 2000.

Rodney Walter, How Europe underdeveloped Africa, Enugu, 1982.

Rose David, Hegel's Philosophy of Right, London, 2007.

Rowell Andy, Marriott James, Stockman Lorne, The next Gulf, London, Washington and Oil Conflict in Nigeria, London, 2005.

Shorter Aylward W.F., Theology of Mission, Theology Today Series, No. 37, London, 1972.

Shorter Aylward, Religious Poverty in Africa, Nairobi, 2001.

Siollun Max, Oil, Politics and Violence, Nigeria's Military Coup Culture, (1966-1976), New York, 2009.

Tenquist Alasdair, Nigeria, A Study on an economically Developing Country, East Sussex England, 1966.

Thiong'O Ngũgĩ Wa, Decolonisisng the Mind, The Politics of language in African Literature, Portsmouth, 2005.

Ukwedeh N. Joseph, History of the Igala Kingdom c. 1534-1854, A study of Political and Cultural Integration in the Niger-Benue Confluence Area of Nigeria, Kaduna, 2003.

Uwechue Ralph, Reflections on the Nigerian Civil War, Facing the Future, Abuja, 2004.

Uzukwu E. Elochukwu, A listening Church, Autonomy and Communion in African churches, Eugene Oregon, 1996.

Walker F. Deaville, Project Canterbury, The Romance of the Black River, The Story of CMS Nigerian Mission, London: Church Missionary Society, 1930, in: http://www.anglicanhistory.org/africa/ng/walker1930/index.html (09.02.15).

Wiemeyer Joachim, Keine Freiheit Ohne Gerechtigkeit, Christliche Sozialethik angesichts globaler Herausforderungen, Freiburg, 2015.

Wilber K. Charles, Catholic Spending and Acting justly, A small- Group guide for Living Economic Stewardship, Indiana, 2009.

Journals, Articles, Speeches, lectures.

Abuh John, The Contribution of St. Kizito's Seminary to the growth of Vocation in Idah Diocese, in: Ed., Pub./Hist. Sub-Committee of the Idah Diocesan Silver Jubilee celebration, Catholic Diocese of Idah at twenty five, Enugu, Pp. 54-56.

Adedeji Adebayo, The Monrovia Strategy and the Lagos Plan of Action,16 Five years after, in: Eds., Adebayo Adedeji, Timothy M. Shaw, Economic Crisis in Africa, African Perspectives on Development Problems and Potentials, Boulder Colorado, 1985, Pp. 9-34.

Ademiluyi Israel A., Aluko-Arowolo Sunday A., Infrastructural distribution of healthcare services in Nigeria, an Overview, in: Journal of Geography and Regional Planning Vol. 2(5), pp. 104-110, May, 2009. Available online at http://www.academicjournals.org/JGRP ISSN 2070-1845 © 2009 Academic Journals, Pp. 104-110.

Aderoju Olaide M., Jantiku Jagila, Fagbemiro Olayinka .A, Aliyu Imrana, Nwadike Blessing K., Ajonye Susan E1, Salman Khalid. S., Geospatial Assessment of 2012 Flood Disaster in Kogi State, Nigeria, in: IOSR Journal Of Environmental Science, Toxicology And Food Technology (IOSR-JESTFT) e-ISSN: 2319-2402, p- ISSN: 2319-2399.Volume 8, Issue 2 Ver. IV (Mar-Apr. 2014), www.iosrjournals.org, Pp. 74-84.

Abdulkadir M.S., Islam in the non-Muslim Northern Area of Nigeria, c. 1600-1960,in; Illorin Journal of Religious Studies, Vol. 1, No. 1, 2011, Pdf, Pp. 1-20.

Adesina Akinwumi Growing Nigeria's Agriculture IITA, speech by the Minister of Agriculture and Rural Development (Nigeria) at the Cassava Forum held in IITA, Ibadan between 11 and 12 August 2011, Pdf, Pp. 1-6.

Adjibolosoo Senyo, The Human Factor and the Failure of Economic Development and Policies in Africa, in: Eds., Fidelis Ezeala-Harrison, Senyo B-S.K. Adjibolosoo, Perspectives on Economic Development in Africa, Westport, 1994, Pp. 25-38.

Adjibolosoo Senyo, The political Economy of Development in Africa: Reflections on Orthodox Thinking and Policy, 215, in: Eds., Fidelis Ezeala-

Harrison, Senyo B-S.K. Adjibolosoo, Perspectives on Economic Development in Africa, Westport, 1994, Pp. 205-218.

Aduku, J.F. Development of Education in Idah Diocese (1978- 2003), in: Ed., Pub./Hist. Sub-Committee of the Idah Diocesan Silver Jubilee celebration, Catholic Diocese of Idah at twenty five, Enugu, 2003, Pp. 33-37.

Afolayan S.F., The Evolution of the Igala Kingdom to 1800, A Reconsideration, in; The Africa Historian, Journal of the History Students' Society, University of Ife, Ile-Ife, Vol. XII, 1986, Pp. 24-31.

Agbali Anthony Attah, Ritualizing Communal Wellbeing: The Igala Anthropology of Healthcare and Contemporary Nigerian Healthcare Delivery, in: Eds., Toyin Falola, Matthew M. Heaton, Traditional and Modern Health Systems in Nigeria, Trenton, 2006, Pp. 305-363

Agbali Anthony Attah, The Catholic Church, Social Justice Teachings and Healthcare Delivery in Nigeria, in: Eds., Toyin Falola, Matthew M. Heaton, Traditional and Modern Health System in Nigeria, Trenton, 2006, Pp. 37-90.

Agbali Anthony, The Igala Response to Colonial Destabilization and Fragmentation, in: Ed., Toyin Falola, Perspectives on Colonialism in Africa, Durham, 2003, Pp. 97-135,

Aguwa C. Jude, Mission, Colonialism, and the Supplanting of African Religious and Medical Practices, in: Eds., Chima J Korieh, Raphael Chijoke Njoku, Molefi Asante, Missions, States and European Expansion in Africa, African Studies, History, Politics, Economics, and Culture, New York, 2007, Pp.127-146.

Ali Anthony Danladi, The Colonial Economy in the Lower Niger Region, in: Arabian Journal of Business and Management Review (Oman Chapter) Vol. II No.7, February 2013, Pp. 47-54.

Allsopp E. Michael, Subsidiarity, in: Ed., Judith A. Dwyer, The New Dictionary of Catholic Social Thought, Minnesota 1994, Pp. 927-929.

Augustinović Maja, Demographie und Entwicklung in Westafrika, in: Ed., Hanns Seidel-Stiftung e.V., Politischer Hintergrundbericht Westafrika, August 2014, Pp. 1-7.

338

Balasuriya Tissa, Globalisation in: Eds., Virginia Fabella, MM, R.S Sugirtarajah, Dictionary of the Third World Theologies, New York, 2000, Pp. 91-94.

Barnett Michael, Humanitarianism as a scholarly Vocation, in: Eds., Barnet Michael, Weis Thomas George, Humanitarianism in Question, Politics, Power, Ethics, Ithaca, 2008, Pp. 235-264.

Barnett Michael, Weiss Thomas George, Humanitarianism, A brief History of the Present, in: Eds., Barnet Michael, Weis Thomas George, Humanitarianism in Question, Politics, Power, Ethics, Ithaca, 2008, Pp. 1-48.

Bartelmus Peter, Moll Stephan, Bringezu Stefan, Nowak Sebastian, Raimund Bleischwitz., Translating sustainable development into practice: a 'patchwork' of some concepts and an introduction to material flows analysis, in: Eds., Raimund Bleischwizt, Peter Hennicke, Eco-Efficiency, Regulation and sustainable Business, Towards a governance structure for sustainable development, Cheltenham, 2004, Pp. 1-32.

Baumgartner Alois, Solidarität, in: Ed., Marianne Heimbach-Stein, Christliche Sozialethik, Vol. I, Regensburg, 2004, Pp. 282-292.

Baus Karl, Von der Urgemeinde zur frühchristlichen Großkirche, in: Ed., Hubert Jedin, Handbuch der Kirchengeschichte, Vol. I, Freiburg, 1985.

Bayart Jean Francois, Stephen Ellis, Beatrice Hibou, From Kleptocracy to the Felonious State, in: Eds., Jean Francois Bayart, The Criminalization of the State in Africa, Oxford, 1999, Pp. 1-31.

Beck B. Roger, All things to all People: Christian Missionaries in Early Nineteenth Century South Africa, in: Eds., Chima J. Korieh, Raphael Chijoke Njoku, Molefi Asante, Missions, States and European Expansion in Africa, African Studies, History, Politics, Economics, and Culture, New York 2007, Pp.11-34.

Bierschenk Thomas, Elwert George, Hohnert Dirk, Long –Term Effects of Development Aid: Empirical Studies in Rural West Africa, Pdf, Pp. 83-112.

Bisong Kekong, The African Quest for Self-Determination within Postmodern globalization and civilization, In: Ed., S. Nnoruka, The Nigerian Journal of Theology, Vol. 21, Ikot-Ekpene, 2004, Pp. 101-120.

Bleischwitz Raimund / Pfeil Florian „Global Resource Governance" Perspektiven nachhaltiger globaler Rohstoffpolitik, in: Eds., Raimund Bleischwitz /Florian Pfeil. Globale Rohstoffpolitik, Herausforderung für Sicherheit, Entwicklung und Umwelt, Nomos, Baden Baden, 2009, Pp. 21-29.

Bohrman Thomas, Subsidiarität, in: Ed., Marianne Heimbach-Stein, Christliche Sozialethik, Bd I, Regensburg, 2004, Pp. 293-301.

Boston J.S., Igala Political Organisation, in: African Notes, Institute of African studies, University of Ibadan Nigeria, Vol. 4, Num. 2, 1967, Pp. 18-31.

Campbell Ian, Army Reorganisation and Military withdrawal, in: Ed., Keith Panter-Brick, Soldiers and Oil, the Political Transformation of Nigeria, Studies in Commonwealth Politics and History, No 5, London, 1978, Pp. 58-100.

Chinweizu, Education for Liberation of Black Africa, Paper presented at the Codesria Conference on 50 years of African independence, Legon, September 2010. Pdf, Pp. 1-10.

Clark Matthew, Understanding Faith-based Organizations: How FBOs are contrasted with NGOs in international development literature, in: Progress in Development Studies 15, I, 2015, Pp. 37-48.

de Waal Alex, The African State and global Governance, in: Ed., Phoebe Griffith, Unbinding Africa, Making Globalisation work for Good Governance, London, 2003, Pp. 11-19.

Desgrandchamps Marie-Luce, Organising the unpredictable': the Nigeria–Biafra war and its Impact on the ICRC, International Review of the Red Cross, Vol. 98, Number 888, Winter 2012, Pp. 1409-1432.

Douzinas Costas, the Many Faces of Humanitarianism, in: Parrhesia number 2, 2007, Pp. 1-28.

Éla Jean-Marc, The Church-Sacrament of Liberation, in: Ed., Maura Browne, The African Synod, Documents, Reflections, Perspectives, Maryknoll, 1996, Pp. 131- 138.

Engel Ulf, Africa images and African Policy, Pleading for Realism, in: Eds., Ulf Engel, Robert Kappel, Germany's Africa Policy Revisited, Interests, images and incrementalism, , Politics and Economics in Africa, Vol. IV, Münster, 2002, Pp. 19-38.

Etu Yusuf, Miachi Tom, The Mahionu War (1916-1917) and the History of Igala, in; Ed., Brian Dawtrey, Journal of Igalaland, Vol. 2, No. 2, Ayangba, 1980, Pp. 34-37.

Ezeala-Harrison Fidelis, What Ails African Economies: Lessons from Over-stretched Underdevelopment, in: Eds., Fidelis Ezeala-Harrison, Senyo B-S.K. Adjibolosoo, Perspectives on Economic Development in Africa, Westport, 1994, Pp. 3-24.

Feason James D., The Rise of Emergency Relief Aid, in: Eds., Barnet Michael, Weis Thomas George, Humanitarianism in Question, Politics, Power, Ethics, Ithaca, 2008, Pp. 49-72.

Fuglestad Finn, How to write African History in the Post-modern era. And how to integrate African history into the mainstream of history, a personal view, 267, in: Eds., Hans Peter, Gerd Splitter, Afrika und die Globalisierung, Vol. 18, Hamburg, 1999, Pp. 258-268.

Gierych Wojciech, The Common Good and the Diakonia-Service of the Church in Society (Forms of Cooperation, Education and Culture), in: Ed., Second Catholic Orthodox Forum, Church and State Relations: From historical and theological Perspectives, Rhodes, Greece, 22 October 2010, Pp. 165-183.

Goldstein Rolf, Landwirtschaftliche Beratung im Gebiet der Diözese Idah/Benue State, Nigeria, in: Ed., Theodor Dams, Integrierte ländliche Entwicklung. Theoretische Grundlagen und praktische Erfahrungen. (Entwicklung und Frieden : Materialen 8), München, 1980, Pp. 237-250.

Griffith Phoebe, Introduction, in: Ed., Phoebe Griffith, Unbinding Africa, Making Globalisation work for Good Governance, London, 2003, Pp. ix-xvii.

Hallahan P.J. Kenneth, Aid, in: Ed., Judith A. Dwyer, The New Dictionary of Catholic Social Thought, Minnesota 1994, Pp. 33-37.

Hammond Laura, The Power of Holding Humanitarianism hostage and the Myth of protective Principle, in: Eds., Barnet Michael, Weis Thomas George, Humanitarianism in Question, Politics, Power, Ethics, Ithaca, 2008, Pp. 172-195.

Harnischfeger Johannes, Zur Entstehung religiöser Konflikte in Nigeria, in: Ed., Josef Thesing, Konrad Adenauer Stiftung (KAS), 11/1996, Pp. 33-74.

Ike Obiora, The Church and Civil Society, the Case of Nigeria, in; Eds., Gerhard Kruip, Helmut Reifeld, Church and Civil Society, The Role of Christian Churches in the Emerging Countries of Argentina, Mexico, Nigeria and South Africa, Bornheim, 2007, Pp. 111-126.

Imam Hauwa, Educational Policy in Nigeria from the Colonial Era to the Post-Independence Period, in: Italian Journal of Sociology of Education I, 2012, Pp. 181-204, Pdf, (03.07.15)

Iwuchukwu J.C., Igbokwe E,M., Lessons from Agricultural Policies and Programs in Nigeria, Journal of Law, Policy and Globalization www.iiste.org ISSN 2224-3240 (Paper) ISSN 2224-3259 (Online) Vol. 5, 2012, Pp. 11-21. Pdf, (01.07.15)

Kaulemu David, Building Solidarity for Social Transformation through the Church's Social Teaching, in: Ed., Daniel McDonald, Catholic Social Teaching in Global perspective, Maryknoll, 2010, Pp. 36-80.

Kemp Mathias, The Governability of the Multinational State of Nigeria, Is Decentralisation the Solution or Part of the Problem? In: Ed., Gerhard Wahlers, Konrad Adenauer Stiftung International Reports, 6/14, Vol. 30, Berlin, 2014, Pp. 7-30.

Korieh J. Chima Conflict and Compromise: Christian Missions and New Formations in Colonial Nigeria, in: Eds., Chima J. Korieh, Raphael Chijoke Njoku, Molefi Asante, Missions, States and European Expansion in Africa, African Studies, History, Politics, Economics, and Culture, New York, 2007, Pp.147-166.

Lamb L. Matthew, Solidarity, in: Ed., Judith A. Dwyer, The New Dictionary of Catholic Social Thought, Minnesota, 1994, Pp. 908-912.

Mabogunje L. Akin, Changes in socio-economic and cultural patterns caused by the industrialization of Nigeria - a regional differentiation, in: Afrika Spectrum, Wirtschaftsplannung und Wirtschaftspolitik in Nigeria, Deutsches Institut für Afrika-Forschung, Hamburg, 1972, Pp. 34-45.

Mabogunje L. Akin, Land Reform in Nigeria Problems, Progress, Prospects, Chairman Presidential Technical Committee for Land Reform, Pp. 1-25, (online) Pdf, (01.07.15)

Mbogori Ezra, African Civil Society, coming to Terms with Globalisation, in: Ed., Phoebe Griffith, Unbinding Africa, Making Globalisation work for Good Governance, London, 2003, Pp. 21-26.

McKenzie David, Identifying and spurring High-Growth Entrepreneurship. Experiment Evidence from a Business Plan Competition, Policy Research Working Paper, World Bank Group, August, 2015.

McNamara Nora, Morse Stephen, Voices from the aid 'Chain': the personal Dynamics of Care, in; Social and Cultural Geography, Vol. 5, No. 2, June 2004, Reading, Pp. 253-270.

McNamara Nora, Nigeria: Diocesan Development Service, (DDS) of Idah, Source: Trocaire, 13th April 2006, Pp.1-8.

Melloni Alberto, Poverty of the church - Poverty of culture: A contribution of Giuseppe Dossetti to Vatican II, in: Ed., David G. Schultenover, Theological Studies. Vol. 75, Number 3, New Jersey, 2014, Pp. 485-501.

Metz Johann Baptist, Compassion: Zu einem Weltprogramm des Christentums im Zeitalter des Pluralismus der Religionen und Kulturen, in: Eds., Johannes Baptist Metz, Lothar Kuld, Adolf Weisbrod, Compassion, Weltprogramm des Christentums, soziale Verantwortung lernen, Freiburg, 2000, 9-19.

Mills Greg; Oppenheimer Jonathan, From Spectator to Player: Strategies for globalising African Trade, 32, in: Ed., Phoebe Griffith, Unbinding Africa, Making Globalisation work for Good Governance, London, 2003, Pp. 32-44.

Morse Stephen, McNamara Nora, Acholo Moses, Sustainable Livelihood Approach: A critical Analysis of Theory and Practice, Geographical Paper No.189, November 2009, PP. 1-67.

Nicholas A. Nwagwu, The state take-over of schools in Nigeria: a controversy", journal of educational administration, 1979, Vol. 17, iss: 1, Pp.75-86.

Nigeria's Dawn, Last Chance for a patchwork state? Understanding Global Issues 99/2 in: Ed., Richard Buckerly, England, 1999, Pp. 1-18.

Nwabuani Ebere, The political Economy of Aboh, 1830-1857 in: African Economic History, Vol. 27 1999, Pp. 93-116.

Nwaokocha A Odigwe., Nzemeke A.D., Aspects of Igala influence on the Oshimili people of western Igboland in pre-colonial times, in: Nsukka Journal of the humanities, No 12, 2002, Pp. 169-179.

Obi Des Obioma, Church's role in alleviation of poverty in contemporary Nigerian Society in: Ed., Sasa Michael Sunday, West African Journal of Ecclesial Studies, (WAJES) Ibadan, 2009, Pp. 79-99.

Ofori-Amoah Benjamin, Technological Change Strategy for Economic Development in Africa, in: Eds., Fidelis Ezeala-Harrison, Senyo B-S-K. Adjibolosoo, Westport, 1994, Pp. 85-102.

Ogbonnaya Joseph, Religion and sustainable Development on Africa, in: African Catholicism and Hermeneutics of culture, Essays in the Light of African Synod II, Eugene, 2014, Pp. 55-74.

Ogbonnaya Joseph, Critical Culture for Integral Development and Responsible Governance in Sub-Saharan Africa, in: African Catholicism and Hermeneutics of culture, Essays in the Light of African Synod II, Eugene, 2014, Pp. 37-54.

Ogbonnaya Joseph, The Role of African Catholicism in the Light of Africae Munus, in: African Catholicism and Hermeneutics of culture, Essays in the Light of African Synod II, Eugene, 2014, Pp. 75-112.

Ogbonnaya Joseph, Theology, Culture, and Sustainable Development in Africa, in: African Catholicism and Hermeneutics of culture, Essays in the Light of African Synod II, Eugene, 2014, Pp. 113-132.

Ogbu U. Kalu, To Hang a Ladder in the Air: Talking about African Education in Edinburgh in 1910, in: Eds., Chima J. Korieh, Raphael Chijoke Njoku, Molefi Asante, Missions, States and European Expansion in Africa, African Studies, History, Politics, Economics, and Culture, New York, 2007, Pp.101-126.

Oguche John, The contribution of the Diocesan Works Department to the infrastructural and social development of Idah Diocese in: Ed., Pub./Hist. Sub-Committee of the Idah Diocesan Silver Jubilee celebration, Catholic Diocese of Idah at twenty five, Enugu 2003, Pp. 38-45.

Oguonu Catherine, The Diocesan Development Services (DDS) in: Ed., Pub./Hist. Sub-Committee of the Idah Diocesan Silver Jubilee celebration, Catholic Diocese of Idah at twenty five, Enugu 2003, Pp. 38-45.

Okpanachi Dorothy, A brief History of Religious Congregation for Women in the Diocese, in: Ed., Pub./Hist. Sub-Committee of the Idah Diocesan Silver Jubilee celebration, Catholic Diocese of Idah at twenty five, Enugu 2003, Pp. 57-59.

Omobolaji Ololade Olarinmoye, Faith-Based Organizations and Development: Prospects and constraints in; Transformation: An International Journal of Holistic Mission Studies 2012 29: 1 http://trn.sagepub.com/content/29/1/1 online: DOI: 10.1177/0265378811427985, Pp. 1-15. (15.10.14).

Oniang'O. Ruth, Agroprocessing: Adding Value to Food Production, in: Ed., Steven A. Brett, Food Security in a Changing Africa, Proceedings of the Workshop on Africa Food Security in a Changing Environment: Sharing Good Practices and Experiences held in Kampala, Uganda, June 6-9, 2001, Geneva, 2002, Pp. 141-162.

Ortlieb Heinz-Dietrich, Entwicklungshilfe für Afrika, Bemerkungen zu den politischen und wirtschaftlichen Entwicklungsproblemen westafrikanischer Länder, in: Ed., Heinz- Dietrich Ortlieb, Veröffentlichungen der Akademie für Gemeinschaft Hamburg, Tübingen, 1961, Pp. 25-44.

Oshio P. Ehi, The Indigenous Land tenure and Nationalization of Land in Nigeria, in: Online- Boston College Third World Law Journal, Vol.10, Iss. 1, Art. 3, 1990, Pp. 42-62 (01.07.15).

Ottaway Marina, The state before democracy, 5, in: Ed., Phoebe Griffith, Unbinding Africa, Making Globalisation work for Good Governance, London, 2003, Pp. 1-9.

Otteson James R. Kantian Individualism and Political Libertarianism, 398-409. Volume 13, Number 3, 2009, in: http://www.independent.org/pdf/tir/tir_13_03_4_otteson. Pp. 389-409, pdf, (15.10.14).

Oyovbaire S. Egbite, The Politics of Revenue Allocation, in: Ed., Keith Panter-Brick, Soldiers and Oil, the Political Transformation of Nigeria, Studies in Commonwealth Politics and History, No 5, London, 1978, Pp. 224-253.

Rolf Hoffmeier, Five decades of German- African relations: limited interests, low political profile and substantial aid donor, in: Eds., Ulf Engel, Robert Kappel, Germany's Africa Policy Revisited, Interests, images and incrementalism, , Politics and Economics in Africa, Vol. IV, Münster, 2002, Pp. 39-62.

Seton R.S., Installation of An Attah of Idah (Nigeria), in: The Journal of the Royal Anthropological Institute of great Britain and Ireland, Vol. LXVI, London, (no year) Pp. 255-679.

Shaibu Albert, Health Policy/History of Health Care Idah Diocese, in: Ed., Pub./Hist. Sub-Committee of the Idah Diocesan Silver Jubilee celebration, Catholic Diocese of Idah at twenty five, Enugu, 2003, Pp. 22-29.

Shikwati James, Redefined Governance – Key to Africa's Development, in: Ed., Johannes Michael Nebe, Herausforderung Afrika, Baden Baden 2011, 176-172.

The Rise and Fall of the Igala State, in: Ed., Onuora Nzekwu, Nigeria, Magazine no. 80, March 1964, Lagos, Pp. 17-29.

The Works of Aristotle, Vol. II, in: Ed., Mortimer J. Adler, Great Books of the Western World, 8, Aristotle II, translated by Benjamin Jowett, Chicago, 2005, Pp. 445- 552.

Turner Teresia, Commercial capitalism and the 1975 Coup, in: Ed., Keith Panter-Brick, Soldiers and Oil, the Political Transformation of Nigeria, Studies in Commonwealth Politics and History, No 5, London, 1978, Pp.161-200.

Van der Woude Aleta, The church as partner in development, in: Ed., Stenger Fritz, Africa is not a dark continent, Tangaza occasional papers, Nairobi, 2005, Pp. 80-85

Veith Werner, Nachhaltigkeit, in: Ed., Marianne Heimbach-Stein, Christliche Sozialethik, Vol. I, Regensburg, 2004, Pp. 302-314.

Verstraeten Johann, The Tension between 'Gesinnungsethik' and 'Verantwortungsethik'. A Critical Interpretation of the Position of Max Weber in 'Politik als Beruf', Pp. 180-187.

Wariboko Waibinte, The CMS Niger Mission, Extra-Territorial Forces of Change, and the Expansion of British Influence in the Niger Delta during the Nineteenth Century, in: Eds., Chima J Korieh, Raphael Chijoke Njoku, Molefi Asante, Missions, States and European Expansion in Africa, African Studies, History, Politics, Economics, and Culture, New York, 2007, Pp. 35-53.

Wariboko Waibinte, West Indian Church in West Africa: The Pongas Mission among the Susus and its Portrayal of Blackness, 1851–1935, in: Eds., Chima J. Korieh, Raphael Chijoke Njoku, Molefi Asante, Missions, States and European Expansion in Africa, African Studies, History, Politics, Economics, and Culture, New York, 2007, Pp.167-186.

Wegh Francis Shagbaor, Neo-Colonialism and the Plight of African Identity, 59, in: Ed., Chudi C Mbanusi, The Aquinas Journal, Volume 1, Number 1, Makurdi, 2008, Pp. 58-69.

Wiemeyer Joachim, Alte und neue soziale Frage, Wilhelm Emmanuel von Ketteler als Arbeiterbischof, in: Eds., P. Klasvogt, M. Vogt, J. Wiemeyer, P Schallenberg, S. Lunte, Amosinternational, Gesellschaft gerecht gestalten, 6 Jahrgang, Heft 2, Münster, 2012, Pp. 47-53.

Wiemeyer Joachim, Business Ethics from Christian Socio-ethical perspective, in: Kirche und Gesellschaft, Nr. 403, 2013, Pp. 1-12. (eine längere Fassung in Englisch)

Wiemeyer Joachim, Globalisierung als Herausforderung der Christlichen Sozialethik, Beobachtungen und weiterführende Überlegungen, in: Ed., Andreas. Fritzsche, Manfred Kwiran, Kirchen und Gesellschaft, Ökumenische Sozialethik, Vol. III, München, 2000, 1-12.

Wiemeyer Joachim, Soziale Ungleichheit und Armut in Deutschland, Ursachen und aktuelle Entwicklung, Bewertung und Maßnahmen zur Begrenzung in: Ed., S. Lunte, Amosinternational, Gesellschaft gerecht gestalten, 10 Jahrgang, Heft 1, Münster, 2016, Pp. 3-10.

Wollasch Hans-Josef, Werthmann Lorenz: Carismacher und Visionär, in: Eds., Neher Peter, Feige Ingeborg, Wollasch Andreas, Wollasch Hans-Josef, Freiburg, 2008, Pp. 17-32.

Yahaya D. Alih, Creation of States, in: Ed., Keith Panter-Brick, Soldiers and Oil, the Political Transformation of Nigeria, Studies, in: Commonwealth politics and history, No 5, London, 1978, Pp. 201-223.

Archive Materials.

Daily Post, Monday April 20, 1970.

Groetz Eugene, The First Contacts of the Spiritans with the Middle Belt.

Weekly Progress Report no. 8, 13/10/69 to 20/10/69.

Weekly Progress Report no. 13, 16/11/69 to 22/11/69.

Church Teachings and documents.

Benedict XVI Africae Munus.

Benedict XVI Caritas in Veritate.

Benedict XVI Deus Caritas est.

Benedict XVI Evangeli Gaudium.

Benedict XVI Spe Salvi.

Benedict XVI, Motu Proprio of the Supreme Pontiff on the Service of Charity.

Catholic Bishop' Conference of Nigeria, (CBCN), The Lord comforts his People, Communiqué at the end of the second plenary meeting of the Nigerian Catholic Bishops conference of Nigeria, CBCN, at the Diocesan Conference Centre, Bishops Court, Effurun, Delta State, 11th-19th, September 2014.

Catholic Bishops Conference of Nigeria (CBCN), Seeking the way of peace, Communiqué issued at the end of the first plenary meeting of the Catholic Bishops Conference of Nigeria (CBCN) for the year 2003, held at the Pope John Paul II Catholic Centre Abuja, from 10th to 14th March 2003.

Catholic Bishops' Conference of Nigeria (CBCN), Conversion for Justice and Reconciliation, Communiqué at the end of the Second Plenary Meeting of the Catholic Bishops' Conference of Nigeria (CBCN) at the Centre of Transfiguration Kafanchan, Kaduna State, 7th to 12th, September 2009.

Catholic Bishops' Conference of Nigeria (CBCN), Faith and the Dignity of The Human Person, Communiqué at the end of the First Plenary Meeting of the Catholic Bishops' Conference of Nigeria (CBCN) at the Daughters of Divine Love Retreat and Conference Centre Lugbe, Abuja, 16th –22nd, February 2013.

Catholic Bishops' Conference of Nigeria, (CBCN), Good Families make Good Nations, Communiqué at the end of the First Plenary Meeting of the Catholic Bishops' Conference of Nigeria (CBCN) at the Daughters of Divine Love Retreat and Conference Centre Lugbe, Abuja, 20th – 26th, February 2015.

Catholic Bishops' Conference of Nigeria, (CBCN), I chose you, The Nigerian Priest in the Third Millennium, September 2004.

Catholic Bishops' Conference of Nigeria, (CBCN), Promoting Authentic Development in Nigeria, Communiqué issued at the end of the Second Plenary Meeting of the Catholic Bishops' Conference of Nigeria (CBCN) at the Bishop Anthony Nwedo Pastoral Centre, Umuahia, Abia State, 8th – 14th, September 2012.

Catholic Bishops' Conference of Nigeria,(CBCN), The Catholic Church in an independent Nigeria, joint pastoral letter of the Nigerian hierarchy, 1st October 1960, in: Ed., Peter Schineller, The Voice of the voiceless, Pastoral letters and Communiqués of the Catholic Bishops' Conference of Nigeria, 1960-2002, Ibadan, 2002, Pp. 1-46.

Congregation for the Doctrine of Faith, Instruction on Christian Freedom and Liberation, 1986.

Deutsche Bischofkonferenz, Den Hungern bekämpfen, Unsere gemeinsame Verantwortung für das Menschenrecht auf Nahrung, Studie der Sachverständigengruppe "Weltwirtschaft und Sozialethik", Bonn, Mai 2012.

Deutsche Bischofskenferenz, Partnerschaft mit den Armen, Wechselseitige Verpflichtungen in der entwicklungspolitischen Zusammenarbeit Eine Studie der Sachverständigengruppe „Weltwirtschaft und Sozialethik", Bonn, März 2004.

Francis, Evangeli Gaudium

Francis, Laudato Si.

John Paul II, Redemptoris Missio.

John Paul II, Sollicitudo rei socialis.

John XXII, Pacem in Terris.

John XXIII, Mater et Magistra.

Kompedium der Soziallehre der Kirche, Päpstlicher Rat für Gerechtigkeit und Frieden, Freiburg, 2004.

Paul VI, Evangelii nuntiadi, Apostolic exhortation.

Paul VI, Gaudium et spes.

Paul VI, Lumen Gentium.

Paul VI, Populorum Progressio

Reports

Food and Agriculture Organisation of the United Nations, (FAO) International Fund for Agricultural Development, (IFAD) World Food Programme, (WFP) The State of food insecurity in the World, meeting the 2015 hunger targets: taking stock of uneven progress, 2015, Rome.

Health /Justice Development & Peace Commission Abuja Province, 2008 Annual Report, 2008, Abuja.

Health /Justice Development & Peace Commission Abuja Province, 2011 Annual Report, 2011, Abuja.

International Finance Corporation, (IFC) World Bank Group, Nigeria Country Profile, 2014, Washington DC.

Library of Congress – Federal Research Division, Country Profile: Nigeria, July 2008.

Millennium Development Goal, End-point Reports 2015, Nigeria, Abuja.

National Human Development Report, Human Security and Human Development in Nigeria, December 2015.

Internet pages

47% of outbound medical tourism in Nigeria go to India, http://www.hatman2010.org/index.php/newsletter/28-47-of-outbound-medical-tourism-in-nigeria-go-to-india (19.03.2016).

Agricultural Research Council of Nigeria, http://www.arcnigeria.org/index.php/explore/the-council/our-vision/152-arcn/about/71-agricultural policies (29.06.15).

Ajayi Femi, The question of mental Dislocation of some Nigerian leaders as Nigeria clocks 51, Nigeriaworld, http://nigeriaworld.com/columnist/ajayi/100911.html. (9.10.2011).

Atiku Abubakar, Restructuring goes beyond resource control, http://www.vanguardngr.com/2017/07/restructuring-goes-beyond-resource-control-atiku/ (30.06.17).

Ayangba Agricultural Development project, The World Bank, http://www.worldbank.org/projects/P002032/ayangba-agricultural-development-project?lang=en (16.07.15).

Catholic Institute of Development Justice and peace (CIDJAP), http://www.cidjap.org/justice-development-and-peace-commission-jdpc-its-implication-in-the-nigerian-church.html (07.10.14).

Catholic Relief Service, http://www.crs.org/ (14.03.15)

Chinua Achebe, Nigeria's promise, Africa's Hope, the New York Times, Jan., 15, 2011, http://www.nytimes.com/2011/01/16/opinion/16achebe.html (12.09.16)

Christian Health Association of Nigeria, http://www.channigeria.org/index.html (08.10.14).

Christian Missions in Many Lands, http://www.cmml.us/about (01.09.15).

DGRV, die Genossenschaften, https://www.dgrv.de/weben.nsf/web/historyofcooperatives (03.07.16).

Dictionary of African Christian Biography, http://www.dacb.org/stories/nigeria/bill_samuelalexander.html (01.09.15).

History, International Federation of Red Cross and Red Crescent Societies, http://www.ifrc.org/en/who-we-are/history/ (15.09.13).

Human Development Reports, http://hdr.undp.org/en/humandev/ (06/05/2010)

Humanitarianism, in: Online Etymology Dictionary. © 2010 Douglas Harper. Retrieved November 24, 2014, from Dictionary.com website: http://dictionary.reference.com/browse/humanitarianism.

352

Idah Diocese Catholic –Hierarchy, http://www.catholic-hierarchy.org/diocese/didah.html (04.02.15).

Internationale Politik und Gesellschaft, IGP, der ausblutende Kontinent, http://www.ipg-journal.de/kolumne/artikel/der-ausblutende-kontinent-942/ (03.06.15)

Justice Development and Peace Commission, Ijebu-ode, http://www.jdpcijebuode.org/. (06.10.14).

Justice Development and Peace Commission, Ikeja office, http://jdpcstleoikeja.org/origin.html (07.10.14).

Kolping Society of Nigeria (KSN), http://www.kolpingsocietyofnigeria.org/edu.php (09.03.16).

Kolping Society of Nigeria (KSN), http://www.kolpingsocietyofnigeria.org/history.php (09.03.16).

Kolping Society of Nigeria (KSN), http://www.kolpingsocietyofnigeria.org/skills.php (09.03.16).

Lawrence O. Obibuaku, Qualitative Education: The Role of Government Take-Over of Schools, Nigeriaworld, http://nigeriaworld.com/articles/2005/sep/061.html (03.07.15).

Nigeria - Mobile Infrastructure, Operators and Broadband - Statistics and Analyses, http://www.budde.com.au/Research/Nigeria-Mobile-Market-Insights-and-Statistics.html (21.08.15).

Nigeria: Food Imports and the Struggle to Eat, Daily Champion, http://allafrica.com/stories/201108100162.html (29.09.15).

Nigerian Red Cross Society, http://www.redcrossnigeria.org/history.html (06.02.15).

Obiora Ike, Human capital development, panacea to national growth, http://www.cidjap.org/invest-in-human-capital-development-don-urges-ngos-government.php (08.03.16).

Odumakin Yimka, Confab: the complete story of the conspiracies, Vanguard Nigerian Newspaper, http://www.vanguardngr.com/2014/08/confab-complete-story-conspiracies-odumakin/(16.09.14).

Powered by WhatIs.com, http://whatis.techtarget.com/definition/four-eyes-principle (04.07.16).

Statista, the Statistics Portal, http://www.statista.com/statistics/262858/change-in-opec-crude-oil-prices-since-1960/ (04.09.16).

The Exam Ethics International, ITV Radio Nigeria, http://itvradionigeria.com/news/nigeria-spends-n1-5-trn-annually-on-students-studying-abroad-says-ngo/(10.09.14).

The Federation of Muslim Women Association of Nigeria, http://www.fomwan.org/about_fomwan.php (05.10.14).

The Roman Curia, Pontifical Council, Cor Unum, http://www.vatican.va/roman_curia/pontifical_councils/corunum/corunum_en/profilo_en/istituzione_en.html (01.07.14).

The World University rankings, Young Rankings 2016, https://www.timeshighereducation.com/world-university-rankings/2016/world-ranking#!/page/0/length/25/country/159/sort_by/rank_label/sort_order/asc/cols/rank_only (19.09.16).

United Nations, General Assembly, A/RES/39/22, 23, November 1984, http://www.un.org/documents/ga/res/39/a39r022.htm (12.04.15).

Utomi Pat, Nigeria is bleeding, needs healing, http://www.vanguardngr.com/2017/08/nigeria-bleeding-needs-healing-utomi/ (12.08.17)

Welcome to Catholic Diocese of Idah, http://netministries.org/frames.asp?ch=ch09029&st=KOGI&name=CATHOLIC%20DIOCESE%20OF%20IDAH&city=IDAH (02.03.15).

Wholesome words, Missionary Biography, http://www.wholesomewords.org/missions/bioslessor2.htm l (07.07.14).

Interview

Interview with Sr. Nora McNamara, (the founder of DDS) in Dublin on 23.07.2015.

Ayebome: What was your general experience of working in the DDS?

McNamara: This has always been the best of challenges. Initiating an instrument or tool to get at the root causes of poverty (which was one of the fundamental reasons for DDS and a response of Vatican II to address poverty) was interesting and exciting though in truth there was little understanding of what this was about. The status quo within the Church was that Religious were looking after health and education which were still worthy causes and of which there was much need. Taking time to understand what were the other needs and causes of inequality were a new concept for most of the Religious and lay community within which I worked. Pioneering was never easy. However there were inspirational and aspirational directives such as working from the grassroots upwards, self-reliance and people becoming the subject and object of their own development. Logically these would come from analysis of needs which I set out to do and had the full cooperation of Msgr. Grimard and the French Canadian CSSps. The parish was the unit where this analysis began. While health and education still needed to be improved upon and expanded there were other very needy areas especially in relation to women. Water emerged as a top priority and while I do not have time to go in this basic need in detail it was this finding from women and indeed supported by men that led to DDS embarking on its first project with self-reliance as its hallmark. The best mentors I've ever had were in this Igala community, priests, religious and laity and while they often were impatient with me, the eventually came round to the notion that in development you cannot make haste. First steps for a good foundation take time. It was clear to me from the advice I received and what I intuitively imbibed was that most of the answers lay within the Igala society. There was a potential that was there to be developed and built upon. In post-civil war Nigeria in Kwara state there were still Ministries that functioned very well. These included Social Welfare, Ministry of Agriculture and Natural Resources, Health and Education among others and always found them most helpful. This was especially true when DDS ran series of what would now be called Sensitisation and Awareness Programmes the length and breadth of Igalaland; it was the personnel from these ministries that helped in many ways.

It is very important to point out that DDS was up to address needs identified by communities throughout the diocese. Agriculture was accidental as it was the only resource that offered any form of self-sufficiency. A study of Igala society also confirmed the existence of many indigenous organizations, meetings or *Ojas*. Much has been written about these organisations which DDS harnessed to the benefit of the society. Many of these became known as the Farmer Councils and became very useful organizational framework through which very useful innovations were channelled. Notable among these were rain water harvesting, primary health care that evolved from kitchen gardening in conjunction with the primary health care team in Ankpa. This is only a small snap shot of what was done in the early years. See one of our more recent publications *Sustainable Livelihood Approach A Critique of theory and practice* gives a complete update of the early years and what gave rise to what. What is important here is that sustainability was being built at every stage within the organisations at community level including the *Ojas*.

DDS changed as the political situation changed as these reflected on needs. The secret of DDS was its ability to respond creatively and ethically to the many changes and turbulences that became part of life in Nigeria. The SAP experience in the wake of AADP in Igalaland was an international catastrophe but we managed to ride it well within DDS. At the request of communities, agriculture expanded and so great was the demand for seeds and seedlings, the normal supplies we enjoyed from places like IITA were not possible. The Ministry of Agriculture had lost its entire staff due to restructuring and were not replaced. DDS in order to be in any way effective had to employ and train extension staff and after much deliberation had no choice but to set up the seed multiplication farm in Iyegu to augment the supplies. We had to pretest some seeds as these improved varieties of seeds were already grown in Igalaland, for example maize, cowpeas, cassava and soy beans.

With the growing awareness to conserve diversity especially in endangered species and with many documents and encyclicals from Rome we managed to identify and save some species. An arboretum was established for that purpose. Many young people and farmers were trained and short courses were organised for recycling of nutrients and compost making etc. There were mainly for farmers who could not attend the full courses. The farm became very attractive as it was professionally laid out to demonstrate soil conservation, recycling of nutrients and the use of crop rotation, inter and under lay cropping. Training took into account soil conservation, a problem identified by the farmers and for which the requested help.

Ayebome: The Iyegu farm for example has been lying fallow with decaying facilities and that gives on some concern.

McNamara: You did not ask me about any other innovation in DDS except the farm but the farm was only there to augment what was happening in the outreach. I refer you to our last publication once again for more details on these. Water in the shape of rain harvesting was one innovation that gave much satisfaction. It was and still is an indigenous system which was improved upon. Some scientific ideas gave a tank that did not leak and all inputs for its completion including the different skills were all available locally. Like most DDS innovations solutions to the problems were found within the community. So much in favour of sustainability.

Ayebome: you just mentioned sustainability, which takes the centre place when one refers to issues of self-reliance. How sustainable were the DDS projects?

Mcnamara: On the issue of sustainability, which was always an important one for DDS it is good to know that from the 1990s onwards water packaging was set up to augment funding or maybe to be free of funders. At least there would be substantial local contribution when required.

Ayebome: One thing I am very certain is that the farm was never a profit generating venture. It was meant to assist the farmers and the yam project for example was obviously a success.

McNamara: One of the biggest achievements of DDS is its work on yam improvement especially with seed yam production. The benefit of this work is spreading far beyond Igalaland; from a historic perspective it is extending into what was once the old Igala kingdom. I am sure you are familiar with this from Chief Okwoli's writings especially on the history of Igalaland. DDS has trained many farmers and trainers in Idoma, Tiv, Illushi and Abuja. The white yam (Dioscorea rotundata) is indigenous to Igala and by far a crop that gives the greatest nutrition and a steady price in the market unlike other crops whose price fluctuates depending on supply and demand.

While in DDS in the 1990s Professor Morse and I did much research into the problems identified by the farmers. Eventually it was concluded that the problems revolved around the availability of affordable healthy seed yam. To make a very long story short we tapped into what was done in IITA and indeed with IITA in finding a solution. First step at tackling this problem began in 1970 when IITA began to improve on the system of mini sett production. There was poor adoption because the sett size was too small and as a nursery stage was required it was too labour intensive. The ware yams cut into pieces on between 30 to 50gr is called a sett – this is sown and produces a healthy seed for the next year)

As we began to address the problem again it was clear that the nursery stage had to be eliminated. The sett size was also increased and treated with a chemical which prevented the treatment the set from tot and eliminated attack by pests and diseases to which a young seed is prone. The treatment is degradable. We called the new sett the Adapted Mini Sett Technique (AYMT). There are boundless possibilities within this system and the end result is that farmers have learned to do this for themselves. They know the steps and provided the work done with the discipline described they can produce clean seed yam for themselves. The problems of affordability and availability are easily managed.

I was out of DDS when the final refinements were made but if DDS could produce a few 1000s of these each year such a saleable product would be a big help not only for sustainability but for extending the technology. It would be a brownie for the church and a way of reaching out to poorer people who could be trained on the farm as well.

Ayebome: Thank you for this wonderful enlightenment into the success story of DDS. Again in your book you did mention about the DDS/donor relationship. From all indications, if I got you right, there was some over bearing control from the donors, how did you come to terms with this factor?

McNamara: Sometimes they could be overbearing and lacking understanding. Again, it is said that the donors are always right, you don't challenge the donors. You do it at your own risk, so you have to take the means of mitigating what happens around the risk. Another interesting thing is the likes of a donor who would ask for the site of demonstration farm be along the side of the road for their own convenience when they come. NO, but where are the people working? You put things where the people are and where the people live. Anyway, if we leave the demonstration along the road they are going to be stolen. But for the most part I would say that we have worked with donors and donors have learnt, so it is a sharing. But the tendency is to believe that the donor is always right and you take a risk when you challenge him. I think it's worth it.

Ayebome: In a resume, what would you say was responsible for the inability of the DDS going further?

McNamara: Transition is always critical and as I prepared to leave DDS Misereor funded two small projects to help address issues that might arise and what extra advice and frameworks needed to be put in place. This of course was all with the approval of the Bishop and the Holy Rosary authorities.

The critical turning point is the transfer of leadership after what was regarded as quite a successful movement. The funds were always going to dry up and funding agencies were not going to keep on supplying subsidies unless the results were noteworthy. Following the principles laid down by Paulo Freire I initiated a period of reflection following from an extended period of action and the organisation began to trim down and let staff go, but the people were glad of such realism and such attempts to make them independent.

Let us not forget that new leaders must have the calibre to adapt and meet inevitable changes which a new future always demands. It is not enough to be trained technically or know the theory; there must be a human relationships component and creativity in the face of unmapped territory. Choosing the leaders of the next phase requires huge perspicacity. There must be a trial period and successful mentoring. There is no magic bullet in the area of development and transition from pioneering stage to the structured organisational stage is never seamless. A different kind of person, a different set of qualifications, a different mentality, is required which distinguishes the originator from the inheritor of any organisation. We have to be honest and humble; and we have to learn from at least 100 years of such experience. The one who begins and the one who carries on from that beginning, require two separate charisms as different as chalk from cheese. St. Francis was a hopeless Franciscan. It requires managerial, legal, administrative and personnel management abilities to carry on from where one left off. Getting the right persons in place is paramount. And when these are carefully chosen they need mentoring, supervision and a lengthy period of probation before they take the reins.

In 2004 and 2005 there was not much appreciation of such approaches and indeed it was not my remit to in any way evaluate what was happening after I left.

Forum Religion & Sozialkultur

Abteilung A: Religions- und Kirchensoziologische Texte
hrsg. von Prof. Dr. Karl Gabriel (Münster)

Wolfgang Belitz; Jürgen Klute; Hans-Udo Schneider; Walter Wendt-Kleinberg (Hg.)
Jenseits der Gerechtigkeit – Kirche in Zeiten wachsender Ungleichheit
Aufstieg und Niedergang kirchlicher Industrie- und Sozialarbeit
Bd. 22, 2018, 352 S., 39,90 €, br., ISBN 978-3-643-13697-8

Riccardo Nanini
An Werke glauben
Theologie, Politik und Wirtschaft bei der Compagnia delle Opere
Bd. 21, 2010, 496 S., 49,90 €, br., ISBN 978-3-643-10982-8

Helmut Jaschke
Wirtschaftsmanagement in benediktinischen Männerklöstern Deutschlands
Bd. 20, 2010, 312 S., 24,90 €, br., ISBN 978-3-643-10560-8

Ansgar Kreutzer
Arbeit und Muße
Studien zu einer Theologie des Alltags
Bd. 19, 2011, 184 S., 19,90 €, br., ISBN 978-3-643-50122-6

Boris Krause in Verbindung mit Karl Gabriel, Reinhard Feiter, Klaus Müller
Religiosität und Kirchlichkeit im Spiegel soziologischer Theorie und Empirie
Gutachten für die Pastoralkommission der Deutschen Bischofskonferenz
Bd. 18, 2009, 176 S., 19,90 €, br., ISBN 978-3-643-10111-2

Rüdiger Gollnick
Benediktusregel und Benediktusvita
Unter modernen Fragestellungen neu erschlossen. Ein interdisziplinärer Leitfaden
Bd. 17, 2008, 128 S., 14,90 €, br., ISBN 978-3-8258-1271-3

Martin Ebner; Karl Gabriel in Verbindung mit Johanna Erzberger, Helmut Geller und
Christian Schramm
Bibel im Spiegel sozialer Milieus
Eine Untersuchung zu Bibelkenntnis und -verständnis in Deutschland
Bd. 16, 2008, 504 S., 39,90 €, br., ISBN 978-3-8258-1252-2

Heiner Katz
Kirchliche Autorität im Strukturwandel der Gesellschaft
Eine religions- und wissenssoziologische Untersuchung zum nachkonziliaren Autori-
tätsproblem der katholischen Kirche
Bd. 15, 2012, 536 S., 39,90 €, br., ISBN 978-3-8258-9623-2

pax christi-Kommission Weltwirtschaft (Hg.)
Der Gott Kapital
Anstöße zu einer Religionskritik
Bd. 14, 2. Aufl. 2006, 208 S., 14,90 €, br., ISBN 3-8258-9316-2

Bernhard Laux
Exzentrische Sozialethik
Zur Präsenz und Wirksamkeit christlichen Glaubens in der modernen Gesellschaft
Bd. 13, 2007, 264 S., 19,90 €, br., ISBN 978-3-8258-9257-9

Jürgen Klute; Hans-Udo Schneider (Hg.)
Auf dem Weg der Gerechtigkeit ist Leben
Sozialethische Anmerkungen (Skizzen) zur Sozialen Gerechtigkeit heute. Festschrift für
Wolfgang Belitz zum 65. Geburtstag
Bd. 12, 2005, 344 S., 29,90 €, br., ISBN 3-8258-8518-6

LIT Verlag Berlin – Münster – Wien – Zürich – London
Auslieferung Deutschland / Österreich / Schweiz: siehe Impressumsseite

Kirchen in der Weltgesellschaft

hrsg. von Prof. Dr. Dieter Becker (Neuendettelsau) und Prof. Dr. Andreas Nehring (Erlangen-Nürnberg)

Liping Tu
Die chinesisch-christlichen Gemeinden in Deutschland
Ihre religionspädagogischen Aufgaben und Möglichkeiten
Bd. 11, 2017, 250 S., 34,90 €, br., ISBN 978-3-643-13654-1

Karl-Fritz Daiber
Protestantismus und konfuzianische Kultur
Aspekte ihrer Zuordnung in China und Südkorea
Bd. 10, 2017, 160 S., 29,90 €, br., ISBN 978-3-643-13653-4

Harald Stuntebeck
Canudos
Eine sozial-religiöse Volksbewegung in Brasilien und ihre pastorale Wirkungsgeschichte
Bd. 9, 2016, 672 S., 69,90 €, br., ISBN 978-3-643-13021-1

Daniel Frei
Die Pädagogik der Bekehrung
Sozialisation in chilenischen Pfingstkirchen
Bd. 8, 2011, 456 S., 31,90 €, br., ISBN 978-3-643-80083-1

Jozef Hehanussa
Der Molukkenkonflikt von 1999
Zur Rolle der Protestantischen Kirche (GPM) in der Gesellschaft
Bd. 7, 2013, 448 S., 49,90 €, br., ISBN 978-3-643-10906-4

Marceli Fritz-Winkel
Zur Zukunft der Evangelischen Kirche Lutherischen Bekenntnisses in Brasilien
Aspekte ihrer Attraktivität im Vergleich mit der Umbanda und der neopentekostalen Igreja Universal do Reino de Deus
Bd. 6, 2012, 248 S., 24,90 €, br., ISBN 978-3-643-10888-3

Milee Woo
Koreanische Gemeinden in Deutschland
Praktisch-theologische Studien zu Problemen und Chancen
Bd. 5, 2016, 272 S., 34,90 €, br., ISBN 978-3-643-10872-2

Han Ho Kim
Beziehungen förderlich gestalten
Eine diakoniewissenschaftliche Vergleichs-Studie zur Arbeit mit Behinderten in südkoreanischen und in deutschen Kirchen und Gemeinden
Bd. 4, 2010, 264 S., 24,90 €, br., ISBN 978-3-643-90008-1

Claudia Häfner
Heimischwerdung am La Plata
Von der Deutschen Evangelischen La Plata Synode zur Iglesia Evangélica del Río de la Plata
Bd. 3, 2008, 464 S., 39,90 €, br., ISBN 978-3-8258-1731-2

Ulrike Sallandt
Der Geist Gottes im Süden Perus
Risiken und Chancen charismatisch-pfingstlicher Verkündigung am Beispiel der „Asambleas de Dios"
Bd. 2, 2007, 280 S., 24,90 €, br., ISBN 978-3-8258-0389-6

LIT Verlag Berlin – Münster – Wien – Zürich – London
Auslieferung Deutschland / Österreich / Schweiz: siehe Impressumsseite

Forum Religionspädagogik interkulturell

hrsg. von Prof. Dr. Engelbert Groß (Katholische Universität Eichstätt-Ingolstadt)
Prof. Dr. Thomas Schreijäck (Universität Frankfurt) und Prof. Dr. Clauß Peter Sajak
(Universität Münster)

Engelbert Groß
Versklavte und verlorene Schöpfung
Lernen für den Rettungsprozess
„Versklavte und verlorene Schöpfung" bietet Dokumentationen. In unterschiedlichen und eigenständigen Tableaus werden informative, kritische und konstruktive Beiträge zu einem „Lernen für den Rettungsprozess" angeboten: Wunder der Natur – Szenarien globaler Zerstörung und Bilder ruinierter Schöpfung – Ursachen globaler Zerstörung der Schöpfung – Wege für Veränderung – Schöpfung entwickeln: Transformation konkret – Rand der Welt und Theologie der Peripherie.
Bd. 32, 2018, 424 S., 34,90 €, br., ISBN 978-3-643-13996-2

Josef Estermann
Südwind
Kontextuelle nicht-abendländische Theologien im globalen Süden
In Südamerika heißt der kräftige Wind aus dem Süden *surazo*. Der *Surazo* ist aber im Gegensatz zu den in Europa üblichen Vorstellungen vom „warmen Süden" nicht sehr angenehm und eher kühl.
Für viele Menschen aus dem Globalen Norden dürfte die vorliegende Publikation auch nicht nur erwärmen, sondern herausfordern, in Frage stellen, aber hoffentlich auch animieren und inspirieren.
Die theologischen Aufbrüche aus dem Globalen Süden können auch für eine ins Alter gekommene und oft als „wiederkäuende" Theologie wahrgenommene Denkfigur des Abendlandes neue und bereichernde Inspirationsquellen sein.
Zugleich ist die Publikation ein Nachschlagewerk für die Entwicklung kontextueller Theologien im Globalen Süden seit rund sechzig Jahren.
Bd. 31, 2017, 202 S., 29,90 €, br., ISBN 978-3-643-80253-8

Peter Egielewa
The Print Media as a Tool for Evangelisation in Auchi-Diocese / Nigeria
Contextualisation and Challenges
Communication in Africa is growing at an unprecedented pace. African governments are investing close to $100bn dollars annually for new infrastructure in communication. There are presently over 500 million mobile phones in Africa. Nigeria remains the economic hub of Africa. With an approximately 50% Christian population, these explosion poses opportunities and challenges for evangelisation in Nigeria. Although, the internet boom is still on the rise, print media has remained an important media of information. This work investigates, how church evangelisation can maximise the opportunities these media explosion bring about.
vol. 30, 2018, 510 pp., 39,90 €, pb., ISBN 978-3-643-90846-9

Elisabeth Dieckmann; Clauß Peter Sajak (Hg.)
Weißt du, wer ich bin?
Initiativen und Projekte für das interreligiöse und interkulturelle Lernen
"Weißt du, wer ich bin?„ Unter diesem Motto haben Juden, Christen und Muslime über mehrere Jahre zusammengearbeitet, um das friedliche Zusammenleben der Religionen in Deutschland zu fördern.
Mit kreativen Initiativen wurden vielfältige Möglichkeiten erschlossen, einander kennenzulernen, Verbindendes zu entdecken und Unterschiede zu verstehen und zu respektieren. Das Projekt "Weißt du, wer ich bin?„ wurde von der Arbeitsgemeinschaft Christlicher Kirchen in Deutschland zusammen mit dem Zentralrat der Juden in Deutschland, dem Zentralrat der Muslime in Deutschland und der Türkisch-Islamischen Union der Anstalt für Religion (DITIB) getragen. Dieses Buch fasst den Ertrag des Projekts zusammen und reflektiert Perspektiven für den Dialog zwischen Juden, Christen und Muslimen.
Bd. 24, 2014, 208 S., 24,90 €, br., ISBN 978-3-643-12299-5

Thomas Schreijäck (Hg.)
Glaubenskommunikation in Afrika
Kontextuelle Herausforderungen und Perspektiven
Bd. 22, 2012, 192 S., 19,90 €, br., ISBN 978-3-643-11591-1

LIT Verlag Berlin – Münster – Wien – Zürich – London
Auslieferung Deutschland / Österreich / Schweiz: siehe Impressumsseite

Afrikanische Theologie /
African Theology /
Théologie Africaine

Joebarth Abba
Philosophy of Thomas Aquinas on Justice and Human Rights
A Paradigm for the Africa-cultural Conflicts Resolution – Nigerian Perspectives
vol. 6, 2018, ca. 304 pp., ca. 34,90 €, pb., ISBN 978-3-643-90909-1

Lotanna Olisaemeka
Socio-Cultural and Religious Conflicts and the Future of Nigeria
A Mission for the Local Church
vol. 5, 2018, ca. 728 pp., ca. 59,90 €, pb., ISBN 978-3-643-90756-1

Claude Adouma Bonsou
Fruchtbarkeit in der Ehe
Überlegungen zur Bevölkerungsentwicklung und Empfängnisregelung in Schwarzafrika
aus theologisch-ethischer Sicht
Die Debatte über die Familie ist aktuell und universell. Schwarzafrika weist das größte Bevölkerungs-
wachstum der Welt auf. Alles dreht sich um das Leben. Es muss bewahrt und weitergegeben werden.
Aus der hohen Fruchtbarkeitsrate resultieren vielfältige Probleme, die die Regierungen durch geeig-
nete Maßnahmen der Geburtenregulierung zu lösen versuchen. Familienplanung ist grundsätzlich
nicht abzulehnen, vielmehr sollen lebensdienliche Handlungsansätze entwickelt werden. In der eheli-
chen Moral muss die Liebe zum Anderen wichtiger sein als das eigene Vergnügen, denn nur so bleibt
sie in der Liebe Gottes.
Bd. 4, 2016, 282 S., 34,90 €, br., ISBN 978-3-643-13331-1

John Chidubem Nwaogaidu
Jesus Christ – Truly God and Truly Man
Towards a Systematic Dialogue between Christology in Africa and Pope Benedict XVI's
Christological Conception
The truth of the Christian message must be interpreted in such a way that Christ as the Incarnate
Word – 'truly God and truly Man' – could become part of the people's way of life.
It is in such interpretation that African Christians in their faith encounter and life experiences might
be able to perceive the reality of Christ-events and find a true home with themselves and with their
God.
vol. 3, 2016, 268 pp., 34,90 €, pb., ISBN 978-3-643-90732-5

Benjamin Nzenekwesi Eze
**Challenges of Health Care Workers Vis-a-vis Evangelical Mission of Jesus Christ in
Igboland, Nigeria**
The call to be a health care worker was, is and will continue to be a special vocation. To be healthy, therefore, becomes a challenge to man, especially to the health care worker whose primary assi-
gnment is to enhance healing. It is a challenge of professionalism, vocation and mission – a challenge
to holistic healing.
vol. 2, 2014, 440 pp., 44,90 €, pb., ISBN 978-3-643-90399-0

LIT Verlag Berlin – Münster – Wien – Zürich – London
Auslieferung Deutschland / Österreich / Schweiz: siehe Impressumsseite